1976

D1073895

revelation

revelation

An Expository Commentary

"God's Last Word"

Donald Grey Barnhouse

**ZONDERVAN**
PUBLISHING HOUSE OF THE ZONDERVAN CORPORATION
GRAND RAPIDS, MICHIGAN 49506

REVELATION
© 1971 by Zondervan Publishing House
Grand Rapids, Michigan
Second printing 1973
Third printing 1974
Fourth printing 1975
Library of Congress Catalog Card Number 77-120051

Printed in the United States of America

CONTENTS

Introduction

INTRODUCTION

Donald Grey Barnhouse, one of the greatest popular expositors of this generation, was convinced the Bible provided a current commentary on the world's passing scene. For many years as editor of *Revelation* magazine and its successor, *Eternity* magazine, he wrote a column called "Window on the World." There, in addition to other sections of the publications, he sought to show how current events were explained by biblical eschatology.

Some of his predictions about a United States of Europe, or revival of the Holy Roman Empire, were made far in advance of the Common Market and the now well-publicized plans for a united Europe.

But it was Dr. Barnhouse's deep conviction that God would restore Israel as a nation that came dramatically true. Once when he was asked why he retained his "antiquated" views of biblical prophecy, he cried out with tears, "I never could abandon the teaching that God has a future place for the Jews as a nation."

Actually Dr. Barnhouse never did depart from the basic theological position held by the late Reuben A. Torrey who was his teacher at the Bible Institute of Los Angeles. The years there put a stamp on Dr. Barnhouse's views that never were changed by his subsequent studies at the University of Chicago, Princeton University, Princeton Theological Seminary and further graduate work in European universities.

The writer of this devotional commentary felt that understanding the prophetic message "provides strength to the believer for the conflict of the days ahead." In the first chapter he declares, "The book of Revelation is the book for the present hour. There is a special blessing promised to those who hear it and treasure the truth God has seen fit to give us."

No doubt Dr. Barnhouse's views of biblical prophecy — now considered by many as a too literalistic interpretation of Revelation and other apocalyptic books of the Bible — gave the thrust to his entire ministry. Yet it is not quite fair to describe him as a literalist if his commentary is studied carefully. Again and again he comments on the symbolism of certain passages. He believed that it was impossible to comprehend Revelation without being conversant with Old Testament symbols. A mountain was the symbol of "government" and the sea for "people," for example. Dr. Barnhouse and other dispensationalists are too often branded literalists. Perhaps they decide on literalistic interpretations of certain passages that others "spiritualize."

Like any man who lives in the Bible and catches glimpses of its elaborate mosaic of unified truth, Dr. Barnhouse amplified and modified some of his less mature positions on what the Bible teaches, yet he never departed from what the theologians call the "pre-trib, pre-mill" position. In other words, he believed the present Church age would be followed by the period known as the Great Tribulation. He was "pre-trib" because he believed the Church—all true Christians—would be caught up in the Rapture *before* the Tribulation. He was a "pre-mill" because he believed that the Church age would antecede the Millennium which he believed would be an earthly kingdom set up in Jerusalem with Christ on the throne. Dr. Barnhouse never could comprehend those who taught there would be no earthly future kingdom.

This commentary is scholarly in the sense that the author always sought to be faithful to the true interpretation of the text. It is also a devotional commentary because Dr. Barnhouse decried the tendency of some Bible students to devour prophetic teaching without seeing it produce practical results in their lives.

Above all, this is a popular commentary, for Dr. Barnhouse always had in mind that his duty was "first to feed God's sheep" and not His "giraffes." However, it is our earnest hope that the "giraffes" will not hesitate to bend their necks to enjoy the sumptuous bounty this book contains.

The last two chapters of the book were written by Dr. Ralph L. Keiper, Associate Professor of English Bible at Conservative Baptist Theological Seminary, Denver, who served for twelve years as the author's research secretary. Dr. Keiper well knew Dr. Barnhouse's thinking on the last book of the Bible so a more competent and sympathetic scholar could not be found to complete the work. Those of us who were colleagues of Ralph Keiper are grateful indeed for his performing this invaluable service, the final hurdle before the book could be published.

The earlier chapters first appeared serially in *Revelation* magazine under the title of "God's Last Word" in the years between 1934 and 1942. Later the messages were broadcast on the radio and subsequently were printed in booklet form. But Dr. Barnhouse did not live to see them published in book form.

Much credit for the editing and copy reading must go to Olive De-

Golia, a former member of our staff, who in her retirement is called in frequently to take over editorial assignments. At 81 she still has not lost her touch!

May this volume bring the same blessing to its readers that other works of Dr. Barnhouse have brought. May all of us give heed to the solemn message of God's Last Word.

RUSSELL T. HITT
Executive Director
The Evangelical Foundation, Inc.

PART I
IN THE SPIRIT

CHAPTER 1

Verses 1-3

The Revelation of Jesus Christ

¹ Revelation of Jesus Christ, which God gave to Him, to show to His yielded servants what must speedily happen; and He made it known, having sent it through His messenger unto His yielded servant, John; ²who attested the Word of God and the witness of Jesus Christ in all that he saw.

³Happy is he who reads and they who hear the words of the prophecy, and treasure what is written therein; for the time is near.
(Rev. 1:1-3, Free Translation)

We are living in the strangest days that man has ever known. The world has passed through terrible times before, but never has the whole earth been so bound together in its wild plunging through one catastrophe after another as today. There have been wars down through the ages, but never wars that have touched so many nations as the conflicts through which we have passed in this generation. There have been political crises, but not on a scale that touched all of the continents.

Civilization has brought so many new means of communication that the matters which affect one nation affect all. Events that take place in Europe and Asia become news that vitally concerns the farmer in the Mississippi valley. Thoughtful Bible students agree almost universally that we are living near the end of the age, and that at any moment the outline of prophetic events preserved for us will begin its course of fulfillment. The world will then rush rapidly through all of the scenes of history which God has written in advance.

The book of Revelation is the book for the present hour. There is a special blessing promised to those who read it and to those who hear it and treasure the truth that God has seen fit to give us. There is always a blessing attendant upon the study of the Word of God, but the blessing promised here is an added one. Our Lord has said, "Where two or three are gathered together in my name, there am I in the midst of them" (Matt. 18:20). That blessing is ours whether we be gathered for prayer, for communion, or even for social joy, if we remember that we are gathered in the Name of our Lord Jesus Christ.

13

The blessing that is promised here is a particular blessing that belongs to the study of this last book of the Bible. There is special strength to be found through the understanding of the prophetic message — a strength that will arm us for the conflict of the days ahead, if our Lord tarries.

If we know this book, we will be kept from any astonishment or fear as the age in which we live becomes dead ripe for plucking. There are terrible judgments coming upon the world. Those who know this book have no fear whatsoever; for the believer may know not only God's plan but his own personal place in that plan. This is why Paul was able to write to the Thessalonians, "But ye, brethren, are not in darkness, that that day should overtake you as a thief. Ye are all the children of light, and the children of the day. . . . for God hath not appointed us to wrath, but to obtain salvation by our Lord Jesus Christ" (I Thess. 5:4, 5, 9).

The God of eternity, who knows the end from the beginning, is saying to His own: "I know the thoughts that I think toward you, saith the Lord, thoughts of peace, and not of evil, to give you an expected end" (Jer. 29:11). He has brought us to a place where we, too, can know the end before it comes to pass. The final results of all the sinister tendencies which we see in the world today, the doom of the world system in which we live, and of the professing church which has so signally failed to live up to the God-given ideal, and the judgments that are to fall upon Israel, are all written in detail in this marvelous book.

In many editions of the Bible, the title page of this book contains the words, "The Revelation of Saint John the Divine." This is not God's title for the book, but a name which was given by fallible men. The true name of this book is found in its opening phrase. It is the "Revelation of Jesus Christ." John wrote it, it is true, but its purpose and its subject are the revelation of our Lord and the accomplishment of His purposes. This is what we are to see in this book. It is not merely the revelation of a prophetic plan, but the revealing of a Person, the Lord Jesus Christ. We shall see Him as the Messiah of Israel, the Lord of the Church and the Judge of the world. If we fail to note His relationship to any one of these three groups, we shall be blinded to the true meaning of this book.

The Greek name of the book is *apokalupsis*—apocalypse—which in its simplest etymological definition means the taking off of a covering—an unveiling. It is used eighteen times in the New Testament and when used of a person always indicates that he is visible. It is a well-known fact that the first use of any Greek word in the New Testament is almost sure to have in its context that which explains the sense of the word and gives it its meaning in all further usages. This word *apokalupsis* is first used in Luke 2:32 where Simeon, the godly old man who waited for the consolation of Israel, took the baby, Jesus, in his arms and blessed Him. "Then took he him up in his arms, and blessed God, and said, 'Lord, now lettest thou thy servant depart in peace, according to thy word: For mine eyes have seen thy salvation, Which thou hast prepared before the face of all people; A light to lighten [this is the word] the Gentiles, and the glory of thy people Israel' " (Luke 2:28-32). Thus the meaning is given. It is a shining forth of a person; it is an unveiling of God. Elsewhere it is translated "appearing," as in I Peter 1:7; "coming," as in I Corinthians 1:7; and "manifestation," as in Romans 8:19. It is a laying bare, a disclosure. There is a sense in which the whole Bible is a revelation. God, who could have hidden Himself had He so desired, has been pleased to disclose, to reveal. This is true of Genesis and Matthew as well as of Daniel and the other prophets; but this last book in the Bible is a special unveiling with a special blessing, showing forth the risen Lord Jesus as God's answer to every problem of the world.

There is an opinion that has been circulated widely from pulpit and pew that this book is too vague, too obscure, too complex to be understood by any ordinary mind. The devil likes to have people believe this. There are men—even men who have been ordained as supposed interpreters of God's Word—who say that it is not a book to be preached, that it contains too much Oriental symbolism which cannot be understood in our day. Others say that it is a book reserved only for the most profound students and the deepest thinkers. Such an attitude is a contradiction of the very name of the book. Revelation is not a puzzle or an enigma. This book is not called the hiding or the mystery of Jesus Christ, but the revelation of Jesus Christ. Practically everyone who reads these words knows the way of salvation, even though some individuals may not appropriate that knowledge for themselves. It is not sufficient to *know* that salvation is through faith in the finished work of the Lord Jesus Christ, but to be born again is to be acquainted with a personal salvation which takes a lost soul out of death and into life; God has told us that all Scripture is profitable, and in the Revelation we find a light that illuminates all the rest of the Bible so that God's plan throughout the ages becomes a clear stream of truth. A pyramid that is built of many stones must have as its peak a perfect pyramid. The whole of God's Word, is indeed, a pyramid of truth, and the book of Revelation is the perfect pyramid that crowns it all.

"The Revelation of Jesus Christ which God gave to Him . . ." What is the implication of this verse? Could God the Father reveal something to the Lord Jesus Christ about Himself? Yes! This verse is the answer to one of the great problems of the Gospels. Jesus Christ was not only perfect deity, but He had a perfect humanity. He "increased in wisdom and stature." He grew from day to day in His sinless humanity. In His deity, He knew all things; in His humanity, He learned.

Speaking to His disciples of the day when He should come again, He said, "But of that day and *that* hour knoweth no man, no, not the angels which are in heaven, neither the Son, but the Father" (Mark 13:32). He did not know these things when He spoke, for in His humanity He had limited Himself, but He knows them now. This Man, obedient in all things, obedient unto death, has been raised from the dead, taken into heaven, seated on the throne of God, and given the full revelation of Himself.

When the disciples asked the Lord some days after the resurrection, "Wilt thou at this time restore the kingdom to Israel?" He answered, "It is not for you to know the times or the seasons, which the Father hath put in his own power" (Acts 1:6, 7). Yes, the times and seasons are in God's power, but in the last book of the Bible they are given over to the Lord Jesus Christ as a revelation for His servants. Now, He knows the exact moment when He will arise from His Father's throne and come forth to set in motion the events that are to take place upon the earth. So in this book God the Father is speaking to the risen Lord Jesus. If the language is difficult for us to understand, this may be the answer: it is the language of the Father. God is speaking with God, revealing His plan.

Another definite reason why some men find this book obscure is that it is a revelation which God gave to Christ "to show to His yielded servants what must speedily happen." The original word is *doulos* and means much more than a servant. Some servants could be sullen, lazy, rebellious. This word, however, is used to translate the Hebrew "bond-slave." Our minds go back to the Scripture record of the days of Jubilee when all the slaves in Israel were liberated. If a slave loved his master and did not wish to go out of his slavery into poverty and misery, he was taken to the door of the tabernacle and a hole was bored in the lobe of his ear with an awl, thus showing that he had given himself over to his master forever as his willing slave. This was certainly in the mind of Paul when he called himself the servant of Jesus Christ.

So this book is the revelation of Jesus Christ which God gave Him to show to His yielded servants. A critic has said that he cannot believe the book of Revelation because to him it is "inacceptable gibberish." This statement is parallel to I Corinthians 1:18, "The preaching of the cross is to them that perish foolishness." The book of Revelation can be nothing but unacceptable gibberish to any but a yielded servant; but if we will go to God with yielded hearts, ask Him to cleanse us of open fault and secret sin, and give understanding, we shall find herein His Word clear and true, and learn that it is possible for a simple believer to have an unconfused grasp of its great teachings. There will be difficulties undoubtedly. The finite mind will always have certain difficulties when facing the infinite Word of God, but the difficulties may safely be left with God, and they will never be barriers to prayerful, devout study.

John was a yielded servant. He was chosen as the channel of this Revelation. John was the disciple whom Jesus loved, the one who leaned on His bosom at the last supper. At that time he was only a boy of eighteen or nineteen. This book was written on the isle of Patmos more than sixty years after the death of our Lord, when John was a very old man. Tradition tells a beautiful story of John, that when too feeble to go out preaching, he was carried in a chair from place to place among the churches of Asia Minor, everywhere lifting up his hands in blessing and exhortation saying, "Little children, love one another." His Gospel and epistles are filled with the warmest love of God. It was he, then, the apostle of love, who was chosen to make known the awful judgments that are to come upon the earth.

John received this message from a messenger. It will be noted that the King James Version says that "He sent and signified it by his angel unto his servant John." The Greek word *angelos* which is translated "angel" is found frequently in classical usage for "messenger." One captain sends an "angel" to another captain in the midst of battle. If the word is transliterated, it will lead to confusion, for it is used many times of different orders of beings in this last book in the Bible. Sometimes, it is true, angels are the messengers; sometimes, men are the messengers; and three times, we believe, the messenger is Christ Himself. So let us become accustomed from the beginning to translate the word as "messenger."

This book demands the attention of believers for many reasons. It calls itself in the opening lines, "the Word of God," "the testimony of Jesus Christ," "this prophecy." It bears the Name of the Lord Jesus Christ. It carries all His authority.

This book is also called the testimony of Jesus Christ. In a court room, when a witness for the prosecution brings in damaging testimony, the defense attorney will quickly move to have the testimony stricken from the record. The judge may sustain the objection or he may overrule it. The judgment will come. This is the testimony of Jesus Christ.

Without the last book in the Bible, other parts of Scripture would lose much of their significance. It is the complement of the book of Genesis which finds its very reason for being in the glory of Revelation. The Bible would be incomplete were the entrance of sin recorded without its judgment and exit. Man's ruin is complete in earlier parts of the Scripture; man's redemption is perfect in Revelation. And Revelation would be just as incomprehensible without Genesis. An English writer says, "The Bible may be likened to a beautiful and complex girdle or belt, with a corresponding connecting clasp at each end, one the complement of the other. Do away with either, the belt is useless, as a belt. So here Genesis and Revelation are the two clasps of the divine Word which link together and enclose between them in 'perfection of beauty' and harmony the whole of the Scripture in which God has been pleased to reveal His eternal purpose."

This Revelation concerns things which must shortly come to pass. We may translate this as the Revelation of "what must speedily happen." The Greek is *en taxei* and refers not to soonness, but to rapidity of execution when once there is a beginning. Scientists have gone to this word for the name of a technical instrument—the tachometer—a device for measuring velocity. In other words, the events of this book are to take place within a brief space of time. God says, "When I begin, I will also make an end" (I Sam. 3:12). There are those who sneer at these words and say that they do not mean much. Have not nineteen hundred years passed? From man's point of view, nineteen hundred years is not soon; from God's point of view, a thousand years is as a day. We are taught here, however, that suddenly shall come the word which shall loose the lightning-like succession of events. Today, the mills of God may grind slowly, but the day will come when the whole machinery of history will be slipped into high gear to run its fatal course to judgment. This is the same word our Lord uses when He says that God shall avenge His own speedily (Luke 18:8). God has borne long with men. This is the day of His patience. In our day we see the furniture of Bible prophecy being moved into place upon the stage of world history. The curtain is ready to be drawn. This shall come to pass in God's moment. Then all that is written in the book of Revelation will come to pass, exactly as written—and it shall come speedily.

Verses 4-8

Alpha and Omega

⁴John, to the seven churches which are in Asia: Grace to you and peace from the One who is and who was and who shall come; and from the seven spirits which are in the presence of His throne; ⁵and from Jesus Christ, the faithful witness, the first-born of the dead, and the ruler of the kings of the earth.

Unto Him who loves us and who has freed us from our sins by His blood ⁶and made us a kingdom, priests unto God and His Father; to Him be the glory and the dominion to the ages of the ages. It is true.

⁷Behold He comes with the clouds. And every eye shall see Him and those who pierced Him; and all the tribes of the earth shall lament because of Him.

Yes. It is true. ⁸"I am the Alpha and the Omega," says the Lord. He who is, who was, and who shall come, the Almighty.
(Rev. 1:4-8, Free Translation)

The yielded servants of the Lord Jesus Christ are brought into the secret of the plan of God, but now a special direction is given to the address of this book. John writes to the seven churches which are in Asia. There were, of course, far more than seven churches in Asia Minor at that time. The itinerary of Paul's missionary journey passes through our minds and we find it a simple matter to name seven others quite as famous as these of the book of Revelation, for example: Colosse, Galatia, Iconium, Lystra, Derbe, Antioch, and Miletus. Why then, is the book addressed to a limited number of churches, and why to these particular ones? Since seven is the number of completeness, we are sure of finding the conditions prevailing in these seven churches sufficient to illustrate God's message. The Lord picks out churches in which there are seven different sets of conditions which will represent the conditions of the churches throughout the age. When we look at the details of the messages to the churches, there are two ways to consider the teaching that is involved. We may think of all seven as illustrative of conditions that exist in the world at any given time in various parts of the Church, or we may think of a successive growth and development since the apostolic time until our day.

Churches differ from country to country and from denomination to denomination. They also differ within any given denomination and within any given city. In almost any great center of the world today, there are some churches with ministers who have departed from the faith; others who compromise; and others who are Bible lovers, faithful to their duty. There are some churches with a large interest in foreign missions; others with a large interest in suppers and socials. There are churches where there is war in the women's groups, and churches that have power for God in prayer. There are churches that are famous for their choirs, their architecture, or their liturgy, and churches that are famous for the depth of the results that are achieved in the ministry of the Word. Paul wrote to the Romans that their faith was famous throughout the world (Rom. 1:8). The seven churches named in the book of Revelation are, therefore, in one way representative of all the churches in the world. There is no condition of faithfulness or unfaithfulness, belief or apostasy, which is not exemplified in the brief compass of the seven messages to Asia.

Though the message of the whole Apocalypse is one of judgment, nevertheless, on this opening page of the Book, there is the benediction of grace and peace. In view of all that is to follow, this is particularly notable. Before the seals of judgment are broken, before the trumpets are blown, before the vials of God's wrath are poured out, God Himself comforts the hearts of those who are in Christ: "Grace to you and peace." God's grace is upon us; we are covered by it. God's peace is within our hearts. These gifts of blessing are ours and cannot be disturbed by the terrible judgments which are about to be announced.

But although grace and peace are called down upon the believer from the very first verses of this book, nevertheless this salutation is not like that which is used in the epistles of Paul. In the writings of the great apostle, we read of grace, mercy, and peace which come from God our Father and from the Lord Jesus Christ. The book of Revelation takes us to God in an entirely different way from that in which He is approached in the Gospels, the Acts, the epistles; in short, in any other New Testament book. Here we have an Old Testament approach. God is spoken of as "the One who is and who was and who shall come." This phrase is not to be found elsewhere in the New Testament. We take a concordance and are led immediately to God's revelation of His Name, Jehovah. Here stands the great I AM who revealed Himself to Moses. It is a well-known fact that the name of Jehovah is made up of parts of three words. We are all of us familiar with the modern trade custom which takes the initials of a firm or the syllables from the names of different men and combines these letters or syllables to make a patent trade name for a product. This can give us a glimmer of light into the meaning of the name Jehovah. The three tenses of the verb "to be" are called into play—"I was, I am, I shall be." A part of each of these three words is put together to form the name Jehovah.

Here, then, in the book of Revelation, we find the fulfillment, the capstone of Old Testament revelation. God speaks as the One who is and who was and who shall come. It should be noted in passing that it is not "who shall be," for the theme of the book of Revelation is not merely the future eternal being of God but the future definite coming back to earth of God. So this name is in perfect harmony with the book it opens which will unfold for us the activity of God as He puts out His hand in government upon Israel and upon the world and upon the church organization insofar as it is a system in the world.

This discovery of the use of the Old Testament name of God in the opening paragraphs of this last of the New Testament books should lead us to a realization of one of the two methods of study which will simplify the understanding of this Book. One evening in a shop on one of the boulevards of Paris, we found a book of fairy tales for children with special illustrations which appeared most confusing at first sight. Red and green lines formed a confused design that gave no appearance of illustrating anything. In a pocket on the inside of the back cover of the book was a cardboard frame with two squares of cellophane—one red, the other green. Look at the design that is meant to illustrate the story of Cinderella. Through the red square, the red lines are not seen and the green lines form a picture of the poor sister weeping beside the fireplace while the others have gone to the great ball; but suddenly shift the frame and look through the green square, and green lines are obliterated and Cinderella in red stands beside a royal coach-and-four ready to go to the festivities. The children are delighted at these changes which seem magical to them but which are all in accordance with a well-known law of physics.

There are two ways of looking at the book of Revelation which will bring clarity to that which to many commentators is confessedly confusion. The one principle of study which we will examine in great detail is that the major portion of this book belongs entirely outside of the age of the Church and that re-gathered Israel is the center of the scene, and the Church does not even appear in the discussion. The other principle is that which has been revealed to us here in the use of the Old Testament name for Jehovah, "the One who is and who was and who shall come." By using the concordance we were pointed back to the Old Testament and discovered the meaning in the phrase. This will be our guiding principle in the study of this book. When we come to the words and phrases which seem to be symbols, we will study the concordance minutely—look through a hundred passages perhaps—but without any doubt, we will find elsewhere in the Bible the same symbol used in such a way that the meaning will become clear.

All that is obscure in the Old Testament prophecies will be known here. The eternal Jehovah moves forth in judgment and reveals His purpose to His servants. There is a great lesson at this point which we must not fail to note. Thousands say that the God of the New Testament is different from the God of the Old Testament, that simple love has superseded what they have called the tribal God borrowed from the Philistines. But "the only begotten Son, who is in the bosom of the Father" (John 1:18) hath declared the God of the Old Testament, in fact, gives us to see God fully. Where there was shadow in the old portrait, light has come; where there was a partial meaning, there is now completeness. The dim gives place to the clear, and we find that the Jehovah of the Old Testament is none other than the glorious God in three Persons. The New Testament reveals to us His glories of which the patriarchs and prophets were themselves ignorant. In the Old Testament, there are many psalms; in the New Testament there are none, because the Spirit sings in every line and the Church joins in praise to Him who loved us and washed us from our sins in His own blood.

When the Israelites, before the time of Christ, sang the psalms they came to "My God, my God, why hast thou forsaken me?" (Ps. 22:1). They understood nothing of the significance of these words, but when in the New Testament we hear them from the lips of Christ, the most stupendous fact in the history of the universe becomes clear to us, that He who knew no sin became sin on our behalf and took on Himself the stroke of the righteous wrath of God so that He was forsaken of the Father in that infinite moment on the cross. All of this we understand when we read the New Testament. The God of one Testament is the God of the other.

The benediction of grace and peace comes not only from this great God, but also "from the seven spirits which are in the presence of his throne." Some would seek to make this phrase mean seven angelic beings, perhaps those who later receive the seven trumpets. But nowhere in Scripture is it indicated that grace and peace come to us from any other than from the Father, Son or Holy Spirit. It is, of course, unusual that the Spirit should be mentioned in the second place in speaking of the Trinity. The usual order is God the Father, God the Son, and God the Holy Spirit. This is the only place in the Bible where this order is reversed. The reason is that Christ is being looked upon here as the risen Son of Man, the One to whom the revelation is being given through the Spirit.

The name given to the Holy Spirit is peculiar — the seven spirits which are before God's throne. In the epistles, the oneness of the Holy Spirit is reiterated. The explanation is that there is one Spirit in a sevenfold perfection. The activities of the third Person of the Trinity are described in Isaiah where we read of the seven spirits which, in all their force, are to be found in the Man Christ Jesus as He comes to reign upon the earth: "And the spirit of the Lord shall rest upon him, the spirit of wisdom and understanding, the spirit of counsel and might, the spirit of knowledge and of the fear of the Lord" (Isa. 11:2). The Spirit is one and yet He works in these manifold activities, not as the Comforter and Teacher as He is in this Church age, for the Church will soon be seen enthroned in Heaven; the Spirit leaving the earth at the time the Body of Christ, the temple of the Spirit, is withdrawn from the earth at the rapture, and He immediately takes on a new character. In passing, let it be noted that this is one more link in the proof that the Church is removed from the earth before the tribulation judgments.

The source of the great benediction is now concluded. Grace and peace come from Jesus Christ to whom a threefold title is now given. He is "the Faithful Witness, the Firstborn of the dead, and the Ruler of the kings of the earth." These are all titles that speak of His humanity. This explains, too, why He is mentioned third in this one place in the Scripture in the order of the Trinity. He is being looked upon essentially as the Son of Man in His threefold office of a faithful prophet, priest who has offered Himself in sacrifice and been raised from the dead, and king over all the kings of the earth.

It was recorded of our Lord, during His life, that He was a faithful witness. "He that cometh from above is above all, . . . And what he hath seen and heard, that he testifieth; and no man receiveth his testimony" (John 3:31, 32). God hath spoken by His Son. As the first begotten from the dead, He is the resurrected One. He had gone to the cross and offered Himself up in obedience to the Father's will. It was a voluntary offering, so He is revealed in the book of Hebrews as our great high priest who is Himself the One who is offered. But the value of an offering to God depends on whether or not He receives it. Abel offered a more excellent sacrifice than Cain and when God received Abel's sacrifice, "he obtained witness that he was righteous, God testifying of his gifts" (Heb. 11:4). But the priest who is greater than Abel and who offered up Himself receives witness from God that His sacrifice is acceptable, and being raised from the dead, becomes our great High Priest forever.

As ruler of the kings of the earth, He is the One who once humbled Himself to death, even the death of the cross. "Wherefore God also hath highly exalted him, and given him a name which is above every name: That at the name of Jesus every knee should bow, of things in heaven, and things in earth, and things under the earth; And that every tongue should confess that Jesus Christ is Lord, to the glory of God the Father" (Phil. 2:9-11).

This triple designation, then, gives great importance to the One who is so named. Where is this Man now? He witnessed among men. He was crucified and raised from the dead. He ascended in glory to Heaven. What is He doing? There is a Man in Heaven, a Man with a body of flesh and bones (Luke 24:39). His work of judgment, exalted above all the kings of the earth, is soon to be described.

But suddenly there is a tremendous break in the thought of the passage. The Church bursts forth in praise. The verses which follow form an antiphonal passage. As in great cathedrals choir answers choir, the singing coming from opposite ends of the church, so here, John speaks, the Church responds, John speaks, and suddenly the Lord Himself breaks in with His exalted voice to make the song complete. John had begun the service saying, "Grace to you and peace from Jehovah, from the working Spirit, and from the Son of Man." The Church answers back, "Unto him who loved us and who has freed us from our sins by his blood and made us a kingdom, priests unto God and his Father, to him be the glory and the dominion to the ages of the ages. It is true." The grace and the peace have come upon the Church. The answer shows a yieldedness to Him. We are won by the attraction of His eternal love, though we had been captives in the chains of sin. The guilt and the chain had been dissolved together by His blood. We are freed. It could never have been done in any other way. It should be noticed that there is what might be considered a grammatical error in this sentence. A present tense and a past tense are linked together. He loves us and has freed us. It was Dr. Tregelles who spent his whole lifetime examining the ancient manuscripts of the Scriptures, who established beyond any doubt of reasonable scholarship, that the verb which describes Christ's love for us is in the present tense. The great scholar said that this one discovery would have been sufficient payment for the whole of his long life's work. Christ's love is not in the past tense; it is present active. He loves us and has washed us.

Note, too, that there are two pronouns put together closely. He has freed us from our sins by His blood. Ours were the sins; His was the blood. Let no man wonder hereafter if salvation is sufficient. And do we wish to measure the magnitude of our rebellion against God, we shall find it in the weight which He placed in the scales to outbalance it and bring us back to Him—the blood of Jesus Christ, God's Son. Is it any wonder that the Church sings this great song of praise? He has redeemed us. He has made us a kingdom. We become priests to God and His Father. The redeemed Church boasts not in herself, but sings, "To him be the glory and the dominion."

Some of the greatest songs of praise in the Scripture occur in the book of Revelation, and it should be noticed that in each, there is an increase in the praise that is offered to Christ. There is something in it like the attitude of a man who receives an unexpected present. A package is handed to him and he says, "Oh, thank you." Then the wrappings are removed and a beautiful wallet is disclosed. He cries out, "Oh, thank you very much." Then he opens the wallet and sees a fifty dollar bill. He says, "Oh, thank you very, very much." Finally, in some little side pocket he finds a check for a very large amount. He exclaims, "I don't know how to thank you. Thank you, indeed, very, very, very much." The praise to Christ in Revelation follows this order. In the first chapter, and the sixth verse, we read, "Glory and dominion be unto him who loves us." In chapter four, verse eleven, it is, "Glory, honor, and power." By chapter five, verse thirteen, the praise is fourfold: "Praise, honor, and glory, and dominion." Last of all, in chapter seven, verse twelve, there is a perfect, sevenfold praise: "Blessing, and glory, and wisdom, and thanksgiving, and honor, and power, and might."

After this cry of praise from the Church, John speaks again, "Behold he comes with the clouds and every eye shall see him and those who pierced him; and all the tribes of the earth shall lament because of him." What is this coming? It is a coming to judge. The first time, He came to deal with sin through the sacrifice of Himself; the second time, He will come with judgment. This statement of John's is not the *hope* of the Church, but the *testimony* of the Church. Our *hope* is that we shall be taken away before these things occur; our *testimony* is that these things will occur. At His first coming, He dealt with sin; at His second coming, He will deal with sinners. We must live either in verses five and six, freed by His blood, or in verse seven under His coming judgment. Every member of the race is living in the sunshine

of the first of these phrases or under the shadow of the other. If you
will not let Him deal with you in love, He must come to you as your
Judge.

When John brought the benediction from all the members of the
Godhead, the Church replied with a song of praise, but when John
announces that judgment will come which will cause men to wail,
God breaks in and speaks. The last phrase of verse seven really belongs with verse eight. "Even so, amen" is spoken by God. The full
utterance is, "Yes. It is true. I am the Alpha and the Omega, He
who is, who was, and who shall come, the Almighty." There is a
combination of two languages here. A Greek and a Hebrew word are
put together. "Even so," is the Greek affirmation—"Yes." "Amen" is
the Hebrew. The double affirmation puts upon this prophecy the seal
of certainty.

Then the paragraph is closed with the recital of titles that particularly belong to His eternal Godhead. Christ had said to Caiaphas and
the council, "Hereafter, shall ye see the Son of man sitting on the right
hand of power, and coming in the clouds of heaven" (Matt. 26:64).
God now says Amen to this declaration. Judgment is always terrible.
Christ is coming to fulfill all that has been spoken of judgment. The
world is full of miseries. The fraud of evil men has robbed the poor,
even the widow and the orphan. Men have nourished their hearts as
in the day of slaughter. God says that He remembers all these things.
The cries of the persecuted are entered into the ears of the Lord of
Hosts. John, in faithfulness to the revelation, announces judgment;
God speaks and puts His seal upon it. It is as though He said, You
spell out your message with your letters, the ABC of judgment. I am
the Alpha and the Omega. All I have said shall come to pass. Judgment is sure for all who have been ungodly. Upon us whom He has
saved through the blood of the Lord Jesus Christ, there is grace and
peace, but His very nature demands that He come to judge the rest.

Verses 9–20

The Son of Man

*⁹I, John, your brother and partaker in the tribulation and kingdom
and perseverance in Jesus, found myself in the isle called Patmos, because of the Word of God and the witness of Jesus Christ. ¹⁰ I was in
the Spirit on the Lord's day; and heard behind me a loud voice, like
a trumpet, ¹¹ saying, What thou seest, write it in a roll and send it to
the seven churches, to Ephesus, and to Smyrna, and to Pergamos, and
to Thyatira, and to Sardis, and to Philadelphia, and to Laodicea.*

*¹²And I turned to see the voice that was speaking to me, and having
turned I saw seven golden lampstands ¹³and, in the midst of the seven
lampstands, someone resembling a son of man, robed to the foot, and
girded about the breasts with a golden girdle. ¹⁴His head and hair,*

white as white wool, as snow; and His eyes as a flame of fire; [15]*and His feet as gleaming brass, as glowing in a furnace; and His voice as the voice of many waters;* [16]*and having in His right hand seven stars; and from His mouth going forth a sharp two-edged sword; and His face was as the sun, shining in His might.*

[17]*And when I saw Him, I fell at His feet as one dead; and He laid His right hand on me, saying; Fear thou not; I am the first and the last,* [18]*and the living One. I became dead and behold I am alive to the ages of the ages. And I have the keys of death and of Hades.*

[19] *Write, therefore, the things thou sawest, and those that are, and those that are about to happen after these;* [20]*the secret of the seven stars which thou sawest in My right hand, and the seven golden lampstands. The seven stars are the messengers of the seven churches; and the seven lampstands are seven churches.*
(Rev. 1:9-20, Free Translation)

The One who died on Calvary has made great claims. The early Church is preaching Him as Israel's true Messiah, as the One who is raised from the dead. John is now to receive a revelation concerning His person and then of the position He occupies and that work which He is yet to do.

First we hear a word concerning John and the manner of his receiving the vision. Writing to the sevenfold Church—in other words, the complete Church throughout the ages—John names himself first of all as brother and partaker in the tribulation and kingdom and perseverance in Jesus. This was the disciple whom Jesus loved, and yet he is a partaker in tribulation. Does this not show us that God's love is faithful? Those who are called according to His purpose (Rom. 8: 28) are loved of Him; yet they that live godly in Christ Jesus shall suffer persecution (II Tim. 3:12). They shall suffer, however, with the knowledge that it is working for their good. To us God says, "Beloved, think it not strange concerning the fiery trial which is to try you, as though some strange thing happened unto you: But rejoice, inasmuch as ye are partakers of Christ's sufferings; that, when his glory shall be revealed, ye may be glad also with exceeding joy" (I Pet. 4: 12, 13).

John was in the Spirit on the Lord's Day. In his commentary, *Apocalypse,* Joseph A. Seiss says that this means that he was carried forward through the centuries until he saw a vision of the great and terrible day of the Lord of which the Old Testament has a great deal to say and of which we will see more in the course of our study. Practically all other commentators, critical and spiritual, believe this to be a reference to the first day of the week. This time we agree with the majority. John, in the midst of the dullness of his island exile, found that the presence of Christ was with him. The Lord had promised to be with His own (Matt. 28:20), and had promised that the Father, Son and Holy Spirit should take up their abode within the heart of the believer (John 14:23, 17). The Christian thus indwelt by God carries his spiritual atmosphere with him. No human courts, and no divine, can ever remove that life from us.

John heard behind him a loud voice like a trumpet. The voice of God in the Old Testament was a still, small voice; but when man would silence the noises of the human heart, that voice will always ring forth like a clarion. I can remember one time riding in a airplane several thousand feet above the earth. It was an old airplane with an open cockpit. The pilot turned and cried out some message to me pointing to earth. I could see his lips move, but the roar of the engine silenced his voice. I indicated with a gesture that I could not hear him. He reached over and moved his throttle, silencing the engine. When he repeated his message, he used the same tone he had used a moment before, but now it sounded like a shout in my ear. So it is with the voice of God. We do not receive His deepest revelations because we are so occupied with the noises in our own lives. The heart of the Old Testament is, "Be still and know that I am God" (Ps. 46:10). Isaiah was a good and faithful preacher in the first five chapters of his prophecy, but it was when King Uzziah died and he saw the vision of the Lord and was cleansed at the altar, that he heard the voice of the Lord saying, "Whom shall I send, and who will go for us?" (Isa. 6:8). God's desire for messengers had been just as urgent before, but now Isaiah was cleansed and listening. So the voice of God came to the Spirit-filled John as the voice of a trumpet.

In the King James Version, the voice is quoted as saying, "I am Alpha and Omega, the first and the last." The earliest manuscripts omit these phrases, but there is no doubt that the One who speaks is Jesus Christ, the Lord Jehovah of Hosts, and that is about to be made most clear in the vision that follows. But the voice did command, saying, "What thou seest write it in a roll and send it to the seven churches." Daniel, upon receiving his vision, was bidden to "shut up the vision" . . . "to shut up the words and seal the book, even to the time of the end" (Dan. 8:26; 12:4, 9). John is to write and send out to the churches that which Daniel had been bidden to shut up and seal. At the close of the book of Revelation, the messenger repeats the command, "Seal not the sayings of the prophecy of this book: for the time is at hand" (Rev. 22:10).

Some men scoff at Christians for preaching that the time is at hand. Nineteen centuries have passed, they say. What could it possibly signify that the day was at hand? They forget that in God's reckoning, not two days have passed. The Old Testament says that Israel will remain in exile for two days, but at the end of that time will be revived and in the third day be raised up and live in the sight of God (Hos. 6:2). This does not mean that we are proposing some method for setting dates for the coming of the Lord. There is no calendar for the Church in the Word of God. All that we can say is that from what God has told us of Israel's future, the time of the coming of the Lord is near—desperately near for the unsaved; gloriously near for us who are redeemed.

Moses at the burning bush turned aside to see this great sight. "And when the Lord saw that he turned aside to see, God called unto him . . ." (Exod. 3:4). John also turned to see. The trumpet voice had done more than attract his attention. God is ever placing burning bushes and sounding trumpets for the eyes and ears of His children. The history of the Church shows us, however, that only comparatively few are willing to turn from their casual living to the extraordinary in which God is waiting further to reveal Himself.

First to meet John's gaze are the seven golden lampstands. We do not have to look for interpretation for the lampstands. We are clearly told that they are seven churches (vs. 20). They are not the source of light but they are bearers of the light and thus they signify the works of the Church. The golden lampstand is a fitting symbol for the Church. The Lord told His disciples that He was the Light of the world, but only while He was in the world (John 8:12; 9:5). It was in anticipation of His departure that He said to them, "Ye are the light of the world" (Matt. 5:14), and the Spirit of God speaks of the sons of God who shine in the midst of the darkness of this age "as lights in the world; holding forth the word of life" (Phil. 2:15, 16).

But now in the midst of the churches, John sees a vision of the Son of Man. This vision of the risen Lord Jesus Christ is one of the most wonderful word pictures in all of God's revelation. Stephen and Paul had seen Him, but they did not describe Him. Here He is in His judicial robes. The believer is secure, for while the seven churches in Asia will be seen in all of the blackness of their earthly failure, the seven lampstands are in the heavenly places with the risen Christ seated in the midst.

If we attempt to visualize the description that the Spirit gives us through John, we will come to confusion. An ancient artist has left us a canvas which now is in one of the museums of Europe, attempting to portray Christ in heaven according to the description here in Revelation. The result is certainly not a masterpiece. One does not need to view the canvas in order to realize how unrealistic is the portrait of a man with hair as white as snow, with face shining like the sun, with flames coming from the eye-sockets, a sword out of his mouth, with feet of burnished metal and with seven stars in his right hand. Such a picture, is, indeed, absurd, and the very incongruity should teach us that the understanding of this passage lies in another direction.

The true method of understanding this vision is to look at it through the rest of the Word of God as the Holy Spirit teaches, comparing spiritual things with spiritual (I Cor. 2:13). Take up a concordance and study all the passages in the Scripture and immediately light breaks. The book of Revelation is seen to be the inspired Word of God, the very capstone of revelation, the explanation of all that is obscure elsewhere in the Scriptures.

A robe, a garment, is seen to be a symbol of character. We are dressed in filthy rags (Isa. 64:6). He is clothed with the garments of light (Ps. 104:2). When He comes to execute judgment as recorded in the end of this great book, He comes as the warrior with His "vesture dipped in blood" (Rev. 19:13). It should be a solemn thought to every believer that though our judgment for sin has been borne for us by the Saviour, nevertheless He sits in the midst of the churches as the supreme Lord, clothed in holiness; and since He has furnished all power for us, He expects that we should avail ourselves of that power and give back holiness to Him.

Isaiah tells us that "righteousness shall be the girdle of his loins" (Isa. 11:5). Here the Son of Man has this golden girdle.

But who is He? An Enoch was taken into heaven after a walk with God. An Elijah was brought to glory in the chariot of fire. How shall we know that this One who died and who rose from the dead is more than these men of old who passed into Heaven without seeing death? Now every item in the description points clearly to the fact that He is none other than the eternal Jehovah. All that may be said of God may be said of Christ. So we find phrases applied to Him here in Revelation that in the Old Testament are applied to God alone. Who is this whose head and hair are white like wool and white like snow? Daniel "beheld till the thrones were cast down, and the Ancient of Days did sit, whose garment was white as snow, and the hair of his head like the pure wool: his throne was like the fiery flame . . ." (Dan. 7:9). There can be no doubt of the fact that in the mind of the writer of this book the risen Lord Jesus Christ is none other than the Ancient of Days of the Old Testament. This is the central figure of divine glory.

His eyes are as a flame of fire; His feet as gleaming brass glowing in a furnace; His voice, the voice of many waters. All of these references symbolize judgment. Habakkuk tells us that His eyes are too pure to behold evil with any compassion; that He cannot look upon iniquity with any kindness (Hab. 1:13). "Neither is there any creature that is not manifest in his sight: but all things are naked and open unto the eyes of him with whom we have to do" (Heb. 4:13).

We read in Corinthians that fire shall try every believer's work, of what sort it is (I Cor. 3:13). Malachi describes Him as sitting as a refiner before his fire (Mal. 3:2). The molten metal that splashes from the furnace is fiery in its gleaming. Brass was the material of the altar where the blood flowed to meet the claims of God's righteousness. His feet shall one day march in judgment. Then shall many of our works be burned, as He must destroy the wood, hay and stubble of our own fleshly providing.

When He speaks, His voice is as the voice of many waters. Twice in the prophecy of Ezekiel this same expression is used of the voice of God (1:24; 43:2). This voice, then, is the Old Testament symbol of the glory and the majesty of God and though this vision be that of the Son of Man, it is thus that our Lord Jesus now appears.

The context tells us that the seven stars which He holds in His hand are the messengers of the seven churches of which we shall see more in their place. Here they are in His right hand, so that His complete authority, whether for blessing or for government or for judgment, is immediately manifest.

The sharp, two-edged sword that goes from His mouth is, of course, the Word of God, living and powerful (Heb. 4:12). How terrible, then, that He has said, "He that rejecteth me, and receiveth not my words, hath one that judgeth him: the word that I have spoken, the same shall judge him in the last day" (John 12:48). And Isaiah tells us, "He shall smite the earth with the rod of his mouth" (Isa. 11:4), while we are also told that the antichrist will be consumed with the spirit of His mouth (II Thess. 2:8).

Is it any wonder, after all this description, that John says, "His face was as the sun shining in his might"? In the beginning of the world, the Lord made the sun to rule by day. Christ is to the world more than the sun is to the earth. His face did shine as the sun on the mount of transfiguration and His raiment was white as the light (Matt. 17:2). Thus we find our Lord robed in the majesty and glory of divine authority in connection with the things that now are; thus He is seated in Heaven. As we see Him in connection with His other works, we will find His titles and His garments quite different.

This is the vision of the Lord Jesus Christ as the Church will one day meet Him. With all of the joyful teaching concerning the coming of the Lord for His own, the Church has been prone to forget that all believers must appear before the judgment seat of Christ to receive the deeds done in the body (II Cor. 5:10). The fact that we shall have been made like unto Himself before this takes place should in no wise mitigate the solemnity of the prospect that is before us. It was to believers and of the believers' judgment that Paul wrote: "Knowing, therefore, the terror of the Lord, we persuade men" (II Cor. 5:11). And who can behold Christ judging the Church without feeling his own responsibility and failure and the responsibility and failure of the Church? Yet, when we fall before Him it is not to listen to words of doom but, with all the gentleness that characterizes the bridegroom's action with His bride, He lays His hand upon us as upon

John and says unto us as unto him, "Fear thou not." And why should we not fear? The only reason why a believer need not fear is that perfect love casteth out fear (I John 4:18). Let no one complain that they fear because they do not have perfect love, for it is not our imperfect love, but His perfect love that casts out fear.

And is this not another way of saying that which He spoke to John, "Fear thou not: I am the first and the last and the living One. I became dead and behold I am alive forever"? Do not fear, because the first and the last, in other words, Jehovah God, has become Man, has died and has risen, was delivered because of our offenses, but has been raised because of our justification (Rom. 4:25). "Herein is our love made perfect, that we may have boldness in the day of judgment" (I John 4:17). And in that trip from Heaven down to death and back to Heaven, He secured the keys of death and Hades. This is a most interesting sequel to the story of the struggle recounted in the book of Hebrews. There we read that our Lord Himself took part of flesh and blood so that through death He might destroy him that had the power of death, that is, the devil (Heb. 2:14). He took a body that He might die in order to destroy the malignant enemy who had the power of death, but though he had it, Christ brought back the keys with Him so that Satan has it no more.

Many people have found great confusion in their Bible study because they fail to see that Hades (intermediate state) contained two divisions—that for the souls and spirits of those in torment and that for the souls and spirits of the believers in joy—and that between the two there was a great gulf fixed (Luke 16:23-26). The bodies of all, believers and unbelievers, crumble into dust. This is spoken of in the Bible as death and sleep. Christ now has its key, so we are guaranteed new bodies like unto His resurrection body (Phil. 3:20, 21). The spirits and souls of all before Christ's death went to Hades. The division in which the righteous abode has been called Abraham's bosom (Luke 16:23). Christ also spoke of it as Paradise, announcing to the believing thief on the cross, "Today thou shalt be with me in Paradise" (Luke 23:43). This is where the spirit of the Lord went in triumph, where He spent the three days between crucifixion and resurrection while His body lay in death. This is the meaning of the phrase in the Apostles' Creed, "He descended into Hell"; that is, into Hades—that division of Hades that was Paradise.

But when He rose from the dead, He emptied the Paradise division of Hades of every soul that was there. Those who had been in a captivity of joy, yet away from the central presence of a holy God, with sins covered but not yet atoned for, now knew what it was to be fully justified and with Him to ascend into Heaven (Eph. 4:8). Indeed, at the resurrection of Christ the firstfruits (I Cor. 15:23; Lev. 23:10), a sheaf of these Old Testament saints, were raised with Christ

(Matt. 27:52, 53). All are now in Heaven. Today, when a believer dies, the body goes to dust in death, in sleep; the spirit and the soul, though absent from the body, are present with the Lord (II Cor. 5:8). They have departed from the body to be with Christ which is far better (Phil. 1:23). They are the living stones built upon Christ the Rock so that the gates of Hades shall never swing shut against them. The One who was dead and who is alive now forevermore has robbed death of its sting, Satan of his power, the grave of its victory. He has in His hands the keys of the prison house of the body on the one hand and of the soul and spirit on the other. This victory sets the heart of the believer at rest and dispels all fear of judgment.

The key that will unlock many doors in the book of Revelation is this nineteenth verse of the first chapter: "Write, therefore, the things thou sawest, and those that are, and those that are about to happen after these." From one point of view, this is the most important verse in the book, since the failure to realize its announcement of three divisions will bring confusion in the interpretation of many of the visions that follow.

It is the outline of the Book. The "things thou sawest" can refer to nothing but the vision of the risen Lord in the first verses of this chapter; "those that are" must be applied to the day of John, therefore, the age of the Church in which we are living; "those that are about to happen after these" will not begin their course until the age of the Church is over.

The last verse of this chapter is the introduction to the seven statements which are given in the following chapters. "The secret of the stars which thou sawest in my right hand and the seven golden lampstands." A secret in the Bible is not something mysterious, but something which has been hidden and is now revealed. The fact that the King James Version has transliterated the Greek word *musterion* should not mislead us.

We have seen that the Greek word *angelos* is almost universally used to mean messenger. The risen Lord is recognizing the ministry of overseers in the church. Scripture clearly teaches that God holds the overseers of the Church responsible for the spiritual condition of the people, and this responsibility is not only upon the pastors but upon all who hold positions of leadership. No angel in Heaven could be held responsible for the state of the Church on earth. This is clearly a word to human messengers, and reveals that even though there is no difference between the clergy and the laity, since God commands all believers to follow His Word and to walk worthy of the calling wherewith they have been called, there is nevertheless an increased responsibility upon those who are spiritual leaders because of the increased opportunity for spiritual service. The oneness of the invisible body of the Church is clearly taught in the epistles, but here the local church is the center of the scene. Every congregation must stand by itself independently and be individually responsible to God. Each lampstand is on its own base, giving forth its own light distinct from the other congregations. Christ in the midst of the lampstands shows us that the individual churches are to be centered in Him, gathered around His Word.

PART II
THE CHURCHES

CHAPTER 2

Verses 1–7

The Church at Ephesus

¹To the messenger of the Church in Ephesus write: These things says He who holds the seven stars in His right hand, He who walks in the midst of the seven golden lampstands.

²I know thy works and toil, and thy perseverance, and that thou canst not bear evil ones; and thou didst test those who say they are apostles and are not; and didst find them liars, ³and thou hast perseverance and for My name's sake thou didst labor and hast not wearied. ⁴But what I have against thee is that thou didst leave thy first love. ⁵Remember, therefore, from whence thou hast fallen, and repent, and practice the first works; if not, I am coming to thee and I will remove thy lampstand from its place, if thou dost not repent. ⁶But this thou hast, that thou hatest the works of the Nicolaitans, which I also hate.

⁷Let him who has an ear, hear what the Spirit is saying to the churches. To him who overcomes, I will give him to eat from the tree of life, which is in the midst of the paradise of God.
(Rev. 2:1-7, Free Translation)

The risen Lord Jesus Christ speaks to the churches. His utterances recorded in Revelation two and three are judicial verdicts, warnings, promises. They lay bare the failures of the church, they call to repentance, and incite to zeal.

Official correspondence in the United States Army is on stationery which has under the letterhead:

> From:
> To:
> Subject:

The first fact that strikes any reader of such correspondence is the author of the letter; then follows the name of the person to whom it is addressed; and finally a one-line statement of subject matter. It is interesting to note that all of the letters that have been found in the papyri of Egypt, contemporary with the writing of the New Testament, and written in the language of the New Testament Greek, open in practically this same form.

All the seven messages of the risen Lord are composed according to a certain structure. Careful analysis will reveal that an identical pattern is to be found in all seven. First, they are addressed to the messenger of the individual congregation; second, the title of the writer is given, each title being one of the descriptive elements of the vision of the risen Christ as recorded in the first chapter; third, to each church the Lord begins by saying, "I know thy works," for "all things are naked and opened unto the eyes of him with whom we have to do" (Heb. 4:13); fourth, the heart of the message is a joyful word of praise, a searching word of blame, or a combination of both; fifth, the message closes with an allusion to His coming. Following this, there are in every case two more details, but the order is reversed after the third letter. The message has been addressed to the congregation as a whole. There is a final word of admonition to the individual: "He that hath an ear let him hear"; and lastly, there is a promise to the overcomer. In the last four messages, the promise to the overcomer precedes the word of admonition. As time went on, was it necessary for the thought of reward to take precedence over the thought of obedience?

The world did not know these churches. Their members were despised in the cities in which they dwelt. Had they all been wiped out in some catastrophe, there would have been little commotion in the world about them. The same is true today.

Let us look at these verses in some detail. Christ speaks here as the One who holds the seven stars in His right hand, as the One who walks in the midst of the seven golden lampstands. We have seen previously that this has reference to the churches. It should be noted that our Lord both holds the churches in His hand and walks in the midst of them. It is obvious that these phrases speak of His double attitude toward believers. We have in Him a standing, or a position, and we have in ourselves a state, or a condition. He holds us in His hand because of what He is, because of the value of His own work, and we are secure. He walks among us because of what we are, because of His desire to bring our lives closer to Himself.

"I know thy works and toil," He says, "and thy perseverance, and that thou canst not bear evil ones; and thou didst test those who say they are apostles and who are not; and didst find them liars." Happy the church that can hear this word of commendation today. Here was a church that was laboring, toiling, persevering. This use of words almost synonymous, each expressing a new shade of kindred meaning, emphasizes the truth of the strong witness of the Ephesian believers. Paul visited the Ephesian church several times. Some sixty years had passed since the day of Pentecost. Two generations of believers had

risen in the history of the church. When for the last time the great
apostle passed near Ephesus, the elders came to meet him. One of the
most moving scenes in all of Scripture is the account of Paul's farewell
to these Ephesian elders. The story is told in the twentieth chapter of
Acts. It is important to us to note a prophecy Paul made. "For I
know this," he told them, "that after my departing shall grievous
wolves enter in among you, not sparing the flock. Also of your own
selves shall men arise, speaking perverse things to draw away disciples
after them." Paul and these elders were now in Heaven, but the words
he had spoken to them that day are shown to be true. The prophecy
is fulfilled. The difficulties of the Ephesian church did not arise from
persecutions from the world; the evil came from within.

One of the most striking phrases of commendation is that this church
could not bear evil ones. So many Christians today find it easy to
bear with the real enemies of Christ who are within the church. Elsewhere we are told that we are to bear each other's burdens, and that
we are to bear with the weak (Gal. 6:2; Rom. 14:1). But we are
told just as specifically that we are not to bear with the false. Too
many churches and too many individuals can and do bear with those
who are evil. The church at Ephesus was commended for a lack of
this kind of tolerance—because they were patient and impatient—patient in their witness, impatient toward the evil ones.

Ephesus had tested them and found them liars. We should not forget that their testing and their judging was in obedience to God's
Word. God tells us that we must judge. Someone interjects, "Why, I
thought Christ said, 'Judge not that ye be not judged.' " True, He did;
but just as truly, He said, "Judge righteous judgment." The command
to abstain from judgment refers to all matters which have to do with
character, actions, works and doings of individuals. "Try the spirits,"
says the Holy Spirit through the apostle John. "Try the spirits whether
they are of God: because many false prophets are gone out into the
world" (I John 4:1). This is a call to judgment. Men say they are
apostles. Should we take them at their face value? God says we
should test them. The Ephesian believers had done so and had found
them liars.

It follows logically that there must be a standard by which men
are to be tested. Paul commended the believers at Berea because they
would not believe him until they checked with the Scriptures in Bible
study to find if he were an apostle or a liar (Acts 17:11). God gives
this very definite standard by which men are to be tested. The question is simply to know whether or not a man is preaching in accordance
with the Word of God. "Whosoever transgresseth, and abideth not in
the doctrine of Christ, hath not God . . . If there come any unto you,
and bring not this doctrine, receive him not into your house, neither
bid him God speed" (II John 9, 10). This is not intolerance; this is

obedience. A man may believe what he pleases, but we, as believers, must be intransigent, standing where God would have us stand. Though we admit the right of any man to believe what he pleases, we deny him that right as a worker in our congregation. We can respect a man who resigns the ministry because he does not believe in the biblical doctrines. We know he is wrong; we do not agree with him, but we respect his honesty. The Lord Jesus Christ commends the Ephesian believers because they have been strict in their stand on apostleship.

Yet in spite of the approbation, there was something lacking. The church had left its first love. We should be careful not to mistake this for brotherly love; this certainly refers to love for Christ. The Spirit speaks through this message to us today. Perhaps we have labored. Perhaps we have been careful to test the belief of those who seek to come among us. Nevertheless, would He have to say, "But what I have against thee, is that thou didst leave thy first love"? When we think of the Lord Jesus Christ, is it with the same freshness of love as at the first?

If we have been carrying a heavy load, and suddenly put it down, there is the feeling of lightness and relief from the burden at first; then we become accustomed to being without it. When our sins were first taken away, we felt the love and joy of resting in the finished work of Christ. But have we slipped back into a drab taking things for granted? David knew what this meant. He prayed "Restore unto me the joy of thy salvation" (Ps. 51:12). As we walk along the years of the Christian life, are we allowing sin to dog our steps more closely? Are we neglecting prayer life, and the study of the Word? Are we a little less faithful and zealous? He misses our first love. Let us return.

It is in this sense that we must think of the fifth verse: "Remember, therefore, from whence thou hast fallen, and repent, and practice the first works." They had fallen from that fellowship that is both high and deep and that is with the Lord Jesus Christ. John tells us elsewhere that "if we walk in the light, as he is in the light, we have fellowship one with the other" (I John 1:7). This verse is sometimes applied to fellowship among Christians. This is not the meaning. The fellowship of which John speaks is vertical and not horizontal. It is the fellowship of the individual with Christ. Fellowship among Christians may exist even without all the parties concerned being in pure fellowship with Christ, for our hearts are not holy enough to discern the spiritual relationship of another soul with Christ, even if that soul be very close to us by blood or friendship. God and our hearts alone know when we have grieved Him and when that fellowship has been momentarily broken. Our fellowship with Him is dependent upon the working of His holiness in our lives. If that first love is not glowing in our moment by moment thought toward Him, we are fallen from the highest place of privilege. It was to the Ephesian church that Paul wrote that the believer's position was in the heavenly places in Christ Jesus. For fellowship with Christ to be broken means that the believer is fallen all the way from Heaven to earth as to the plane of his living. Is it any wonder that He says, "Remember, therefore, from whence thou art fallen"?

The call to repentance is not to be confounded with that which comes to souls under conviction of sin. It is something far more spiritual. In the shops of one of the great railroad systems, we have seen scales so delicate that the film of human breath blown on one of the balances is sufficient to outweigh the equal balance. Some such thought as this is to be found in the call to repent. The breath of the flesh has touched the lever. Spiritual yieldedness is thrown out of balance. We are here called back to that silence of soul where the heart goes up to Him with the look of full contrition which He knows so well and which He is so eager to turn into a smile by the reflected light of His own smile. For we are brought back to our first works, not to those described in the phrase, "not of works lest any man should boast" (Eph. 2:9); but to those which result from the inner relationship to God. The believer should be able to sing, "If ever I loved Thee, my Jesus, 'tis now," but too often, if we are honest, we must say, "We have not loved Thee as we ought." When love goes, work that has any value in His eyes, of necessity, goes with it. Any half-hearted service can do no more than dishonor the Lord. We may, indeed, profess, and loudly, that we have found in Him our "all in all," but if we contradict this by our lives, do we not prove ourselves to be untrue, and show that we have not found in Christ full salvation for the heart?

It is to be noted that no question of doctrine is raised in all this. The difficulty of these believers was that they were holding to orthodoxy without a heart of personal devotion to Christ. This is the real meaning of the letter without the Spirit. This loss of love showed the soul's distance from Christ, for we do not think longingly of those we have ceased to love; but true love ever annihilates distance, even though half a world lies between love and its object. The heart bridges the distance constantly.

These believers were told that they were to return to that early attitude of fellowship, and if not, they were to sustain a great loss. "If not, I am coming to thee, and I will remove thy lampstand from its place." It goes without saying that there is no reference here to the loss of salvation, although this verse has been quoted by those who, for some reason difficult to comprehend, seek to prove that salvation is not safe. An example will perhaps show the true meaning of this passage. A certain church had a pastor who led the congregation in deep devotional life for several years. During his ministry the church attained a reputation for faithfulness and spiritual life. Its lampstand was in a prominent place; its witness for God was unquestioned. The pastor received a call to minister in another city. The church whose pulpit thus became vacant turned its eyes away from the Lord and toward its own reputation. The leaders did not seek God's man to minister to them, but sought someone with a big name, capable of filling their pulpit. Within a year or two the congregation had dwindled; the church no longer stood in a prominent spiritual position in the community. Another church almost unknown before that time, came forward to the place of faithful witness. The lampstand of the first church had been removed from its place. The history of Christendom is marked by the wreckage of such churches. This was the awful danger that threatened the Ephesian church. In their case, the risen Lord gave them a timely warning. In our day, the warning has been given, and is sounded no more, save through the pages of God's Word.

But the grace of the Lord found even one more thing to commend in this church. In spite of their enfeebled love, they hated the works of the Nicolaitans, and in solemn words, the Lord adds, "Which I also hate." Later on, in this same chapter, writing to the church at Pergamos, He speaks again of the Nicolaitans and their doctrine and announces His hatred thereof. Who were these Nicolaitans whose deeds grew into doctrine, hated by the Lord? The commentaries say it was some unknown sect. We have no knowledge from history. In fact, there is nothing but the name itself, and yet I believe that this is sufficient.

The etymological meaning of the word itself is sufficient. Break the word in two. The first syllables come from the same root as the Greek word *nike* which means "victor" and "victory." In the very next verse the same root is to be found in the word that is translated "overcometh." The last half of the word, both in the Greek and in our own English, means "the laity." Back in the second verse, there were those of whom it is said they were found to be liars. Here, then, as early as the days of John, was the claim to apostolic succession already presented by men and denied by God. Paul brought credentials from Heaven and rejoiced in the fact that His Gospel was not man's, that it was not received from men nor by teaching, but by the revelation of Jesus Christ. Timothy and Titus, though taught of Paul, could certainly have said that God had revealed His truth to their hearts. Any attempt to alter this spiritual order is Nicolaitanism—the exaltation of a clergy over the laity. This thing God hates. In Corinth, by the time of Paul's second epistle, these "false apostles and deceitful workers" were at work in the Corinthian church, "transforming themselves into the apostles of Christ." It was then that the Holy Spirit gave us the great declaration which tells us that when we look for the devil we are not to forget to look in the pulpit. Sometimes people are startled when they hear for the first time that God has said to look in the pulpit for Satan, but this is certainly the implication of the Corinthian passage. Paul says that it is no marvel that the false apostles and deceitful workers should transform themeslves into the apostles of Christ because "Satan himself is transformed into an angel of light. Therefore it is no great thing if his ministers (and we must not be thrown off the scent by the fact that they may be called doctors of divinity) also be transformed as the ministers of righteousness" (II Cor. 11:14, 15).

The true apostolic succession is not by the ordination of men, nor is it by the claims of men; it is by the empowering of God. No man with spiritual common sense would believe for a moment that the hand of bishop, classis, synod, presbytery, conference or any other ordaining body could be a substitute for the supernatural calling and the divine infilling. Wherever God has called His man, there will be an example of the flock and not a lording over the charge allotted to him (I Pet. 5:3). God has called ministers and not lords. Nicolaitanism may begin with the idea of ministering, but its deeds prove its satanic source, while its supposed rights to its heritage become a vested interest, which God says He hates.

The message to the church at Ephesus is now concluded. God has spoken to the congregation. Will the congregation follow His leading? As to the application of the message, it makes no difference to you and to me whether the group obeys or not. Obedience is commanded of the whole church, but each individual has his particular place in the plan of God. The Spirit now speaks to each believer. "Let him who has an ear hear what the Spirit is saying to the churches." No believer has the right to excuse himself on the grounds that the church is in a low spiritual condition and that he, therefore, is not to be expected to rise above the average. God orders him to hear the Spirit's word. The hearing is not merely becoming aware of what is being said; it is acting upon it. In the early morning the child hears his father say, "It is time to get up." Only the child who gets up can be said truly to have heard.

The first of the promises to the overcomer is now given. To the one who faces the necessity of partaking in strong church discipline, and who is not willing to stop short because of an implied slur in the epithets that will be applied to all who name heresy or who fight against vested interest in the church of Christ, the Lord Jesus Christ promises that he shall be given to eat from the tree of life which is in the midst of the paradise of God. Some have said that eating from the tree of life was the equivalent of receiving eternal life, but this is most evidently a false interpretation. Eternal life is the prerequisite for membership in the true Church. Eating of the tree of life is a reward that shall be given to the overcomer in addition to his salvation. His work, built upon the foundation that is Christ Jesus, abides the test of the Lord's appearing, and he receives over and above his entrance into eternal life, a place in the Heavens in the midst of the paradise of God. We are aware that the conception of Heaven depicted by medieval artists placed the apostles on front seats, the popes and bishops near at hand, and the rich who had given largely to the church only one step farther away. The apostles' place is secure. The Lord Jesus Christ has told us that they would sit upon twelve thrones judging the twelve tribes during the millennial kingdom (Luke 22:30). But for the rest, He has said that earth's first shall be Heaven's last. We need not worry about the frown of the world if we have the smile of the Lord.

Verses 8–11

The Church at Smyrna

⁸*And to the messenger of the church in Smyrna write: These things saith the First and the Last, who became dead and lived* AGAIN. ⁹*I know thy tribulation and thy poverty, (but thou art rich); and the blasphemy from those who are saying they are Jews, when they are not, but are a synagogue of Satan.* ¹⁰*Have no fear of the things thou art going to suffer; behold the Devil is going to cast some from among you into prison, in order that ye may be tested; and you shall have tribulation ten days: become faithful until death, and I will give you the crown of the life.* ¹¹*He that hath an ear, let him hear what the Spirit saith to the churches. He that overcometh cannot be hurt in any way by the second death.*
(Rev. 2:8-11, Free Translation)

It is not easy to suffer. God Himself tells us that "no chastening for the present seemeth to be joyous, but grievous" (Heb. 12:11). To the suffering saints of all ages, the risen Lord Jesus Christ speaks in His Word to the messenger to the church at Smyrna.

The city of Smyrna received its name from one of the principal products for which it was renowned in commerce. It was the port of myrrh. It is most significant, therefore, that our Lord should speak as He does to the church at Smyrna. It will be the suffering church. Myrrh was used to embalm the bodies of the dead. Carefully the linens were prepared, and wound around the bodies of the loved ones, while myrrh was packed between the folds of the cloth. Thus was the body of our Lord embalmed. They brought Him myrrh with the gold and frankincense at His birth, because He was to receive death at the hands of men before He should leave this world. When He comes again, they will bring Him gold and frankincense but no myrrh (Isa. 60:6).

In the midst of the Church today, there is suffering. They that "live godly in Christ Jesus shall suffer persecution" (II Tim. 3:12).

"In the world ye shall have tribulation" (John 16:33). There is one sense in which this message, then, applies to all who suffer at any phase of the history of the Church. The passage can certainly be applied to the suffering Church of our day. We are inclined to forget that there have been perhaps more martyrs who have literally shed their blood for their faith during the time in which we have been alive on the earth than during any other generation of history. Thinking of the great persecutions of the early centuries and of the time of the Inquisition, some will immediately say that this is preposterous, but out over the world in our generation, there have been many martyrs. The Waldensians and Albigensians, the Huguenots, the true believers who came under the Inquisition, were all of the line of the church of Smyrna. We in the Occident are relatively free from persecution, yet there is a growing intolerance that may easily lead to more martyrdom.

The witness of honest and intelligent people shows us the church of Smyrna in Russia. From 1920 to 1923 it was permitted to circulate the Bible, even Soviet presses printed it, and creditable witnesses report that hundreds of thousands were converted; but in 1924, the authorities began to shut down, the persecution began and has grown more and more violent. There was the absolute interdiction of the printing of the Bible. Christians by the thousands were exiled to Siberia. Here is real persecution and real suffering.

But there is a primary sense in which the message must be applied to another day. As Ephesus characterizes the apostolic age, so Smyrna characterizes the period of the great persecutions. This was the martyr age of the Church, and Polycarp, one of the most renowned of the early Christians, who gave his life for his Lord, was himself a bishop of the church at Smyrna.

The Lord tells this suffering church that they will have tribulation ten days, and even the secular historians are in accord that there were ten great persecutions about this time. Their trouble is not to last forever. It was to be for ten days, but their Lord was to endure forever. Not for always will there be suffering. The Lord will come and put an end to tears. Who is it that speaks to this church? It is the One who was dead and is alive. It is as the Sufferer that He speaks to His suffering ones. He understands the contradiction of sinners. He suffered a death that was infinitely worse than it is possible for man to experience, for He was the Holy God and His death was not only the suffering of the body, but the greater anguish of becoming sin for us.

Does any believer have to go through suffering? The Lord Jesus knows all about it. He was dead and is alive. When He thus reminds the suffering ones, He calls them to think of the cross. No believer ever passes through any trial that the Lord has not known. His lips have drained every cup we can ever know.

These suffering ones of Smyrna were wretched because of all they were suffering, but God knows them. He found the treasure that was hidden in the field and hid it once more for Himself. He found the pearl of great price and for joy thereof sold all that He had to redeem it by His blood. What though we be unknown to the world? We are known to God. The tired heroes are brought before the hosts of the universe to be distinguished as members of the legion of honor, for though God knows their trouble and poverty and knows how the world looks upon it, He adds that little phrase that makes riches out of poverty, that touches trouble with the kiss of God, and makes this world's sufferings not worthy to be compared with the glory that shall be revealed in us.

Here is one of the greatest contrasts of the Bible. "I know thy poverty, but thou art rich." Everything depends on the point of view. Some linguists have claimed that the word "Huguenot" is from the root word *gueux* meaning "beggars." The world has frequently looked upon persecuted Christians as upon some desperate rabble, but the beggars press invisible gold in their palms and go on for God "having nothing, and yet possessing all things" (II Cor. 6:10). What matters the frown of the world if we have the smile of God? Men hear an evil report. God records the good report. Deceivers to men, yet true to God; unknown to the world, well known to God; dying, and behold we live with life that is eternal and abundant; poor, and yet making many rich.

We cannot pass by this parenthesis without referring to the church of Laodicea. There we hear God speaking to the unfaithful church. Like sword thrusts, the divine words pierce them. "Thou sayest, I am rich, and increased with goods, and have need of nothing; and knowest not that thou art wretched, and miserable, and poor, and blind and naked" (Rev. 3:17). What a contrast with Smyrna! The poor church God calls rich. The rich church God calls poor. All this is current history. How many congregations possess great stone buildings, beautifully furnished, with equipment sufficient to compete with the world in providing amusement and entertainment! Bond issues may be floated to build churches and missions and schools; but without the touch of God, it is all dead. Increasingly every believer must take his stand for the rich poor church or the poor rich church. We must stand with the world or with God. Our appraisal of poverty and riches will depend on whether our eyes see material things only or whether we are able to consider the invisible and discern spiritual realities.

Suddenly the scene changes. Here where all has seemed strength, we find a weakness. In the midst of the saints were blasphemers. There were some here who said they were Jews but were not. This was a peril more terrible than the martyrdom that awaited some of them. They had been told that there was no need to fear the enemy

which could destroy only the body, but that they were to fear God
who could destroy both body and soul in hell (Matt. 10:28). Persecution was an open assault from without. The blasphemy was a pious-
tongued danger which rose from within.

Here in the church of Smyrna Satan had introduced his children.
They were in opposition to God's true people as blasphemy is always
in opposition to truth. As the Gospel spread among the Gentiles,
Jewish voices were not lacking to demand the circumcision of each
convert along Old Testament lines. Because the law had been "holy,
just, and good" (Rom. 7:12), many failed to see that it was a carnal
commandment which had to be set aside because of its "weakness and
unprofitableness" (Heb. 7:16-18).

The first church council was called to settle the matter. Some were
saying, "Except ye be circumcised after the manner of Moses, ye cannot be saved" (Acts 15:1). Peter, certainly moved by the Holy Spirit,
not only told of God's great work among the Gentiles, but asked why
anyone would want to "tempt God to put a yoke upon the neck of the
disciples which neither our fathers nor we were able to bear?" (Acts
15:10). He definitely discarded law as a means of salvation and announced that his hope was in the grace of the Lord Jesus Christ.

The decision of the council was certainly God-inspired, since we
read in the findings that were sent to the churches that it was the decision of the Holy Spirit. Those who had preached salvation through
legalism were said to have "troubled [the believers] with words, sub-
verting [their] souls" (Acts 15:24). But Peter, ever prone to follow
the flesh rather than the Spirit, evidently fell into the hands of some
strong-minded exponents of legalism, abandoned his God-given position, and lapsed in his practice though probably still keeping his faith.
The Judaistic minority, evidently disgruntled, followed Paul to Antioch
and the struggle grew so great that Paul was forced to reprove Peter
publicly (Gal. 2:11).

Writing to the Galatians, Paul quoted at length from his answer
which so effectively silenced Peter. One statement therein shows why
this doctrine as found in the church of Smyrna was called blasphemy,
and its followers members of the synagogue of Satan. For Paul showed
definitely that the attempt to be saved by law degrades Christ and
makes Him the minister of sin. "If, while we seek to be justified by
Christ, we ourselves also are found sinners, is therefore Christ the
minister of sin? God forbid. For if I build again the things which
I destroyed, I make myself a transgressor" (Gal. 2:17, 18).

The council at Jerusalem had been meant to settle the question forever, but tares grew with the wheat. Judaistic Christians multiplied in
the church and followed Paul everywhere. Even in Galatia, almost
entirely Gentile, the evil was so great that Paul devoted almost the
entire epistle to it. The message to the church at Smyrna covers a

period from two to eight generations after the epistle to the Galatians was written, yet the tares were growing. Peter had been definitely convinced, and a few years later wrote that "the longsuffering of our Lord is salvation; even as our beloved brother Paul also, according to the wisdom given unto him, hath written unto you." He accepts by faith that which he could not comprehend and continues, "As also in all his epistles, speaking in them of these things; in which are some things hard to be understood, which they that are unlearned and unstable wrest, as they do also the other scriptures, unto their own destruction" (II Pet. 3:15, 16). That position which he once practiced, he now definitely names "the error of the wicked" and calls his readers "to grow in grace."

Our Lord told us that the tares would grow in the same field with the wheat throughout this entire age. In the church today we find a legalism which has not grown less blasphemous because it has grown more respectable. In the churches today there are still two schools of legalism: those who, like Peter, aware of the truth, nevertheless fall into legalistic practices which they will one day be forced to recant, if not in this life, at least before the throne of their Lord; the other school is made up of the tares—blasphemers who substitute character for Calvary. They are "false teachers . . . who privily bring in damnable heresies, even denying the Lord that bought them" (II Pet. 2:1).

A Christian must never forget that salvation is by grace, and if it be by grace, then it is no more of works, and that if we are saved by grace we are also kept saved by grace.

The true believer will not be easily trapped by those who would call Christians into the bondage of the law and subject them to the keeping of the seventh day rather than the first, but the believing heart must be careful that its keeping of the first day is in grace and not of the law. The true believer will not be easily trapped by those who would make all salvation on the basis of many works, but the believing heart must be careful lest it hold for a moment that its salvation could be lost after once the Lord Jesus has implanted the divine life. There are many Peters in the church today who need the Spirit's proving. They must be resisted to their face, for they are to be blamed. They are not standing fast in liberty. They have been entangled again in the yoke of bondage. These, true believers, are not to be confused with the blasphemers of the synagogue of Satan who carry their legalism to the place where it dethrones Christ.

And now the Lord turns back again abruptly to His faithful saints. "Fear none of these things which thou shalt suffer," He tells them, and this is both a prophecy and a promise. It shows that He knows in advance all that is to happen to His own. It shows that He has conquered every situation which may face His children. It shows us that His perfect love has cast out the fear that might go with suffering. The

Lord has not promised us grace even to think of how it might feel to be burned at the stake, but the Lord has promised us the grace to support us in any circumstance, even if we should be burned at the stake. We are to live our lives one day at a time—yes, one moment at a time.

Since we know that all things work together for our good, why should we fear? Has not every bit of suffering been measured out by the hand of love more carefully than the mother portions out the milk that goes into the bottle for her infant child? No formula was ever so carefully followed as that of the love of the risen Saviour toward those who are to share some of the suffering He knew. To the Colossian church, Paul wrote of filling up that which was lacking in the affliction of Christ (Col. 1:24). This raises an immediate question. Is there anything lacking in the suffering of Christ? Careful thought will show us that there is. Christ suffered in three ways. First of all, He suffered as man—all the sufferings that go with human nature. This suffering He shared with us. Secondly, He suffered for man. This was a substitute and in our place. There is no sharing of this suffering. He took it all—and alone. But lastly, He suffered from man. This suffering is not yet complete. During the age in which we live, He is still suffering from man, but in the person of His saints. This suffering we share with Him. What difference, then, does it make if the devil casts some of us in prison that we may be tested? He has measured out all the suffering in advance. In this case, ten days. Wave after wave came upon the Church. When the tenth great persecution had taken place, God saw that it was stopped.

To the individual, a reward is offered. "Be thou faithful unto death, and I will give thee a crown of life." Mark well that this is not a promise of life but the crown of life. Life is not a reward for faithfulness. Life is a gift of grace. The crown of life belongs not to all, but only to that select few whom He chooses to suffer with Him, even unto physical death. It would appear, indeed, that one does not have to go all the way to active martyrdom to receive this reward, since He tells us elsewhere, "Blessed is the man that endureth temptation: for when he is tried, he shall receive the crown of life, which the Lord has promised to them that love him" (James 1:12).

Once more the Spirit warns, "He that hath an ear, let him hear what the Spirit saith unto the churches." And the final word is, "He that overcometh shall not be hurt of the second death." We have heard somewhere the story of a small boy who was led out with his father at the time of the Roman persecutions to be given to the wild beasts of the arena. As the cages were opened and the ferocious animals appeared, the little boy said, "Will it hurt, Father?" and the father, placing his arm around the lad's shoulders, looked off to the invisible and said, "Perhaps for one swift moment, but he that over-cometh shall not be hurt of the second death."

What difference does it make how we leave this world so long as we know we are to triumph over it at the first resurrection? Death may be a sleep for the body, but it is entrance into life abundant for the soul and spirit. "To be absent from the body, and to be present with the Lord" (II Cor. 5:8). "To depart is to be with Christ; which is far better." With joy we face all eventualities, knowing that for us "the second death has no power" (Rev. 20:6).

Verses 12–17

The Church at Pergamos

[12]And to the messenger of the church in Pergamos write: These things saith He who hath the sharp, two-edged sword; [13]I know where thou dwellest, where Satan's throne is; and thou holdest fast My Name, and didst not deny My faith, even in the days in which Antipas was My faithful witness, who was slain among you, where Satan dwelleth.

[14]But I have a few things against thee, because thou hast there those who hold the teaching of Balaam, who taught Balak to cast a stumbling block before the sons of Israel, to eat things sacrificed unto idols, and to commit fornication. [15]So hast thou also those who hold the teaching of the Nicolaitans, in like manner.

[16]Repent, therefore; if not, I am coming to thee speedily, and will make war against them with the sword of My mouth.

[17]Let him who has an ear hear what the Spirit is saying to the churches. To him who overcomes, I will give of the hidden manna, and will give to him a white stone, and on the stone a new name written which no one knows but the one who receives it.
(Rev. 2:12-17, Free Translation)

Degeneration is the law of all life apart from God. Rust, decomposition, decay and corrosion are the common lot of every material thing in the universe. The sun, the rain, the air itself—all carry resistless arms of destruction. The very stars grow old.

The risen Lord Jesus Christ, speaking to the churches, shows that the same law is at work in spiritual life. He said, "Apart from me, ye can do nothing" (John 15:5). At first thought, it would appear that this statement made to the disciples the night before the crucifixion, would indicate that the Church would stand still apart from Christ, that there would be no forward movement. The message to the church at Pergamos shows that it means even more. The Church does not stand still apart from Christ; it degenerates.

Ephesus had been the church of the wheat sown on good ground, bringing forth fruit, but the first love had been lost. By the time of

Smyrna, the tares had taken root, and, within the boundaries of the
visible church were those whom the risen Lord saw as the synagogue
of Satan. By the time the Pergamos stage was reached the third of
the parables was finding its fulfillment. The mustard seed which the
Lord meant to be nothing more than an herb grows up to be a tree,
and the birds of the air — the devil's birds — come to lodge in its
branches.

The Lord appointed twelve apostles; the Holy Spirit ordered the
choosing of a few deacons and commanded that elders should be
ordained in every place. This simple organization would have been
sufficient for all the Lord intended to do by His Church in the world.
Whence, then, has come the hideous monster which parades the world
today in pious mask under the name of the Church? It was Pergamos
which saw the sudden cancerous growth from the mustard seed which
the Lord had planted.

When did the church thus virtually change its nature? History
shows us that it was not a gradual development, but that in large
measure, one sudden event took the church out of its proper place of
hated but faithful witness and into the place of pampered privilege in
the world. The paragraph to the church of Pergamos describes the
change and warns believers today against acquiescence in traditional
ways. The very word "Pergamos" has in it the same root from which
we get our English words for bigamy and polygamy. It is the word
for marriage. The particle which forms the first syllable frequently
calls attention to something that is objectionable. "Pergamos" signifies
a mixed marriage in the most objectionable sense of the word, for it
is the marriage of the organization of the church of Jesus Christ with
the world in defiance of the distinct command of the Spirit, "Be ye
not unequally yoked together with unbelievers: for what fellowship
hath righteousness with unrighteousness? and what communion hath
light with darkness? And what concord hath Christ with Belial? or
what part hath he that believeth with an infidel? And what agreement hath the temple of God with idols?" (II Cor. 6:14-16).

How did the world come to fall in love with the church? The Lord
had said to believers, "If the world hate you, ye know that it hated
me before it hated you. If ye were of the world, the world would
love his own . . ." (John 15:18, 19). It follows logically that when
the world came to love the church, the church had first become part
of the world.

In the early part of the fourth century, the monarch of the Roman
Empire died, leaving the question of succession in dispute. The leader
of the forces of the west marched his army toward the leader of the
forces of the east. Near a little river in northern Italy, at a place
called the Milvian Bridge, the two armies bivouacked over against
each other waiting for the coming day and the order to battle. The

western general, who had come into some minor contact with Christianity, that night made a vow. If he won the battle, he would become a Christian. Later tradition added much to this event. Some say that he saw a vision of a cross in the sky with the Latin inscription, *in hoc signo vinces* ("by this sign conquer"). We can ignore all this accretion to truth. The stark fact remains — Constantine made a bargain with some supernatural power to join the church organization if he won his battle. Succeeding events would indicate that the bargain was made with the prince of this world, the god of this age, the spirit who blinds the minds of men that they should believe the lie. Constantine was "converted." There is no evidence that he was born again.

Imagine the whispering that went around Rome. The Emperor had become a Christian. Out of the catacombs they came. Instead of being persecuted, they found themselves popular. Like a youngster among heavy drinkers, the church's head was turned by the wine of the world.

The priests of the pagan temples had been paid from the purse of the Empire, but now Caesar was a Christian and the priests of Mars and Venus hastened to their baptisms. For the first time in the history of the church, salaries were paid to Christian workers. Tradition has it that Constantine's mother was the first to give the money for the erection of a church building. Before, kitchens and catacombs, humble dwellings or humbler dungeons had echoed with the quiet hymns of the believers whose songs of praise were frequently changed to the shout of the martyr as the believers were dragged forth to the arena.

All this was over now. The rags of persecution gave way to softer garments, and the church began to enjoy the feel of silk upon its flesh. Thus the Pergamos stage of church history came into being, the church was married to the world.

The risen Lord Jesus, in order to speak to such a church, selects among His many titles the one of judgment connected with the Word of God. It is "He who hath the sharp, two-edged sword." This sword is spoken of in two other passages of Scripture. In Hebrews 4:12, it is the discerner of the thoughts and intents of the heart. The Greek word for "discerner" is *critikos* and shows us that the Word is the standard by which God judges the heart and life of the believer. But in the nineteenth chapter of the book of Revelation, the same sword is in evidence, not as a critic of believers, but as an instrument of war with which He smites the nations. This same thought is seen in the sixteenth verse of the message to Pergamos where He says, "I am coming to thee speedily, and will make war against them with the sword of my mouth." One commentator tries to say that these letters cannot apply to any events of church history because of the threat of war, saying that Christ does not war against His Church. This is to entirely misread the passage. In the midst of the worldliness of the

newly intoxicated church, there are those who stand faithful to the
Word of God. Most surely, the wheat will never be burned, but most
surely, the tares will be burned. "I will come to thee." Indeed, the
hope of the believer is this. "And will make war against them" is the
judgment upon ecclesiasticism which slumbers but which will one day
break forth.

Outwardly, the Pergamos church was the dwelling where Satan's
throne was located. The Greek word is clearly "throne," but the translators of the King James Version softened it down to "seat." Let us
not be afraid of the phrase. It is Satan's throne.

It should be noted that Hislop in his famous book, *The Two
Babylons,* traces the removal of the Babylonian priesthood to Pergamos. There is, therefore, a distinct connection between the ancient
devil worship of Babylon and Pergamos where Satan's throne was
declared at one time to be.

In view of all the terrible implications of the presence of Satan's
throne in a city, it can readily be seen that the risen Lord is not com-
plimenting the church at Pergamos when He tells them that they are
dwelling near that throne. The believer is in the world, but he is not
of it. As it was counted a matter of faith for Abraham to live in tents
and a lack of faith for Lot to dwell in Sodom, so there is a shadow
on the believers in Pergamos who had their root too firmly in the
ground that was polluted. No believer is responsible for being in the
world, but we are responsible for our attitudes toward the world. A
man may own much property and yet be heavenly-minded, while another may lack title even to a grain of sand and yet mind earthly
things. This is the contrast which Paul made to the Philippian believers when he warned against those who walked unworthily, minding
earthly things, and called true believers to remember that their citizen-
ship was in Heaven (Phil. 3:18-20).

Yet even in such surroundings the believers held fast Christ's name
and had not denied His faith. It is wonderful that the risen Lord
can find something to praise in this church. He who has said that at
the best we are unprofitable servants (Luke 17:10), sees a doctrinal
faithfulness to praise, even in the midst of His condemnation of the
evil in the church. While it is the personal belief of the writer that
orthodoxy of life is to be counted almost as a doctrine, since "the fruit
of the Spirit" (Gal. 5:22) can be considered not only as life but as
doctrine, we must note, nevertheless, that the Lord here praises those
who were dwelling in the shadow of Satan's throne for their faithfulness to His Name and the body of Christian doctrine. This should
make us very slow to deny the salvation of individuals in any body
of Christianity where true doctrine is held.

One in this church had died for his faith. In that place where believers were fellow-dwellers with Satan, one man had stood out so faith-

fully that death had resulted. Here he stands in the imperishable Word of God, unknown to historians, but eternally remembered by the Lord Jesus Christ. Believers may be the object of ridicule by those who set up their own standards of intellectual worth and value. But the record stands that all who are His own are known to God. Though Antipas is not to be found in any secular history, we shall meet him before Heaven's throne, in the day when the Lord Jesus Christ shall say, "Well done, thou good and faithful servant."

But the doctrinal faithfulness of this group in Pergamos is over-balanced by error. Nicolaitanism is fully accepted. What were mere deeds in Ephesus had become doctrine. The clergy are exalted and are lording it over God's heritage (I Pet. 5:3). Furthermore, Balaam-ism was prominent in this church. It should be remembered that the Nicene and Athanasian Creeds date from this period of history, creeds that are orthodox as to the Person of Christ, but which omit so much truth that they cannot be acceptable as standards to the one who would hold the whole Word of God. Creeds were drawn up by councils where members of the clergy were in complete domination, and at one of which Constantine, the emperor, not yet even baptized, proceeded to a golden throne, while all present stood waiting for him to take his seat as the honorary president of the highest assembly of the church.

The church was orthodox, but with a dull, dead orthodoxy that per-mitted error to grow. The reality of justification was almost unknown. More and more confidence was being placed in the ceremonial rites of the church. None of the creeds contained articles reflecting any real knowledge of salvation. In these centuries which preceded the Dark Ages, many people had come in contact with Christianity. They fre-quented the churches, and yet refused baptism so that they might ask for it at the time of their death, in order to have more sins of their lives behind them at the time the washing took place.

Those who lord it over the people will soon begin to destroy them. The word Balaam means "the destroyer of the people." If we turn back to the history of this strange figure as recorded in the book of Numbers, we find that which clarifies three passages in the New Testa-ment where "the error of Balaam" (Jude 11), "the way of Balaam" (II Pet. 2:15) and "the doctrine of Balaam" are discussed. It will be remembered that Balak, having heard of the victorious advance of the children of Israel, attempted to hire Balaam to prophesy against them that they might be cursed of God. Balaam, who possessed some knowl-edge of God, sought his own way until he was in the hands of the wicked king, though God stopped him from speaking against His people, and put in his mouth a blessing three different times. When "Israel abode in Shittim" (Num. 25:1), they were settled on the bor-ders of Moab, and this was what made possible the doctrine of Balaam. Israel had no business abiding in the wilderness any more than the church should have been dwelling where Satan's throne is. Israel should have proceeded in true separation from the world straight on through the wilderness to the promised land. As long as they were thus separated, they were under the promise of God, and nothing could touch them. As soon as they yielded their special character, and settled down among the idolatrous nations, the way was open for the enemy to seduce them from their blessing and to bring upon them the justice of God.

Balaam must have whispered to Balak that though he could not curse Israel, he could tell the king how to bring them to the place of cursing. Let the choicest of the women of Balak's kingdom display themselves before the eyes of God's people who had gotten out of the pilgrim pathway. These men would take the daughters of Moab unto themselves. They would be thus joined to idolaters, and the curse of God would speedily follow. And so it came to pass. As soon as the men of Israel had taken the daughters of the Moabites, these women drew them on to pagan altars where sacrifices were offered to demons. They put this food to the lips of the sons of Israel and made them partakers in fellowship with demons (I Cor. 10:20, 21). The fornication which they committed was not that of taking these Moabite women. It was the full yieldedness to demon power at the demon altars in the demon rites.

It is to the believers that the Lord Jesus speaks. There is a sharpness in the tone which cannot be overlooked. It is the ringing cry, "Repent!" To Ephesus He had said quite kindly, "Remember, therefore, from whence thou art fallen and repent" (2:5). Here, there is a sharp command. If there is not obedience, there must be judgment. He will come for the wheat; He will make war on the tares.

The message to the church at Pergamos is over. The Lord now speaks to the individual. "Let him who has an ear hear what the Spirit is saying to the churches." How far are we, individually, keeping the church and the world separate? When we hear the command against the unequal yoke, do we realize its importance? The real mixed marriage is one between a born-again believer and one who is not a born-again believer, though the two may sit in pews in the same church building and take of the bread and cup from the same Communion table. The unequal yoke is the formation of friendships with unbelievers for purely social fellowship. The Holy Spirit will teach a believer what friendships he may have in the world in order to witness for Christ. Balaam will whisper to the believer that he must have such contacts for witness when, in reality, he wishes them only for the satisfaction of the old nature.

The overcomer may sometimes seem to be lonely. The world may think that the believer's strong stand has kept him back from honor and privilege that might have been rightfully his. Did not Balak blame the Lord to Balaam's face? "I thought to promote thee unto great honor; but, lo, the Lord hath kept thee back from honor" (Num. 24: 11). The world will look upon the Lord as being a hinderer, but God whispers to the individual heart, You shall partake of the hidden manna. It is Jesus Christ who is the living bread which came down from Heaven (John 6:51). It is upon Him that the separated heart feeds. As at first we partook of His very death in order that we might be passed out of death and into life, so now we continue to partake of Himself—all that He is, all that He has done, all that He is now doing, and in hope of all that He yet shall do. Thus we live above the world. Thus the honors of Balak appear to us as dust. Thus we consciously weigh all the offers of the world and day by day reject them. The world comes to the place where it seeks to cut us off from its larder. It is then that we feed most surely from the hidden manna.

But the reward of the overcomer does not include merely the hidden manna of spiritual food. It includes something that is both more glorious and more intimate. The overcomer is to receive "a white stone, and on the stone a new name written which no one knows but the one who receives it." The commentators are strangely silent as to the meaning of this white stone. One or two go so far as to note that the Greek word *psephos* is the name for the stone that was used in ancient rings for seals, and have thought that the symbol might be connected with the safety and sealing of the Christian. But throughout the New Testament, the sealing of the Christian is not made dependent upon works, but is part of salvation. At the same time the believer is born of the Spirit into the family of God, He is also sealed with the Holy Spirit unto the day of redemption (Eph. 4:30).

The meaning of the white stone is possibly found in quite another direction. Before the court of the Areopagus where all criminal cases involving the death penalty were tried, the judges had little stones, white and black. When the case was finished, the judges walked by an urn and dropped one stone into the urn. The black was for condemnation; the white was for acquittal. Plutarch writes that Alcibiades once said, "If I should be accused in a capital case, I would not put my trust in anyone. I would not put my trust even in my mother for fear that through error she might put in the urn a black instead of a white stone." The word for stone thus became the common word for ballot.

The overcomer thus receives from the Lord Jesus the authority to judge in His name. "Do ye not know that the saints shall judge the world? . . . Know ye not that we shall judge angels?" (I Cor. 6:2, 3).

But, more than the delegated authority of the Lord, is the intimacy that is to be found in the name that is to be written on it. One has no secrets with casual acquaintances. A secret is a mark of intimacy, and the Lord has promised that there will be this deep fellowship that is indicated by the new name. I am called Doctor by those who know me least, Pastor by some who know me more closely. My given name is used by close friends. My children call me Father or Daddy. A mother has called me Son, while in the most intimate of all human relationships, there is a place for endearing names which refinement will not permit to be bandied about in public. Not even in letters will these names be used. The actual presence of the loved one is demanded for the use of the names which even the children of the family do not know.

This is the intimacy promised to the overcoming believer by the Lord Jesus Christ. The Bridegroom will speak to the bride. He will have a tender name for her that shall not be known, even to the cherubim and the seraphim.

Verses 18–29
The Church at Thyatira

¹⁸*And to the messenger of the church in Thyatira write: These things saith the Son of God, the One having His eyes like unto a flame of fire and His feet like unto polished brass;* ¹⁹*I know thy works, and love, and faith, and service, and thy perseverance, and thy works; and the last more than the first.*

²⁰*But this I have against thee, thou dost tolerate the woman, Jezebel, who calls herself a prophetess; and she teaches and seduces my bondslaves to commit fornication, and to eat things sacrificed unto idols.* ²¹*And I gave her time in order that she might repent, and she is not willing to repent of her fornication;* ²²*Behold I do cast her into a bed, and those committing adultery with her into great tribulation, except they repent of her works;* ²³*and I will kill her children with death, and all the churches shall know that I am the One who searcheth the reins and hearts; and I will give to each one of you according to your works.*

²⁴*But unto you I say, and to the remnant in Thyatira, as many as hold not this teaching, and who know not, as they say, the depths of Satan, I lay not upon you any other burden;* ²⁵*but that which ye have, hold fast till I come.*

²⁶*And to him who overcomes, and keeps my works until the end, I will give to him authority over the nations;* ²⁷*and he shall shepherd them with a sceptre of iron as the vessels of a potter are broken in pieces, as I also have received from My Father;* ²⁸*and I shall give to him the morning star.* ²⁹*Let him who has an ear, hear what the Spirit is saying to the churches.*
(Rev. 2:18-29, Free Translation)

The firstfruits of an evil sowing were now reaped. Iniquity was ripening fast. The evolution of the church may be traced in Thyatira to its logical conclusion. In Ephesus, the believers lost their first love, became occupied with other things, and developed a class which was a sort of clergy, to whom the preaching of the Gospel was entrusted. These preachers lowered the doctrine to suit the coldness of their hearers. By the time of Smyrna, the doctrine of true grace had been diluted with legalism until the synagogue of Satan was in the midst of the church. Married to the world, Pergamos exalted clericalism to a doctrine and low levels of conduct became common.

In Thyatira, the last step to apostasy is taken. Jezebel is exalted in the church and from her throne ministers unto Satan.

If we read these messages from the risen Lord at one sitting, a striking change in the tone of the letters is most noticeable when we reach Thyatira. Heretofore, the thought had been toward the past. The Lord had given the church a call to repentance (2:5, 16). Here, the Lord announced that time had been given for repentance, but she was not willing to repent. The burden of judgment is against the organization, and the body of believers seems to be but a remnant. Thus we find that the Lord looks toward the future and that to Thyatira is made the first mention of the second coming of Christ.

For the terrible judgments now pronounced, the Lord assumes His supreme title, Son of God, which has not been used up to this time. To the other churches He had revealed Himself in attributes that would stimulate faith and call for dependent trust. Here He takes the symbols of judgment and presents Himself as One with flaming eyes and feet of polished brass. These eyes will some day look men through and through, for there is no "creature that is not manifest in his sight: but all things are naked and opened unto the eyes of him with whom we have to do" (Heb. 4:13). In this connection it is worth noticing that in the midst of this letter, for the first and only time, the Lord returns to the attack and gives Himself yet another name and announces still further judgment. He is the One who searches the reins and the hearts. So all the hidden things of darkness shall be brought to light. And those feet of polished brass shall come forth to judgment when the Faithful and True returns. "In righteousness he doth judge and make war . . . and he treadeth the winepress of the fierceness and wrath of Almighty God" (Rev. 19:11, 15).

Before the Judge speaks His word against the apostates, He pauses to comfort the little remnant. We must distinguish carefully between the wheat and the tares, between the organism and the organization. Even under Jezebel there were the few who remained faithful to the truth of the Lord and to the Lord of truth. But before we speak of them, let us see the vileness of the ground in which they were flowering. For while this remnant was personally faithful, there was a toleration of great evil; and the Lord held it against His own that they did tolerate Jezebel and all she stands for.

In the parable of the leaven, it was a woman who hid the leaven. So it is a woman, Jezebel, who leads the apostasy of the church. To understand the inner meaning of all that follows, we must turn back to the Old Testament to the time of the worst apostasy in Israel when this Zidonian queen introduced idolatry among God's people and caused the faithful prophets to be slain. Jezebel must be seen as the leading figure in the pageant of apostasy. "As if it had been a light thing for him to walk in the sins of Jeroboam, . . . Ahab took to wife Jezebel, the daughter of Ethbaal, king of the Zidonians and went and served Baal, and worshipped him" (I Kings 16:31). This was Ahab's Pergamos—marriage with the world. His Thyatira was soon to follow. He built a pagan temple and pagan altars and we read that "Ahab did more to provoke the Lord God of Israel to anger than all the kings of Israel that were before him" (I Kings 16:33). The period of Jezebel has in it that which is the worst of all the periods of the Old Testament. Thyatira is the period which sees "the depths of Satan" reached in the church. What was it that Jezebel let Ahab to do, that brought forth the supreme anger of the Lord?

First, the nature of the apostasy which Jezebel introduced into Israel was nothing more than the most depraved sex worship, with actual prostitution brought into the very temple of Jehovah. This fact is hidden in the language of the translation, but a comparison of Scripture passages speedily uncovers the awful blot on Israel's history. In I Kings 18:19 we read that Elijah challenged Ahab to gather the forces of apostasy at Mount Carmel. These were four hundred and fifty prophets of Baal, and "the prophets of the groves, four hundred, which eat at Jezebel's table." Formerly, writers on Old Testament history understood the groves which are mentioned so frequently to be places of worship somewhat like the Druidic grounds. The very use of the English word which suggests a clump of trees shows that the translator knew nothing of the terrible reality that was behind the Old Testament statements. The revised versions have never used the word grove but have always transliterated the Hebrew *Asherah, Asherim* or *Asheroth.*

It is true that the Mosaic law ordered that no grove of trees should be planted near the altar of the Lord (Deut. 16:21). The reason for that will come out when we realize the use to which such altars were put. But that there was something far more than trees outside the temple is evident from the story of Josiah's reforms. We read that "he brought out the grove from the house of the Lord . . . and burned it . . . and stamped it small to powder . . ." (II Kings 23:6). Such statements authorize us to conclude that the Asherah was an idol in the form of a tree. Stone slabs in the British Museum show carvings representing a king making an offering to a tree. There was the religious ceremony in connection with the fertilization of a date palm. One authority speaks of it as "the trunk of a tree with the branches chopped off regarded as the wooden symbol of the goddess, Asherah, companion and consort of Baal, type of abounding fecundity." The Greek form of this name is Astarte and this is none other than the Roman Venus.

"There are many variations of nature worship besides the Phallic and Venus cults, such as the beliefs in the fertilizing effect of the sun upon the earth—hence sun-worshipers—and the association of human sexual practices with the fertility of the fields.

"The best known examples of sacred or religious prostitution are those that are practiced in the temples of the Chaldean *Venus* whose name was Mylita as described by Herodotus, Strabo, and others from first-hand observation. Identical voluptuous rites were practiced in Phoenicia, Carthage, and Syria where the Mylita or Venus was known as Astarte . . ."

It was this worship with its male and female prostitution that Jezebel introduced into Israel. The previous references to Josiah's reforms demonstrate this fact, for after speaking of the cleansing of the temple and the bringing forth of the phallic symbol from the house of the Lord, we read that Josiah "brake down the houses of the sodomites, that were by the house of the Lord, where the women wove hangings for the grove" (II Kings 23:7). Ezekiel (16:15ff) describes the action and accompaniments of this idolatry.

During the first centuries of the Christian era, the pagan world was filled with this type of thing even as it is in India today. From Daremberg and Saglio, foremost archaeological authorities in the French language, we translate a brief paragraph justifying this statement. "The temples were the ordinary places of seduction; above all, those which were frequented by women. Ovid names among others, the temple of Venus, patron goddess of the courtesans, where the worship of Adonis was celebrated according to the Syriac rite; the temple of Isis whose priests were also panderers; the temple of Diana Erycima, situated in forests near the Appian Way. According to the witness of early Christian and even pagan, writers, there was not a sanctuary in a sacred wood, not a place of worship, which was not at the same time, an asylum of debauchery and adultery."

Christianity contained in its teaching a revulsion against such filth. The burden of the letter to Thyatira is that these practices were accepted in the church and that their ritual was introduced into the organization.

The second sin of Jezebel is in her treatment of Naboth. Ahab coveted Naboth's vineyard because it was near his house and he wanted it for a garden. He asked for it as a gift, then offered to purchase it.

But to Naboth it was sacred; it was the inheritance of his father, something that was not to be bartered or given away. Ahab sulked and would not eat for covetousness, and Jezebel came to him saying, "Why is thy spirit so sad that thou eatest no bread? . . . Dost thou now govern the kingdom of Israel? Arise, and eat bread, and let thine heart be merry: I will give thee the vineyard of Naboth the Jezreelite" (I Kings 21:5, 7). We then have the story of the plot. This wicked queen wrote letters in Ahab's name, sealed with his seal, to the nobles of Naboth's city. A fast was declared and Naboth was set in a high place. False witnesses came in, children of Belial, who swore that Naboth had blasphemed God and the king, and he was carried forth out of the city and stoned to death. News was sent to Jezebel, and Ahab made haste to take possession of the inheritance of Naboth.

Oh, the remnant of the faithful who suffered for their faith! Their great crime was the possession of property, or the faith of their fathers, a priceless inheritance; not lightly to be bartered. How many witnesses were suborned, how many inquisitors rose up against them, because they would not surrender their inheritance for a price! Here in the message to Thyatira is the imperishable record that they are not forgotten. But the Son of God says to these faithful ones, some of whose names lie dishonored on history's pages with the truth distorted and concealed, "I know thy works, and love, and faith." How this love and faith were put to the test! "I know thy service." How they kept on with unflagging zeal in the midst of discouragement! "I know thy perseverance." How every ounce of it was called forth in the dark centuries when Jezebel ruled without hindrance! But lastly, there comes the greatest compliment of all. He repeats, "I know thy works" and says that the last were more than the first. So in this chain of the attainments of the believers in those dark days, we see the very power and presence of the Lord.

In the south of France, there is a famous tower where Marie Durand and other believers were imprisoned in days of great persecution. She was a noblewoman, and orders had been strict that she, personally, should not be molested. How gladly would her tormentors have released her if she had abjured her faith, but through the years she remained, comforting the women who were imprisoned with her. She saw the horrors round about her. She comforted the anguished virgins who were robbed of their honor. She brought into the world the children that the jailers had inflicted upon her fellow captives. Yet through all the years, she went day by day to the wall of her prison and with her bare hands rubbed the rock until the French imperative *Resistez!* was graven in the stone. But the risen Lord Jesus Christ had engraved that resistance in her heart before ever it was transferred to stone. Her last works were more than the first. The lightness and vigor of youth could have accounted for her first refusal, but only the divine strength could account for the divine perseverance of years. She would not sell the inheritance of her fathers.

But Jezebel is rightly chosen as a symbol of the days of Thyatira because of the nature of Jezebel's office and claims. It is to be noted that the risen Lord states that Jezebel "calleth herself a prophetess." That was her own assumption. She was an idolatrous queen; prophetess, never. By the choice of Ahab, she occupied the throne of Israel. Her pretension of religious leadership was in line with her character.

This is the logical climax of ecclesiasticism. It begins with the deeds of the Nicolaitans; the deeds are transformed to doctrine; the clergy is married to the world and exalted over it in power; it then pretends to speak for God. We are never to forget this evolution.

The conflicting claims of Jezebel and the Scriptures present an interesting comparison. Both pretend infallibility. The Roman prophets claim infallibility which must not be tested, but which must be received, without question. The Scriptures, which everywhere claim for themselves finality and infallibility, submit themselves to every possible test. In China, we were amused at first to note that every silver coin exchanged in commerce is carefully sounded to hear its ring. Only the one who presents a counterfeit would be afraid of the test which would reveal its base coinage.

Before we leave Jezebel for the concluding portion of this message to Thyatira, we should note one other shadow cast by the idolatrous queen who calls herself a prophetess. She said to Ahab, "Dost thou now govern the kingdom of Israel?" (I Kings 21:7). So the name and seal of the king were appropriated by the wicked queen. The Church of Jesus Christ has no such place in this world. God has not called us to politics but to preaching. The Lord Jesus, in His last instructions to His disciples before His crucifixion, pointed out the enmity that would exist between the world and the believer. "If the world hate you, ye know that it hated me before it hated you. If ye were of the world, the world would love his own; but because ye are not of the world, but I have chosen you out of the world, therefore, the world hateth you . . . All these things will they do unto you for my name's sake, because they know not him that sent me" (John 15:18, 19, 21). Any time that Christians become so popular with the world that their rule is acceptable, the Church has abandoned its sacred calling. We are witnesses, not governors. Our time of ruling is future. Today is man's day. Only Jezebel can ever be popular with the world that crucified Christ.

Judgment is prophesied upon ecclesiasticism. It is definitely stated here that the Jezebel form of Christianity shall pass through the great tribulation (vs. 22). We will see, however, when we come to the message to the church of Philadelphia, that the real believers will be kept from the hour of tribulation that is to come upon the earth. The details of God's judgment upon ecclesiasticism occupy a large section of this prophecy. Suffice it to say that God here promises to give to everyone according to his works: to those who follow Jezebel, great tribulation; to those who work the work of God, believing on Christ whom He hath sent (John 6:29), there will be glory promised to those who are Christ's. They are to receive the morning star. The Lord Jesus Himself explains this statement further in the Revelation: "I, Jesus, have sent my angel to testify unto you these things in the churches. I am the root and the offspring of David, and the bright and morning star" (Rev. 22:16). The Old Testament closes with a glorious promise of the rising of the Sun of Righteousness with healing in His wings (Mal. 4:2). The glory of the Lord shall be established in all the earth. The New Testament, seeing the Church, which is the Body and the Bride of Christ, invisible to the Old Testament, ends with a promise which explains the Lord's own word, "I will come again, and receive you unto myself; that where I am, there ye may be also" (John 14:3). The morning star shines before the sunrise. The rapture is to take place before the revelation. Jezebel and her daughters and those who have companied with them will, indeed, be cast into a bed of great tribulation, but the Church of Jesus Christ shall not pass through this tribulation.

God knows the pressure that will be brought to bear upon those who stand out for God. As the age draws on toward its end, perilous times shall come. For whom can they be perilous but for those who are God's? That which is lacking in the sufferings of Christ (Col. 1: 24) must be borne by those who hold His cross. How patient God is with them! No other burden is placed upon them. Hold fast! We look for the morning star to break over the horizon. This is our blessed hope.

And after we have gone to be with the Lord and after the tribulation of those days has passed, the Sun of Righteousness shall arise. As He comes forth to reign upon the earth, He brings us back to reign with Him. Here is a problem for those who would teach that there is no literal kingdom, who say that the coming of Christ is a single event. When is this promise to the overcomers of Thyatira to be fulfilled? There is to be a literal kingdom. We who have believed and who form the invisible Church of this age are to come back with the Lord. "Behold, the Lord cometh with ten thousands of his saints" (Jude 14). The overcomer is to exercise the power of Christ upon the earth. This is the only way this promise may be interpreted. The overcomer is to have authority over the nations; he is to rule with a rod of iron. He is to dash the enemy to pieces as a potter breaks a vessel into shards. We repeat, this is nothing less than the exercising by the believer of authority on earth at Christ's second coming to rule

His kingdom. In the second Psalm, all these words are distinctly spoken of the Lord's anointed, Jesus Christ, God's King. Here the same promise is given to the overcomer as a part of his reward.

Once more the Lord pleads with the individual believer. "Let him that hath an ear hear what the Spirit is saying to the churches." What a message for our day! The Lord is coming. He is to take us out of the world before its hour of tribulation. We are to go to be with Him. We are to return—not as Jezebel, the false queen, but as the bride, loved by the husband, joined unto Him as one. This is why the Saviour came, choosing and cleansing the Church, presenting it to Himself glorified without spot or wrinkle or any such thing, but holy and without blemish. This is the fulfillment of the great mystery of the spiritual marriage of Christ and the Church (Eph. 5:22-32).

CHAPTER 3

Verses 1–6

The Church at Sardis

¹And to the messenger of the Church in Sardis write: These things saith He who hath the seven spirits of God, and the seven stars; I know thy works, that thou hast a name that thou livest, and thou art dead. ²Become vigilant, and strengthen the things remaining that were ready to die: for I have not found thy works completed in God's sight.

³Remember, therefore, how thou hast received and heard, and observe and repent. If, therefore, thou wilt not watch, I will come as a thief and thou shalt not know what hour I shall come upon thee. ⁴But thou hast a few names in Sardis which defiled not their garments; and they shall walk with Me in white, for they are worthy.

⁵The one who overcomes, he shall be clothed in white garments, and I will in no wise blot out his name out of the scroll of life, and I will confess his name before My Father and before His messenger. ⁶Let him who has an ear, hear what the Spirit is saying unto the churches.
(Rev. 3:1-6, Free Translation)

There is a distinct break between the messages spoken to the first four churches and those which now follow. The whole character of the last three messages differs greatly from the first four. This can be brought out in a most striking fashion by a further comparison with the parables of the thirteenth chapter of Matthew.

Our Lord had been busy on that Sabbath morning when these parables were spoken. He had been in controversy with the Pharisees because His disciples had picked grain on the holy day. He had healed the man with a withered hand. He had spoken to the multitude, and cast out a demon which possessed a man. He had spoken in terms of such sharp judgment against the leaders of the people that some thought He was beside Himself and called His mother and His brethren to give Him into their custody. But Jesus had taken the occasion to give another great message on the relationships between Himself and those who were doing the Father's will, and then withdrew into some home, possibly for noonday rest and refreshment.

When He went out of the house to the seaside, all of the houses in the village emptied themselves, and the crowd speedily followed Him. He spoke to them from the boat the great parables which prophesied the outward characteristics of Christendom. We have seen how the first four of these parables correspond with the first four letters to the churches of Asia. But when the Lord had completed the parable of the leaven, He rose from His place in the boat, dismissed the crowd, and went into the house where His disciples followed Him. It can readily be seen that the first four parables are what we might call "outside" parables and the last three may be called "inside" parables.

Something of the same difference may be noted here as we turn to the message of Sardis. The development of evil seems to have ceased. The work of Satan had progressed throughout the time of the first four churches until in Thyatira we find "the depths of Satan." Nothing can go beyond this. But the purposes of God are not frustrated, and in the message to Sardis begins a new course in the flow of spiritual thought.

For the first time, there is no word of commendation. From the first word, there is nothing but censure. One commentator has said, "Their state is described in a single word—soulless profession—they had a name to live but were dead. It was not scandalous wickedness, but decent death; the form retained, the heart gone; Christ owned in word, ignored in deed; creeds correct, conduct respectable, life departed . . . sound doctrine and outward propriety . . . affections not only waning, but gone. His name held, His Word read, His truth owned, Himself forgotten." Such was Sardis. It had become just a decent part of the world, as barren and lifeless toward God as any other portion.

It is very significant that the Lord speaks to Sardis as the One who has the seven Spirits of God and the seven stars. This goes back to the vision of the first chapter (1:4, 16, 20) where these symbols are explained: the perfect work of the Spirit and the full Church in every century and in every climate.

In other words, here is the reassertion that the Lord Jesus Christ wishes to control His Church by the effective work of the Holy Spirit. In the epistle to the Corinthians, we are told that Jesus the Lord administers the gifts of the Holy Spirit to the Church (I Cor. 1:5). Though there are diversities of gifts, it is the same Spirit. Four times we read of "the same Spirit" and again of "the selfsame Spirit," the "one Spirit" (I Cor. 12:4-13). The authority of the Spirit of Christ is "in all the churches of the saints" (I Cor. 14:33).

The analogy drawn in Corinthians lies in the fact that the Church is presented as a body. The human body is directed by a governing spirit. Where there is a normal condition, the spirit articulates every joint and moves every muscle at will. Under proper training, the body of an athlete is so smoothly directed that the runner can dash a hundred yards in less than ten seconds. The human spirit can so control a human body that the ten fingers may be made to go through thousands of precise movements in the few brief moments necessary to play a great sonata on the piano.

When the human spirit does not control some part of the body, there is said to be a partial paralysis. Some pressure upon a nerve center or some other abnormality may cause one foot to be dragged or one hand to be withered instead of maintaining the normal participation in the life of the body.

The Holy Spirit should govern and direct the Church which is the Body of Christ. Every part should work in perfect harmony with every other part. "Where the Spirit of the Lord is, there is liberty" (II Cor. 3:17). And yet this liberty is within "the unity of the Spirit" (Eph. 4:3).

When Christ was here upon earth, men cried, "We will not have this man to reign over us" (Luke 19:14). When the Lord ascended into Heaven, men took hold of the church organization and argued that the place of the absent Lord had to be taken by some earthly substitute. But from the beginning the Lord had announced that He would send the Holy Spirit to lead and guide His Church. The Spirit would bring to the remembrance of the disciples the teachings of the Lord and would not only direct the believers in their lives, but even in their very praying (Rom. 8:26).

It is of most striking significance, therefore, that after the church organization reaches a place which the Lord characterizes as "the depths of Satan" (Rev. 2:24), He should speak once more as the One who holds the churches and directs them by His Holy Spirit. The Reformation of the sixteenth century was, indeed, a new beginning. Sardis described that which flowed out of the Reformation. Insofar as the Reformation was God's work, it does not need to be brought into the message to the seven churches. It was the work of the Holy Spirit, and, of course, needs no judgment from the risen Christ. We must not fail to see, however, how short-lived this work of the Holy Spirit really was. Luther and Calvin with the lesser reformers moved forth on a high spiritual plane but the devil's birds flocked into the branches of the new organization as they had come at the "conversion" of Constantine. German nobles found this pretense tailored to their desires, and used it to seize the lands of the church and to enrich themselves. The spiritual movement had flowed forth from the wells of God like a clear, life-giving stream, but as the waters passed over the desert sands of unregenerate desire, they were stopped short. The mighty advance which the Reformation made in the first decades was arrested.

The risen Lord Jesus Christ expressed the verdict in a single sentence, "I know thy works, that thou hast a name that thou livest, and thou art dead." There is nothing wrong with the Augsburg Confession, with the Thirty-nine Articles, with the Heidelberg Confession, with the Westminster Confession. Go throughout Christendom, however, and you will often find the Gospel in a coffin. The very fact that a church is called a Christian church gives it a name that it lives. Go into churches, however, and see how far you have to travel before you find salvation. And the sterility of churches in America is nothing compared to that which is to be found in the Protestantism of the Continent. There are, indeed believers, but dead, formal orthodoxy too frequently characterizes the scene.

"Become vigilant, and strengthen the things remaining that were ready to die: for I have not found thy works completed in God's sight." Here is the beginning of five exhortations to be found in this single passage. "Become vigilant." It is far more than the "watchful" of the King James Version would indicate. They have been in the sleep of death. In Paul's epistle to the Ephesians, the sleeper was told to awake and to arise from the dead (5:14). The exhortation to Sardis is more than this. It is not merely the call to be awake; it is to remain awake, to keep a vigil as a watchman in the midst of a sleeping encampment. There is in the word the idea of a continuing alertness.

The second exhortation is that the one who becomes vigilant should strengthen the remnant that is about to go into this death sleep. Ezekiel gave a similar message. "Woe be to the shepherds of Israel that do feed themselves! Should not the shepherds feed the flocks? . . . The diseased have ye not strengthened, neither have ye healed that which was sick, neither have ye bound up that which was broken, neither have ye brought again that which was driven away, neither have ye sought that which was lost" (34:2-4).

If ever we should be inclined to believe that "the messenger of the church" is the spiritual leader of the congregation, as God distinctly commanded that elders should be ordained in every place, it would be in such passages as these. In the epistle to the Hebrews, the individual believers are commanded to give obedience to those who guide them. "Remember them which have the rule over you, who have spoken unto you the Word of God . . . Obey them that have the rule over you, and submit yourselves: for they watch for your souls, as they that must give account, [obey in such a way], that they may do it with joy, and not with grief: for that is unprofitable for you" (Heb. 13:7, 17).

If yieldedness to the spiritual guides is commanded in the epistle to the Hebrews, faithfulness on the part of the guide is commanded here as in other passages where the elders and overseers are exhorted. There is no hint of what the world today would call "the clergy" but rather the exhortation, "Let each esteem other better than themselves" (Phil. 2:3). Every true believer must heed this call to become vigilant. All those who become vigilant will see round about them in the midst of a church organization which will never be pure, masses of people in the midst of nominal Christianity, who will listen readily to the life-giving message of salvation. God needs missionaries in all the churches, just as much as He needs them in Africa, Borneo and China. Experience agrees with this Word of God. Whenever a vigilant believer sets out to strengthen the feeble remnant, he will find blessing upon his work as well as the persecutions which inevitably arise against those who will live godly in Christ Jesus (II Tim. 3:12).

The works of these believers in Sardis were said to be incomplete. Does this not mean that just as Paul, entering a city, was told by the Lord that He had many of His elect in that place (Acts 18:10), so we may be sure that God has many in the midst of Sardis who are His own? The first work required of any individual is to believe in the Lord Jesus Christ as personal Saviour. Following this, we are to live in yieldedness to the Holy Spirit to maintain good works not for salvation, but because we have been saved. But we have a work to witness and that work must be completed. God is calling out a people for His Name (Acts 15:14) and He is using human voices for the calling.

The exhortations of the following verse are most enlightening. The believers are told to remember, therefore, how they had received and heard. The reference is clearly to the manner of receiving and hearing. In all ages, the Church has received and heard in the same way. When one is born again, one receives the Holy Spirit. He comes to dwell in the human heart. The receiving has to do with the Person of God, Father, Son and Holy Spirit, as He comes in all His fullness to take up His abode in the believing heart which becomes His temple. Believers are to remember this. Forty thousand delegates to one of the greatest denominations, meeting in a general convention, heard one of their leaders state that part of their purpose in gathering was "to devise business methods by which the Holy Spirit of God may be regulated and made efficient." How could such a statement ever have been made if the speaker had obeyed the injunction of this verse and remembered how the Holy Spirit was received? He is not a machine to be regulated; He is a Person to take control.

The manner of hearing of the Gospel refers to the doctrine of Christ. "Faith cometh by hearing, and hearing by the Word of God" (Rom. 10:17). Sardis had received a whole Bible. In the days of the apostles, the full counsel of God had been declared. Nothing that was profitable had been kept back from this (Acts 20:20, 27). If this full revelation had been obscured during the Dark Ages, the Reformation had brought the whole message of God into the language of the common people. They were to observe the things which they had received and heard. They were to repent. They were to become vigilant.

We find in the resurrection of Lazarus a spiritual analogy to all we are reading here in the message to Sardis. The whole Reformation movement was life from the dead. Unquestionably the true doctrine of God is to be found in the great creeds of the Reformation bodies, but these organizations are bound hand and foot with the grave clothes of tradition. We must cut these, that the believers may walk freely in normal life and fellowship.

There is a warning given to those who will not watch. The Lord says He will come as a thief and that they will not know the hour. We must disagree with those commentators who say there is no reference here to the Lord's second advent but only to a sudden visitation in judgment. This passage rightly understood is the preparation for much that follows in this great prophecy. The Lord's second coming is not an isolated event, but a series of events. As His first coming was over thirty years long, so His second coming is at least seven years long, and in one sense can be considered to be a thousand and seven years long. The first phase of the Lord's coming is as a bridegroom and the second phase is as a thief. He does not come upon His bride as a thief and He does not come upon the apostates and unregenerate world as a bridegroom. The heart of this message to Sardis is that those who trust in the fact that their names are written in some church book are dead. If they refuse to leave this death for life, if they remain in their unregenerate state, they will miss the Lord's coming as a bridegroom. They will remain upon the earth in their ever-deepening sleep through the darkest hour at the end of which the Lord comes upon them in judgment, suddenly like a thief.

The only approach to commendation is in the words that are now spoken of the few names in Sardis. The emphasis upon names in this message should be noted. The church had a name to live but was dead. There were a few names which did not defile their garments. The overcomer would not have his name blotted out, but his name would be confessed before the Father and His messengers. This repetition is not accidental. Sardis had a church roll. It had a name in the first place, a name that it was Christian. Of course, there should have been as many real believers as there were names on the roll of the church, but only a few of the official list could be counted among those who had passed from death into life. The fact that they were believers was demonstrated not only in the sight of God who looks upon the heart and sees true faith, but in the sight of men. The garments were undefiled. To them a promise is given. "They shall walk with Me in white, for they are worthy."

This is repeated in the promise of the next verse: "The one who overcomes, he shall be clothed in white garments." Throughout the whole of the Scripture, righteousness is to be found under this symbol of garments. Man's false righteousness is as filthy rags in God's sight (Isa. 64:6). But the believer is to "put on" the Lord Jesus Christ (Rom. 13:14), for Christ is made unto us righteousness (I Cor. 1:30).

Before the fall, man was undoubtedly clothed in garments of glory and beauty. As we read of God who "clothest Thyself with light as with a garment" (Ps. 104:2), as we remember Christ at the transfiguration with raiment white as light, so we have every right to draw the analogy and believe that man was thus clothed before his fall. This will explain perfectly the nakedness which the first pair discovered and which troubled them so even after they had prepared the fig-leaf garments. Since the light was gone, fig leaves could never satisfy God, but He Himself shed blood in order to provide skins for them (Gen. 3:21). So it is said of the saints on many occasions that they shall be clothed in white, that they have made their robes white in the blood of the Lamb (Rev. 6:11; 7:9, 14; 19:8).

Their worthiness, of course, is the worthiness of Christ. The true believer has counted all of self but dung that he might win Christ and be found of Him not having his own righteousness which is of the law, but that which is through the faith of Christ (Phil. 3:9).

The further promise is given to the overcomer that his name shall not be blotted out of the book of life, but shall be confessed before His Father and His messengers. The positive promise needs no comment. It is a combination of both Matthew's and Luke's accounts of a promise given by Christ. The Lord said in Matthew that the one who confessed Him before men would be confessed before the Father. In Luke it is reported that the Son of Man would confess him before the messengers of God.

A problem has arisen in the minds of some. If the Lord states that He will not blot out the name of the overcomer from the book of life, does this not mean that other names can be blotted out of the book of life? In other words, does this verse not teach that it is possible for one who has really been born again to lose his salvation? Such a problem could never arise in the minds of those who have a real knowledge of the comprehensiveness of salvation or the true meaning of justification. The problem will disappear when we realize the principle of Scriptural interpretation that no obscure passage should ever be quoted in contradiction to a clear line of Scriptural teaching for which there are plain statements and great masses of teaching.

Life in the Scripture is eternal life. Salvation is eternal salvation (Heb. 5:9). This is the only kind of life and salvation the Scriptures know anything about. Let us build upon the great, clear passages of Scripture and not create a doctrine based upon the "What-might-be-is" of human experience. The Word of God is our clear guide.

Once more the message concludes with the definite word to the individual in the midst of the congregation, "Let him who has an ear, hear what the Spirit is saying to the churches."

Verses 7–13

The Church at Philadelphia

⁷*And to the messenger of the Church in Philadelphia write: These things saith the Holy, the True, He that hath the key of David, Who opens and no one shuts, Who shuts and no one opens; ⁸I know thy works; behold, I have set before thee an opened door, and no one can shut it; because thou hast a little strength, and thou didst keep My Word, and thou didst not deny My Name.*

⁹*Behold, I give out of the synagogue of Satan, those who say they are Jews, and are not, but lie; behold, I will compel them that they shall come and worship before thy feet, and may know that I have loved thee.*

¹⁰*Because thou hast kept the word of My patience, I also will keep thee from the hour of the tribulation, the one which is about to come on all the inhabited world, to test those dwelling on the earth.*

¹¹*I come speedily; hold fast that which thou hast, that no one take thy crown. ¹²The one who overcomes, I will make a pillar in the sanctuary of My God, and he shall not go out any more; and I will write on him the Name of My God, and the name of the city of My God, the new Jerusalem, that cometh down out of Heaven from My God; and My new Name. ¹³Let him who has an ear hear what the Spirit is saying to the Churches.*
(Rev. 3:7-13, Free Translation)

Out of the living death of Sardis flow two streams—Philadelphia, in which there is nothing to rebuke, and Laodicea, in which there is nothing to praise.

To each of the churches, the risen Lord Jesus Christ presents Himself in a different character and always in keeping with the need of the church. The titles chosen for the addresses to the first five churches are all taken from the description by which He reveals Himself in the first chapter of this Book. All of them are more or less indicative of judgment. He has spoken as the One holding the churches in the right hand of authority, as the One who is risen to take that authority, the One who has the two-edged sword, eyes as a flame of fire, feet like fine brass to march in judgment against the iniquitous. It is most significant, therefore, that the titles by which He reveals Himself to the church in Philadelphia are not only taken from another part of the Bible to which there has been no previous reference in the Revelation, but also that there is no suggestion of judgment.

To the church which has really desired to "speak the matchless worth" and to sound forth the glories which shine in the Saviour, He reveals Himself in a personal way, quite different from anything we have seen before.

He begins with two of His attributes which show Him to be very God, the One who is holy and true. In the law, He revealed Himself as the Holy One. This was one of His Jehovah titles. "I AM holy" (Lev. 11:44). But in Isaiah, God has revealed Himself in a very special way. "For thus saith the high and lofty One that inhabiteth eternity, whose name is Holy; I dwell in the high and holy place, with him also that is of a contrite and humble spirit, to revive the spirit of the humble, and to revive the heart of the contrite ones" (Isa. 57:15). The risen Christ is declaring Himself to be God.

In the same way, He claims to be the One that is true. Christ Himself, when He was here upon earth, had prayed in that last intimate moment with the Father before the crucifixion, "This is life eternal, that they might know thee, the only true God, and Jesus Christ whom thou hast sent" (John 17:3). Here He is claiming oneness with the Father. John was particularly fond of this word "true," and we find it frequently in his writings. Thus he closed his first epistle which sums up all of these declarations. "And we know that the Son of God is come, and hath given us an understanding, that we may know him that is true, and we are in him that is true, even in his Son, Jesus Christ. This is the true God and eternal life" (I John 5:20).

The church which has seen the Lord in this double revelation of holiness and truth can stand unshaken in the world. The course of this age is presented in II Thessalonians under the symbols of lawlessness and delusion. Opposite these stand holiness and truth. It is the vision of Christ as the Holy One which will keep the true Philadelphian when "the mystery of lawlessness" ferments around us. It is the vision of Christ as the True that will keep us when the whole world has fallen into strong delusion and is laughing at the believer because he will not believe "the lie."

The Lord further speaks of Himself as the One who has the key of David. The concordance takes us to the only passage in the whole Bible which contains any reference to this symbol. It is the climax of "the burden of the valley of vision" (Isa. 22). Hezekiah was king. The horsemen of Assyria had come against Israel. The choicest valleys were full of chariots, and the dismantled people were able to see that "the breaches of the city of David were many." God gave the people a definite call to repentance, "In that day did the Lord God of hosts call to weeping, and to mourning, and to baldness, and to girding with sackcloth." But instead, as in many other periods of history when men have danced upon a volcano and cried, "After us the deluge," the people turned to "joy and gladness, slaying oxen, and killing sheep, eating flesh, and drinking wine." Their cry has become a proverb even unto today. "Let us eat and drink: for tomorrow we shall die." Their leader was one Shebna who was the treasurer and "over the house." It was to him, because of his failure to repent, that the Lord said, "I will drive thee from thy station, and from thy state shall he pull thee down. And it shall come to pass in that day, that I will call my servant Eliakim the son of Hilkiah: and I will clothe him with thy robe, and strengthen him with thy girdle, and I will commit thy govern-ment into his hand . . . And the key of the house of David will I lay upon his shoulder; so he shall open, and none shall shut; and he shall shut, and none shall open. And I will fasten him as a nail in a sure place; and he shall be for a glorious throne to his father's house. And they shall hang upon him all the glory of his father's house" (vss. 19-24).

The significance of the key of David is immediately plain. It is the lordship of the Son of David over His house. After a time like Sardis, where there was nothing but nominal Christianity, the Lord Himself shall take over the authority. "The government shall be upon His shoulder" (Isa. 9:6). The enemy may come in like a flood, but One more stable than Eliakim holds the key. The world will deride or pity, but no weapon that is formed against the believer shall prosper.

He opens a door of deliverance, and it cannot be closed. An hour of testing was about to come upon the world, but Philadelphia should be delivered out of it. The authority of the Lord Jesus Christ would open a door, and by His own Heavenly power would see to it that those who were of His own should not pass through the great tribula-tion.

This is also indicated in the epistle to the Philippians. "Our citizen-ship is in heaven," says Paul, "from whence also we look for the Saviour, the Lord Jesus Christ: who shall change our body of hu-miliation that it may be fashioned like unto his glorified body, accord-ing to the working whereby he is able even to subdue all things unto himself" (3:20, 21).

We cannot think with some commentators that the open door is merely that of service of which Paul wrote three times (I Cor. 16:9; II Cor. 2:12; Col. 4:3). There is something far greater involved here. It is a door of deliverance from the tribulation that is about to come upon the world.

The rallying center in Sardis had been a name. It was the church rather than Christ. Here, it is Christ rather than the church. Thus the Lord reveals Himself and smiles upon those who seek Him. "I know thy works," and so the reward was theirs.

They had "a little strength." It was not the fault of the Lord that they did not have more. The history of power in the Scripture is very marked. "God hath spoken once; twice have I heard this, that power

belongeth unto God" (Ps. 62:11). But that which belongeth to God
is given to Christ. "All power is given unto me in heaven and in
earth (Matt. 28:18). What does He do with this power? The very
last words He spoke on earth, before ascending into Heaven, refer to
this. "But ye shall receive power, after that the Holy Spirit is come
upon you . . ." (Acts 1:8). It was acting upon this sequence that Paul
was able to say, "I can do all things through Christ which strengtheneth me" (Phil. 4:13).

It is to be noted that even in Philadelphia there was no revival of
Pentecostal power. Pentecost will not be repeated any more than will
Calvary. This does not mean that there may not be another great
time of blessing upon the Church before the Lord comes. There have
been many such periods before. They may occur again. But at their
best, they are times of "little strength."

The church of Philadelphia is commended for keeping the Word of
the Lord and not denying His Name. Success in Christian work is
not to be measured by any other standard of achievement. It is not
rise in ecclesiastical position. It is not the number of new buildings
which have been built through a man's ministry. It is not the crowds
that flock to listen to any human voice. All of these things are frequently used as yardsticks of success, but they are earthly and not
heavenly measures. The strength of Philadelphia in the presence of
the risen Lord lay in the fact that the believers had kept His Word
and not denied His Name. "This book of the law shall not depart out
of thy mouth; but thou shalt meditate therein day and night, that thou
mayest observe to do according to all that is written therein: for then
thou shalt make thy way prosperous, and then thou shalt have good
success" (Josh. 1:8). The world today will laugh at the one who keeps
the Word of the Lord. We are asked by some to abandon Genesis
to "science," salvation by redemption to anthropology, the life of the
Spirit to psychology, the very Word itself to the higher criticism. The
Philadelphian, however, has his delight in the law of the Lord and
his whole life is lived within the sphere of the Book. But there is an
orthodoxy of word which is elsewhere condemned in the Scripture. It
has the letter without the Spirit. Here the church is commended for
holding the letter, but also for not denying the Name of Christ. To
keep the Name of Jesus Christ is to

> . . . sing the characters He bears,
> And all the forms of love He wears,
> Exalted on His throne.

It is the highest expression of individual fellowship of the soul with
our God, the Lord Jesus Christ.

At first glance, it would appear that the next verse leads us to an
abrupt change of theme. If we have really understood the symbol of
the key of David, however, we will see that there is no change. "Be-

hold, I give out of the synagogue of Satan, those who say they are Jews, and are not, but lie; behold, I will compel them that they shall come and worship before thy feet, that they may know that I have loved thee." Sennacherib's messengers had ridiculed the Israel of God and the God of Israel. Hezekiah spread the letter before the Lord and was answered. Though the inhabitants of Israel were "of small power" (Isa. 37:27), like the Philadelphians of "little strength," yet the Lord brought the enemy to naught in their presence. Thus will it be for those who elect to keep God's Word and the Name of the Lord Jesus Christ. How often is the true Christian ridiculed because he believes, for example, that this world came into being by the direct creative act of God? He does not deny any of the facts of modern discovery, but refuses all interpretations of those facts which deny the Word and the Name of His Lord. In the heart of the organized church today, there are those who claim to be a people of God. They have buildings, pastors, orders of service, hymns, prayers, Bible readings and sermons. But they are not the people of God; they lie. They talk about the Fatherhood of God, but have not been born again. They despise those who would center their fellowship in a Christ who is God, and in a Word which He has magnified above His Name (Ps. 138:2). "But they shall proceed no further: for their folly shall be manifest unto all . . ." (II Tim. 3:9). There is an absolute limit beyond which God will not allow them to pass. The true believer is to be patient. The day is to come when these tares in the midst of the wheat will be gathered out. The tares' religious pretense will not avail. They shall be revealed for what they are—the synagogue of Satan. Here the veil is lifted, and we are allowed to see into Heaven.

These false brethren are compelled to come and worship before the feet of the believers, and to know that God has truly loved those whom they despise. This is the only passage in the Bible where worship is used of an act that is forced upon anyone. It is the explanation of prophecy "that at the name of Jesus every knee should bow . . . and that every tongue should confess that Jesus Christ is Lord, to the glory of God the Father" (Phil. 2:10, 11). The passage does not mean that the believers are to be worshiped. It is merely at their feet that the unbelievers shall kneel as they are forced to acknowledge that Christ is God, and that every detail of the Scripture is eternally true.

Those who keep the Word of God are aware that great judgments are to come upon this world. They look about them in the world and see that the hatred which crucified Christ still reigns, and that wherever there is not active hatred, there is polite indifference to the claims of God. They know that the clouds of God's wrath have been gathering for ages, and that the judgment stroke must one day fall upon the inhabitants of the earth. Will the Church pass through the great tribulation? Let the risen Lord answer this question most definitely. "Because thou hast kept the Word of my patience, I also will keep thee from the hour of the tribulation, the one which is about to come on all the inhabited world, to test those dwelling on the earth." Escape was definitely promised by the Lord Jesus Himself (Luke 21:36). If the Church is to come through the tribulation judgments that are to come upon this earth, then, say it plainly, there is no blessed hope in the Bible.

But the believer is not to presume upon the grace of God because he knows that he is to escape the vials of wrath which are to be poured out upon the inhabitants of the earth. The judgment for rewards he is to face, and the Lord says, "I come speedily; hold fast that which thou hast, that no one take thy crown." Shebna had been the treasurer over the house of Israel (Isa. 22:15). He did not walk in righteousness before the Lord, and Eliakim superseded him and received his reward.

The scene has been such a quiet one that the promise to the overcomer is more striking than in the previous letters. Ephesus had lost its first love; the overcomer returned to it. Smyrna was in the midst of persecution; the overcomer stood fast in the face of it. Pergamos was about to be drowned with worldliness; the overcomer resisted the flood and stayed above it. Thyatira was being seduced by Jezebel; the overcomer resisted her blandishments. Sardis had a name to live but was dead; the overcomer did not defile himself with the corpse. But in Philadephia there is only commendation; there is no blame. What does the believer overcome then? The only answer lies in the fact that though there be no blame, there is warning. The danger for the believer in Philadelphia is that he will let slip his true character, while keeping the Word and loving the Name of the Lord Jesus Christ.

How many believers there are who, having begun in the Spirit, seek to be made perfect by the flesh (Gal. 3:3)! Clearly the one who believes that our continuation in salvation depends upon ourselves, in short, the one who does not believe in the finality of salvation, cannot be counted an overcomer in the Philadelphia sense of the word. The crown of righteousness is for them who love His appearing (II Tim. 4:8), and can be lost by following the seducing teachers who put any event between the believer and the rapture.

But there are those who keep the Lord's Word about the security of the believer and the return of the Lord Jesus Christ and who are yet in danger of losing their crown. Apostasy in good works is a real danger, for the failure to live according to holiness "is contrary to sound doctrine" (I Tim. 1:10), and the believer must ever be "careful to maintain good works."

The fourfold reward to him who maintains the Word and the Name of Christ in the midst of the church that is in the world is most beautiful. First, he shall be made a pillar in the sanctuary of Christ's God, and he shall not go out any more. Once more, let the concordance reveal to us the meaning of this promise. The pillars are spoken of in I Kings 7:15-22. Solomon had two pillars cast by a fine workman. "And he set up the pillars in the porch of the temple: and he set up the right pillar, and called the name thereof Jachin: and he set up the left pillar, and called the name thereof Boaz" (vs. 21). What are these pillars to which names are given? Jachin means "He establishes" and Boaz means "in Him is strength." This is a fitting reward for the Philadelphia overcomer. He has had a little strength, so he is made a pillar of strength. His very reward will testify that he has been sustained from the beginning by the Word and the Name of the Lord. Henceforth, he does not go out of the presence of God anymore.

Upon the overcomer also three names are written. The Lord has revealed Himself in this letter as being the One who is holy, who is true. Holiness and truth, with all else that we have seen the Name of God to mean, will be upon the believer. He has been the object of his vision, so he shall see Him and be like Him (I John 3:2). They have been called Philadelphians in this earth because they have been dwelling in that city. But they did not look upon that city as their home. They, too, have "looked for a city which hath foundations, whose builder and maker is God" (Heb. 11:10); and since they desired a better country, that is, a heavenly, God is not ashamed to be called their God, for He hath prepared for them a city (Heb. 11:16). They will have upon them the name of the city of Christ's God, the new Jerusalem, as a mark that they are citizens of Heaven.

Finally, Christ promises that the believer will bear His new name. Toward the end of the Apocalypse, this new name is revealed to us. It is "King of kings and Lord of lords" (Rev. 19:16). The overcomer, then, is to reign with Christ forever and ever (Rev. 22:5).

Once more the message closes with the solemn call of the Spirit, "Let him who has an ear hear what the Spirit is saying to the churches." No one can disclaim the warnings given here on the ground that they are addressed to a local church in John's day which has long since passed from the earthly scene. To all who have the quickened ear comes the definite command that they are to hear not what is said to a church, but what is said to the churches. The message to each is for all.

Verses 14–22

The Church at Laodicea

[14]*And to the messenger of the Church in Laodicea write: These things saith the Amen, the faithful and true Witness, the Beginning of the creation of God;* [15]*I know thy works, that thou art neither cold*

nor hot: I wish thou wert cold or hot. ¹⁶So because thou art luke-
warm, and neither hot nor cold, I am about to spew thee out of My
mouth.

¹⁷Because thou sayest, I am rich and have been made rich, and have
need of nothing, and knowest not that thou art the wretched one, and
the miserable one, and poor, and blind, and naked: ¹⁸I counsel thee
to buy from Me gold refined by fire, so that thou mayest become rich;
and white raiment, that thou mayest clothe thyself, and the shame of
thy nakedness be not made manifest; and eye salve to anoint thine eyes
that thou mayest see. ¹⁹As many as I love, I convict and discipline:
Be zealous, therefore, and repent.

²⁰Behold I stand at the door and knock: if anyone hear My voice,
and open the door, I will come in to him and sup with him, and he
with Me. ²¹The one who overcomes, I will grant to him to sit with
Me in My throne, even as I also overcame, and sat down with My
Father on His throne. ²²Let him who has an ear hear what the Spirit
is saying to the Churches.

(Rev. 3:14-22, Free Translation)

Laodicea was the church for which Paul had had great conflict (Col.
2:1). Some of his epistles were possibly written in duplicate, with the
name of some church other than that under which we today possess
the epistles written in the salutation. Certainly the epistle to the Colos-
sians was to be read to the church at Laodicea, and they, in turn, were
to read an epistle which he had addressed to the Laodiceans (Col.
4:16).

Philadelphia was to be removed before the tribulation, but there
is no such promise to Laodicea. This is the apostate church out of
which the Lord will call some individuals, for He watches over it in
love; but the main stream flows on into the great Babylon.

The risen Lord now speaks, and for this church so sorely in need
of judgment, He takes the character of the Amen, the faithful and
true Witness, the Beginning of the creation of God. It is necessary
that He should speak in this character, so low had the church fallen,
so far from what He had meant it to be. Centuries had now passed
since the Church was planted in the world. It had been born looking
for the return of the Lord. As this first hope was lost, so its first love
was lost. Rare are the voices through all the ages of the fathers and
the reformers that even mention the Lord's return. Those who had
begun their days with the pulse-quickening thought that perhaps He
would rend the clouds, returning before the night should fall, now
looked with eagerness for the aggrandizement of the church, and the
domination of the world by what they now called a spiritual kingdom.

We are especially told that it was "while the bridegroom tarried,
they all slumbered and slept" (Matt. 25:5). A sleeper, awakened by
a call, may sit bolt upright for a moment, and, hearing nothing further,
fall back into a torpor more profound. It was in this sleep after the

moment of power at the Reformation, that the church dreamed of power and greatness upon the earth. Instead of believing God's Word, and following the line which He had marked out for her to be a true witness to the saving grace of God in Christ, a body called out from the world, she went forth to conquer her place as a king in the midst of kings. She learned to stoop to every artifice, to dissemble, to cheat, to trick, to persecute, to kill, if only she could advance her rule and increase the domination to which she fancied herself called in the world, the world out of which she had been taken.

One of Aesop's fables is the well known story of the dog who saw the image of a dog reflected in the pool beneath his feet. Though he had a bone, he was jealous of the bone which he saw in the other dog's mouth. He opened his jaws to snarl, and to snatch at the other bone, and lost his own which fell into the water. How this pictures the church which has finally come to the Laodicean state! The promises of God were not enough for her. She laid them aside to grasp at earthly power and dominion. Not only was this dominion denied her, but she has irretrievably lost the high position to which God called her.

To her the Lord speaks. She may, indeed, have failed, but He is still the Amen, the faithful and true Witness. In Isaiah 65:16, God is twice called the God of truth. The Hebrew is most significant. It is God of the Amen. We find it stamped upon our Lord's speech. Every time He said what is translated in the King James version by "verily, verily," it was really, "Amen, Amen" — "It is true, it is true." All the fullness of the Godhead dwelt in Him, and He introduces Himself now as the God of all truth who has come to confound the faithless church who has played the harlot with the nations.

This, then, is an announcement that His testimony is true. The warnings which He pronounces shall, indeed, come to pass. Men may, indeed, say, "Where is the promise of His coming? For since the fathers fell asleep, all things continue as they were from the beginning of the creation" (II Pet. 3:4). Men have imperfect ideas of justice, and, therefore, have imperfect justice. But the Lord has spoken and all shall come to pass. Years ago, Judge Cambo of Malta, from his own window, saw a murder committed, but condemned an innocent man to death after having him tortured till he confessed, because the judge believed that his private knowledge ought not to be added to the evidence brought before him officially. Not so our Lord. Elsewhere we have seen that His eyes are as a flame of fire. He sees all. Here He announces the certainty of the judgments that are spoken and the certainty of His promises, "for all the promises of God in him are yea, and in him Amen" (II Cor. 1:20).

But why does He add to His judgment title, when speaking to Laodicea, that He is "the Beginning of the creation of God?" We go back to Isaiah where He is called the Amen and find in the next verse a marvelous promise, "For, behold, I create new heavens and a new earth . . . but be ye glad and rejoice for ever in that which I create: for, behold, I create Jerusalem a rejoicing, and her people a joy" (Isa. 65:17, 18).

The followers of Pastor Russell and Judge Rutherford interpret this phrase to mean that Jesus was an angel, the very first Being ever created by God. How foolish! Rather do we see that He who takes all the attributes of the God of creation announces that He is about to be through with the age of the Church and that the new day, the day of the Lord, which is to be a brief moment of judgment, will usher in an absolutely new creation. It will begin with Himself. "The former [creation] shall not be remembered, nor come into mind" (Isa. 65:17).

This church in its nauseating condition was thoroughly known to the Lord. "I know thy works, that thou are neither cold nor hot." How many people there are today who fit this description perfectly. Certainly, they cannot be called cold. Even more certainly, they cannot be called hot. The first love has gone and they are in no wise like the Philadelphians who yet glowed with the fire of the Spirit. In other words, they are completely indifferent.

To them the faithful Witness says, "I wish thou wert cold or hot." Why should the Lord desire that they should rather be cold than lukewarm? This wish of the Lord can be understood by His statement to the Pharisees at the time He had healed the man born blind . . . Christ had come into the world, He said, "That they which see not might see; and that they which see might be made blind . . ." and had concluded, "If ye were blind, ye should have no sin: but now ye say, We see, therefore your sin remaineth" (John 9:39, 41). So the Lord is saying, If instead of being lukewarm, you were so cold that you should feel that coldness, then the very feeling of your need might drive you to the true warmth, but now in your lukewarmness, you have just enough to protect yourselves against a feeling of need.

But they did not have the true fire that comes from God in the regeneration of the soul. They did not have the true life of God. It was for this reason that they were to be spewed from His mouth. There is no more terrible image in the Word of God. Laodicea is the church rich in its own worldly eyes, which God says is poor It declared itself to be rich and to be enriched; in short, to have need of nothing. In God's eyes, that church was wretched and miserable, poor, blind and naked.

Yet upon a church that has sunk as low as Laodicea, the risen Lord still showers His love. He is standing there, the faithful and true Witness, counseling them, calling them away from their self-styled riches, pleading with them to repent, promising to supply every need. He holds before them the wonderful promise of fellowship and closes with the amazing promise that in one step they can go from the Laodicean state to His very throne. How great is the grace of God!

Poor, blind, and naked, they most assuredly were, but His counsel is that they might receive from Him gold tried in the fire. This would change their poverty into riches. He offers them white raiment that their nakedness might be covered. He offers them eye salve that their blindness might be cured. Some people have found a difficulty in that the Lord's counsel should be to buy these riches from Him. With what shall we purchase, and are these things for sale? Listen to the great invitation: "Ho, every one that thirsteth, come ye to the waters, and he that hath no money; come ye, buy, and eat; yea, come, buy wine and milk without money and without price" (Isa. 55:1).

What is this gold that is tried in the fire? David sings of the glories of God's revelation in the Heavens and in His Word (Ps. 19:7-11). Successively, he refers to the law of the Lord, the precepts of the Lord, the commandment of the Lord, the ordinances of the Lord, Then he says, "More to be desired are they than gold, yea than much fine gold." Fine gold is the jeweler's way of expressing gold that has been refined in the fire. In another psalm (12:6) we read, "The words of the Lord are pure words; as silver tried in a furnace of earth, purified seven times."

The call of the Lord to Laodicea, then, is to come back to the Word of God. The poverty of this church lies in the fact that the Word of God is not given its proper place. In our theological seminaries, men are too often taught much about the Bible, but not true expository preaching. Pick up one of our great metropolitan dailies on any Monday morning and read the summaries of the sermons that have been preached in the churches of our cities the day before. Politics, economics, literature, social service, ethics, philosophy and plain bombast are all to be found in the record. But in how few is there any indication of any real knowledge of the plan of God! Some, indeed, still retain a Biblical text as a point of departure but too frequently that departure has no return. Laodicea's pride is fattened on sermons; Laodicea's soul is starved for the Word of God.

Next, the Lord counsels the Laodicean to buy of Him "white raiment, that thou mayest clothe thyself, and the shame of thy nakedness be not made manifest." It is the Lord who clothes Himself with light as with a garment (Ps. 104:2). The transfigured Lord has garments as white as the light (Matt. 17:2). And later in this book, we are told that the Bride is to be "arrayed in fine linen, clean and white: for the fine linen is the righteousness (the word is plural in the Greek) of the saints" (Rev. 19:8). Good works, in the Bible sense of the term, a definite following after righteousness, are commanded of God. Failure to have them is "contrary to sound doctrine" (I Tim. 1:10). The Laodicean is naked because his life is not producing good works in

God's sight. These can come only when "we are his workmanship, created in Christ Jesus unto good works, which God hath before ordained that we should walk in them" (Eph. 2:10).

Finally, the Lord counsels the Laodicean to come to Him for eye salve that his eyes might be anointed and that he might see. The anointing in the Scripture is always a symbol of the Holy Spirit. Without this there can be nothing acceptable to God. There may be might and power, but this is not God's method for the life of the Church. Do we not read, "Not by might, nor by power, but by my Spirit, saith the Lord of hosts" (Zech. 4:6)? How many churches there are today which are dependent upon might and power. Every committee is organized, everything functions smoothly, every contingency is taken care of and yet they are blind.

How He wants to supply all this wonderful merchandise to His children! He stands and pleads with them to take it. He is willing to cause them some pain if only they see their need. "As many as I love, I convict and discipline: Be zealous, therefore and repent." The verses that have preceded are, indeed, one of the sharpest rebukes in the whole of the Bible. Does this proceed from a heart of judgment or a heart of love? Surely the latter. One of the Lord's definite ways of working is revealed here. He does not want to punish His children. No one is more delighted than He when hearts turn in simple yieldedness for full communion and fellowship. He knows us so well. Some will come at the first call of love. Others must have the sternest rebuke. Still others, unheeding the rebuke, must feel the stroke of His rod. Thus He calls them to be zealous. Zeal is consuming. It is the opposite of lukewarmness. It is the call to be on fire for Him.

There now follows the great invitation, "Behold, I stand at the door and knock: if any man hear my voice, and open the door, I will come in to him, and sup with him, and he with me." The Christ we see in this letter to Laodicea is a pleading, all-providing, loving, disciplining Lord. The climax that is reached here is to let these poor Laodiceans know that He is near at hand, that they can count upon Him to deliver the supplies they so sorely need, at the very moment when they will make the first gesture toward Him. It is the picture of a wealthy father whose son launches out into business for himself and who tells the son that he is ready to stand back of him and can be called upon for supply in any emergency.

Yet there is a tragic note in this great invitation, for the story is unfinished. Some years ago, a writer told an interesting tale of a palace where captives were cast into an arena, being asked to choose between two doors. Behind one was a beautiful woman with a priest standing near to marry them, and behind the other was a tiger. Previous captives had been killed by the tiger; but along came the hero of the story, poor, but in love with the princess of the palace, now cast into the arena. By a signal she could tell him which door to choose. Did she really love him? Would she rather he be killed or marry another woman? The writer skillfully brought the tale to the last page describing the emotions of the man, and ended his book with a sentence asking when the door was chosen "Who came out the lady or the tiger?"

What is Laodicea going to do? The Lord stands so near. He brings all supplies with Him. If only the door shall be opened, full communion shall be entered into immediately. What does Laodicea do? Eternity alone will reveal the answer, some in glory on His throne, some spewed from His mouth.

And this invitation is the narrowest in all the letters to the churches. In Thyatira there was remnant (2:24); in Sardis there were a few names (3:4); but here it is "if any man hear my voice." Do we see here that as the centuries roll on, the wheat is producing a hundred-fold, sixtyfold and thirtyfold? At any rate, no heart can refuse the invitation on the ground that it belongs to the whole Church. It is for the individual.

And now we come to the last promise to the overcomer. "The one who overcomes, I will grant to him to sit with me in my throne, even as I also overcame, and sat down with my Father on his throne." The one who leaves Laodicean lukewarmness, who recognizes the depths of his need, who turns away from self, who buys the full supply that the Lord gives without money and without price, shall rise to the very throne of Heaven.

There is a most important dispensational teaching in this verse. There are those who think that the Church is the kingdom and that there is to be no literal kingdom upon the earth. Here the Lord says that at the present time He is not upon His own throne. He has, therefore, one purpose. He lives to make intercession for us (Heb. 7:25). The individual who, even in the midst of apostasy and lukewarmness, turns to Christ and passes out of death and into life shall be a part of that glorious company clothed in light that makes up the Bride which is the fullness of Him who filleth all in all (Eph. 1:23). His throne is about to be established. His kingdom is about to begin.

And now for the seventh and last time comes the call, powerful in its recurring rhythm, "Let him who has an ear hear what the Spirit is saying to the churches." Today, the age of grace still runs. The sevenfold call still sounds, and the Spirit still speaks.

PART III
CHRIST, THE LAMB

CHAPTER 4

Verses 1–5

The Throne of God

¹After these things I looked, and behold, a door had been opened in Heaven; and the first voice which I heard was as of a trumpet speaking with me, saying: Come up hither, and I will show thee what things must come to pass after these things. ²And immediately I came in the Spirit; and behold, a throne was set in Heaven, and One was sitting on the throne. ³And the enthroned One was in semblance like a stone, a jasper and a sardius; and there was a rainbow round about the throne in semblance like unto an emerald. ⁴And round about the throne were twenty-four thrones; and upon the thrones twenty-four elders sitting, clothed in white garments; and on their heads were crowns of gold. ⁵And from the throne proceeded lightnings and thunderings and voices; and seven lamps of fire were burning before the throne, which are the seven Spirits of God.
(Rev. 4:1-5, Free Translation)

Following the letters to the seven churches of Asia, there is a sharp break in the continuity of the thought. Entirely new matters are discussed, and a proper interpretation of the new situation is the key to the understanding of all that follows in the great symbolic scenes of judgment which are depicted in the rest of the Revelation.

The delineation of the churches covers the full scope of time and place in our age and world. There will never be local churches unlike those described in these previous chapters, and the whole of the age of grace runs under our gaze as we look at the successive steps in the degeneration of the organization, and of the spiritual measures taken by the Lord Jesus to insure that His plans shall triumph and that all the wrath of man, yea, the wrath of Satan, shall ultimately praise Him.

"After these things I looked, and behold, a door had been opened in Heaven." John was, of course, already in a state of spiritual contemplation. God had unveiled certain lines of truth and John had

87

written the things which he had seen, and the things which are (1:19). Apparently there was a break in the vision and John had written down that which had been given to him.

Now his spiritual desire for more truth turned his face Heavenward, and the Lord revealed to him a door that had been opened in Heaven. The same voice which he had heard in the first instance now called to him again in the same trumpet tones, saying, "Come up hither, and I will show thee what things must come to pass after these things." But the Lord spoke no longer of the lamps of testimony. That age is ended. He now called His servant to Heaven that he might look down upon all that should follow from the point of view of Heaven itself. There are many truths here that are almost self-evident. Any revelation of truth must come from the Lord Jesus Christ. Any true understanding of the course of world events must be based on Heaven's perspective of those events.

Further, it may be said that here is a typical teaching in the very act of John's translation to Heaven for the vision that is to follow. Enoch was caught up to Heaven before the judgment flood poured over the earth. John is caught up to Heaven before receiving the vision of the flood of judgment that is yet to come upon the earth. Those are the types. The anti-type lies in the fact that all believers will be caught up to Heaven before the judgment is actually poured out upon the earth. We are confronting here another indication that the Church is not to pass through the Tribulation, but is to be removed before the prophesied terrors. There is to be a description of the hour of tribulation. The Lord has said that He would keep His believers from that hour (3:10).

So, in the Spirit, John is carried into Heaven. And what does he see? There are undoubtedly many objects in Heaven, but one object fills his vision at first to the exclusion of all else. It reminds me of an incident that took place in our home when our children were young. In many a home in the days that precede Christmas, the children are talking about all the gifts they are going to receive and about the tree which they know will be trimmed for them. They retire the evening before, and the tree is set up and lighted and all the presents are placed beneath it. The room still has all its accustomed furniture. In the morning, however, when the blinds are drawn and the tree is lighted and the children are suddenly introduced into this scene of joy, their eyes will see first of all the blaze of light that illumines the tree. Later, they will see the packages at its foot and begin to enter into the joy of their possessions. In spite of the imperfections of the comparison, this may help to throw some light on what now occurs. John, suddenly introduced into Heaven, saw Heaven's throne and the One who was sitting upon it.

It is, of course, the throne of God.

We do not need to take the time to discuss the reality of Heaven.
Heaven is; and Heaven as a part of the revelation of the Lord Jesus
Christ can be known to all who, like John, are introduced by the Spirit
of God. Nor will we spend time discussing the fact that Heaven is a
material place. John saw a throne. If the objection is that he was in
the Spirit and that it might be a spiritual throne, we would answer
that the body of Jesus Christ was raised from the dead and that our
Lord said, "Handle me, and see; for a spirit hath not flesh and bones,
as ye see me have" (Luke 24:39); and it was that body which
ascended into Heaven. There must be a material Heaven or there
was no ascension, and if there was no ascension, there was no resurrection, and if there was no resurrection, there is no salvation.

It is very important to note that this is the throne of God the Father.
To the church at Laodicea the Lord had said, "The one who overcomes, I will grant to him to sit with Me in My throne, even as I also
overcame, and sat down with My Father on His throne." There are
those who seek to teach that there will be no future material kingdom
of God established upon the earth. They try to teach that the Church
is the kingdom, and that Christ is now enthroned in Heaven as king
over the Church. This view is distinctly contrary to biblical teaching;
yet one commentator says, "The main purpose of this vision as a whole
is to reveal our glorified Saviour in the act of occupying His Father's
throne," and further continues, "It is not conceivable that any other
event could evoke this outburst of praise from all creation." Now
if there is anything which this vision is not, it is not a vision of Christ
in the act of occupying His Father's throne. The great prophetic
psalm outlines the events. "The Lord said unto my Lord, Sit thou at
my right hand, until I make thine enemies thy footstool" (110:1).
The commentator whom I have quoted makes this vision of Revelation to be that of Christ taking His seat at the Father's right hand.
This, however, was no revelation but a fact already known to the
Church. Peter had preached it on the day of Pentecost (Acts 2:33).
Stephen had proclaimed it at the moment of his martyrdom. The
epistle to the Ephesians is built upon Christ's presence there.

Rather, this is a vision that perfectly fulfills the psalm. "Sit on my
right hand until . . ." It is the "until" we are to see now. It is not
Christ taking the throne before the age of grace, but it is Christ rising
from the throne at the end of the age of grace. It is perfectly conceivable that this event evokes the greatest of all outbursts of praise. The
day of evil is about to close. The eternal plan and righteousness of
God is about to be vindicated forever. The day of the Lord is about
to dawn. So this vision is in reality that of Christ about to leave His
Father's throne where He has been throughout the age of the Church.
At present He is there as our Mediator. He ever lives to make intercession for us. All this will come out much more clearly in chapter

five where we shall see Christ in the interval between His descent from the Father's throne and the ascent to His own throne. In all the scenes that follow, we will see Christ, for the moment unoccupied with His work of intercession—another proof, of course, that the rapture precedes the tribulation—but in the quite different work of judgment upon different groups that shall be revealed as our study progresses.

In the vision of the Lord sitting upon the throne, there is a comparison with two precious stones, the jasper and the sardius. The jasper is "clear as crystal" (21:11), and to it is likened the light of the holy Jerusalem which comes from "the glory of God" (21:23). The jasper is indeed the symbol of the glory of God. So the glory of the Lord is that which first strikes the eye of John, even as it did that of Isaiah.

The sardius, better known in our day as the carnelian, is red. Hengstenberg quotes ancient authorities who call it "blood-colored" and takes it to describe the righteous wrath of God, the color of the fire of the divine anger. Certainly this fits in with the judgment scene that is about to take place, for our God is a consuming fire (Deut. 4:24; Heb. 12:29).

Up until the present time, no man has seen God at any time. In the Old Testament, there had been appearances in which He manifested Himself under some form for His purposes in revelation and redemption. In Christ, God the Father was fully manifested (John 1:18) so that all who see Christ have seen the Father (John 14:9). Now, however, those who have been made pure in heart are to see God in His essential glory and separate from the Son, who is shortly to come and stand before this throne.

Round about the throne was a rainbow, resembling an emerald. In the Old Testament the rainbow was introduced as God's pledge to Noah and the race that the earth should never again be destroyed by a flood. But judgments are now to break forth which will ultimately end in the destruction of the world, though not by a flood. An anonymous writer has said, "God has never said that the continuance of this world is either necessary to His plans or dependent upon His divine pleasure. It rests upon the maintenance of the conditions of Noah's covenant." If men reject the covenant that is offered in Christ, that rejection has no bearing upon the existence of this world. It is, in fact, a matter that shall be judged after the world has passed away before the Great White Throne. "While the earth remaineth" the present order of natural events will continue unaltered (Gen. 8:22), but this is only while the earth remaineth. The Bible certainly teaches that all is to pass away. What prevents this? This same writer points out that God has overlooked times of ignorance but that now, since the nineteenth century, men have willfully set scientific guesses which may or may not be proved in opposition to the sure foundation of the

Scriptures, and have put these hypotheses as of equal, if not greater
authority, than the Scriptures. The very existence of Noah, the man
who undertook the contract with his Lord and Creator on behalf of
all his descendants, is now denied, and the responsibilities of man
toward God which Noah accepted for mankind are thereby repudiated.
The restraint which God Himself placed upon man through the centuries has now been removed, and within the last century it has been
proposed in Christendom for the first time since Babel, to abolish marriage, capital punishment, and the use of meat for food which were
involved in the instructions to Noah following the flood. The simultaneous appearance of all these social issues is an indication that the
restraint is likely to be completely removed at no distant date by Him
who placed it, and that a rebellion will soon break out which the
man of sin will head. Then will the covenant be fully broken. Then
will God set in motion those events through a thousand and seven
years which will end in the utter destruction of all things material.

But before the wrath of God is thus poured out, He shows His
own that there is a rainbow round His throne. Today we see but half
the circle. Then, it shall be seen in all its perfection. For those who
see the rainbow, there is certainty that the storm has already passed
by the place on which they stand. The believers are already in Heaven,
already in their eternal bodies, already like Christ. Eternal life is theirs.
They are in Christ Jesus and there is no condemnation. No judgment
can ever touch them again.

Round about the throne were twenty-four other thrones and on these
twenty-four elders. All commentators have united in seeing here the
representatives of Israel and the Church. That this is true and that
they are not angels is certain from the fact that their song in chapter
five is a swelling confession of praise and worship. "Thou hast redeemed us to God by thy blood out of every kindred, and tongue,
and people, and nation" (5:9). Here then is yet another proof that
the Church shall not pass through the Tribulation, for we find these
singers in Heaven before the beginning of the judgments.

That these twenty-four represent the heads of the twelve tribes of
Israel and the twelve apostles is abundantly confirmed in Scripture.
When we come to the description of the new Jerusalem, we find twelve
messengers at the gates and on the gates the names of the twelve
tribes of the children of Israel, while the names of the twelve apostles
are on the foundations of the city (Rev. 21:12-14). Our Lord promised the disciples that they should sit upon twelve thrones judging the
twelve tribes of Israel (Matt. 19:28; Luke 22:30). So it is that believers of all ages are seen here. These saints are clothed in white
garments, the righteousness of the Lord Jesus Christ upon them. White
is never to be found in the Scripture as the color of innocence. The
high priest Joshua (Zech. 3) did not receive white garments instead

of his filthy garments, but clean ones, while the Tribulation saints not only washed their robes but made them white in the blood of the Lamb (Rev. 7:14). The white is a righteousness which belongs to Christ alone and which is ours only through our being in Him.

The twenty-four elders wear crowns of gold. They are here as rulers. Now this does not necessarily mean that these crowns are literal, this is symbolic of judgment. The believers are to share judgment with our God. One commentator has spoken of them as "the Heavenly Senate of the Church"; but certainly their rule is not at all over the Church, for in the Church which is the Body of Christ, all members are articulated directly from the Head. The answer rather is to be found in the great promises to the believers that they shall rule with the Lord over the world. "Do ye not know that the saints shall judge the world? . . . Know ye not that we shall judge angels?" (I Cor. 6:2, 3). This is the glorious future of the redeemed ones. The Bride is lifted to the throne of the King of kings and Lord of lords, and rules with Him in His own righteousness, shining forth as the sun in the kingdom of their Father (Matt. 13:43). This authority is derived from the Lord, and all who wear the crowns recognize that it is from Him, for in a moment they cast their crowns before the Lord (4:10). When all earthly crowns and thrones have perished, the redeemed ones of Christ will be at the beginning of their reign. How small then will appear the great majesties of earth, and how insignificant the powers they have to bestow!

From the throne proceed lightnings and thunderings and voices. This is the first faint rumbling of the judgment that shall come forth against mankind out of Christ, against the empire of Satan, and the farthest worlds of the universe. Now there is a premonition of judgment, but soon worlds shall perish. They shall wax old as doth a garment. They shall be folded away like a vesture, and they shall be changed (Heb. 1:11, 12). These three sounds, heard from the throne of God, can be interpreted only with the concordance. They are the three sounds which proceeded from Sinai when the law was being given. "And it came to pass . . . that there were thunders and lightnings, and a thick cloud upon the mount, and the voice of the trumpet exceeding loud" (Exod. 19:16). The people trembled but did not obey, and now the time of Jacob's trouble (Jer. 30:7) is about to be introduced, and the nations of the earth are to be brought into judgment. Again and again in this study of Revelation lightnings announce the judgments of God. The voices are not merely the claps of thunder, but are the articulate announcements of the judgment of God which the earth will soon feel.

Seven lamps of fire were burning before the throne, and these are stated to be the seven Spirits of God. We have already seen in earlier passages that there is but one Holy Spirit, but that He is in a seven-fold perfection of activity in carrying out the purposes of God. His oneness with the Father is here manifest in the fact that He is spoken of as a source of light. The source of Heaven's light is threefold and yet it is one. "The glory of God did lighten it [the holy city] and the Lamb is the light thereof" (Rev. 21:23), and here the Holy Spirit is a sevenfold lamp. Father, Son and Spirit are one.

Verses 6–11

Prelude to Judgment

⁶And before the throne there was a glassy sea, like crystal: and in the midst of the throne and round about the throne four living ones, full of eyes before and behind. ⁷And the first living one is like a lion; and the second living one is like a young bullock; and the third living one has a face as a man; and the fourth living one is like a flying eagle.

⁸And each of the four living ones has six wings; round about and within they are full of eyes; and they have no rest day and night, say-ing: Holy, holy, holy is the Lord God, the Almighty who was and who is and who is coming.

⁹And when the living ones give glory and honor and thanks to the One who sits upon the throne, who lives to the ages of the ages, ¹⁰the four and twenty elders fall down before the One who sits upon the throne and worship Him who lives to the ages of the ages, and cast their crowns before the throne, saying, ¹¹Worthy art Thou, our Lord and our God, to receive the glory and the honor and the power; for Thou didst create all things, and because of Thy pleasure they were, and were created.

(Rev. 4:6-11, Free Translation)

Human language is not fitted to describe Heavenly things, and the symbols merely point us to certain Old Testament scenes which shed further light on the meaning of these words. Most important perhaps is the clue that is given to us in Hebrews 9:23. There we are told that the tabernacle built by Moses, and its appointments, the specifica-tions of which were given by God Himself on Mount Sinai, were the patterns or representations of things in the Heavens.

When a priest entered the holy place of the tabernacle for the first time, certainly the first object his eyes would have perceived would have been the seven-pronged candlestick with its seven lights by which all his ministrations were to be illuminated. As soon as John's eyes had become accustomed to the glorious Presence on Heaven's throne, he saw the seven lamps burning there which symbolize the perfection of the work of the Holy Spirit in God's universe.

Before the throne there was a glassy sea, like crystal. The concordance immediately takes us to the temple built by Solomon after the model of the tabernacle. "And he made a molten sea, ten cubits from the one brim to the other: it was round all about, and its height was five cubits" (I Kings 7:23). This great basin, fifteen feet in diameter, was supported on the backs of twelve oxen of brass, facing outward. Here the priests came for their cleansing. Each time before they entered the holy place they stopped for the cleansing ceremony. It is worthwhile noting that Moses made the laver in the tabernacle out of the mirrors of the women. These were of metal, highly polished. How soon human vanity and pride, typified by these mirrors, are melted down in the presence of God. When we see Him, our comeliness fades and we must go to His laver for cleansing.

But the laver, the sea, that John saw before the throne of God was not filled with water. When we are saved, we are justified, and all our sin is removed forever. This is why our Lord refused to wash Peter's head and hands again. But Peter still needed the laver. The daily contact with the world demanded a repeated coming to the throne of God. All this reached its climax for us in the Holy Spirit's great promise, "If we confess our sins, He is faithful and just to forgive us our sins, and to cleanse us from all unrighteousness" (I John 1:9). This is our font of cleansing.

But thank God the laver will be turned to crystal. The day will come when none of the saints will ever need confession. We begin each morning with earnest prayer. Our hearts flow out to God in the poignant silence of a great desire that we might live lives that would be free from sin, and would be stamped by the presence of Christ, that would be filled with victory. Yet, no matter how nearly we may have attained this ideal, we end each evening asking God to look back over the hours and by His searching Spirit to show us the things wherein we have displeased Him. Some word spoken in haste, or perhaps some word of witness left unspoken, some moment of defeat when the flesh has caused our thoughts to wander from God, His Word and His work—these and many other things are brought to our hearts under the light of the Spirit. Then it is that He points us to the laver. No matter what our day, we have need for it at the end. If we say that we do not need it, we deceive ourselves, and worse, we make God a liar (I John 1:8, 10).

One of the greatest joys in the anticipation of Heaven is that the laver is of crystal. I shall never have to go to the Heavenly Father again to tell Him I have sinned. I shall never have to meet that gaze of Christ that caused Peter to go out and weep bitterly. The laver is of crystal only because I and all the saints of all the ages will have been made like unto the Lord Jesus Christ. There will be no more sin. This is one of the reasons why it will be Heaven.

In the midst of the throne and round about the throne, John saw four living ones. Nothing could be more unfortunate than the King James translation which calls these creatures "beasts." They are creatures of the highest order, and from comparison with many other passages in the Word of God we can see immediately that they are none other than the cherubim. When we come to the account of their participation in the song of redemption (5:7-10), we shall discuss their nature and earlier history. Here the reference is to their office and work.

It should be noted, first of all that Satan before his fall was of this order. He was, in fact, the anointed or set apart cherub. The passage in Ezekiel 28, which describes him in his unfallen state reveals him as being of the utmost power and beauty. He is called "the anointed cherub that covereth." One of the French versions casts further light on this point. "Thou art the cherub who wast set apart to protect" (Ezek. 28:14). He was set by God in some authority connected with God's government. Lucifer fell from this high office and became Satan.

It would thus seem that the office of the cherubim has always involved some special distinction in connection with the throne or power of God. The first time we find them in the Scriptures they are working as instruments of authority and government. The main visions in which they are seen show them in close association with the throne of God and the very heart of His divine glory. Some of these passages should be noted. The first appearance of these living ones is in connection with the expulsion of Adam and Eve from the garden of Eden. The casual reader will be led to think, as I for so many years thought myself, that the flaming swords of the cherubim which turned every way were merely for the purpose of keeping the banished pair from any attempt to return to their former abode. I am convinced that this was the least important factor in the work of the cherubim on behalf of Adam and Eve. They were sent to keep, that is, to guard, to protect, the way of the tree of life. I found an exact parallel to this phrase in one of the addresses of the late President Roosevelt. At the time, he was giving over-age destroyers to Britain, talking about our advance into the Atlantic Ocean, he said, "We are determined to keep the way to Iceland." We are determined to keep the way. That was the meaning of the cherubim. God put them with swords flaming to keep the way of the tree of life. What was this way?

In every age God has had one means of approach to Himself. These have all been symbols of Christ Himself who said, "No man cometh unto the Father but by me" (John 14:6). If we look at all the details of the early chapters of Genesis, we find that Adam and Eve were driven to a spot outside the garden. They and their children had been ordered to bring a blood sacrifice. This we know from the fact that Abel obeyed this unrecorded command "by faith" (Heb. 11:4). Cain, after his sin, "went out from the presence of the Lord" (Gen. 4:16). Do not these passages taken together prove beyond a shadow of doubt that God put up an altar in the east of Eden where He ordered a blood sacrifice to be the basis of approach to Him by fallen man? Satan, as in all ages, would have sought to hinder man from his approach to God. The cherubim were placed there, greater in might than Satan, with the ability to ward off his attempts to destroy the altar. There, between the cherubim, the sacrificial blood was brought, and sinful man had access into the presence of a holy God through the Lamb who was to come.

In the holy of holies of the tabernacle, which was a part of the "patterns of things in the heavens," stood the ark. Its cover was a picture of the scene which had taken place at the eastern gate of Eden. Inside the ark were the tables of the law which man had outraged. Above the holy of holies was the pillar of cloud by day and fire by night. What prevented these symbols of holiness and justice from flaming out to destroy the people round about? Nothing but that which was symbolized by the cover of the ark of which the two cherubims of gold were a very part. On the day of atonement, the great high priest came into the holy of holies with the blood of the sacrifice and placed the blood on the top of the cover of the ark between the two cherubims. This God Himself called the mercy seat. "And the cherubims shall stretch forth their wings on high, covering the mercy seat with their wings, and their faces shall look one to another; toward the mercy seat shall the faces of the cherubims be . . . And there I will meet with thee, and I will commune with thee from above the mercy seat, from between the two cherubims which are upon the ark of the testimony . . ." (Exod. 25:20, 22).

There were four of these living ones, each with a different semblance—the one like a lion, the second like a young bullock, the third with a face as the face of a man, and the fourth like a flying eagle. In Ezekiel's great vision of the throne of God these same creatures are described in such detail that there can be no possible confusion. The first chapter of his prophecy is given up to their description which parallels almost entirely that of John. In the tenth chapter, he sees them again, recalling the earlier vision by the river of Chebar and he says, "I knew that they were the cherubims . . . and the likeness of their faces was the same faces which I saw by the river of Chebar" (Ezek. 10:20, 22).

Once more we repeat that these are symbols. Most certainly, there are not monstrosities in Heaven with the faces of animals, a bird and a man, any more than the Lord Jesus at the present time is a Lamb with seven horns and seven eyes. It is Hengstenberg who quotes the old Jewish saying, "There are four which take the first place in this world: men among the creatures, the eagle among birds, the ox among cattle and the lion among wild beasts." Through all the history of the Church, too, it must be remembered that these same symbols have been used to portray various characteristics of our Lord Himself. There are sculptures and windows with these symbols representing the four Evangelists: Matthew showing us Jesus as the Lion of the tribe of Judah; Mark revealing the Lord as the ox, the Servant of all; Luke portraying the Lord as the Man above all men; and John manifesting Christ as the eternal Word who was in the beginning with God, who indeed was God (John 1:1). It is in these portrayals and not in any question of manuscript sources that the differences in the four Gospels are to be found.

All of the characteristics of rule and dominion are upon these mighty beings whom God has placed at His very throne. He is about to exercise His Lordship over all creation, to bring man to the bitterest judgments of all human history. Satan, the anointed cherub, has long resisted Him. Here are living ones, in every way his equals, yes, infinitely his superiors, since they have access to all of the power of God. These are not with him in his rebellion. They are ready to carry into effect the orders of divine judgment.

The fact that these living ones are twice said to be filled with eyes "before and behind," "round about and within" is symbolic of the fact that these beings are not blind instruments who act as automatons, but sentient creatures who perceive and know and understand.

Their cry is like that of the seraphim in Isaiah's vision—the three-fold holiness of the Lord. One commentator, a century ago, remarked that all of the wonderful description of the cherubim and seraphim "serves not for the glorifying of the cherubim and the seraphim but of God. How glorious must He be, how rich in supply of help for His people, how mighty for the destruction of His enemies, before whom the concentration of created life so profoundly humbles itself, and with reverence obeys."

The starry hosts of Heaven never cease to proclaim God's majesty and glory. By day the sun, by night the moon and the stars speak of Him. And as the heavens declare the glory of God, so the angelic hosts "rest not day nor night." Men have turned away from God and have followed one of the cherubim into rebellion. The earth bears the mark of the curse upon sin. Yet God will be worshiped and His creation, animate and inanimate, will continue to praise Him.

It is perhaps proper to note the names of God in this passage. As Lord, He is Jehovah, the God of redemption. As God, He is the Strong One with all power in Himself. The Almighty takes us back either to the Lord of Hosts which speaks of Him as the Creator of the infinite armies of Heaven or to the revelation to Abraham where He gives Himself the name El Shaddai, the Almighty, but which really means the Breasted One, the One who nourishes, the One who is the source of life and strength. The cry of the cherubim ends with the eternal character of God. This is the One who always was; this is the One who now is; and this is the One who is coming. The last clause does not refer to the fact of continued future existence merely. This, of course, is implied, but the present participle is the announcement that He is about to come in a special way. Great judgments are now to be poured out. It is this God who will act.

Here in this description we have the first two appearances of a phrase which we shall find frequently throughout the book of Revelation. God lives to the ages of the ages. This is the strongest possible expression for an unending eternity. We make special mention of it because later we shall see that the same phrase is used of the duration of the punishment of Satan, his captains and those of earth who have followed him. Some have tried to claim that such punishment will come to an end and have argued that the phrase was one which indicated a period with a final termination at which such punishment would end. How we would love to believe this! But we dare not sacrifice the holiness and justice of God to pamper our emotions. It is the time of the duration of God's existence!

The effect upon the four and twenty elders is now described. We have seen that they represent the redeemed saints from this earth. They see these wonderful beings, symbols of power and holiness, and they see them prostrate before God. They see them ascribing glory and honor and thanksgiving to this One who sits upon the throne and who lives to the ages of the ages. Immediately the elders fall down before Him and worship Him. Satan may have seduced the world through millenniums of struggle to accept him as the prince of this world and as the god of this age, but now beings mightier than he show the way of true worship. God alone is to receive the homage of men. The redeemed saints have learned this lesson and are glad not only to prostrate themselves before Him but to take the crowns which they wear and cast them down at His feet. What are these crowns? As we have seen earlier in our study, they are the symbols of reward. They are the prizes which have come from God's heart of grace, given unto those who, at the best, were unprofitable servants. When we shall see the worship of the mighty cherubim, we shall realize therefore, that no crown belongs to us rightfully and we shall cast them down before the presence of Him who lives forever.

It is this God who created all things, and because of His sovereign pleasure they were called into being. His works have been sullied by sin. His Name has been brought into disrepute among men because of the existence of sin in His creation and because of the effects of judgment upon that creation. He who moved at first to create, now moves to restore. Righteous judgment is to be poured out upon the earth and the eternal plan of God, seemingly frustrated by the entrance of sin, will be shown to be that which shall manifest before all creation's host—men, angels, fallen beings—that all things are after the counsel of His will.

CHAPTER 5

Verses 1–7

The Lamb Becomes a Lion

¹And I saw upon the right hand of Him who was sitting upon the throne a scroll, written within and on the back side, having been firmly sealed with seven seals. ²And I saw a mighty messenger proclaiming in a great voice, Who is worthy to open the scroll and to loose its seven seals? ³And no one in Heaven, neither the earth, nor under the earth was able to open the scroll nor to look thereon.

⁴And I was weeping much because no one was found worthy to open the scroll, neither to look thereon. ⁵And one of the elders saith unto me, Weep not; behold the Lion which is of the tribe of Judah, the Root of David, prevailed to open the scroll and its seven seals.

⁶And I saw in the midst of the throne and of the four living ones, and in the midst of the elders, a Lamb standing, as having been slain, having seven horns and seven eyes which are the seven spirits of God sent forth into all the earth. ⁷And He came and took the scroll from out of the right hand of Him that sat upon the throne.
(Rev. 5:1-7, Free Translation)

When John's eyes had become accustomed to the light of glory, he began to see more of the details of the heavenly scene. A scroll, and the word indicates that it was a small scroll, was seen in the right hand of the One who was sitting upon the throne.

In the scene before us Christ is not on the Father's throne; the age of His intercession has come to its close. We shall see Him acting in an entirely new character. Every symbol points to it. Every name indicates it. Every gesture demonstrates it. The age of the Church is over. This is now prophecy of the future. The four and twenty elders representing the body of believers already have been glorified and have begun their praise for eternity. In other words, this is the scene in Heaven after the rapture of the believers.

The scroll had been written on both sides and had been sealed— it is an intensive word, closely sealed or tightly sealed — with seven seals. Is there any reference to a sealed scroll in the Scriptures? There

100

are two passages in the prophets which will demand our attention. One in Ezekiel, is of a scroll that is written within and without, but which is spread open before the prophet; the other in Daniel, is tightly sealed.

When the stupendous visions of Daniel had been recorded, a definite order was received from God as to the disposal of the prophecy. "But thou, O Daniel, shut up the words, and seal the scroll, even to the time of the end: many shall run to and fro, and knowledge shall be increased" (Dan. 12:4). But Daniel was filled with the wonder of his subject. He knew just enough to know that he did not understand the meaning of the amazing things he had seen and with intense desire he longed for a revelation of the meaning of his own prophecy. What a lesson on the inspiration of the Scriptures! God had spoken; the prophet had recorded, but he was as dependent on the Holy Spirit for a knowledge of what he had written as we are today for that same knowledge.

Those who are justified in Christ are given the right to understand. So John was shown the vision of what is to occur in the future when the Lord Jesus Christ shall rise from the Father's throne, divest Himself of the robes of mediation, and take upon Him the character of Judge, bringing to accomplishment every word which has been spoken by God, pouring history into the channels that God has dug for it.

One of God's mighty messengers now proclaims in a loud voice, "Who is worthy to open the scroll and to loose its seven seals?" Without doubt, the messenger in this case is one of the angelic host. But we shall continue to use the word messenger, because as we have already seen, the word is applied to very different categories of beings: to the human messengers of the seven churches; here to an angelic being; and in passages that are yet to come, probably to the Lord Jesus Christ Himself when He undertakes certain work for the Father.

The cry of the messenger reveals that there is no one in the Heavens, nor the earth, nor under the earth who is able to open the scroll or to look thereon. Neither angels, men, nor demons can know anything of the plans of God until He is pleased to reveal them. They may possess great wisdom either angelic wisdom, human wisdom, or Satanic wisdom. This avails nothing. "And the vision of all is become unto you as the words of a book that is sealed, which men deliver to one that is learned, saying, Read this, I pray thee: and he saith, I cannot; for it is sealed" (Isa. 29:11). There is over the future, as Hengstenberg points out, not a partial but a complete darkness. The redemptive work of Christ contains the only key for prophetic problems—the only light for the future.

But why could no one look upon this book? Knowledge of the future is a very part of God, and one of the proofs of His deity. To look upon the future is to look upon God and no man may do this except through Christ.

John had not yet learned this and so he was weeping. He had seen the unworthiness of all others, but had not yet realized the worthiness of Christ to meet this problem as He meets all others. We may ask ourselves if we are thus concerned at the spiritual ignorance of those around us. Does it cause us to weep that God's people are in error because they do not know the Scriptures? Have we shed any tears because defeat comes to His people through lack of knowledge (Hos. 4:6)? It is only as we enter into this divine love that we can be of any use in the edification of God's people. It was Bengel who said, "Without tears the Revelation was not written, neither can it without tears be understood." Let not that man think to understand the pages of these prophecies who approaches them as apocalyptic curiosities or interesting specimens of first century literature.

The end of John's weeping comes at the place where all tears are dried. He was pointed to Christ where tears are turned to joy. One of the elders stopped his tears with the command, "Weep not: behold the Lion which is of the tribe of Judah, the root of David, prevailed to open the scroll and its seven seals."

Here is one of the important passages of the Apocalypse for its special revelation of the meaning of the whole. The elder comes to the weeping John and says, "Behold the Lion of the tribe of Judah." What did John have every right to expect to see? There is only one answer. He had the right to expect to see a lion. If I am driving with my children and say to them, "Look at the train," they may expect to see a train and not a vegetable garden. Were I to point them to a train which they could not see, they would ask for further explanation. If I were to reply, "I mean that vegetable garden," they would have every right to say, "But why do you call a vegetable garden a train?"

In this book of Revelation, this book of symbolic language such a change in symbols is of extreme importance. John was told to behold a Lion, but when he looked he saw a Lamb. What is the explanation?

Thus far in this book of Revelation Christ has been described by title twenty-four times, from the fourth verse in the first chapter where He is spoken of as the One who is and who was and who is to come, down to the message to Laodicea where He is called, "the Amen, the Faithful and True Witness, the Beginning of the creation of God." They are peculiar titles which apply to Him in His present state and office. They are, one might say, Church titles, titles which the Church may give to her Lord, titles by which the Lord would reveal Himself to His Church.

But now something is about to happen on the earth. The Lord is about to pour out judgments upon the earth. The Church at this point in the prophecy has already been removed from the earth. The four and twenty elders are in Heaven. Earthly promises are now to be fulfilled. It is inexcusably selfish to attempt to steal all of the promises in the Bible for the Church of today, an error of some commentators which accounts for the utter disregard of Israel, God's earthly people. The Holy Spirit is not talking about a spiritual people, but the physical descendants of Abraham when He speaks through Paul of the brethren, "kinsmen according to the flesh: who are Israelites; to whom pertaineth the adoption, and the glory, and the covenants, and the giving of the law, and the service of God, and the promises . . ." (Rom. 9:3, 4). To these brethren, kinsmen according to the flesh, belong the promises. Every word in the Old Testament which speaks of a kingdom is Israel's promise. Christ's inheritance is not only the Church which is the pearl of great price for which He sold all that He had, but it also includes Israel which is the treasure hidden in the field and which He purchased with His own blood and which He hid again.

Without the fulfillment of all the earthly promises made to Israel, the full redemption is not accomplished. Any attempt to spiritualize these promises and to apply them to the Church is doing violence to the Word of God. If the Author of the Book may make promises to the children of the loins of Abraham and then fulfill them in a "spiritual" way to the children of Gentiles who have become Christians, then He may well cast off the believers in Christ and fulfill His promises to them by calling out some new people or by creating some new species. No, God is not a God of caprice. "The gifts and calling of God are without repentance" (Rom. 11:29). And it is in this precise connection—the announcement of the certainty of His promises to the physical descendants of Israel—that God thus binds His promises to a literal fulfillment.

Israel has been temporarily set aside and their fall has become the riches of mankind through the preaching of the Gospel. Their diminishing has become the riches of the Gentiles who now have access in this age of grace (Rom. 11:12). But at the same moment that the Holy Spirit was giving this promise through Paul He was looking forward into the future and saying, "How much more their fullness . . . For if the casting away of them be the reconciling of the world (through the preaching of the gospel) what shall the receiving of them be, (in the future when God restores them) but life from the dead?" (Rom. 11:12, 15).

This is the lesson that John learned in his heavenly vision. He wept when he found no answer to all of the problems of prophecy and then he learned that the Lion of Judah, the root of David, *prevailed* to open the scroll and its seven seals. The Greek word which is translated "prevailed" is the same as "overcome" in the letters to the churches of Asia. It is the word which Christ uses of Himself: "I also

overcame and am set down with my Father in his throne." Jesus Christ
prevailed at the cross. He may not take His place as ruler of Israel
until He has become the Redeemer through the sacrifice of Himself.

All the promises to Israel are to become effective by virtue of the
death of the Lord Jesus Christ. Our Lord was exalted by the Father
because of His first work. Because He left Heaven's glory and humbled
Himself to the death, even the death of the cross, God hath highly
exalted Him and given Him the Name that is above every name. This
had been promised of old. "Therefore will I divide him a portion with
the great, and he shall divide the spoil with the strong; because he hath
poured out his soul unto death: and he was numbered with the transgressors and he bare the sin of many, and made intercession for the
transgressors" (Isa. 53:12).

He comes to the fore in virtue of this new power that He won at
the cross. The time of His intercession for our sins is over. He now
has other things to do. Here He is presented to begin His future work,
but this future work will be founded upon His past work. It is in virtue of what He has been that He becomes what He shall be.

Hearing of One who possesses the highest titles of Israel, John
looks and sees a Lamb—in the Greek it is a little lamb—standing
within the circle about the Father's throne. This Lamb stands "as
having been slain, having seven horns and seven eyes." Several artists
of the Middle Ages attempted to paint this scene. With the background of an Italian palace or surrounded by Flemish burgher saints,
they have painted a lamb with a bloody wound showing on its fleecy
coat, seven eyes painted into its horrible head, and seven horns proceeding forth at various angles wherever there was any room left. Such
paintings are monstrosities. To describe them is to show the folly
of any explanation beyond the symbolic. These are symbols. Jesus
Christ, with the marks of His death upon His resurrected body, was
seen by John. But He was seen not merely as Thomas saw Him in
the day in which he was called to put forth his hand and touch those
marks; now He is seen with something more. He has the symbols of
government and the force and ability to execute the decrees of God.
The horn in Scripture is the symbol of authority and government.

When Samuel was born, Hannah came into the temple and prayed
a prophetic prayer. In this the symbol of the horn is to be found for
the first time in Scripture. Hannah said, "My heart rejoiceth in the
Lord, my horn is exalted in the Lord: my mouth is enlarged over
mine enemies; because I rejoice in thy salvation." There follows an
outline that is in harmony with the order of events of history and
prophecy. Israel is asked not to talk in pride and arrogancy. The
alternating periods of strength and weakness in Old Testament times
are described. The death and resurrection of Christ are symbolized.
"The Lord killeth and maketh alive: he bringeth down to the grave,

and bringeth up." Grace then operates in all freeness and, "He raiseth up the poor out of the dust, and lifteth up the beggar from the dung-hill, to set them among princes, and to make them inherit the throne of glory." This is certainly a picture of what God is doing today in the Church. Then suddenly, judgment breaks. "The adversaries of the Lord shall be broken to pieces; out of heaven shall he thunder upon them: the Lord shall judge the ends of the earth; and he shall give strength unto his king, and exalt the horn of his anointed" (I Sam. 2:1-10).

He shalt exalt the horn of His anointed, of His Messiah. The same symbol is to be found throughout the psalms. Among many instances we may note the following. "In my name shall his horn be exalted" (89:24). "His horn shall be exalted with honor. The wicked shall see it and be grieved" (112:9, 10).

The horn, then, is the symbol of power and of government, and since the Lamb is seen with seven horns, it means that the meek and lowly Jesus is to receive, when the days of His intercession are over, the full power of the government of God, to accomplish all of the purposes which have been eternally determined. But among all the animals of sacrifice which typify our Lord Jesus, it is the lamb that is chosen. He is not seen as the dove that was slain, or the ox, or bullock, or goat; but as the lamb, most fitting of all the sacrificial symbols to represent His holiness, His righteousness and especially His patience in suffering and His submission to the Father's will, the Lamb without blemish and without spot (I Pet. 1:19). At the trans-figuration scene, the prophets spoke to Him of His decease which He should accomplish at Jerusalem (Luke 9:31). Again and again the Heavens burst into song at the thought of His death. Here we have the declaration that even in the day of His power, when He shall come forth to pour out the wrath of God upon a deserving earth, when He shall come as Judge of the nations to break them into pieces, when He shall come vested with all of the authority of the Almighty Creator, He will nevertheless act in full harmony with all that He was when He was dying upon the cross.

In his essay on Victor Hugo's work, Robert Louis Stevenson writes of the injustice of human law. Of *Les Miserables* he says, "It is the moral intention of this great novel to awaken us a little, if it may be— for such awakenings are unpleasant—to the great cost of this society that we enjoy and profit by, to the labour and sweat of those who support the litter, civilization, in which we ourselves are so smoothly carried forward . . . A sort of mocking indignation grows upon us as we find Society rejecting, again and again, the services of the most serviceable; setting Jean Valjean to pick oakum, casting Galileo into prison, even crucifying Christ. There is a haunting and horrible sense of insecurity about the book. The terror we thus feel is a terror for

the machinery of law, that we can hear tearing in the dark, good and
bad between its formidable wheels with the iron stolidity of all machinery, human or divine . . ."

But there will be no such tearing machinery in the judgments of
Christ. There will be no action upon partial knowledge. He has
seven eyes, the perfection of vision that goes with omniscience. He
knows all and sees all. "All things are naked and opened unto the
eyes of him with whom we have to do" (Heb. 4:13). And He works
with all the sevenfold perfection of the perfect Spirit of God.

It is He, the risen Lord Jesus Christ, finished with His age-long work
of mediation, who comes and takes the scroll from out of the right
hand of Him that sits upon the throne. It is He, Judah's Lion, the
Root of David, who is about to fulfill all the promises which yet remain to be accomplished for Israel. Jacob's dying blessing shall be
accomplished. The brethren shall praise Judah. His hand shall be on
the neck of His enemies . . . Judah is a lion's whelp. The people shall
now be gathered to the Lawgiver who holds the scepter and who shall
know how to enforce His every wish (Gen. 49:8-10).

And with the taking of the scroll, action is about to begin. Once
more we insist upon the importance of Christ's position in this scene.
He is walking in Heaven. He came to the throne. He is not sitting
there as Mediator. He stands as Judge. And when the great moment
of praise shall have ceased, He will tear the seals from the scroll, pre-
cipitating that tribulation which He Himself said was greater than any
since the beginning of the world.

Verses 8–14

The Lamb Takes the Scroll

*8And when He took the scroll, the four living ones and the four
and twenty elders fell down before the Lamb, having each one a harp
and golden bowls, full of different kinds of incense, which are the
prayers of the saints. 9And they sang a new song, saying, Worthy art
Thou to take the scroll and to open its seals; for Thou wast slain,
and didst purchase to God in Thy blood, out of every tribe and tongue
and people and nation; 10And didst make them for our God a kingdom and priests, and they shall reign over the earth.*

*11And I saw, and I heard the voice of many messengers round about
the throne and the living ones and the elders; and the number of them
was ten thousands of thousands and thousands of thousands; 12saying
with a great voice, Worthy is the Lamb that was slain to receive the
power, and riches, and wisdom, and strength, and honor, and glory,
and blessing. 13And every creature which is in Heaven and on the
earth, and on the sea, and all that are in them, I heard saying, Blessing, and honor, and glory, and power, be unto Him that sitteth upon*

the throne, and unto the Lamb, unto the ages of the ages. ¹⁴*And the four living ones said, Amen; and the elders fell down and worshiped.* (Rev. 5:8-14, Free Translation)

We have insisted that the scene before the throne in the fifth chapter of Revelation is a vision of that which is to take place in the future at the end of the Church age and at the outset of the Great Tribulation period. There are positive indications which show that the scene is future, and there are the negative indications which show that the scene cannot possibly be in the past.

We have already pointed out several of the former. The fourth chapter begins with "the things which must be after" the Church age. The elders, representing the Church, are already in Heaven, and have already received their crowns of reward. There is before the throne the laver which is of crystal, a symbol that there is no more need for daily cleansing from sins. Finally, the Lord Jesus Christ does not appear as One who is seated upon the throne, which most certainly is the place of His present activity as our Intercessor, but He is presented to us as One who has laid aside His work in behalf of the Church and has assumed titles indicative of His work for Israel. There is still a further proof which will come out as the prophecy unfolds. We will demonstrate from passages of Scripture that the series of events begun in chapter six is absolutely in the future and that Christ pointed to one event in the series as the fixed mark from which prophetic time and events were to be determined. Answering the disciples' question as to the sign of His coming and the end of the age, the Lord announced events which parallel the series of judgments.

The negative proofs are just as impressive. Let us note first of all what the Lord Jesus did upon being received into Heaven. What honors were bestowed upon Him at the time of His ascension? He had prayed the Father that He might receive again the glory which He had had with Him before the world was (John 17:5). And if we turn to the book of Peter we read that God raised Him from the dead and gave Him glory. This refers to the majesty of the Godhead with which He had been clothed before the incarnation and of which He had emptied Himself at His incarnation (Phil. 2:7). And thus He was set by God "at his own right hand in the heavenly places, far above all principality, and power, and might, and dominion, and every name that is named, not only in this age, but also in that which is to come" (Eph. 1:20-22), and all things were put under His feet.

There seems to be, however, a clear recognition that this elevation by God was more in the character of a potential announcement of what should become fact later, for we find in the New Testament not only that there is no record of Christ's reigning; but that there is a positive record that He is not yet reigning, that He is, in fact, occupied in the work of intercession for the believers. In both Ephesians and Corinthians, we read that all things have been put under Christ's feet. In the epistle to the Hebrews, however, we are told that this is potential and not actual. "Thou hast put all things in subjection under his feet. For in that he put all in subjection under him, he left nothing that is not put under him. *But now we see not yet all things put under him*" (Heb. 2:8). Indeed, the whole argument of the epistle to the Hebrews is to tell the children of Israel who had been living their lives with their eyes upon Moses and Aaron—Moses to tell them what to do and Aaron to make a sacrifice for them when they had failed to do it—that Christ was now occupied as the Moses and Aaron, the Apostle and High Priest of the new profession. "Now of the things of which we have spoken this is the sum: we have such an High Priest, who is set on the right hand of the throne of the majesty in the heavens; a minister of the sanctuary" (Heb. 8:1, 2). It is said that as Moses sprinkled the tabernacle with the blood on the day of dedication, so Christ has gone to prepare a place for us, taking the value of His death to purify the Heavens themselves, entering not "into the holy places made with hands, which are the figures of the true; but into heaven itself, now to appear in the presence of God for us" (Heb. 9:24). This is His temporary occupation. He is "from henceforth expecting till his enemies be made his footstool" (Heb. 10:13). "He shall appear the second time without sin unto salvation" (Heb. 9:28) to complete the work of salvation which involves the destruction of the forces of evil, a work which He has not yet undertaken except in providing a basis for their destruction by His death upon the cross.

There is an Old Testament prophecy also which must be taken into consideration in the settlement of this problem. The second Psalm is the first of the great prophecies concerning Christ and His rule. It is a dialogue in the Godhead—the Father, Son and Spirit speak together. The nations of the earth array themselves against God and the rulers take counsel together against the Lord and His anointed. Some have imagined that this was completely fulfilled by Israel's rejection of Christ and His crucifixion. This Psalm is quoted in the fourth chapter of Acts as referring to the trial and death of Christ. Yet that array of earth's forces against God is as great today as it was in Pilate's hall, and is to come to its climax yet in the future. In spite of man's rejection, God has set Christ upon His holy hill. We are quite willing to accept that this was done at the time of the resurrection. It does not follow, however, that the rest of the Psalm was fulfilled at that time. Here we have the great unprayed prayer of Christ. The Father says, "Ask of me, and I shall give thee the nations for thine inheritance, and the uttermost parts of the earth for thy possession." Some may contend that Christ has already asked the Father for the nations, and that He has already received them.

We reply that if this be so, He has not yet done anything about it, for the prophecy goes on to state, "Thou shalt break them with a rod of iron; thou shalt dash them to pieces like a potter's vessel." Here is the whole point of the argument. The Lord Jesus Christ must literally fulfill this prophecy at some future date.

This scene is laid at the end of the present age after the Church has been gathered to Heaven, after our Lord has risen from His work of intercession. No longer seated at the right hand of God, He is seen walking in Heaven, coming to take the book out of the right hand of God, and proceeding with His work for His own in Israel and among the nations, and proceeding with His work of judgment upon the enemies whom God is now about to make His footstool.

It is when He assumes this character that Heaven breaks forth anew in worship. I have pointed out elsewhere that there are four things out of place in the universe. The Church is out of place; she ought to be in Heaven. Israel is out of place; she should be in the land that has been sworn to her and possessing every part of it. The devil is out of place; he ought to be in the lake of fire while he is still roaming free. Christ is out of place; He should be through with intercession and seated upon His own throne reigning instead of upon His Father's throne interceding. Here in the vision of the throne of God in Heaven we hear successively cries of praise and worship. The saints come home to Heaven, their proper place. Christ ceases His work in their behalf, for they are now made like Him. He moves to assume titles which show that He will now fulfill the promises made to Israel. All these presage the doom of Satan who will so soon be cast forth from Heaven to his proper place. Is it any wonder that when Christ walks in Heaven and takes the book, the unloosing of whose seals means fulfillment of promise and judgment, the righting of all wrongs, the living creatures and the four and twenty elders fall down to worship? Each one of the elders has a harp. This is a symbol of praise. Each one has a golden vial of incense. This is a symbol of worship.

It should be noticed in passing that there is incidental teaching here concerning prayer. The literal translation is that the golden vials are full of incenses which are the prayers of the saints. Today, prayer consists of confession, intercession and worship. When we confess, we are occupied with our sins; when we intercede, we are occupied with human needs, ours and others; but when we worship, we are occupied with Him alone. The day will come when prayer will be emptied of its need for confession. There will be no more laver. Prayer will be emptied of its need for intercession. There will be nothing remaining but that which may be symbolized under the bowls of incense, and all our prayer shall be praise and worship.

A new song is then sung. If we take it in the wording of the King James Version, the living creatures join with the elders and sing it about themselves. If we take it in the American Revised Version, the song would be impersonal. If the living creatures are included in the song of redemption, there are implications which take us back to past mysteries at the dawn of time. Are there cherubim who have been redeemed? We know that Lucifer was of this order and there may be a hint of things unknown concerning which we have no right to dogmatize, but which might lead us to hope that many of the creatures who originally followed Satan had been offered salvation and had availed themselves of the offer. Certainly it would not be out of harmony with the nature of God. If this be true, how delighted we shall be to see them in Heaven, and to hear their harmony with our own.

In any event, the song is one which centers in the worthiness of Christ. Paraphrased, its words run, "Because Thou didst die, because Thou didst purchase by Thy blood a body of believers, called out of every tribe, and tongue, and people, and nation, and because Thou didst make of them for our God a priestly kingdom that shall reign on earth; because of all this, Thou art worthy to take the book and open the seals thereof."

Is it not wonderful to see that when God moves to right the wrongs that are in the world, that when God moves to pour out judgment upon those that deserve it, He does not move with the arbitrary autocracy of a self-willed despot, but with the ordered righteousness of His own perfect justice? He is worthy to wrest the kingdom away from Satan because He died on the cross and prepared a body of believers to take the power and reign.

The definite statement should be noted that the believers shall reign over the earth. This is in keeping with other Scriptures. The Corinthian believers are commanded to stay away from worldly law courts in the settlement of their disputes in view of the fact that they themselves have in their destiny the high position of judge of all mankind (I Cor. 6:2). The overcomers in Sardis are promised future power over the nations to join with Christ in this rule of the rod of iron, to join with Him in the crushing judgments of the nations. It is not possible to spiritualize these statements. The Church is not ruling today. The Church was never meant to rule in the present age. "In the world ye shall have tribulation" (John 16:33). No place of power and triumph in the present earthly scheme of things is ever promised to the believer. He is in the world, but not of it. Satan is the world's prince and the god of this age. Yet, nevertheless, Christ is to rule on the earth. He is to rule the nations. The idea of symbolic language cannot be pushed to the point where one can take such a phrase as "They shall reign on the earth," and say that symbolically this means "They shall not reign on the earth."

And now all of Heaven's host take up the cry. Many angels round about the throne and the cherubim and the saints all join in the response, "Worthy is the Lamb that was slain." It should be noted in this connection that there are definite indications of angelic interest in the details of the plan of God. Peter, speaking of the Old Testament prophets, pointed out that their great pronouncements had caused them to study their own writings to find out their meaning. The Spirit of Christ spoke through them and they then searched diligently to find out when the great victories of which they spoke should be accomplished. "Of which salvation the prophets have inquired and searched diligently, who prophesied of the grace that should come unto you: searching what, or what manner of time the Spirit of Christ which was in them did signify, when he testified beforehand the sufferings of Christ [the first coming], and the glory that should follow [the second coming]. Unto whom it was revealed, and not unto themselves, but unto us they did minister the things, which are now reported unto you by them that have preached the gospel unto you with the Holy Spirit sent down from heaven . . ." (I Pet. 1:10-12). But this statement is not finished. There is one more sentence. It would have been important enough to tell us that the writers of the Old Testament were eager students of their own writings, that they had been inspired of God to speak of things of which they knew nothing, had recorded faithfully that which they heard, and had given themselves with diligence to the study of the problems involved. But the Old Testament records are of even more sacred interest than this, for the Holy Spirit concludes this sentence through Peter, "which things the angels desire to look into." The verb is a strong one. They want to fasten their attention upon the Scriptures, to study these problems thoroughly.

The angels are Bible students and human beings may well learn a great lesson from them in this day when the Scriptures are being taken more and more casually by so many people and dismissed altogether by so many others.

The angels are interested in prophecy, and when the Lord ends His intercession and takes the scroll from the hand of the Father, every angel knows that this is the signal that God's long day of patience is ended. They know that action, fierce, strong and just, is about to begin against those who have offended so long, and that soon the Lord will go forth "To execute judgment upon all, and to convince all that are ungodly among them of all their ungodly deeds which they have ungodly committed, and of all their hard speeches which ungodly sinners have spoken against him" (Jude 15).

The subject of the new song is not the blessing of redemption already old, but the joy of the host is expressed that Christ is about to take the power and exercise dominion. The prayer we often sing is about to be answered,

> "Fill up the roll of Thine elect.
> *Then,* take Thy power and reign . . ."

The number of those who join in the praise when this occurs is beyond count. It might well be translated, "And the number of them was armies multiplied by armies, and armies of armies." The world sometimes sneers at the Church on the ground that the believers form a feeble company. Jokesters will seek for a laugh by answering the question, "Do you want to go to Heaven?" with some such phrase as, "No, I want to be with the majority," or "I never like being lonesome." But Heaven's number of earth's redeemed will be hosts of hosts, myriads of myriads, not counting the infinite armies of the angelic beings. There will be far more people of earth in Heaven than in the lake of fire. Even in the vast nations of paganism, God will not be mocked. God knows how to reach out and take His own unto Himself even where Satan's power seems to be most strongly entrenched.

When Daniel sees the vision of Heaven with the Ancient of Days seated upon the throne, he writes, "His throne was like the fiery flame, and his wheels as burning fire. A fiery stream issued and came forth from before him: thousand thousands ministered unto him, and ten thousand times ten thousand stood before him: the judgment was set, and the books were opened" (Dan. 7:9, 10). The vision is the same. The hosts of Heaven are first to acknowledge the Lordship of the Lamb. In chapter four, the praise was to the Father; here, the praise is to the Son. Heaven's cry is, "Worthy is the Lamb that was slain to receive power, and riches, and wisdom, and strength, and honor, and glory, and blessing." It should be noted that this is worship of Jesus Christ. It is not in His character as the eternal Jehovah that He receives this worship, but as the Lamb that was slain. "Thou shalt call his name Jesus for he shall save his people from their sins" (Matt. 1:21). It is "at the name of Jesus" that every knee shall bow (Phil. 2:10). Here is the fulfillment of this prophecy. "And every creature which is in heaven, and on the earth, and on the sea, and all that are in them" are heard to say, "Blessing, and honor, and glory, and power be unto him that sitteth upon the throne, and unto the Lamb, unto the ages of the ages." Very clearly this has not yet taken place. It did not take place when Christ ascended into Heaven, but lies in the future when He will begin to enforce His plan.

Does this mean that even the devil and the hosts of the lost will join in praise to Christ? Hengstenberg believes that it does and that they shall be forced in spite of themselves to praise Christ, by whom all things were made. For their very existence came from Him and the gifts with which they are furnished are a telling proof of His greatness and love. At all events, praise shall be universal in His creation. The inanimate things by their very existence show forth His praise, and He will know how to call forth praise even from His enemies, just as every knee shall bow and every tongue confess that He is Lord.

Again we point out that this praise is to endure unto the ages of the ages. This is the third use of this phrase in the book of Revelation. The Father who sits upon the throne liveth unto the ages of the ages (4:9). The elders worship Him that liveth unto the ages of the ages (4:10). Praise shall be unto the Lamb unto the ages of the ages. We would build our impression of this unending eternity from the timelessness of these phrases, for we shall need to call them to mind when we come to judgment scenes.

The voice of praise dies down. The cherubim cry, "Amen." These mightiest agents of the execution of God's will announce, when praise is ascribed to the Lord Jesus Christ: So shall it be. The redeemed ones—we ourselves—who have had such an active part in all this scene fall down and worship Him. There is something majestic in the silence of this phrase. Never will such music have been heard in the universe. Never will so many voices have intoned such mighty praise. The armies of armies come to the last note. The mightiest of God's creatures sound the amen. We gaze upon the scene with no voice for utterance and, prostrate, we worship the Lord Jesus Christ who now proceeds to the most awful scenes of judgment with actions that are rooted in His cross.

PART IV
THE SEALS

CHAPTER 6

Verses 1–2

The First Horseman

¹And I saw when the Lamb opened one of the seven seals, and I heard one of the four living ones saying as with a voice of thunder, Come. ²And I saw and behold a white horse, and the one sitting on him having a bow; and a crown was given to him, and he went forth conquering, and to conquer.
(Rev. 6:1, 2, Free Translation)

At some time in every commentary on the Book of Revelation, it is necessary to go back to the Book of Daniel and to the great prophetic utterance of our Lord in His last discourse on the Mount of Olives, a few days before His death. The events in the breaking of the seals are pictures which need to be framed, and the framework is to be found in the passages we have indicated.

Daniel had a vision which concerned certain periods of time. Just as John wept when he thought that there was no one worthy to open the scroll, so Daniel received his prophetic knowledge after definitely setting his face unto the Lord God "to seek by prayer and supplications, with fasting, and sackcloth, and ashes" (Dan. 9:3). The humiliation of the soul of the prophet was preparation for divine revelation, and no one can lay hold of prophetic truth who is not willing to pass by the same low road. His final prayer was for the sanctuary at Jerusalem, the Holy of Holies, symbol of the presence of God on earth among His people. "Now, therefore, O our God, hear the prayer of thy servant, and his supplications, and cause thy face to shine upon thy sanctuary that is desolate, for the Lord's sake . . . O Lord, hear; O Lord, forgive; O Lord, hearken, and do; defer not . . ." (Dan. 9: 17, 19).

It was in the midst of this plea that Gabriel was sent from Heaven to talk with Daniel and to inform him. "I am now come forth," he said, "to give thee skill and understanding." Daniel was then informed that seventy periods of time were determined upon Israel and upon

117

Jerusalem. In the English translation, the phrase has been rendered "seventy weeks." The Hebrew word which is translated "week" is one which means a seven. The new Revised Standard Version rightly translates it, "weeks of years." Just as the period of ten years is called a decade, so we could well translate this word "heptad," a period of seven years. If we do this, the meaning of the passage becomes clear. "Seventy heptads are determined upon Thy people and upon Thy holy city." Within this period of four hundred and ninety years, certain things were to be accomplished. This time was determined "to finish the transgression, and to make an end of sins, and to make reconciliation for iniquity, and to bring in everlasting righteousness, and to seal up the vision and prophecy, and to anoint the most Holy" (Dan. 9: 24). Now it is readily seen that some of these points have been fulfilled, and that others have not, although far more than four hundred and ninety years have passed. When the Messiah came forth to die, He did make reconciliation for iniquity, but everlasting righteousness was certainly not brought in at that time.

Only two explanations are possible. All that was prophesied did not take place in four hundred and ninety years, therefore, the prophecy is false; or, the years are not consecutive, and a gap is to be sought somewhere. The latter interpretation is immediately seen to be the correct one. Gabriel was very specific. The period of seventy heptads, seventy weeks of years, was to be divided into three sections: forty-nine years plus four hundred and thirty-four years, plus seven years.

Let us read more closely. "Know therefore and understand, that from the going forth of the commandment to restore and to build Jerusalem unto the Messiah the Prince shall be seven heptads and sixty-two heptads" (Dan. 9:25). The beginning of the time measure was the royal decree promulgated by Artaxerxes in the twentieth year of his reign, and recorded in the second chapter of Nehemiah. After seven heptads the city had been restored in the midst of great troubles. From this time, the sixty-two heptads run. Daniel's narrative continues, "And after sixty-two heptads shall Messiah be cut off but not for himself." Here, of course, is a very definite date, the crucifixion of Christ as a substitute for the sins of Israel. We do not need to go into the details of the chronology. Sir Robert Anderson, former head of the Criminal Investigation Department of Great Britain (Scotland Yard), and well-known student of the Old Testament, has done this admirably in his book, *The Coming Prince.*

Following this tragedy there was to be a judgment upon Jerusalem. "The people of the prince that shall come shall destroy the city and the sanctuary; and the end thereof shall be with a flood, and unto the end of the war desolations are determined" (Dan. 9:26). Now we know historically that it was the Roman people who destroyed the city and the sanctuary under Titus. This identifies "the prince that

shall come" as being one who shall become the head of the Roman
Empire. The argument has been set forth many times and by many
writers. It fits all the circumstances perfectly and accords with the
definite statements of Christ, the prophecies of Paul and the visions
of John in the book of Revelation.

Sixty-nine heptads have thus been accounted for. One remains, seven
years which we declare to be future, to begin after a great lapse of
time between the death of Christ and the events which shall set this
seventieth heptad in its course. We ourselves are living in this parenthesis between the sixty-ninth and seventieth periods.

When the disciples came to the Lord on the Mount of Olives during
the last week before the crucifixion, they asked Him certain prophetic
questions. They wanted to know the sign of His coming and the end
of the age. They knew nothing of the Church age. It was at that
time a mystery hid with God "which in other ages was not made
known unto the sons of men" (Eph. 3:5). The age concerning which
they inquired was the age of God's dealings with Israel, the age covered by Daniel's prophecy with which we are concerned. How did the
Lord answer? He began to recount a series of events: false Christs,
wars, and rumors of wars, famines, pestilences and earthquakes. And
He announced that these were but the beginning of sorrows (Matt. 24:
5-8). One most significant prophecy then occurs by which we are
able to tie all prophetic utterances together in their proper sequence.
"When ye therefore shall see the abomination of desolation, spoken of
by Daniel the prophet, standing in the holy place, whoso readeth,
let him understand" (Matt. 24:15).

According to the Lord Jesus Christ, an event spoken of by Daniel
is the key to the understanding of the events at the end of the age.
It is when they shall see something which He calls "the abomination
of desolation" placed in the Holy of Holies in the sanctuary at Jerusalem.

Let us go back to Daniel's prophecy to discover the meaning. He
has spoken of this sinister figure, the prince that will come, one whose
people would destroy Jerusalem. We read, "And he shall confirm the
covenant with many for one heptad: and in the midst of the heptad
he shall cause the sacrifice and the oblation to cease, and for the
overspreading of abominations he shall make it desolate, even until
the consummation, and that determined shall be poured upon the desolate" (Dan. 9:27).

The prince that shall come is the Antichrist. Our Lord said, "I am
come in my Father's name, and ye receive me not: if another shall
come in his own name, him ye will receive" (John 5:43).

The picture now becomes clear. The Antichrist will make a treaty
with the majority of the Jews for seven years. They will immediately
begin the Levitical sacrifices. When the period has run half its course,

that is after three and a half years, the Antichrist will order the sacrifices to cease and then will perform some act which our Lord calls "the abomination of desolation." A concordance will quickly reveal to us that idolatry is frequently called an abomination unto the Lord, but we have a more definite description in the second epistle to the Thessalonians (2:1-8) of what the Antichrist will do.

In this chapter Paul had taught personally that Christ was to come at any moment to take the believers out of the world. Following this rapture there would be a time of great tribulation upon the earth. When the first persecutions came, there were some who thought that Paul's prophecy was being fulfilled and that, therefore, somehow they had been left behind in the rapture. Satan desired to foster this false doctrine in order to increase spiritual confusion. The New Testament had not been written, and spiritual truth was communicated in supernatural ways and was beginning to be communicated by the inspired epistles of Paul. When Thessalonian believers came to him with the problem, he wrote, "Now we beseech you, brethren, by the coming of our Lord Jesus Christ, and by our gathering together unto him, that ye be not soon shaken in mind, or be troubled, neither by spirit [Satanic spirit], nor by word [someone speaking a false word in the meeting], nor by letter as from us [someone had undoubtedly stooped to counterfeit Paul's epistle] as that the day of the Lord is now at hand" (II Thess. 2:1-2). No false doctrine should be believed. The Scripture definitely pointed out that God's great judgments could not take place until certain things occurred. So he goes on to explain, "Let no man deceive you by any means: for that day shall not come, except there come a falling away first, and that man of sin be revealed, the son of perdition" (II Thess. 2:3). Here is the announcement that the Antichrist must come, and there follows a definite description of the act of which Daniel hints and which the Lord announced to be the fixed point from which prophetic events were to be understood. What does this Antichrist do when he comes?

"He opposeth and exalteth himself above all that is called God, or that is worshipped; so that he as God sitteth in the temple of God, showing himself that he is God" (II Thess. 2:4). This is "the abomination of desolation" spoken of by Daniel and then again by Jesus Christ.

Paul reminds them that this was precisely what he had preached about when he had visited the church in Thessalonica. He then went on to complete the teaching. The Antichrist may not be manifest until another great event takes place. "And now ye know what withholdeth that he might be revealed in his time: for the mystery of iniquity doth already work: only he [the Holy Spirit] who now letteth will let, until he be taken out of the way" (II Thess. 2:6-7). The Holy Spirit came down into the world at Pentecost in a special sense in which He had

never been in the world, to dwell in the Church, the body of believers
which is called the temple of the Holy Spirit (I Cor. 6:19). When
all believers are removed to Heaven according to the promise made
to the church in Philadelphia (Rev. 3:10), and which we have seen
prophetically accomplished in the vision of the elders around the throne
of God, the Holy Spirit goes out of the world in the sense that He
came into it at Pentecost. When, therefore, "he be taken out of the
way, then shall that Wicked be revealed, whom the Lord shall consume with the spirit of his mouth, and shall destroy with the brightness of his coming" (II Thess. 2:7-8).

Putting all of these prophecies together, we see that there is a seven-
year period marked by a treaty between the Antichrist and Israel, the
central point of which will be the betrayal of Israel by the Antichrist
and the setting up of his statue in the Holy of Holies as though he
were God. The Lord Jesus Christ divides the events in the twenty-
fourth chapter of Matthew by this point. It should be noted that we
have no way of tying this event into the dates by which we now count
time. There is no connection between events of the twentieth century
and these prophetic outlines. In the future, however, believers of the
last seven-year period will be able to mark their calendars day by day
and know the course of events by means of the prophecies which are
spread before us.

Today this explanation must be understood if we are to arrive at
a true understanding of the book of Revelation. From the opening of
the first seal when the first earthly event in this seven-year period takes
place, and up to the nineteenth chapter of Revelation, is the detailed
history of earth events after the Church has been removed to Heaven
and while Satan is making his last bold bid for earth control.

From the twenty-fourth chapter of Matthew, certain conclusions
must be drawn from our Lord's teaching. A series of events is described up to the fourteenth verse. The abomination of desolation is
announced in the fifteenth verse. Following this, a second series of
events is described, including the phrase, "for then shall be great tribulation," which term has frequently been extended to cover the whole
of the seven-year period. For the sake of harmony with all Biblical
utterances we shall not use the term Great Tribulation of the whole
seven-year period but only the last half of the period, and shall call
the whole time by the phrase "the seventieth heptad" or "the seventieth week" or, more briefly, "the seven years." There is absolute parallelism between the events as described by Christ in His prophecy of
this period and the detailed prophecies of the Apocalypse.

When the Lord Jesus began to answer the questions of the disciples,
He said, "Take heed that no man deceive you. For many shall come
in my name, saying, I am Christ; and shall deceive many" (Matt. 24:

4, 5). The first earth event then of the seven years is a special manifestation of the power of Satan counterfeiting the return of Christ.

With this announcement we are ready to see the first seal removed
by the Lord. "And I saw when the Lamb opened one of the seven
seals, and I heard one of the four living creatures saying as with a
voice of thunder, Come. And I saw, and behold a white horse; and
the one sitting on him having a bow; and a crown was given to him
and he went forth conquering and to conquer."

It is strange that more commentators have not detected the counterfeit. But just as many people are deceived by counterfeit coins, for
if they were not, no one would go to the trouble of making them, so
many have been deceived by this counterfeit Christ who rides forth as
soon as He who hindereth is taken out of the way. Many have looked
upon this rider of the white horse as being Christ.

If we wish to see Christ coming forth as a conqueror, we must
turn to the nineteenth chapter of the book of Revelation. "And I saw
heaven opened, and behold a white horse; and he that sat upon him
was called Faithful and True, and in righteousness he doth judge and
make war . . . And his name is called the Word of God . . . And
he hath on his vesture and on his thigh a name written, KING OF
KINGS, AND LORD OF LORDS" (Rev. 19:11, 16).

The Antichrist is a counterfeit Christ. He has no power to create.
He is going to imitate. He is going to seek to fulfill the world's idea
of what the Messiah should be, since the world has rejected God's
Word as to what the Messiah must be. We have only to look at the
details of the prophecy to see how far removed this is from the Lord
Jesus Christ of the Scriptures. The counterfeit is revealed by a detailed comparison of the two riders. The One whose name is the Word
of God has on His head "many crowns." The symbol is of all royalty
and majesty. The Greek word is *diadema*. The horseman of the first
seal wears no diadem. The false crown is the *stephanos*. Its diamonds
are paste. It is the shop girl adorned with jewelry from the ten-cent
counter imitating the lady born and bred who wears the rich jewels
of her inheritance. All is not gold that glitters. No amount of gaudy
trappings can deceive the spiritual eye. Clothes do not make the man
in spite of the proverb.

The weapon of this rider is the bow. The Lord of glory is quite
differently armed. He carries "a sharp sword, that with it he should
smite the nations" (Rev. 19:15). Thus is the Faithful and True armed.
But this Don Quixote moves forth with a weapon that strikes terror
only to the uninitiated, for those who are marked out as God's own
carry the shield of faith with which they shall be able to quench all
the fiery darts of the wicked one (Eph. 6:16). No, this is not the
Christ, though he may be dressed up to look like Him. On the walls
of the great museums are masterpieces of painting. Before these, on

easels, are the copies of students. It takes no very practiced eye to distinguish between genius and what often amounts to caricature.

Commentators who have attempted to interpret this rider as being the Lord Jesus have been hard put to it to explain the riders which follow, scourge upon scourge, especially when they have tried to fit these prophecies into some event of Church history. The best they have been able to imagine is that the wrath of God was moving in the little chastisements that have come upon the earth through the years. But how could these, which are at the most rehearsals, be called a tribulation greater than any that ever was or ever shall be?

It has been rightfully said that nothing but hopeless confusion "can result from the attempt to show that a future event has already been fufilled. It is no wonder that the book has remained sealed to many, simply because they will not admit that all this is future. The facts of history together with the plain language of revelation, have been strained to the last limit to produce an agreement; and the many tongues of interpretation testify to the hopelessness of the effort. Nothing has ever transpired in history to fill up the measure demanded by the majestic language of this part of Revelation. Let us remember that God has purposes yet to be fulfilled, and we shall escape from the bewildering confusion of the historical interpreters, and, at the same time, rescue the Book from the dishonor put upon it."

Verses 3–8

The Train of the Antichrist

³And when he opened the second seal, I heard the second living creature say, Come. ⁴And there came forth another, a red horse; and it was given to the one that sat on him to take the peace from the earth, in order that they might kill each other; and there was given unto him a great sword.

⁵And when he opened the third seal I heard the third living creature saying, Come, and I saw, and behold a black horse; and THE ONE THAT SAT ON HIM *had a balance in his hand. ⁶And I heard as it were a voice in the midst of the four living creatures saying, a measure of wheat for a denarius and three measures of barley for a denarius; and hurt thou not the oil and the wine.*

⁷And when he opened the fourth seal, I heard the voice of the fourth living creature saying, Come. ⁸And I saw, and behold a livid horse, and the one sitting on him is named Death, and Hades followed with him. And authority was given unto them over the fourth part of the earth to kill with sword, and with famine, and with death, and by the wild beasts of the earth.

(Rev. 6:3-8, Free Translation)

The world in its moment of greatest need will turn to a man who goes forth with a plan for peace. Our Lord stated when He was here on earth, "I am come in my Father's name and ye receive me not: if another shall come in his own name, him ye will receive" (John 5: 43). This is the rider on the white horse. His true character is not long hidden. When he takes possession of the power over the nations, he is swiftly followed by the judgment of God. After the white horse there comes forth the red, the black and the livid. No sooner do these appear than war is unloosed, famine breaks forth and death stalks the earth. It is not without reason that the Holy Spirit calls the Antichrist "The Beast." He comes out of the abyss (Rev. 17:8), his character is that of a beast (13:2, 3), his power, his throne and his authority are from Satan, (13:2). And finally, God deals with him as a beast (19: 19, 20).

From him we see the nature and the character of this rider of the white horse, for at first the world will take him to be Christ, the Messiah. He is, however, the counterfeit Christ, the anti-Messiah.

The order of events follows closely that which was announced by our Lord in answer to the disciples' questions on the Mount of Olives, "For many shall come in my name, saying, I am Christ; and shall deceive many" (Matt. 24:5). This is the white horse. "And ye shall hear of wars and rumors of wars . . . for nation shall rise against nation and kingdom against kingdom . . ." (24:6, 7). This is the red horse of war. There are some who apply this passage to our day, thinking that the wars which trouble this age are those spoken of in prophecy. Nothing could be farther from the truth. The wars of our day are but rehearsals, but the wars which Christ prophesied take place after the believers are removed from the earth, after the man of sin has been revealed (II Thess. 2:3). These campaigns are described in the book of Daniel.

There is a well-known type of biblical narrative in the Old Testament in which the Holy Spirit leads a prophet to consider some event that is taking place before the gaze of the world at that moment. The inspired writer presents some of the details of what is to him contemporaneous history. Then, suddenly, without so much as a break in the paragraph, the Holy Spirit carries the writer forward more than two thousand years to the time of the end and speaks of prophetic events which have some similarity with those taking place before the eye of the prophet. We might liken this type of prophecy to the stereopticon slide. Take it in your hands and examine it and dimly you see certain lines and patches of light and shade. Place it in the projector with the proper light shining through it and on the screen in proper focus and you see the great image clear and distinct. So it is with prophecies in the Word of God, for Isaiah brings a message of comfort to Jerusalem because of some armistice that has ended a local warfare (Isa. 40:1, 2). The next verse carries us on to John the Baptist comforting the nation because the final peace has been proclaimed. Ezekiel rebukes the king of Tyre because of pride that lifted him up to the place where he accepted worship from his subjects and is carried on into the spiritual realm to describe the fall of Lucifer who through pride turned the worship of creation away from God toward himself (Ezek. 28).

The Word of God enables us to trace some of the movements of Antichrist after his first rise to power. We see from the verses that are under discussion in the Revelation that the rider of the second horse is permitted to take peace from the earth. Christ tells us that following the manifestations of false christs come wars and rumors of war. It is Daniel who describes the campaign. The details of the beginning are not given to us. They do not concern the land of Israel, but suddenly we see two kings pushing against the Antichrist (Dan. 11:40). His army is first seen marching forward in the neighborhood of Asia Minor and Syria. "He shall enter into the countries, and shall overflow and pass over" (vs. 40). Perhaps in the light of other scriptures this might be taken to describe the campaign that united the former Roman Empire. At any rate, we next see him enter Palestine, "He shall enter also into the glorious land, and many countries shall be overthrown" (vs. 41). Knowing our geography it is easy to follow the narrative when he comes from Syria into Palestine. Will he turn to scale the terrible ramparts that protect Jordan? Daniel shows us that the situation in Egypt is evidently urgent. He does not have time for a thrust against the Arab people. "These shall escape out of his hand, even Edom and Moab, and the chief of the children of Ammon" (vs. 41). He reaches Egypt and conquers it. Some of his forces break over Ethiopia (vss. 42, 43). But it is a wave that has dashed itself too high upon the shore and must break and recede, "Tidings out of the east and out of the north shall trouble him: therefore he shall go forth [out of Africa] with great fury to destroy, and utterly annihilate many" (vs. 44). His headquarters were established in Palestine, "Between the seas in the glorious holy mountain" (vs. 45).

Now the stage is set for later events of the seven year period. The conquest of Palestine and the rehabilitation of the Roman empire are by no means the climax of the defeats and disasters of the time of the end. In fact, our Lord said—and what a word of comfort this will be to those who have the true nature of the Antichrist and whose hearts have turned in repentance toward the true Christ—"See that ye be not troubled: for all these things must come to pass, but the end is not yet" (Matt. 24:6).

We think that we are living in a day of war and rumors of war, but all that we have seen is nothing compared with what shall be when the second horseman of the Apocalypse rides forth. We see just enough to know the great outline of what will come to pass. What will it not take of marching armies and Satan's flying air squadrons to bring the nations into the alliances that face each other at Armageddon? Russia leading her forces and those of the Germans she has absorbed; Persia turned from other influences and swinging into line with the great northern confederacy; the Arab peoples uniting to join with them; republics turning to kingdoms; western Europe, in dismay at the power of the coalition that rises in the north and east, melts together under the rule of the Antichrist.

The historian, trained in research, faces a problem of history with delight; but here lying before us in a prophetic word and even visible on the not too distant horizon of world events is the greatest cataclysm of all time. God in His own inscrutable purpose takes His restraining hand from the world and permits Satan to have his way. Yet He in His omniscience knows how Satan's force will move and has written down the outline in His Word.

So clear is this picture that it is almost a pity to turn aside to answer false interpretations. To us it is almost incredible that serious interpreters of the Bible record should go so far from the truth, yet we have before us a commentary accepted by many which makes of the first horseman the Lord Jesus and the red horse to be that strife or variance that comes from the preaching of the Gospel. Quoting as a parallel, Christ's words, "Think not that I have come to send peace to the earth: I came not to send peace, but a sword" (Matt. 10:34), it seems almost childish to speak of persecutions and wars that have followed the spread of Christianity as the fulfillment of this prophecy. Such interpretation comes from a low view of God's wrath against sin. There is no realization of the meaning of "Great tribulation, such as was not since the beginning of the world to this time, no, nor ever shall be" (Matt. 24:21). If it be said that the words we are discussing cannot apply to the last days, for there will be then no peace to be taken away from the earth, we must realize that it is as a man of peace that the false christ will be able to get his hold on a tired world. Mankind, refusing the substance that is in Christ, takes the "peace" that the Antichrist offers but finds that the white horse is followed by the red scourge of war.

The third horse is black. In the sequence of events given by Christ it is famine which follows the war and rumors of war. Here we have great scarcity indicated. The climax where men die of hunger comes with the fourth horseman. The black horse, however, does bring great scarcity. He carries the balance indicating that food must be weighed carefully. Ezekiel prophesies that the children of Israel in the midst of their desperation will know this scarcity. "And thy meat which thou shalt eat shall be by weight, twenty shekels a day; from time to time shalt thou eat it. Thou shalt drink also water by measure . . .

behold, I will break the staff of bread in Jerusalem: and they shall eat bread by weight, and with care" (Ezek. 4:10, 11, 16). This is part fulfillment of the judgment announced in Leviticus, "When I have broken the staff of your bread . . . in one oven, and they shall deliver your bread again by weight; and ye shall eat, and not be satisfied" (Lev. 26:26).

It will be seen as we continue our study of the Revelation that following the greatest strokes of suffering there are breathing spells as though to test humanity. Will they turn to God or will He be forced to bring forth greater and heavier artillery of punishment? From the midst of the four living creatures comes a voice commanding the rider of the black horse. The voice speaks of the measurement of wheat and barley and gives command to protect the oil and the wine. The measure spoken of here is the Greek measure of capacity of very ancient usage, the choenix. As early as the time of Homer it was indicated as the amount of wage given to a workman for a full day's work (Odyssey XIX:XXVIII). Herodotus also gives this as the measure of wheat consumed by each soldier in the army of Xerxes (VIII:CLXXXVII). The coin was the denarius, the amount of wages given to a day laborer (Matt. 20:2). If the poor barley grain were consumed, it was found to be three times cheaper than the wheat. The prices are certainly high. A man would be giving all of his income for the bare necessities of life, but he could scrape through. Some have seen in this passage nothing but famine. Rather, we believe, must the contrast with luxury be seen. "Hurt thou not the oil and the wine," the voice commands. The poor are getting poorer; the rich are still able to retain their luxuries.

Just after World War I, I spent a few days in Vienna at the time when misery was very great. The British commissioner had just reported in the London *Times* that it was not uncommon to see the streets of the capital blocked by funerals of which three out of four were children. There was a shortage of coal and the police had ordered everyone off the streets by nine o'clock. The city was filled with wealthy refugees from Russia and other countries. Walking along the boulevard one afternoon as the crowds were coming out of the opera which began early to conform with the curfew regulations, I saw men with bare feet in the snow, their skeletons covered with rags, their ribs seen through the holes in the cloths with which they attempted to cover their bodies. From time to time there was blood on the snow from their feet. Out of the opera came men escorting women with fortunes in jewels upon them. Never have I seen more wonderful displays in any of the capitals of the earth. The beggars blocked the way to the fine limousines that came for the rich. I saw the men striking the beggars with their canes to clear the way for the women. Poor girls not clad in the gaudy finery of prostitutes, but with poor clothing and in wooden shoes, clattered about clutching at the passer-by and offering to sell themselves for a coin which at that moment could be purchased for one-five hundredth part of a dollar. Mark well, there was no famine in Vienna. There was scarcity in the midst of plenty, but there was no hurt to the luxuries.

One of the great criticisms of the present time is that there is scarcity in the midst of plenty. This is the situation which will be accentuated a thousandfold when the Antichrist begins his reign. It is a social maladjustment.

Yet there is no repentance. Nations do not turn to God, but go on their way without Him. Bengel has said, "The balances of this rider serve as a sign, that all the fruits of the ground, and consequently all Heaven with its progressive influences, all the seasons of the year and the course of events, with their manifold changes and vicissitudes, are subject to Christ." All the happenings of earth, the movements of crops, the order of events are in answer to His Word, yet men will not believe.

There is, of course, a spiritual interpretation of these symbols. There are other verses in the Bible where bread and oil and wine are mentioned together. "He causeth the grass to grow for the cattle, and herb for the service of man: that he may bring forth food out of the earth; And wine that maketh glad the heart of man, and oil to make his face to shine, and bread which strengtheneth man's heart" (Ps. 104:14, 15). Can it be that in the midst of famine for the bread of God, where it will be impossible for the Bible to be circulated, where every precious copy will be protected as in the days of great persecution, that the people will nevertheless have the wine of gladness and the anointing of the Spirit of God? The Holy Spirit indeed will have left the earth when the Lord withdraws the Church at the rapture. But He will have left only as the One who indwells the heart of man. He will yet be here as He was in Old Testament times, pouring Himself forth upon those who believe and making glad their hearts in the midst of spiritual lack.

At the opening of the fourth seal, the last horse is seen. The color of this horse in the Revised Standard Version is given as pale. The Greek word is very interesting. It is *chloros,* from which the name of chlorine gas is taken. The same word is found elsewhere in the New Testament and is translated "green" (Mark 6:39 and Rev. 8:7; 9:4).

The rider of this horse is named. He is none other than death. Hades follows with him as though to gather up the victims, which are mowed down by the sickle of death.

The devil is the one who had the power of death (Heb. 2:14). We see him exercising it upon the family of Job, the moment he has the permission of God. What he does now is definitely by the command of Christ. John saw in the first chapter, the One who said, "Behold, I am alive for evermore, Amen; and have the keys of Hades and of death" (Rev. 1:18). As we behold the four horsemen ride forth, we must not forget that they come at the express command of the One who opens the seals. What comfort for us today and what comfort for the persecuted ones of the future, to know that no movement of Satan is apart from the knowledge of the will of God.

There are two possible explanations of what follows. We can look upon these symbols as describing something literal and something spiritual. I am inclined to think that both explanations are true. Christ included it in His list of events; false christs, wars, rumors of wars to be followed by famines and pestilence and earthquakes in divers places. Here we see the rider of the greenish horse going forth with power over the fourth part of the earth. "Kill with sword and with hunger and death and by the beasts of the earth." It is very simple to give the material explanation. Modern methods of war in this age of atom bombs and hydrogen bombs have made it possible. One-fourth of the earth's population, if taken in the large sense, or one-fourth of the population of the Holy Land, if taken in the small sense, could be destroyed in a very brief time. Today the great armies have the means to make ruthless war against the civil population of a possible enemy. This includes war by gas, war by bombs from the air, and worst of all, bacteriological warfare by test-tubes filled with germs to be dropped into the water supply of the enemy. A very few months would suffice to do away with one-fourth part of the earth's population.

Spiritually, however, following the rise of Antichrist, there comes war, together with social unrest and great scarcity. If the symbols describing the character and actions of the fourth rider are spiritual, our task again is not difficult. The devil, who is the power of death is also called "a liar and the father of it" (John 8:44). His desire to kill is also seen in this same verse, "He was a murderer from the beginning, and abode not in the truth, because there is no truth in him." Here he goes forth to kill with his sword. "The sword of the Spirit is the Word of God" (Eph. 6:17). The weapon of Satan (not the same Greek word) is, of course, counterfeit. It would represent the spiritual lie as opposed to the truth of God. God's truth makes alive: Satan's lie kills. There particularly is a reference to this in Paul's great prophecy concerning the Antichrist. "Even him, whose coming is after the working of Satan with all power and signs and lying wonders, and with all deceivableness of unrighteousness in them that perish; because they received not the love of the truth, that they might be saved. And for this cause God shall send them strong delusion, that they should believe a lie" (II Thess. 2:9-11). In the Greek it is "that they should believe *the* lie" as though some specific lie were in view. As we proceed we shall see that demons are sent to the earth to propagate false doctrines. Here is the beginning of something that is as yet in the shadows, but which certainly will take definite form after the man of sin is revealed. There have been lies before, but this is the climax as though Satan had held back the ace of trump to play in the last desperate moment of his game.

The spiritual hunger is readily understood where there is no feeding on the Word of God. This famine is always sore. We must not forget the definite prophecy that in the last days there shall be a famine of the Word of God (Amos 8:11).

Spiritual death follows spiritual hunger. The lie spreads like a pestilence carrying its awful toll of victims to Hades which follows, holding them until they shall be cast into the lake of fire (Rev. 20:14). And this propagation of the lie shall be done officially. Governments will connive to support Satan's thrust. Evangelically-minded nations, notably Germany, Scandinavia, Holland and Great Britain—all have done much to spread the truth. Their benevolent attitude was once a great factor in the preaching of the Gospel. But all of the governments, "the wild beasts of the earth," will follow the lead of the rider of the deathlike horse. And the lie will spread with its famine and death.

Well may the heart that is out of Christ tremble at the thought of so much judgment. But, well may the heart of every believer rest in our Lord. He said, "See that ye be not troubled." The reason for such a statement is that He knows the end from the beginning and that we are in Him.

Verses 9–11
Confusion, Martyrdom and Vindication

⁹And when he opened the fifth seal, I saw under the altar the souls of them who had been slain because of the testimony which they held. ¹⁰And they cried with a great voice saying, How long, O Sovereign Lord, the holy and true, dost Thou not judge and avenge our blood on them that dwell on the earth? ¹¹And to each one was given a white robe, and it was said unto them that they should rest yet a little time, until the number of their fellow-bondslaves and their brethren that are about to be killed, even as they also had been, should be complete.
(Rev. 6:9-11, Free Translation)

With rapid pace the four horsemen have ridden forth to open earth's most momentous years. At the time these seals are broken, earth is practically as it is today. Before seven years will have passed, the kingdoms of this world will have become the kingdom of our Lord and of His Christ. The prince of this world will have had his power wrested from him. The god of this age will have lost all claim to divinity.

But now these seven years lie before us. The Antichrist, followed by the other horsemen, has come forth.

With the opening of the fifth seal, a cry is heard, the cry of the martyrs slain for their faithfulness to the Word of God, and for their testimony to His truth.

This again follows exactly along the line of our Lord's prophecy on the Mount of Olives: "All these are the beginning of sorrows. Then shall they deliver you up to be afflicted, and shall kill you: and ye shall be hated of all nations for my name's sake. And then shall many be offended, and shall betray one another, and shall hate one another" (Matt. 24:8-10). We can better understand the religious confusion of tomorrow if we see that of today. It is also true that we shall understand our own times better if we realize what is just in the future. When the body of true believers is caught away from the world, all of unbelieving ecclesiasticism will be left in control of the organization. There will be some people who will see immediately after the rapture that the Word of God is true, that there has been gigantic and Satanic deception in the midst of Christendom. Though these people will not be indwelt by the Holy Spirit, since the day of the Church will then be over, they will nevertheless bear testimony to the truth of God's Word. For this they shall die.

The foundation work for this bigotry and intolerance is laid today in the fanaticism of many liberals today. Those who make a shibboleth of liberalism are the most intolerant. In seeking to be abreast of the times, they have adopted the oldest errors with the most recent masks. The main creed of those who fight creeds can be expressd in language as old as the human race. "Yea, hath God said?" is the question of Satan to the woman in the Garden of Eden, and it is the question of the apostates of our day. The credulous and the skeptical of our day are united with Cain in their hatred of a sacrifice of blood. The one who glories in being a freethinker is bound in the slavery of all who have hated God's truth in His revelation. Even those who have kept the outward form of Christianity have diluted the content of faith until salvation is taught by some watery gospel of works while a hopeless confusion of the Church and the kingdom releases its dark mist in the minds of men.

The causes of this situation are not far to seek. The church organization has abandoned its unique position as the channel of God's salvation in favor of a more popular activity of dispensing words not always weighty on the social and political problems of the day. The bride of the Lord has become the mistress of the world. This is the inner significance of apostasy. The surface study of the Bible is responsible. Men have been unwilling to pay the price necessary for a true understanding of God's Word and way. A young doctor told us that he had been in great confusion. We recommended a certain pamphlet to him, telling him that it contained all of the basic essentials for a knowledge of the Word of God. His face fell when we showed him the pamphlet. With some shame, he confessed that his mother had been attempting to have him study that very booklet for almost ten years.

It is the lack of knowledge of the Word of God that leads men into confusion. They do not know God's ways and so they do not know Satan's ways. They do not know God's righteousness and fail to see Satan's righteousness. Of this one writer has said, "As God sends ministers to proclaim His righteousness, so Satan employs ministers to proclaim his, the imitation. We have to question the very common thought that Satan's effort is to make good men bad, and bad men worse, as they appear in the sight of their fellowmen. His desire is the very opposite; he wishes to make men good, not only in the sight of other men but also in their own sight . . . Satan urges men to do good, to be governed by a high moral code, to support all movements for the betterment of the race, to support ecclesiasticism, to be exercised about morals of the community . . . His ministers make much of civic and social righteousness, of national and international righteousness, but have no word to say concerning 'the righteousness of God which is by faith in Jesus Christ.' Their appeal is to 'make something good of the world,' to 'scatter sunshine.' "

Anyone can see the width of this river of thought in our day. In the future, all restraint is removed at the coming of Christ for His saints, and these forces of "righteousness" will kill those who stand for the Word of God and His testimony in the final seven years.

The reason men hate the Bible is that it is the written Word of God and reveals to us Christ, the living Word of God. "The carnal mind is enmity against God" (Rom. 8:7). Men do not hate the world's idea of God. They hate the Christ in God. This points us to the age-old conflict which God announced in the Garden of Eden. "I will put enmity between thee and the woman, and between thy seed and her seed; it shall bruise thy head, and thou shalt bruise his heel" (Gen. 3:15). The hatred that was announced on the day of the fall has manifested itself unceasingly through the ages, and will not change its nature when restraint is removed from it.

This section of Scripture is the first intimation that the reign of Antichrist is to witness the greatest revival that the world has ever seen. More millions will be saved under the preaching of God's witnesses in these seven years than in many times that period in this present age. These seven years are the time of God's wrath upon the world bcause of its rejection of His Christ and His truth. Yet even in the midst of tribulation He will send His witnesses into the world insisting upon His claim. "Woe unto them!" This is the true meaning of "the gospel of the kingdom" which "shall be preached in all the world for a witness to all nations" (Matt. 24:14). Today we preach the Gospel of grace. It is the free offer of salvation to all who rest in Christ, with the promise that God Himself will come to dwell in the heart the moment we have turned to Him. The Gospel of the kingdom includes all the Gospel of grace but contains also the proclamation that God is about to overthrow and condemn all man has done in order to establish by force of the rod of iron, the kingdom of God's rule upon the earth, with Israel the central human factor of the government, and Christ the divine center of it all. Righteousness for which the world has so long waited is about to come upon the earth. The Lord Himself is about to appear. This is an announcement of hope for those who are willing to bow their hearts before God, but it is a cry of doom to those who know not God and obey not the Gospel of our Lord Jesus Christ. These fall upon the witnesses of this truth with great wrath, and the result is seen immediately. The witnesses are broken on the first turn of the wheel of persecution. John now sees their souls in Heaven.

It should be noticed that these souls are conscious and speaking. This is one more blow to the idea of soul-sleeping. There are those who are led astray by the use of the word "sleep" in connection with the death of the body into the belief that the souls also sleep. The truth can be seen by the teaching of the Word of God concerning the resurrection. It is said of the same body of believers that they "rise" and also that God will "bring" them with Christ when He comes (I Thess. 4:14-16). How can they both rise from the earth and be brought from Heaven? In finding this answer, the whole question of soul-sleeping is settled forever, and the truth about our dead is revealed. Sleep is applied only to the body of the believer, and never to the soul. When death comes to a believer, there is the departure of the soul from the body and the immediate entrance of that conscious soul into the presence of Christ. Thus "to be absent from the body" is "to be present with the Lord" (II Cor. 5:8). It is "to depart, and be with Christ, which is far better" (Phil. 1:23).

This great truth outlasts the present age of the Church which is the body of Christ. Here it is definitely taught that the tribulation saints also are in the presence of God.

These souls are said to be "under the altar." We are not to think that John had a vision of an altar with souls peeping out from underneath. The whole teaching of the Old Testament is that the altar was the place of the sacrifice of blood. To be "under the altar" is to be covered in the sight of God by that merit which Jesus Christ provided in dying on the cross. It is a figure that speaks of justification. It is practically the equivalent of David's cry, "Purge me with hyssop, and

I shall be clean: wash me, and I shall be whiter than snow" (Ps. 51:7). Hyssop was that small Palestinian plant which hung beside the altar and, according to Levitical prescription, was used by the priests who dipped it into the blood and sprinkled the people with it. When, therefore, David cried out to be purged with hyssop, we are not to think of the absurdities of an ancient commentator who spoke of the purgative qualities of the plant when taken internally. It is one of the countless pageants of the cross to be found portrayed in Scripture. These martyred witnesses are covered by the work of the Lord Jesus Christ (Rom. 13:14). Adam and Eve were covered with coats of skins obtained by the shedding of the first blood upon this earth. This replaced the fig leaves of their own good works which, in turn, had been an attempt to replace the light of innocence which had undoubtedly clothed them before the fall. Little by little all that is lost in Genesis is regained in Revelation.

Now these martyrs cry to God, "How long, O Sovereign Lord, the holy and true, dost thou not judge and avenge our blood on them that dwell on the earth?" This cry constitutes one more proof that we are no longer occupied with events taking place in the day of grace. This is clearly after the rapture. Contrast, for example, this cry for vengeance with that of Stephen, the first martyr of the Church. "Lord, lay not this sin to their charge" (Acts 7:60). Can it be considered for one instant that these souls who, of course, have left their old nature far behind, can be crying out for vengeance to God in Heaven in a time that is still in the age of grace? This is impossible. Rather this is in keeping with the cry of the Old Testament martyr who died saying, "The Lord look upon it and require it" (II Chron. 24:22). Though such a cry would have been out of order at any time during the centuries since Christ died, it is here quite in order, even as Stephen's pleading for grace is of the Holy Spirit at the beginning of the day of grace. We must not forget that judgment from God is to fall upon this earth. David sings prophetically of the doings of Jehovah "when he maketh inquisition for blood" (Ps. 9:12). This cry of the martyrs is almost the last that will be heard from God's saints, for soon after this God will bring the agony of His people to an eternal end.

God calls them to patience. He knows every cry of His children, but the hour of His judgment is fixed, and shall come upon the world in His own moment. All the stored-up cup of wrath is about to be poured upon the earth.

God's word is that they should rest for a little season. How long this is we know definitely from Revelation 20:4 where these souls are again brought into view. There John says, "And the souls of them that were beheaded for the witness of Jesus and for the Word of God . . . lived and reigned with Christ a thousand years." This passage also includes the remaining number of the tribulation saints who have not yet been killed at the time the fifth seal is opened. It should be pointed out, however, that there are two different words used in connection with the position of the tribulation saints during the millennium. In one place (7:15) it is said that they serve the Lord day and night in His temple, while in another passage (20:4) it says that they reign with Christ. These points will be considered when we come to the passages in question.

It is to be noted that the persecutions follow in seasons, or it might be said, using another figure, that they come in successive waves with intervals between until in the last half of the tribulation week, persecution shall be a veritable tide so that Christ had to say, "Except those days should be shortened, there should no flesh be saved; but for the elect's sake those days shall be shortened" (Matt. 24:22).

The fifth seal shows us the first sheaf of these martyred ones crying out to God for vengeance which He will not be slow to send. Will this judgment bear fruit? Will those who have been fighting against God cease their enmity? This will not be the case. The carnal mind is enmity against God, and this enmity attaches itself to all those who stand for His Word. Just as the plagues of Egypt caused Pharaoh's heart to harden, and the tasks of God's people were made more grievous, so each persecution brings more judgment, and each judgment more persecution as the Holy Spirit takes out individuals from the world and as Satan hurls his power against them. The end will come only with the coming of the One who shall break them with a rod of iron and dash His enemies to pieces like a potter's vessel.

While the sixth seal brings a tremendous fright to the world, nevertheless the Scriptural division of the subject proves that the breaking of the seals is introductory in its character and demonstrates the truth of the Lord's words, "All these are the beginning of sorrows" (Matt. 24:8). Even with the four horsemen and with the first martyrdoms, the Great Tribulation has not yet begun. All this is in the first half of the seven years. It is not until the middle of the period, when the abomination of desolation is seen, that the Great Tribulation really begins. This must be realized, especially in view of the fact that many people speak of the Great Tribulation as the seven-year period, while in reality it is the last three and a half years of the seven-year period.

Even in the midst of this story of bloodshed and judgment, there is a word of wonderful comfort for the believer. These martyrs are told that their waiting for judgment upon their enemies is only "until the number of their fellow-bondslaves and their brethren that are about to be killed, even as they also had been, should be complete." This shows in advance that God has ordained the details. The One who numbers the hairs of our heads also has numbered the host of the martyrs. What God in effect is saying to the first martyrs of the tribulation week is this: You have been martyred, but do not be impatient. I have the affair well in hand. I chose you before the foundation of the world for the very purpose you have just seen realized in your suffering bodies. You have been horribly treated, but I look upon it as having been suffered for the name of My Son, and I shall bless you for it forever. You are only the first of those whom I have thus chosen to die for My name. There are many others. I have marked them out for this purpose. I know all about them and about you. You may rest in peace.

All this teaches in a very beautiful way that nothing can ever touch the believer unless it has passed through the will of God. There is a definite plan for the life of every one of God's children. One of our favorite verses was spoken by the devil, for when you can get the father of lies to tell the truth, you may be sure that he is forced into such a narrow corner that there is no hope for him. Thus when God points out to Satan that Job is upright, Satan replies, "Hast not thou made a hedge about him?" (Job 1:10). Thus the enemy confesses: It is not my fault that Job is righteous. I would have gotten at him if I could.

Face all of your problems in the light of this truth.

Verses 12–17

Black Sun and Bloody Moon

¹²And I saw when he opened the sixth seal and a great earthquake came to pass; and the sun became black as sackcloth of hair; and the full moon became as blood; ¹³and the stars of heaven fell unto the earth as a fig tree casts its unripe figs when it is shaken by a great wind; ¹⁴and the heaven was rent asunder as a scroll rolling itself up and every mountain and island were removed out of their places.

¹⁵And the kings of the earth and the great and the military commanders and the rich and the strong and every bondman and freeman hid themselves in the caves and in the rocks of the mountains; ¹⁶and they say to the mountains and the rocks, Fall upon us and hide us from the presence of the one that sits upon the throne and from the wrath of the Lamb: ¹⁷Because the great day of His wrath has come; and who is able to stand?

(Rev. 6:12-17, Free Translation)

One of the most vivid experiences of my boyhood was the rude awakening on the morning of the San Francisco earthquake: fires, destroyed buildings, restless people, atmosphere tense with expectation of further disaster; a glow in the sky that enabled us to read at midnight by the light of the burning city, wild stories running from person to person with imagination fattening upon rumor.

Earthquakes were not unknown in Bible lands. Amos (1:1) dated his prophecy by an earthquake. Zechariah described the flight of the people before an earthquake in the time of King Uzziah (Zech. 14:5). It is this figure of speech that God now uses to describe the cataclysmic upheaval which is to take place when the Lord Himself breaks the sixth seal.

If some people wish to see in this passage a real earthquake, we have no criticism to offer. We believe, however, that the Holy Spirit is pointing to something far more significant than a mere seismological disturbance. The first time that the Greek word is used in the New Testament is in the story of the storm that arose when the Lord was asleep in the ship and the disciples were afraid. It is in the phrase, "There arose a great tempest in the sea" (Matt. 8:24). Still more striking, however, is the classical use of this word. Plato uses it of disturbances, disorders and commotion.

In the light of the context and the references in the Old Testament, we believe that the passage before us indicates the shaking of all political and ecclesiastical institutions.

Isaiah, in one of his great chapters, speaks of the confusion that shall come upon the earth. "Behold, the Lord maketh the earth empty, and maketh it waste, and turneth it upside down and scattereth abroad the inhabitants thereof . . . the land shall be utterly emptied, and utterly spoiled . . . the earth mourneth and fadeth away . . . the earth is utterly broken down, the earth is clean dissolved, the earth is moved exceedingly. The earth shall reel to and fro like a drunkard, and shall be removed like a cottage; and the transgression thereof shall be heavy upon it; and it shall fall, and not rise again" (Isa. 24:1, 3, 4, 19, 20). Again immediately following this, as in our passage in Revelation we read, "Then the moon shall be confounded and the sun ashamed . . ." (vs. 23).

A further passage that is most evidently parallel with this paragraph in Revelation reads, "For the indignation of the Lord is upon all nations, and his fury upon all their armies; he hath utterly destroyed them, he hath delivered them to the slaughter. Their slain also shall be cast out, and their stink shall come up out of their carcasses, and the mountains shall be melted with their blood. And all the host of heaven shall be dissolved, and the heavens shall be rolled together as a scroll: and all their host shall fall down, as the leaf falleth off from the vine, and as a falling fig from the fig tree" (Isa. 34:2-4). The references to the heavens, to the scroll and to the falling figs are more than sufficient to bind this passage to the one upon which we are commenting.

The accompaniments of this great shaking are phenomena that concern the sun, the full moon and the stars. In the Bible the explanation of these symbols is referred to constantly as symbols of authority.

From the very first page of the Scripture, the sun was spoken of as the ruler of the day, the moon and the stars as the rulers of the night. If we see in the figures that are now presented to us a collapse of supreme authority accompanied not only by a collapse of derived authority such as state, provincial and colonial authority, but also of local authority, we will begin to catch the picture of the great terrors that will now come upon the earth. Lawlessness, which has been held in restraint through hundreds of years, will now be permitted to break forth. And how simple this is in the light of modern discovery. Perhaps men would not have thought of the destruction of so much central government before the atomic era, but now, of course, a few bombs delivered in the right places and central government would be destroyed, supreme authority would collapse. Central authority, itself, would be shaken, and perhaps there would be little more than local authority, and in many places this, too, would be broken down.

We are told in the great revelation given through St. Paul to the Thessalonian church that the day of the Lord would not come until there had first come an apostasy and the man of sin, or rather the lawless one be revealed. The heart of the passage is "For the mystery of iniquity doth already work: only he who now letteth will let, until he be taken out of the way, and then shall that Wicked be revealed . . ." (II Thess. 2:7, 8). A mystery in the Scriptures, as is well known, is not something that is mysterious in the modern sense of the word; but something which has been secret in the councils of God and which because of His good pleasure He makes known to His servants. The presence of the principle of lawlessness working as a ferment in the midst of the world, restrained by the presence of the Holy Spirit in the Church, breaking forth after He is taken out at the rapture in the sense in which He came at Pentecost, is one of the great truths of the New Testament revelation.

There is a general feeling that the stream of history is drawing near a cataract. There is everywhere in the social frame an outward unrest which as usual is the sign of a fundamental change within. Lecky in his great *History of Rationalism* states it clearly in saying, "It has long been a mere truism that we are passing through a state of chaos, of anarchy and of transition. During the last century the elements of dissolution have been multiplying all around us." And more recently Toynbee has spoken of our era today as the Post Christian Era—dismissing Christianity as Voltaire dismissed the Bible more than a century ago.

All of these tendencies, so clear to the great thinkers of yesterday and today, move onward toward the moment when human authority shall break up, when national, provincial and local governments will disappear.

The disappearance of central authority is not of great primary importance so long as local authority continues, but the stars, the symbols of local authority, fall like unseasonal fruit. In the warm climate of Palestine, the fig trees, after the harvest of the autumn crop, bud again in the winter. From these buds come fruit that remains small and hard, the growth checked by the intermittent cold of winter. When the warmth of spring finally comes and the sap begins to flow in the trees, all of this unseasonable fruit drops off in a shower. Within a few days the trees are cleared to make ready for the true crop that follows.

This is the picture that our Lord uses. A great wind would, of course, hasten the fall, if it came at the propitious moment. It is said of our Lord that His fan is in His hand, His winds of judgment will blow according to His desire and local government will fall like the wind-blown false fruits. The wind is frequently the symbol of such a judgment. It was a wind that blasted the seven lean ears in Egypt (Gen. 41:6, 23) and the ungodly "are like the chaff which the wind driveth away" (Ps. 1:4).

Where shall people turn for authority? The next phrase says that the Heaven "was rent asunder as a scroll rolling itself up" (Free Translation). Does this mean that no vestige of ecclesiastical power remains? The true Church will have disappeared from the earth before these troubles come upon the waiting world. It is hard to believe that men who have so much contempt and so little reverence for an ecclesiasticism which yet contains a mass of true believers, will retain respect for a Satanic ecclesiasticism of which all will be clouds "without water, carried about of winds, trees whose fruit withereth, without fruit, twice dead, plucked up by the roots; Raging waves of the sea, foaming out their own shame; wandering stars to whom is reserved the blackness of darkness forever" (Jude 12, 13).

Take from the bottom of some drawer a diploma which has been tightly rolled for years. Open it out and then release it. See how it snaps back into the form it has taken through the years. As quickly will the hold of ecclesiasticism over the hearts and minds of men be broken, as a scroll rolls up with a snap, so organization will disappear from this earth.

Every mountain is overthrown and every island is cast into the sea. The mountain is the symbol of government. From the time that Satan desired to "sit also upon the mount of the congregation, . . . I will be like the most High" (Isa. 14:13, 14) until the time when the stone cut out without hands shall become a great mountain and fill the whole earth (Dan. 2:35) the mountain will have this significance. The islands are symbolic of smaller powers. All will be affected, there will be no stability, no permanence.

All this prepares us for the final picture. Conditions become so terrible that men think that the famous "end of the world" has come. From time to time even today we hear people speak of some catastrophe in a hysteria that includes such a phrase as, "I thought the end of the world had come." We who know the Scripture know of course that many things must come to pass before the last great and terrible day of the Lord. Previous judgments have reached some classes of people, but there have always been those who through the advantage of wealth or fortuitous circumstance have been able to find some refuge. But now every class is reached, from kings to slaves. The vast disruption of all authority, accompanied no doubt by natural phenomena, fills every heart with dismay. Men have known of the prophecies of Scripture and they have scoffed at them even as the world scoffed at Noah's prophecies of impending judgment. Now the chaotic conditions that reach every sphere recall the prophecies, and the population is seized by a premonition of coming judgment. Yet there is no repentance, no prayer to God, no cry for mercy. There is nothing but terror and a frenzied desire to escape from the just judgment of God. The greatest prayer meeting that the earth has ever seen now takes place, but like most prayers that have been offered throughout the ages by fallen humanity these are not addressed in the right way. Whosoever calleth upon the Name of the Lord shall be saved, but there is no promise made to those who call upon the rocks and the mountains. And there are many people, too, who address O God, O God without coming to the God and Father of our Lord Jesus Christ, and recognizing that access is only by the finished work of the Saviour.

But even this world horror is premature. We must not be confused by the false theology of this frantic population. Though they say, "the great day of his wrath has come," this is not true. Christ said, "All these are the beginning of sorrows" (Matt. 24:8). Little do they know that all they have seen and experienced is no more than a shadow of the terrors which must yet come. These are but the judgments that precede the great day of His wrath. The day itself has not yet dawned, for the tribulation, which has the distinction of being called the Great Tribulation, does not begin until after the abomination of desolation.

It is significant to note that men are seeking refuge from the wrath of the Lamb. This proves, of course, that they know about the Lamb, that they know the mercy which has been offered for so long must be withdrawn and that wrath must take its place. Now "every shaft of judgment is barbed by the memory of slighted grace" which is proof that "the carnal mind is enmity against God" (Rom. 8:7). The hearts that cried, "We will not have this man to reign over us" (Luke 19:14), will run to the desolate places of the earth to escape from His wrath just as they ran to every expediency of excess to escape His grace. Thus the unregenerate heart of man will act even after the millennial reign of Christ (Rev. 22:11) and one of the chief characteristics of eternal punishment is that the conscience of man will never be stilled. "Their worm shall not die, neither shall their fire be quenched" (Isa. 66:24).

At the time of the New York World's Fair, I saw a very interesting cartoon. It was one of these pictures without a caption. It showed the sketch of General Electric's exhibit at the New York World's Fair. Across the outside was the great sign, "Come in and see the man-made lightning." Those of us who had been at the World's Fair, and who had entered that building will never forget how bolts of lightning were shot from machine to machine, bolts that would jump 20 or 30 feet in space between the poles that had been made for it. But the point of the cartoon, "Come in and see the man-made lightning," was in the fact that the people who were running for refuge in the building, were running away from a storm, and from bolts of lightning that were falling from Heaven. Is it not true that men will go even to man-made lightning to escape from the God-made lightning? I remember reading that the destruction that was caused by the earthquake in the southern part of Japan three or four years after the destruction of Hiroshima has caused far more damage than the atomic bomb itself. Then our picture is almost as though men say— "Oh, Dear God, please, please send us atomic bombs. We would rather deal with such things than with Thee. Thy judgments are too terrible. We cannot stand them." And men will pray to the inanimate objects, cry to the rocks and the mountains, and ask that these fall upon them to hide them from the wrath of the Lamb. Today the door of mercy is still open, and these great apocalyptic stories are great calls to evangelism—calls to those outside of Christ that they might come and build their hope in Christ alone.

CHAPTER 7

Verses 1–8

Arrested Judgment

¹After this I saw four messengers standing on the four corners of the earth, holding fast the four winds of the earth so that a wind should not blow on the earth, nor on the sea, nor on any tree, ²and I saw another messenger ascending from the rising of the sun, having the seal of the living God: and he cried with a great voice to the four messengers to whom it was given to hurt the earth and the sea ³saying, Hurt not the earth, nor the sea, nor the trees, till we have sealed the bond slaves of our God upon their foreheads.

⁴And I heard the number of the sealed: a hundred and forty-four thousand sealed from every tribe of the children of Israel. ⁵Out of the tribe of Juda, twelve thousand sealed; out of the tribe of Reuben, twelve thousand; out of the tribe of Gad, twelve thousand; ⁶out of the tribe of Asher, twelve thousand; out of the tribe of Naphtali, twelve thousand; out of the tribe of Manasseh, twelve thousand; ⁷out of the tribe of Simeon, twelve thousand; out of the tribe of Levi, twelve thousand; out of the tribe of Issachar, twelve thousand; ⁸out of the tribe of Zabulon, twelve thousand; out of the tribe of Joseph, twelve thousand; out of the tribe of Benjamin, twelve thousand.

(Rev. 7:1-8, Free Translation)

The scene that comes with the opening of chapter seven is startling in its sudden change. Imagine that you are gazing upon a motion picture where the action has been swift and terrible. A great storm has been raging, waves have torn at the rocks, a lighthouse gives way and the parapet starts to fall toward the sea below. Suddenly something happens to the projector and the continuity of the picture is suspended. One scene remains upon the screen. A giant wave has risen to its crest and the foam stands suddenly still. The stones that have begun to fall from the lighthouse hang suspended in mid-air.

In the midst of the clamor of the world's upheaval, black sun and bloody moon, terror of humanity in its naked cowardice, four messengers suddenly appear. They lay hold upon the winds of judgment—the Greek word is a strong one, like the hold of death upon the body

(Acts 2:24)—and all judgment is suspended. The winds may not blow on the earth, nor on the sea, nor on any tree. These symbols are easy to interpret. The earth is Israel; the sea, the Gentiles; the trees, as we know from the famous parable in the ninth chapter of the book of Judges, refer to those in authority.

In verse one, the messengers are undoubtedly angelic beings. We would make the distinction clear, for we will find One who is called a messenger, miscalled an angel in our translations, who is none other than the Lord Jesus Christ Himself.

"The four corners of the earth" has two possible meanings. It may include "the uttermost parts of the earth," or it may be restricted only to that portion which is in view in the prophecy, a localized judgment covering either Palestine or the land that is in the revived Roman Empire. As a general rule in this last book of the Bible, the judgment scenes do not cover the whole of the earthly globe, but that portion of the earth which comes under the rule of the Antichrist. Outside and beyond these dominions, another power is rising which will come in sharp conflict with the forces of the man of sin at the battle of Armageddon.

At all events, the fact that the four messengers stand on the cardinal points, indicates that they are far removed from each other and that the judgment that is now arrested is wide in its extent.

In many places in the Scriptures, the wind is used as the symbol of divine judgment and the fact that there are four winds, shows that in this case the judgment is wide-spread. "And upon Elam will I bring the four winds from the four quarters of heaven" (Jer. 49:36) is clearly a picture of the judgment of the Lord coming from every side. A little farther on in the same prophecy God will raise up against Babylon a destroying wind (Jer. 51:1). In the second book of Samuel the same figure is used (22:11) in a manner that is clearly indicative of the judgments of God. A marginal reading of Zechariah 6:1-5 speaks of the chariots which come out from the presence of the Lord. In verse 5 they are said to be "four spirits of the heavens." The Hebrew word is that which is usually used for wind.

That we are considering a moment when judgment is temporarily suspended is evident, not only from the tone of the chapter under discussion, but also from the direct statement of the other messenger who ascends from the rising sun, having the seal of the living God. He cries to the four messengers of judgment, ordering them to arrest their activities. He clearly states, however, that this is only "until . . ." When God's elect shall have been marked in order to preserve them in the midst of the judgment, the indication is clearly that the winds will blow once more. The motion picture will begin to turn. The waves will dash on, the suspended stones will fall and the scene will proceed as though there had been no interruption. This may also be seen from the fact that as soon as the elect of God are sealed, the angels sound forth the trumpets of judgment, carrying on their avenging work for God.

God now proceeds to set His seal upon a great body of men before the judgment trumpets will sound and the vials of His wrath will be turned out upon the earth. Let us consider the nature and the purpose of this sealing. We know, of course, that the salvation of any individual in any dispensation is, from one point of view, the result of the active grace of God, and from man's point of view is the result of the individual's belief in God's Word about the Lord Jesus Christ. There is, of course, no change in the Tribulation period. These children of Israel who are now sealed have been chosen by God for His purposes and have come in their own souls to put their trust in the Lord Jesus Christ, who is still at the time of this scene the "despised and rejected of men" (Isa. 53:3). Now upon their faith the seal of God will be effectually set. The grace that saved them gave them their position as saints of God. There will be a great change in their position. They had been a part of Satan's goods, but now they will have become the property of the Lord who redeemed them. Upon them, therefore, God will set His seal so that they may be distinguished from the world which He disowns. As blood was put upon the door of the houses of Israel in Egypt so that the angel of death would pass over these houses and strike only those which were not marked, so the seal of God is put upon the forehead of His own so that the angels of judgment, passing through the world, will know those who are God's.

The seal on the forehead of those who are the Lord's servants takes us back to a great picture in the book of Ezekiel. A man clothed with linen and who carries a writer's inkhorn is ordered by God to go through the city and "set a mark upon the foreheads of the men that sigh and that cry for all the abominations that be done in the midst" of Israel (Ezek. 9:4). Others were then ordered to go through the city and to "slay utterly old and young, both maids, and little children, and women: but come not near any man upon whom is the mark; and begin at my sanctuary" (vs. 6). From the context it is clear that it is a prophecy of God's dealings with Israel at the time of the end.

The Lord may indeed for His own purposes permit that some of the wrath of Satan shall touch those who bear His seal upon their foreheads, though the worst of his agents will be unable to touch those who are thus sealed. This will be working out the plan of God. Judgments that come from God Himself will never touch His own. It is expressly stated in the ninth chapter that the Satanic forces which are released from the bottomless pit will be able to hurt "only those men who have not the seal of God in their foreheads" (Rev. 9:4). When we read further in this same chapter of the nature of the tor-

ments which demon hosts will bring to men, we see the reality of the
protection which is then afforded to those who are the Lord's own.
"The foundation of God standeth sure" in every age and on this foundation He tells us there is a seal, "The Lord knoweth them that are
his" (II Tim. 2:19). Then as now this certainty of position is a call
to holiness of life, to practical separation in accordance with our posi-
tional separation and sealing.

There are two questions in connection with this portion of the vision
which remain to be discussed; the number of those who are sealed
and their identity. According to the record, each of the twelve tribes
mentioned furnish twelve thousand of those who receive the mark in
their foreheads.

The number twelve in the Scripture has a special association with
the idea of completion and it is also attached inseparably to the destiny
of God's chosen earthly people, Israel. Immediately, of course, we
think of the twelve tribes and the twelve apostles. In the last great
vision of Scripture of the eternal home of all the company of the redeemed, these two are united. The New Jerusalem has *"twelve* gates,
and at the gates *twelve* angels, and names written thereon, which are
the names of the *twelve* tribes of the children of Israel" (Rev. 21:12).
Furthermore, "the wall of the city had *twelve* foundations, and in them
the names of the *twelve* apostles of the Lamb" (21:14). Thus Israel
and the Church are united in one eternal structure and yet separate
one from the other. The idea of completion is found yet again in
this vision of the Heavenly city for its dimensions are given in terms
of twelve. The wall is one hundred and forty-four (the square of
twelve) thousand cubits, while the city itself is *"twelve* thousand furlongs" in length, breadth, and height (21:16). In this symbol of the
perfect cube of twelve, the idea of completion is carried out to its
utmost in the Scripture.

The thousand is ten raised to its third power. The number ten is
constantly used in the Scripture in connection with government and
has even been called "the number of government and responsibility,"
as exemplified in the Ten Commandments. We see now in this description of the sealing of twelve thousand from each of the twelve
tribes of Israel, the perfection of God's dealings with His own during
the Tribulation. These numbers then may be either literal or symbolical. This will be seen more clearly when we discuss the identity of
those seen in the vision.

Rightly dividing the Word and rightly joining the Word are both
good principles. If we read the promises made to Israel throughout
the whole of the Word of God, and if we read them honestly, we must
be convinced that the Church has never succeeded to this inheritance
in any adequate way and there is no possibility that these promises
ever can be fulfilled in the Church. While we have constantly affirmed

the necessity of seeking the true meaning of symbols, we must see the vast difference between such a method of interpretation and the "spiritualizing," which certainly does not come from the Holy Spirit, who would never treat the Word of God so lightly. Christ came not to destroy but to fulfill, and the promises made to the literal descendants of Abraham, Isaac and Jacob must certainly be included in that which God swore by Himself that He would perform.

The great Catholic scholar, Crampon, has devastatingly dealt with the historical method of interpretation. He points out that Joachim de Flore, who lived at the end of the twelfth century, divided up the seals, trumpets and vials to cover the centuries which had preceded him, thus demonstrating that the time of the end had come. Five hundred years later, Holzhauser performed the same operation, assigning the seals, trumpets and vials to other historical facts, bringing it up to his day.

We cannot too strongly insist on the error of the historical school of interpretation and would wish to consider most earnestly Crampon's summary with his own italics, in which he shows the impossibility of the historian's interpretation of the Apocalypse. "But are not many of the symbols much too great and out of all proportion with the events to which they are applied? Bossuet himself and most of those who have followed him have felt this difficulty and to protect their system have recognized that their historical applications indeed do not exhaust the whole of the meaning of the apocalyptic visions. We would then ask the partisans of this method a direct question. If on your own admission the events to which we apply the prophetic texts answer only feebly and partially to the great symbols and energetic expressions of these texts, on what do you base your right thus to apply them? Since you have no true exegetical reasons, is it that you have taken up your interpretation because you have found some authorization in the tradition of the fathers? There is no such tradition. Before the sixteenth century *not a single father or commentator* ever applied the great prophecies of the Apocalypse to the events that brought about or accompanied the fall of the Roman Empire and the history of the Church." That is a magnificent summary and one that has never been answered by any theologian, Catholic or Protestant.

There are Catholic commentators that take the position opposed to the Catholic I have quoted—as there are Protestant commentators on both sides of this question, but unhesitantly I take my position with those who see that the entire book of the Apocalypse is prophetic from chapter four to the end, and all the events that are described there, are yet to happen in this world, after God comes to the end of His use of the Church in this earth.

The twelve tribes then must be taken as literal Israel and not as the Church. At the time of the division of the kingdoms, the faithful of the northern tribes obeyed the Word of the Lord and went to Jerusalem in sufficient numbers to guarantee the succession of all of the twelve tribes and before the death of Rehoboam God looked upon the tribes as a unity, seeing "all Israel in Judah and Benjamin" (II Chron. 11:3). This of course destroys the claims of those who have looked upon Britain and America as being the ten lost tribes, who have imagined that there is a difference between the Jews and Israel. They are the same, and most definitely all the tribes are now seen in Judah and Benjamin.

Thus Nathanael was an Israelite indeed (John 1:47), Anna was of the tribe of Aser (Luke 2:36) and the twelve tribes were represented in the multitude of scattered Jews who had come from various parts of the earth and who were in Jerusalem on the day of Pentecost and who were addressed in the opening verses of the epistle of James and the first epistle of Peter.

Verses 9–17
The Great Awakening

⁹After this I saw and behold a great multitude which no one was able to number from out of all nations and tribes and peoples and tongues, standing before the throne and before the Lamb, clothed with white robes, and palms in their hands; ¹⁰and they cry with a great voice saying, Salvation to our God who is sitting upon the throne, and unto the Lamb.

¹¹And all the messengers were standing in the circle of the throne and of the elders and of the four living creatures, and fell down before the throne, upon their faces and worshiped God, ¹² saying, Amen: the blessing, and the glory, and the wisdom, and the thanksgiving, and the honor, and the power, and the strength be to our God, through the ages of the ages; Amen.

¹³And one of the elders asked, saying unto me, These who are arrayed with the white robes, who are they and whence came they? ¹⁴And I said unto Him, My Lord, Thou knowest. And He said to me, These are the ones who come out of the great tribulation, and they wash their own robes and made them white in the Blood of the Lamb. ¹⁵For this reason they are before the throne of God and serve Him day and night in His temple; and He who is sitting on the throne shall dwell over them. ¹⁶They shall hunger no more, neither thirst any more; neither shall the sun fall upon them nor any heat; ¹⁷because the Lamb who is in the midst of the throne will shepherd them and will lead them to fountains of waters of life; and God will wipe away all tears from their eyes.

(Rev. 7:9-17, Free Translation)

When the forces of chaos were unleashed in France more than a century and a half ago and when terror followed revolution, it was the great spiritual movement that occurred under the Wesleys which kept England from following in the same path. Historians have called the movement, "The Great Awakening." Both of these events, the Revolution and the Awakening, are but faint shadows of what shall take place in the future when the Antichrist is reigning upon the earth. The world's great tribulation, chaos indescribable, will certainly come to pass. We have the Word of the Lord Jesus that it will be the greatest of all time (Matt. 24:21). Just as surely, the world's greatest spiritual movement will take place at the same time. This passage is one proof of this fact.

We will consider the preachers used by God in this great awakening, the message that was delivered by them, and the host that was led to the knowledge of the Saviour through their preaching.

That these are undoubtedly literal Israel may be seen not only in the mathematical way in which they are linked each to his tribe but also by the fact that their destiny differs from that of the Church seated with Christ on the throne and that of the multitude who will serve God day and night in the Temple. This company is seen rather as a special retinue, a glorious bodyguard to accompany the Lord Jesus on all His movements during His glorious reign on earth (Rev. 14:4). That literal Israel is in view may also be seen from certain details in connection with the enumeration of the tribes.

A careful examination of the dozen places in the Bible where all the twelve tribes are mentioned will reveal some very beautiful truths. Jacob had twelve sons who were the fathers of the twelve tribes. Joseph had two sons, Ephraim and Manasseh, whose names later were added to the list of the tribes. This gives us fourteen names out of which twelve are selected, but not always the same twelve, in presenting the truths concerning Israel. Levi, the priestly tribe, had no military duties to perform and was not given a portion of the land when the tribes entered Palestine. The portion of Levi was to be the Lord Himself (Deut. 18: 1, 2; Josh. 13:14). In order to fill His place both in military affairs and in the land, a new tribe had to be found so Joseph was replaced by his two sons. Leaving out the name of Levi and that of Joseph, twelve names remained. In this list of tribulation messengers the twelve tribes include, however, the name of Levi and that of Joseph and also one of Joseph's sons, Manasseh. Ephraim and Dan are omitted. Why is there this particular choice in the book of Revelation? The answer is to be found in some of the Old Testament teachings concerning Dan and Ephraim.

During the wanderings of the children of Israel in the desert, an incident occurred which brought a curse on the tribe of Dan. A young man, the son of an Israelitish woman, Shelomith, the daughter of Dibri, of the tribe of Dan (Lev. 24:11), blasphemed the name of Jehovah and cursed. By a definite order of the Lord, the young man was brought out and stoned to death. This blasphemy was in direct disobedience to the nature of God and had a certain curse attached to it, which was later recorded by Moses. In the Palestinian covenant, we find God's statement against blasphemy, "The Lord will not spare him, but then the anger of the Lord and his jealousy shall smoke against that man, and all the curses that are written in this book shall lie upon him, and the Lord shall blot out his name from under heaven. And the Lord shall separate him unto evil out of all the tribes of Israel, according to all the curses of the covenant that are written in this book of the law" (Deut. 29:20, 21). In the passage that precedes (vs. 18) we read, "Lest there should be among you any man, or woman, or family, *or tribe* . . ." According to this the name of Dan would have to be blotted out.

But there were also other serious charges against Dan. Jacob in his dying blessing prophesied of Dan, "Dan shall be a serpent by the way, an adder in the path, that biteth the horse heels, so that his rider shall fall backward" (Gen. 49:17). When Deborah and Barak delivered the children of Israel in the time of the judges, the other tribes sent men to fight but Dan remained back in a cowardly way. In the song of victory, though there are praises for the other tribes, all that could be said of Dan was, "Why did Dan remain in ships?" (Judg. 5:17).

Far more serious than this, however, is that Dan seemed to have been a leader in apostasy. Jeroboam caused golden calves to be made and set one in Bethel, "and the other put he in Dan. And this thing became a sin: for the people went to worship before the one, even unto Dan" (I Kings 12:29, 30). Almost a hundred years later, this calf of gold was still to be found and worshiped in the days of Jehu (II Kings 10:29). Jeremiah tells us that Dan was a "voice of calamity" (Jer. 4:15, Heb.). Amos had to cry out against the people who were still walking in the way of idolatry crying out "Long live Dan! Long live the way of Beer-sheba" (Amos 8:14, Heb.).

It was in Ephraim that Jeroboam built his city of idolatry. It was from Ephraim that he set up his attempt to gain control of all power. It was of Ephraim that God said he was joined to his idols and was to be let alone (Hos. 4:17). Dan and Ephraim will not be protected by God's seal during the great tribulation. Though they will come to salvation with all Israel, they will not be used as God's witnesses.

It may be easily understood, why the Lord did not include Dan and Ephraim in the list of the tribes who are to do the tribulation preaching. Those who have a weakness for idolatry cannot be permitted to witness in a day when the false prophet of Antichrist is pointing to a statue of the man of sin and calling upon people to worship him.

The question may arise in the minds of some as to how the tribes will be discovered and identified since they are scattered today. They reckon, of course, without the power of God. Just as the Lord Jesus will be able to sort out all of the bodies that have gone back to the dust of the earth and raise them from the dead, "according to the working whereby he is able even to subdue all things unto himself" (Phil. 3:21), so God will know the tribal identities.

In all this we see one of the most beautiful truths in the Bible shining forth with great brilliance. Though Ephraim and Dan have had their candlesticks removed from their places (Rev. 2:5) and are not permitted to take part in the preaching of the gospel of salvation and the accompanying gospel of the kingdom, they are not yet cast off from God. Just as the risen Lord Jesus Christ took care to send word to the erring disciple, Peter, that he was still the object of His love, Dan is singled out for mention in connection with the ultimate inheritance of the people, "Go tell my disciples *and Peter . . .*" (Mark 16:7). How this thrills our hearts as we realize the safety of the believer when once the Lord Jesus Christ has set Himself to his redemption. How wonderful, therefore, that along with all these terrible things in the history of Dan, Jacob should have been able to prophesy of "that which shall befall you in the last days" (Gen. 49:1), especially of the erring one, "Dan shall judge his people as one of the tribes of Israel" (Gen. 49:16). Finally in the last chapter of the book of Ezekiel, the tribes are seen in the millennial glory and Dan is among them. The grace of God shines out, for when the land is divided for the millennial reign, Dan's portion is put first of all the tribes (Ezek. 48:1). In no other place in all the Scriptures is Dan mentioned first. This honor usually goes to the eldest, Reuben. In Revelation, Judah, tribe of the Lord Jesus Christ, is first. Everyone of us can be thankful that, "the gifts and calling of God are without repentance" (Rom. 11:29).

There is but one message that can reach the hearts of men. The preaching that will be delivered by these sealed servants necessarily must be occupied with the redemptive work of the Lord Jesus Christ. Salvation in every age has been on the basis of what Christ accomplished on Calvary. Adam and Eve believed God's Word about the Redeemer who was to come, and they were covered with garments provided by the shedding of blood which typifies the righteousness of Christ (Gen. 3:21). Abel, offering the lamb by faith, presented to God an acceptable sacrifice. Abraham saw Christ's day (John 8:56) and was glad. Moses esteemed the reproach of Christ (Heb. 11:26). We today are saved by looking back to the cross as they were by looking forward to it. During the Great Tribulation when the Church has been removed, the sealed Israelites, as well as the multitude that no man can number, will all be saved because Christ died. It is also true of those who shall come to God during the millennial reign of Christ.

Let us make it plain. Not one human being will be in Heaven unless he has come through faith in God's Word about His Son. Some may understand it better than others; some, like those who were near the center of camp when Moses lifted up the serpent in the wilderness, may get a close view; others from the edge of the camp may see the dim shadow in the distance. The important thing is that they have faith to look to the lifted Christ. Only God can touch those who are dead in trespasses and sins and cause them to look. But of this it is certain that all who look shall live.

There is an important addition which many people overlook in their study of the Word of God. To the central truth of the redemption accomplished by Jesus Christ upon the cross is added a distinct message for every different age. While we are saved today in the same way that Moses and David were saved under the law, there is a difference in the way that preaching is carried on from one age to another. The man who asked the Lord Jesus "What shall I do to inherit eternal life?" (Luke 10:25) received quite a different answer from that given to the Philippian jailer who asked Paul the same question, "What must I do to be saved?" (Acts 16:30). At one time in God's dealing with men, it was necesary to bring a lamb or some other blood sacrifice and offer it before God. It was also necessary from Moses to Christ that anyone who was saved should be circumcised and adopted into one of the Jewish tribes.

In the age in which we live, all of this has been done away. Christ admitted to the woman at the well that the Jews were correct in worshiping at Jerusalem rather than at Mt. Gerizim, saying that salvation was of the Jews (John 4:22). At the same time, however, He said that the hour was coming and already had come when men should stop approaching God on the basis of the Jewish altar and should come to Him in spirit and in truth.

In the days preceding Christ's coming and in the early part of our Lord's ministry, John the Baptist and Jesus preached the "gospel of the kingdom." No man could go to Heaven by that gospel. It was indeed good news that the Messiah was at hand. Men ought, therefore, to repent and turn to the gospel of God's grace regardless of the form of presentation. Today we cannot preach the gospel of the kingdom. It will be preached again, however, since our Lord says that the gospel of the kingdom is to be preached in all the world for a witness before the end shall come (Matt. 24:14). In view of all the teaching of the Word of God on this subject, it is undoubtedly the gospel of the kingdom which is the added special message of the

144,000. Of course, they present Jesus as the Saviour. Many look to Him and are saved. But they also preach the gospel of the kingdom presenting Jesus as Messiah. They are the sealed witnesses, the 144,000 like Paul who go out with all the gifts of the Holy Spirit, having the prophecies of Joel fulfilled in themselves, as the first faint occurrences at Pentecost cannot possibly be the complete fulfillment which comes to full fruition in the last days. Note that the story of Pentecost not only links the occurrences of that day with the prophecies of Joel but, in a method that is frequently used in the Bible, carries the reader in the next phrase over thousands of years to future time. The last verses of the chapter (Acts 2:16-21) definitely link these prophecies to the Great Tribulation.

Multitudes accept the Lord Jesus as their Saviour as a result of this Tribulation preaching. The greatest awakening of all time will take place while the Antichrist is consolidating his power and while he is spending his most vigorous effort to exalt himself in the Holy of Holies in Jerusalem, crushing those who refuse to bow before his statue.

A numberless company is now seen, from every nation and kindred and people and tongue. They are clothed in robes of white, symbol of the righteousness which they have received from Him. They have in their hands palms, symbol of victory and glory.

Though this multitude is taken out of every tongue, nevertheless, it cries with a single voice. The verb is in the "vivid dramatic present" tense. Their cry is one of praise to God for the salvation He has accomplished in their behalf. It has been accomplished by the Father and the Son and to Them all praise is given.

At this cry of praise all the angelic beings standing round about the great circle of the elders and the living creatures, the cherubim around the throne of God, fall down upon their faces and worship God. We know that the angels are Bible students (I Pet. 1:12). Here in the minds of this angelic host they are aware of the awful conditions that have prevailed because of the presence of sin in the universe. Why has God been patient? Why has God been so forbearing with the enemy? This is a mystery. But now the multitude cries out that salvation has come and the hosts of Heaven worship God. Here is the sevenfold perfection of praise: blessing, and glory, and wisdom, and thanksgiving, and honor, and power, and might.

One of the elders now asks a question of John and then gives the answer. Who are these people which compose the great multitude and from whence have they come? It should be noted that those commentators who identified the elders in the earlier chapters as representing the Church and who now identify this great multitude also as being the Church, are in the anomalous position of seeing the Church as being in Heaven as the glorified Church, telling John who is on

earth as a prophet of the Church that the great multitude is none
other than themselves, the Church. Into such depths fall those who
are not willing to admit that there is a restoration of literal Israel.

Why are men unwilling to take the decisive voice that the Spirit of
God gives to us in this passage? "These are they which came out of
great tribulation and have washed their robes and made them white
in the blood of the Lamb." In other words they do not constitute
the Church at all. We, the body of Christ, are already seen in Heaven
at the time of this vision. Our calling, our service and our destiny are
all different from that of the great multitude. In the twenty-fourth
chapter of Matthew our Lord speaks of that time of terror which He
Himself calls the Great Tribulation. It is while that reign is upon the
earth that this multitude of Gentiles is saved through faith in the death
of the Lord Jesus Christ.

As their calling and service differ from ours, so does their destiny.
We, as the bride with the Bridegroom, sit upon the throne to rule and
reign with the Lord of Glory. Our destiny is said to be that of rulers
and judges. We are to be kings and priests (I Cor. 6:2, 3; I Pet. 2:9;
Rev. 1:6). The 144,000 are to be the glorious bodyguard, the retinue
of the Lamb, following Him whithersoever He goeth (Rev. 14:4).
The destiny of the Gentile multitude, however, is that of temple servants. Any reader of the book of Ezekiel knows, of course, that the
Temple will be the central earthly feature of the millennial reign. Here
we are told that the great multitude which has come out of the tribulation period is to carry on the priestly work of that Temple.

The day of their tribulation is now over; they shall hunger no more,
neither thirst. The reason is given in the next verse. They shall be
fed by the Lamb who shall lead them unto living fountains of waters;
they who have forsaken all for Him and who have not been able to
buy or sell since they have refused the mark of the beast, and who as
a result have been in the midst of hunger and thirst are now fed by
the Lord Jesus, Himself.

We have seen the sun as the symbol of government. These who
have suffered from the authority that is centered in the Antichrist
shall thus suffer no more, neither shall the sun light on them; nor shall
they know any heat. Heat is the Bible symbol of persecution and
suffering. The trial of their faith, being much more precious than of
gold that perisheth though it be tried with fire, will have been found
unto praise and honor and glory at the appearing of Jesus Christ (I
Pet. 1:7). This suffering is over forever. God, Himself, shall wipe
away all tears from their eyes.

CHAPTER 8

Verses 1–5

Fire From the Altar

¹And when He opened the seventh seal, there came a silence in Heaven for about half an hour.

²And I saw the seven messengers which stand in the Presence of God; and to them were given seven trumpets. ³And another messenger came and stood at the altar, having a golden censer; and there was given to him much incense, in order that he might add it to the prayers of all the saints upon the golden altar which is before the throne.

⁴And the smoke of the incense with the prayers of the saints, went up into the Presence of God out of the messengers' hands, ⁵And the messenger had taken the censer, and filled it with the fire from the altar, and cast it into the earth; and there followed voices, and thunderings, and lightnings, and an earthquake.

(Rev. 8:1-5, Free Translation)

Suddenly with the opening of the last of the seals all of the sounds of Heaven cease and there is silence for a period which in John's conception of time, is half an hour long, but which even in the measure of eternity must be one of the most astounding incidents known by the Heavenly hosts throughout their existence.

What is the meaning of the silence of God? Perhaps we may come to the answer as we survey the revelation of God from the Old Testament through to this last Word. Perhaps the explanation is that the silence in Heaven is occasioned by the end of what in the Old Testament, has been called the silence of God. Throughout the Old Testament, the men of God cried out against the seeming triumph of evil. The Spirit of God gave the answer through David, "Our God shall come, and shall not keep silence: a fire shall devour before him, and it shall be very tempestuous round about him. He shall call to the heavens from above, and to the earth, that he may judge his people" (Ps. 50:3, 4). The prophet's view was, of course, that God was going to bring righteousness and judgment to the earth, but buried in

154

the midst of unrighteousness their impatient souls cried, "How long shall the wicked triumph?" (Ps. 94:3). They "inquired and searched diligently . . . searching what, or what manner of time, the Spirit of Christ which was in them did signify, when it testified beforehand the sufferings of Christ, and the glory that should follow" (I Pet. 1:10, 11). There is an eager desire in Heaven and on earth to know when God will break His silence and effectively end the ills of earth.

The seventh seal is opened and Heaven is silent for the space of half an hour. The seventh seal is not a judgment, it is a new beginning. From it come forth seven messengers each with trumpets to sound further judgments. The Word of Christ has been vindicated: "All these are the beginning of sorrows" (Matt. 24:8). We can understand this development by a simple illustration. We have all seen firework displays in which giant rockets are shot into the air exploding into a great ball of fire. This, as it falls toward the earth, bursts into a great number of balls of fire of various colors which, as they fall further toward earth, burst again into smaller balls of various colors.

So it is with the judgments of God. At first we see nothing but a sealed scroll. As the seals are removed each one appears to be a judgment and we would expect that when we come to the last seal, it would be the last judgment. But instead, the last seal discloses seven angels, each with trumpets. These, in turn, are various judgments, and the seventh trumpet, in turn, reveals not another single judgment, but seven vials of the wrath of God. In both instances there is a series of seven with the last disclosing seven more. In addition to this structure there is a parenthesis between the sixth and the seventh in all three series.

In all the symbolism here and in the verses which follow, the Spirit of God multiplies the evidences that judgment comes from God. It is the Lord Jesus Christ himself who opens the seal and sends forth the first judgment. It is the Holy Spirit Himself who appears in the form of the seven messengers to blow the seven trumpets.

Still another messenger now appears and his work will reveal the whole basis of the judgments that are to follow. He is seen standing at the altar. Later he is seen with the prayers of all the saints upon the golden altar which was before the throne. At first glance these two altars may appear to be the same but a careful study will reveal that they differ from each other.

It will be best at this point to go back to the Old Testament for a moment to present a background against which many points in Revelation will become clear. The last verse of Revelation 11 will speak of the Temple of God and the ark of the testament in Heaven. Still later we will find reference to "the temple of the tabernacle of the testimony in heaven" (Rev. 15:5). These passages can be interpreted only in the light of the Old Testament and we shall proceed there by way of the epistle to the Hebrews. This book, the name of which gives it its great significance, has important material to present to us with reference to the ancient tabernacle and Temple.

Describing the consecration of the tabernacle by the rites of sacrifice and sprinkling of the blood, the author of the epistle to the Hebrews goes on to say, "It was therefore necessary that the patterns of things in the heavens should be purified with these; but the heavenly things themselves with better sacrifices than these. For Christ is not entered into the holy places made with hands, which are the figures of the true; but into heaven itself, now to appear in the presence of God for us" (Heb. 9:23, 24). The Revised Standard Version strengthens this by speaking of the earthly tabernacle and its appurtenances as being "the copies of the heavenly things." When Moses was about to make the tabernacle he was admonished of God in definite terms. "See, saith he, that thou make all things according to the pattern shewed to thee in the mount" (Heb. 8:5). It is certain then, that the tabernacle and the Temple which was constructed later on the same plan, were but the earthly manufacture, scale models, so to speak, of a great reality that is to be found in Heaven.

A worshiper approaching the tabernacle would have come first of all to an altar in the courtyard. On this altar a fire was lighted to consume the body of the lamb after its blood had been shed. Beyond this altar was a laver filled with water so that the priests might wash their feet before penetrating into the holy place.

After passing the altar and the laver the priest entered the main room of the Tabernacle or Temple called the sanctuary. In it he saw first of all, the seven-branched candlestick, symbol of Christ the Light. Then he found the table of shewbread, Christ the Bread of Life, where the saints feed; then at the far end of the room, a golden altar which is called the altar of incense. No blood sacrifice was offered on this altar, though the incense which was burned before it had to be lighted with fire procured from the altar where the blood of the lamb had dripped. That fire had originally been lighted from the holy presence of God, and it was the failure on the part of Nadab and Abihu to light their incense with the fire from this altar which caused their death, when they brought strange fire into the presence of God. This teaches, of course that all worship must be on the basis of the redemption accomplished by Christ.

Behind the altar of incense was the great veil separating the sanctuary from the Holiest of all (Heb. 9:1-3). This veil in the Temple was the one which was torn asunder from top to bottom at the moment Christ was dying upon the cross (Matt. 27:51). Only the great high priest could go beyond this veil and on only one day in the year, the day of atonement. All this is clearly described in the first half of Hebrews 9. Within the Holiest of all, the ark of the covenant was located.

Over this was the mercy seat where the high priest placed the blood on the day of atonement. It was here that God dwelt in the midst of His people and where could be seen the pillar of cloud by day and the pillar of fire by night. All of the ministrations of the priest were carried on in these surroundings. Every object, every activity was filled with the meaning of Christ and His redemptive work. Every detail, however, was a copy of a reality that was in Heaven, in the presence of God. It would appear that this is the architectual plan of the space before the throne of God. It is only by respecting the details of this plan, and especially by recognizing the spiritual significance attached to each detail by the Holy Spirit Himself in the interpretation to be found in the book of Hebrews, that these great realities can be understood.

The messenger standing at the altar has in his hand a golden censer which he uses for two purposes, first for intercession and then for judgment. At the golden altar, that is the altar of incense, the altar of worship, the messenger brings the prayers of the saints. These are, of course, the saints who are on the earth. The prayers that are offered are from the saints on earth and the intercession of the saints in Heaven has already been turned into praise and adoration (Rev. 5: 8-10). It should be noted, of course, that by saints, I mean any man or woman who has built his hope in Jesus Christ. The term saint is a technical one, it does not necessarily mean someone who is saintly, but someone who has been saved through Christ—the meanest, lowest, most humble believer is in the sight of God and in the definition of the Bible a saint.

The messenger now moves through the Temple to the altar of sacrifice. The censer which has held incense for the worship of God is now filled with fire from the altar, and this fire is cast upon the earth. The judgment fire which is to rage upon the earth comes from the very altar where the Lamb has been slain and His body consumed. In other words the wrath of God that is to be poured out upon the earth is solemnly based upon the sufferings of the Lord Jesus Christ on Calvary. When Satan rebelled against God, the Lord did not arbitrarily move against him to take his power away, but in the ordered plan of the ages put the tremendous forces into operation which brought us to the consummation of the cross. There it was that the Lord Jesus Christ spoiled principalities and powers, making a show of them openly and triumphing over them (Col. 2:15). Just as a sheriff executes a writ in virtue of the judge's decree, so the Heavenly messenger now pours forth judgment which is in full harmony with the absolute righteousness and holiness of God.

One of the greatest of the prophets was one day permitted a vision of the Heavenly Temple. He saw the Lord high and lifted up. He heard the cry of the seraphim as they led the worship of the universe and announced that the whole earth was filled with His glory. Immediately Isaiah saw himself in contrast to the holiness that was there revealed and he cried, "Woe is me! for I am undone; because I am a man of unclean lips, and I dwell in the midst of a people of unclean lips; for mine eyes have seen the King, the Lord of hosts" (Isa. 6:5). We know from the New Testament that this was a vision of the Lord Jesus Christ in the presence of the Father (John 12:41). When Isaiah had seen the uncleanness that was in himself, the Lord met it by fire from the altar. One of the seraphim came with a live coal in his hand which he had taken with the tongs from off the altar and laid it upon the mouth of the prophet and announced that his iniquity was taken away and his sin purged (Isa. 6:6, 7).

How terrible it is to contemplate the fact that the fire from the altar which cleansed Isaiah's lips is the fire that is now poured out on the earth in judgment. If the world will not have Jesus Christ as its Saviour and King it must have Him as Judge. That is the truth so tellingly presented in this majestic picture of the courts of Heaven. It is a well deserved judgment that is poured out upon the earth in a way that is inextricably bound up with the holiness of God, the sacrifice of the Lord Jesus Christ, and the worship of the Creator by the universe.

Voices, thunderings, lightnings and an earthquake come from the contact of Heaven's fire and earth's sin.

The seven messengers prepare to sound their trumpets. The second of the great series of judgments begins.

PART V
THE TRUMPETS

Verses 6–12

A Star Called Wormwood

⁶And the seven messengers having the seven trumpets, prepared themselves in order that they might sound. ⁷And the first sounded, and there came hail and fire mingled with blood, and they were cast upon the earth; and the third part of the earth was burnt up, and the third part of the trees was burnt up, and all green grass was burnt up.

⁸And the second messenger sounded, and as it were, a great mountain burning with fire was cast into the sea; and the third part of the sea became blood; ⁹And the third part of the creatures which were in the sea, which had life, died; and the third part of the ships was destroyed.

¹⁰And the third messenger sounded, and there fell from heaven a great star, burning as a torch, and it fell upon the third part of the rivers, and upon the fountains of the water. ¹¹And the name of the star is called The Wormwood; and the third part of the waters was turned into wormwood; and many of the men died from the waters, because they were made bitter.

¹²And the fourth messenger sounded, and the third part of the sun was smitten, and the third part of the moon, and the third part of the stars, in order that the third part of them should be darkened, and the day should not shine for a third part of it, and the night likewise. (Rev. 8:6-12, Free Translation)

The first four of the trumpet judgments seem to be somewhat in the nature of an anti-climax. They differ from the earlier judgments. They are not as universal in their extent. They cannot be compared with the horrors that will follow in the great woes and in the final outpouring of the bowls of God's wrath.

An electric wire that is made for carrying the small voltage of house needs will stand currents which will burn out filaments and blow out fuses. A transformer will enable these wires to send power that transcends ordinary needs if the occasion arise. So it is with human suffering. Man may think that he can stand only so much, but when a great emergency comes he finds that he can live on and on under conditions which would ordinarily seem intolerable.

In the midst of great pain there is a moment when the overworked nerves are incapable of transmitting further misery. One is conscious that the pain is continuing unabated, but it seems as if there is some surcease. Then, as though the nerves had become used to the increased intensity of suffering, they are enabled to carry an anguish that had not yet been deemed consistent with the retention of life.

At the close of the sixth chapter suffering humanity had already

161

reached the point where all men from kings to slaves were crowding into the dens of the rocks under the false impression that the pains and sorrows of the first series of judgments had exhausted the possibilities of the wrath of God. They come out of the rocks to carry on a life that has long since ceased to be worth living. Judgments that are worse than any they have known fall upon them and they make shift to endure a little more.

These first judgments are partial, and they deal only with matters which touch the bodies of men. There is a mixture of mercy to be seen in them all. Why should the Lord spare the two-thirds? Why should only one third part of humanity suffer? Is it not a call to the others to turn to God and live? We have every right to believe that some indeed are called out from among those who escape these torments, but the multitude remain in unbelief and call from God further woes and final wrath.

In order to avoid confusion it should be remembered that the great day of God's wrath is yet future, not only from our point of view but from the point of view of those who fall under the trumpet judgments. The fact that the people of earth cried unto the mountains and the rocks (Rev. 6:16, 17), saying that the great day of God's wrath had come, did not make their statement true any more than the cry of someone today in the midst of natural calamity that the end of the world was here would really end the world!

All these difficulties will be done away with if it is recognized that, terrible as the seal and trumpet judgments are, they are not the judgments of the great tribulation which must come after the abomination of desolation in accordance with the definite prophecy of the Lord Himself (Matt. 24:15, 21). The seals and the trumpets are still in the phase of the beginning of sorrows.

The first messenger sounds his trumpet and hail and fire, mingled with blood, are cast upon the earth, causing the burning of the third part of the earth, of the third part of the trees of the earth, and all of the green grass of the earth. If this is literal, it needs no explanation whatsoever. It would be the announcement of a catastrophe resulting from causes that are not ordinarily to be found in nature or that might well be found in man's new discoveries that rise out of nuclear fission. The "earth" here does not necessarily mean the whole globe, but may be limited to the sphere of Israel, or at most, to the sphere of the old Roman Empire.

Seiss has shown that it is possible to interpret these phenomena with exact literalness. He gives examples of such natural phenomena during the nineteenth century, and calls to our attention as all commentators do, to the fact that in Egypt, "the Lord sent thunder and hail, and the fire ran along upon the ground; and the Lord rained hail upon the land of Egypt. So there was hail, and fire mingled with the hail, very grievous . . . and the hail smote every herb of the field" (Exod. 9: 23-25).

Hail is always used of judgment. The plague of hail in Egypt is but one example. Against Ephraim God announced the mighty and strong one, "as a tempest of hail and a destroying storm" (Isa. 28:2). To Job, the Lord revealed that He had reserved "treasures of the hail . . . against the time of trouble, against the day of battle and war" (Job 38:22, 23). And this time of trouble, described by Jeremiah (30:7), and Daniel (12:1), can be none other than the judgment scenes of the future which shall come primarily upon Israel, and then in a wider way, upon the nations which have persecuted Israel.

Fire is another symbol of judgment. It comes from the Lord, it devours, it consumes, it is divine judgment. Blood, which is mingled with the hail and the fire, can speak but of more judgment. Here is violence and death.

The second messenger sounds his trumpet and as it were, a great mountain burning with fire was cast into the sea; and the third part of the sea became bloody; and the third part of the creatures which were in the sea, which had life, died; and the third part of the ships was destroyed.

The first thing to strike our attention is the little clause "as it were." Here is a definite indication of symbolism. The mountain it is said is not a literal mountain, but as it were a mountain. There are two possibilities, then; it is all symbolism, or the mountain alone is symbolic. We have previously noted that the earth is frequently a symbol of Palestine and that the sea by contrast represents the Gentile nations. This judgment, then, if taken symbolically, is a judgment that falls more especially upon the Gentile nations. The concordance will give us one clue. Jeremiah speaks of a burnt mountain. "Behold, I am against thee, O destroying mountain, saith the Lord, which destroyeth all the earth; and I will stretch out mine hand upon thee, and roll thee down from the rocks, and will make thee a burnt mountain" (Jer. 51:25). Our Lord also spoke of a mountain that should be removed and cast into the sea when the disciples would have unwavering faith (Matt. 21:21). There is in view here a great power filled with eruptive forces which shall be cast into the midst of the nations. Many commentators have pointed out the analogy with the French Revolution. An even greater analogy has come into being in our times in Russia, the Russian experiment was bound to succeed and every year brings greater proof to the world that Satan's mightiest efforts have succeeded beyond all thought of those who appraised Communism in its early decades. Some power nearer the western nations, nearer Palestine will know such an upheaval, and will have such mighty social and economic success that the surrounding nations will be thrown into turmoil as Satan demonstrates his ability to do great things for the suppressed classes and the toiling masses. The result is catastrophe for the surrounding nations; death and destruction of trade and commerce. How pregnant these words become in our day.

The other possible interpretation of this trumpet judgment is again that of Seiss. He sees symbolism in the phrase "as it were," but believes that only the mountain is not literal. It is, he thinks, something that looks like a mountain, and he judges it to be a literal meteoric mass from Heaven that falls into the sea, most likely the Mediterranean. He believes that the catastrophe would cause the death of the living creatures in the sea and would destroy the third part of the commerce that moves upon it.

Choosing between these two possible meanings of the phrase, I would be inclined to accept the first, as it seems much more in keeping with the spirit of the Bible as I read it. There are, however, prophecies in the Old Testament that speak of the destruction of the fish of the sea and the commerce of the earth (Hos. 4:3; Zeph. 1:3; Isa. 2:16). And again I say that since the coming of the age of nuclear fission, all of these things become much more literally possible than we had ever thought before. We know that a whole island was lifted up bodily by the explosion of a hydrogen bomb and that it was cast into the sea, and that fish were filled with radioactive elements and were capable of causing sickness—hundreds of miles away. We know how that burns came upon men away outside the limits of the destructive explosion. And so in the light of the fact that all of these judgments may be the result of man's own sinfulness and willfulness, it is very possible that these things will have a literal fulfillment in the light of history and the Word of God.

With the sounding of the third trumpet, John saw a star named the Wormwood, burning like a torch, fall from Heaven. Falling upon the third part of the rivers and springs of the earth it turned them to wormwood and many people died from the bitter poison of the waters.

Here again we must present the two interpretations, literal and symbolical. If the vision is a symbol, we must, of course, brush aside all of the historic vaporings of men who have tried to see some incident of the past in this scene. Whatever it means it is a picture of something that lies in the future.

The only possible symbolism would be found through the identification of the rivers and springs as the sources of spiritual refreshment in life. Our Lord spoke to the woman at the well, saying, "Whosoever drinketh of this water shall thirst again: but whosoever drinketh of the water that I shall give him shall never thirst; but the water that I shall give him shall be in him a well of water springing up into everlasting life" (John 4:13, 14). In the Psalms we are told that those who go from strength to strength have been turning the valley of trouble into a well, and dwelling in a place of springs (Ps. 84:6, 7,

Heb.). The same symbol is found in the last chapter of the Bible as
the river proceeding from the throne of God. After leaving Egypt the
children of Israel came to the place in the desert where "they could
not drink of the waters of Marah, for they were bitter . . . And the
Lord showed him [Moses] a tree, which when he had cast into the
waters, the waters were made sweet" (Exod. 15:23, 25). If the tree
represents the cross of Jesus Christ, then the waters without the tree
would be religion without redemption. If in addition there is the
positive introduction of poison, the situation is still worse. A star
called the Wormwood falls from Heaven. Here the star that is fallen
is a Satanic messenger who poisons the streams of spiritual life with
false doctrine which is compared to wormwood. The Greek word for
this is that from which we get our word *absinthe.* This we know is
a drink so intoxicating that the French government had to take the
sternest measures to keep it away from the Indians who, maddened
by its effect, went forth to commit the most desperate crimes. All this
is in line with those prophecies which speak of the deceptions of the
last days. "The Spirit speaketh expressly, that in the latter times some
shall depart from the faith, giving heed to seducing spirits, and doctrines of devils" (I Tim. 4:1). Those who "received not the love of
the truth, that they might be saved" are given over by God to a
"strong delusion, that they should believe a lie" (II Thess. 2:10, 11).

If this, on the other hand, be taken as a description of a literal
phenomenon, the passage would need reading but not explanation.
A meteor of some kind, falling from the literal heavens might well
embitter the third part of the waters of the earth, or some explosion
of a device invented by man, some vast nuclear fission that would set
forth a chain reaction beyond the control of the physicists who invented it, could indeed explode entailing "fearful distress on account
of the absence of wholesome drink, and great mortality among men."

The fourth trumpet judgment reaches into the heavens. Some blight
touches sun, moon and stars, darkening them by one third, and lessen-
ing in consequence, the proportional amount of light that reaches
earth. As we have seen in our discussion of the judgment under the
sixth seal, the sun, moon and stars are symbols of human government.
Even though the rule over the earth may be in the hands of those
who are described as "principalities . . . powers . . . the rulers of the
darkness of this world . . . spiritual hosts of wickedness in high places"
(Eph. 6:12), all of the powers upon the earth are "ordained of God"
(Rom. 13:1). The sixth seal showed us the cataclysm of anarchy and
the breakup of all authority. There has been, naturally, the attempt
to restore order out of chaos. We know from many passages in the
Bible that the power of the Roman dictator will be formed during this
period and that Satan will come to dwell within him as the Antichrist.

Our Lord, in Luke's record of the last great prophetic utterance, spoke along lines which closely parallel the judgments announced under the four trumpets. "And there shall be signs in the sun, and in the moon, and in the stars; and upon the earth distress of nations, with perplexity; the sea and the waves roaring; men's hearts failing them for fear, and for looking after those things which are coming on the earth: for the powers of heaven shall be shaken" (Luke 21: 25, 26). This passage should be read in the light of a prophecy in the epistle to the Hebrews. "Yet once more I shake not the earth only, but also heaven. And this word, yet once more, signifieth the removing of those things that are shaken, as of things that are made, that those things which cannot be shaken may remain. Wherefore we receiving a kingdom which cannot be moved, let us have grace . . ." (Heb. 12:26-28). The "powers of heaven" that are to be moved are very probably the spiritual rulers of this world's darkness, and the result of that shaking will be increasingly felt upon the earth as all attempts at human government are proved to be abortive and as it is increasingly demonstrated that only the coming of the Lord can bring peace and order upon the earth. Thus Isaiah prophesies, "Moreover the light of the moon shall be as the light of the sun, and the light of the sun shall be sevenfold, as the light of seven days, in the day that the Lord bindeth up the breach of his people, and healeth the stroke of their wound" (Isa. 30:26). And all this will lead on to that perfect time when there will be no further need of human leadership, since the Lamb will be all the light and there will be no need of lesser lights (Rev. 21:23).

We could not pass this way without noticing a tremendous coincidence, if you wish to speak of coincidence in the Scripture, in this phrase, "the powers of heaven be shaken." The word for Heaven in Greek is the same word (*ōuranos*) from which we get our word "uranium." The word for power is *dunamis,* explosive power, from which we get "dynamite." And the word which is used for "shaken" in the Greek means "to be set off balance." Very literally, then, the Greek could be translated to read, "the explosive force of uranium shall be set off balance." I am willing to regard this as coincidence, but it must be recorded as a coincidence that is so striking that it must be considered in the evidence when we discuss the prophecies of the Word of God. How wonderful for us who are believers to know that God is on the throne, that no weapon that is formed against us shall prosper, that God will always take care of His own, and that He knows how to deliver the godly out of testing.

CHAPTER 9

Verses 8:13–9:12

The Irruption of Demons

[13] And I saw, and I heard one eagle flying in midheaven, saying with a great voice, Woe, woe, woe, to them dwelling on the earth, from out of the other voices of the trumpet of the three messengers which are about to sound.

[1] And the fifth messenger sounded, and I saw a star from the heavens, fallen to the earth, and to him was given the key to the pit of the abyss. [2] And he opened the pit of the abyss, and there arose a smoke out of the pit, like the smoke of a great furnace, and the sun and the air were darkened from the smoke of the pit.

[3] And from out of the smoke locusts went into the earth, and unto them was given authority, as the scorpions of the earth have authority. [4] And it was said to them that they should not hurt the grass of the earth, nor any green thing, nor any tree, but only the very men who have not the seal of God upon their foreheads. [5] And it was given to them that they should not kill them, but that they should be tortured five months; and their torture was as the torture of a scorpion when it strikes a man. [6] And in those days shall men seek death, and in no wise shall find it; and they shall desire to die, and death fleeth from them.

[7] And the likenesses of the locusts were like unto horses prepared unto battle; and upon their heads as it were crowns like unto gold; and their faces as the faces of men; [8] and they had hair as the hair of women; and their teeth were as those of lions. [9] And they had breastplates like breastplates of iron; and the sound of their wings as the sound of chariots, of many horses rushing to war. [10] And they have tails like scorpions; and there were stings; and their authority was in their tails to hurt men five months. [11] They have a king over them, the messenger of the abyss; whose name in Hebrew is Abaddon, but in the Greek he has the name, Apollyon.

[12] The one woe is past; behold, there come yet two woes after these. (Rev. 8:13; 9:1-12, Free Translation)

The book of Revelation describes wrath of two different kinds, that which comes from God Himself and that which comes from the devil.

The closing verse of the eighth chapter belongs properly to the passage that is before us and is the introduction to the most horrible scene we have yet encountered in our study of the Apocalypse, since it describes a plague in which God for His purposes, increases the forces of the devil on earth.

An eagle, not an angel, is seen flying in the midst of the heavens announcing three woes upon the inhabitants of the earth. The three woes are for the trumpet judgments which are yet to come. It is the eagle who speaks (the English translation is quite an error), being the strongest of birds and sometimes a symbol of vengeance since it is a bird of prey. "For wheresoever the carcase is, there will the eagles be gathered together" (Matt. 24:28; cf. Rev. 19:17, 18).

And now the fifth messenger sounds the trumpet and the first woe begins. A star is seen that has fallen to the earth. In the last chapter we saw it in the course of its falling. The result was the bitterness of wormwood. We now see it fallen to the earth. One commentator sees this star as one of lesser dignity than the one which fell from Heaven at the third trumpet. May it not be merely that the great star has lost much of his power and is now a fallen star? It is none other than Satan himself and we shall see the details of this coming to earth in the twelfth chapter. This is prophesied by Isaiah (14:12) and by the Lord Himself (Luke 10:18). That Satan still has access to Heaven and that his fall is still future is certain from the general teaching of the whole of the Word of God.

A key is given to this fallen one to unlock what is called in the common translation, "the bottomless pit," but which is literally "the pit of the abyss."

Reference to the abyss is found nine times in the New Testament and more than thirty times in the Septuagint. A careful study of all the passages shows very clearly that the abyss is a place in which are to be found restrained, certain beings which have come under the judgment of God. This prison house is described in II Peter 2:4 in a passage which should be translated, "If God spared not angels when they sinned, but cast them down to Tartarus, and committed them to pits of darkness, to be reserved unto judgment . . ." A. T. Robertson, one of the greatest Greek authorities of the past generation, is the source of the statement that the word which is translated in the King James Version, "chains of darkness," should be "pits." Jude also speaks of fallen angels in like terms as "angels which kept not their first estate, but left their own habitation, he hath reserved [them] in everlasting bonds under darkness unto the judgment of the great day" (Jude 6).

Tartarus would seem to be more terrible than Hades. It is interesting to note that Homer (Iliad 8, 16) uses the word to describe "the dark and doleful abode of the wicked," as far beneath Hades as earth is below Heaven.

All of this throws great light on a passage in the Gospel of Luke and on this passage. When Christ went into the country of the Gadarenes, He met a certain man who had the legion of demons who besought the Lord "that he would not command them to go out into the abyss" (Luke 8:31). These demons preferred to be incarnate in swine, so deep was their horror and dread of the abyss to which some of their fellows were already confined.

All of these passages taken together reveal very clearly that "the pit of the abyss" to which Satan is given the key, harbors some of the most terrible of the fallen creatures which followed Lucifer in his rebellion. In the story (not parable) of the rich man and Lazarus, Hades was the abode of the spirits of all of the dead, both righteous and unrighteous. The two compartments were separated by "a great gulf" (Luke 16:26). Does this not contain an indication that there is indeed lower than the abode of the lost souls, a pit of darkness to which fallen angelic creatures are committed? In further chapters of the book of Revelation we shall see the one that is called "the beast," ascending out of the pit of the abyss (Rev. 20:1, 3). Isaiah further speaks of the punishment that shall come upon the angelic host. "The Lord shall punish the host of the high ones that are on high [that is, Satan's hosts], and the kings of the earth upon the earth. [For this earth is to be terribly judged, but God never forgets that behind the wicked of this earth there are the wicked of the angelic hosts.] And they shall be gathered together, as prisoners are gathered in the pit, and shall be shut up in the prison, and after many days shall they be visited" (Isa. 24:21, 22).

How frightful then to contemplate the horror that shall come upon the world at the opening of the door of this prison house of fallen angels. The smoke of the great furnace comes out of the pit of the abyss, darkening the sun and the air, reminding us of the destruction of Sodom and Gomorrah (Gen. 19:28), where we read of the smoke of a furnace in judgment, and reminding us of the giving of the law on Sinai, where we read of the smoke of a furnace in connection with the righteous holiness of the Lord in the giving of the law (Exod. 19:18).

Out of this smoke come the most vicious of Satan's hosts. They are as locusts to cover the earth. We know that when the swarms came in the plague in Egypt, every green thing was devoured by them (Exod. 10:15). The star of wormwood was bad enough in its bitterness; the smoke blinding and confusing, and symbolizing a smothered fire that will yet break forth in judgment was even worse. The demon forces that come out of the smoke are even incalculably worse. "A day of darkness and gloominess, a day of clouds and of thick darkness, as the morning spread upon the mountains; a great people and a strong; there hath not been ever the like, neither shall be any more after it, even to the years of many generations" (Joel 2:2). This same prophet describes the armies which were to come upon Israel as locusts and we read, "The appearance of them is as the appearance of horses" (Joel 2:4). This may indicate a military invasion, hordes that would come upon the land with utter ruthlessness because of the Satanic power which energized the army. This, of course, would be in keeping with the rest of the Word of God for we are told of the spiritual hosts of wickedness in the Heavenly places who are the rulers of the darkness of this world (Eph. 6:12).

These demon powers have authority upon the earth even as scorpions. A concordance may give us a double reference here. Rehoboam followed the counsel of his younger advisers and said, "My father did lade you with a heavy yoke, I will add to your yoke: my father also chastised you with whips, but I will chastise you with scorpions" (I Kings 12:11). In this case according to some authorities, the scorpion was a knotted whip worse than an ordinary lash. Others believe it indicated a punishment marked for its great cruelty. Our verse may speak then of the cruelty of the attack of the Satanic hosts. We shall see further a comparison between these demons and the insect itself.

The horror of this judgment is that torture comes to the demon-driven men but they are not able to end the torment. The enemy does not have power to kill the victims but during a space of five months the violence of the pain and madness is upon them without surcease.

In those days men will seek death and in no wise will find it; they will desire to die and death will flee from them. When Job was first stricken with the sore boils that came from Satan, his wife asked him to curse God and die; but while he cursed the day he was born, he was willing to accept evil, when God permitted it, as well as the good which he had so often received from God. He wished for death but he did nothing to bring it upon himself. In his great misery Job cried that in death, "The wicked cease from troubling; and there the weary be at rest. There the prisoners rest together; they hear not the voice of the oppressor. The small and great are there; and the servant is free from his master" (Job 3:17-19). He went on to wonder why light was given to those that were in misery and life to those who were bitter in soul and who longed for death when it did not come and who dug for it more than for hidden treasures, who rejoiced exceedingly, and were glad, when they found the grave. But though Job found life bitter, he was not willing to speak against God nor in any way seek to take his own life. Here in the book of Revelation the case is quite different. These men seek death. We have all read stories of people who have attempted suicide and have been rescued from their attempt only to be quite happy that they had failed since life, after all, was desirable. There will be no such joy here when death escapes one, so great is the driving torment of these demon-possessed ones. It would seem from the sixth verse that there is an intimation of suicide attempts which are frustrated by God.

The account now turns to a description of the demon forms, and in the language there is a hint of a spiritual meaning which must not be overlooked. One commentator has said, "In the description of the locusts certain moral features are probably delineated. Resistless fury and show of power would seem to be indicated in the war horses and the crowns, the appearance of boldness and independence along with real weakness and subjection in faces of men with the hair of women; destructive violence in the teeth of lions, and a conscience steeled against pity and remorse in the breastplates of iron; while their progress causes a mighty commotion like war chariots hastening to battle. These may well be biblical sentences which describe the ruthless advance of troops from an atheistic land like Russia, for men can become terrible beasts when they are not restrained by any thought of God. Another commentator says of this passage in the book of Revelation, "The horse-like appearance would show the active energy of battle against the truth and against Christ, the crown, the rewards given them, the glorying in this falsehood of those who never crowned Christ, though they may have sung, 'Crown Him Lord of All.' Their faces, like men, would suggest intelligence and humanity and mercy, as sure as the movements of that day will assume the humanitarian methods. The hair gives an idea of glory. Mary, as a picture of God's own people, used her hair to wipe the feet of Christ, laying her glory there, a true type of the Church of God; here it is borne for themselves. Their teeth . . . tearing and threatening, show the persecution of the Jewish people . . . The whole judgment is described as the rapid spread of falsehood for truth."

As we look through the concordance to find the symbolism of various words, one of the most interesting details appears in connection with the phrase which describes the sting in the tail of the scorpion. What follows becomes even more important if we follow the revised versions of the tenth verse, "And they have tails like scorpions, and stings; and in their tails is their power to hurt men five months." In one of the great judgment passages of Isaiah the Lord announces that He "will cut off from Israel head and tail . . ." and then explains "the ancient and honorable, he is the head; and the prophet that teacheth lies, he is the tail" (Isa. 9:14, 15). Here is an interesting comparison. The ancient and honorable, or as it is in one version, the elders and the magistrates, are the leaders. They will be cut off because they have caused the people to err. In addition, the false prophet teaching lies is called the tail. False doctrine is like the sting of the scorpion. First it poisons, but it leads ultimately to madness. This horde of demons out of the pit lays hold on the part of Israel which is not sealed with the name of God and devastates it like locusts which turn a fruitful field into a desert, and stings the heart and the conscience with scorpion-like anguish.

This plague lasts for an exact period of five months. One phase of wrath will give way to another as every phase of human life will come under the judgment of God during these awful years. Men flee from one plague only to find themselves in a worse. "The day of the Lord is darkness, and not light. As if a man did flee from a lion, and a bear met him; or went into the house, and leaned his hand on the wall, and a serpent bit him" (Amos 5:18, 19).

Is not this all a fulfillment of the prophecy made by the Lord Jesus? "When the unclean spirit is gone out of a man, he walketh through dry places, seeking rest, and findeth none. Then he saith, I will return into my house from whence I came out; and when he is come, he findeth it empty, swept, and garnished. Then goeth he, and taketh with himself seven other spirits more wicked than himself, and they enter in and dwell there: and the last state of that man is worse than the first. Even so shall it be also unto this wicked generation" (Matt. 12:43-45). Thus the locust swarm of Satanic power brings Israel to a state of strong delusion where they are driven on from lie to lie, coming eventually to a state of final judgment from God.

Some commentators have tried to place this scene in past history and have said that these locust armies were the Saracens. This cannot be, however, because the day of the Lord did not follow.

Nor, in this plague can they be literal locusts, as some have tried to claim. That this is not a literal picture is certain from the verse that now follows. These locusts which came out of smoke "have over them a king, the messenger of the abyss." Our Lord takes particular pains to tell us "The locusts have no king" (Prov. 30:27).

The king of these locusts is named in both Hebrew and Greek. The name that God gives to him is Abaddon or Apollyon. The word, *Abaddon,* is not to be found in the English translation elsewhere in the Bible but the Hebrew word itself occurs six times. Speaking of God, Job says, "Hell is naked before him, and Abaddon hath no covering" (26:6). Job says, "Abaddon and death say, We have heard the fame thereof with our ears" (28:22). A third time Job uses this word, on this occasion, speaking of the effects of adultery, "For it is a fire that consumeth to Abaddon, and would root out all mine increase" (31:12). David uses it once in the sense of the abyss. "Shall thy lovingkindness be declared in the grave? or thy faithfulness in Abaddon?" (Ps. 88:11). Finally the word is to be found twice in Proverbs. "Hell and Abaddon are before the Lord. . . ." (15:11). "Hell and Abaddon are never full" (27:20). In all six cases in the

King James Version this word is translated "destruction." John gives the Greek translation, *Apollyon,* a participle of the verb, "to destroy." Since it is used here as a name, it is "Destroyer." Men have made foolish attempts to identify this king.

In it, of course, is one of the titles of Satan of which there are so many in the Bible. We are reminded of the two passages in Matthew's Gospel where the Lord Himself speaks of the prince of the demons or rather where He comments on the Pharisee's use of the name, Beelzebub, whom they call the prince of the demons. The commentators have made many conjectures as to the meaning of this name. Whether it be "the lord of a dwelling" with a pun on "the master of the house" (Matt. 10:25) or whether it means "lord of lies," we do not know. The Lord said, commenting on the Pharisees' thought, "If Satan cast out Satan, he is divided against himself" (Matt. 12:26), thus linking the name of the one they called prince of demons to Satan himself.

How well the believer may rejoice that we stand "in Christ" and that there we are beyond the reach of his attacks. So it will be with the sealed ones of that future day. Satan's locust hordes may not touch those who have the seal of God upon them.

As though to prepare us gradually for the greater horrors that are yet to come, the Spirit completes the vision of the fifth trumpet judgment and points off to the future. "The woe is past; behold there come yet two woes after these."

Verses 13–21

The Euphrates Angels

¹³And the sixth messenger sounded, and I heard one voice from the horns of the golden altar which is before God, ¹⁴saying to the sixth messenger which had the trumpet, Loose the four messengers which are bound at the great river, Euphrates, ¹⁵And the four messengers were loosed, which had been made ready for the hour and day, and month and year, in order that they should kill the third part of men.

¹⁶And the number of the armies of the horsemen was twice ten thousand times ten thousand [or, twice myriads of myriads], I heard the number of them. ¹⁷And thus I saw the horses in the vision, and them that sat upon them, having breastplates of fire, and of hyacinth, and of brimstone; and the heads of the horses are as the heads of lions; and out of their mouths go forth fire and smoke and brimstone. ¹⁸By these three plagues was the third part of men killed, by the fire, and the smoke, and the brimstone, which is going forth out of their mouths, ¹⁹for the authority of the horses is in their mouth, and in their tails, for their tails are like serpents, having heads, and with them they do harm.

²⁰*And the rest of the men, who were not killed with these plagues did not repent of the works of their hands, that they should not worship demons, and the idols of gold, and of silver, and of brass, and of stone, and of wood; which are neither able to see, nor to hear, nor to walk;* ²¹*and they did not repent of their murders, nor of their sorceries, nor of their fornication, nor of their thefts.*
(Rev. 9:13-21, Free Translation)

To the sounding of the sixth trumpet is added a voice which comes from the golden altar which stands in the Presence of God. It is unspeakably solemn that the great judgments which come up on the earth in the last days are directly linked with the atonement that God has made for sin.

The abomination of desolation spoken of by Daniel the prophet (Dan. 9:27; Matt. 24:15) has already taken place at this period. The altar on earth has been desecrated; the sacrifice and the offerings have been made to cease; the naked altar in Heaven cries out for judgment; the desecration must be avenged; Antichrist must reap the fruit of his rashness and his rebellion. The golden altar was the altar of incense. Upon it every evening and every morning the priest burned sweet incense. Of the golden altar it was also written, "And Aaron shall make an atonement upon the horns of it once in a year with the blood of the sin offering of atonements; once in the year shall he make atonement upon it throughout your generations: it is most holy unto the Lord" (Exod. 30:10). The man of God in the time of Jeroboam's apostasy "cried out against the [false] altar in the word of the Lord, and said, O altar, altar, thus saith the Lord; Behold, a child shall be born unto the house of David, Josiah by name; and upon thee shall he offer the priests of the high places that burn incense upon thee, and men's bones shall be burnt upon thee. And he gave a sign the same day, saying, This is the sign which the Lord hath spoken; Behold, the altar shall be rent, and the ashes that are upon it shall be poured out" (I Kings 13:2, 3). The apostasy that will come under the Antichrist has already occurred at this point, and it has desecrated the altar. And it is from the horns where the blood was wont to be applied that a cry goes forth to God for vengeance.

The horns of the altar of incense had been touched with blood by the high priest and thus cried out to God for mercy for His people. Now these selfsame horns cry out to God for judgment upon those who had so thoroughly offended. When sin cries out to God for punishment it is a most solemn matter, but when the altar, the only place where sin could find forgiveness, and the horns of the altar which received the touch of the blood which bled for the sinner, unite in crying to God for judgment the climax of vengeance has been reached. "He that despised Moses' law died without mercy under two or three witnesses: of how much sorer punishment, suppose ye, shall he be thought worthy, who hath trodden under foot the Son of God, and hath counted the blood of the covenant, wherewith he was sanctified, an unholy thing, and hath done despite unto the Spirit of grace?" (Heb. 10:28, 29). That "much sorer punishment" is now to be meted out.

The cry that has come from the horns of the altar is "Loose the four messengers which are bound in the great river, Euphrates." The river Euphrates must be considered in three ways. First, it was the situation of the ancient Babylon. Second, it was the frontier of the promised land (Gen. 15:18; Deut. 1:7; 11:24; Josh. 1:4). Third, the Euphrates was the boundary of the old Roman Empire which is to be restored under the rule of the Antichrist.

The river, however, is of greatest importance in the fact that it is a double frontier, that of the land promised to Israel and that of the empire of the Antichrist. Satan's kingdom is to be divided against itself and therefore it shall not stand. The Euphrates is a most significant border of this division in Satan's kingdom.

Very definitely it is shown that God has placed at this barrier four great messengers, supernatural powers, to forbid the passing of evil forces from the east to the west. At this period in the future these barriers are removed and an innumerable company of horsemen is now released and pours toward the land of promise. There are two ways in which this passage can be taken, literally or figuratively, or rather naturally or supernaturally. Are these forces which come from beyond the Euphrates armies of men or are they demon forces?

Once before the Lord stirred up the spirits of a great leader to come from the east upon His people. "Thus saith Cyrus king of Persia, All the kingdoms of the earth hath the Lord God of heaven given me; and he hath charged me to build him an house in Jerusalem, which is in Judah" (II Chron. 36:23; Ezra 1:2). The Lord further said of Cyrus, "He is my shepherd, he shall perform all my pleasure" (Isa. 44:28). Yet again, "Thus saith the Lord to his anointed, to Cyrus, whose right hand I have holden, to subdue nations before him, and I will loose the loins of kings, to open before him the two leaved gates [of Babylon]; and the gates shall not be shut" (Isa. 45:1). Here is abundant proof that God led one great leader from beyond the Euphrates, broke the power of Babylon before him and subdued the nations to bring them under his will. The question arises: Was he a type of yet another force that shall come from beyond the Euphrates? Is there another who is to be thus led as an instrument of judgment in the hand of God?

Many passages in the Old Testament prophets speak of the invasion of Palestine in the last days by the great forces from the north. Ezekiel devotes two chapters (38, 39) to a description of the great invasion of the armies of the north in the last days.

The fact that John adds to his statement, "I heard the number of them," would increase the possibility that it is an exact number. If this vision is material and literal, it is the picture of the innumerable hordes of the north and east forced ever onward by the supernatural power which directs this judgment. The angels who are directing the movement are said to have been prepared for the hour and day and month and year. History is in the hand of God and runs in the channels that have been dug for it. The result is the death of one-third of mankind. This does not seem at all incredible with two hundred million men on the march. How many millions of them must fall by the wayside in addition to those that fall before them? Of the army that comes down from the north it is said, "Thou shalt ascend and come like a storm, thou shalt be like a cloud to cover the land" (Ezek. 38:9). Of this army it is also said, "The chariots shall be with flaming torches in the day of his preparation . . . The chariots shall rage in the streets, they shall justle one against another in the broad ways: they shall seem like torches, they shall run like lightnings" (Nah. 2:3, 4).

The three words used in verse 17 translated fire, hyacinth and brimstone are found in no other place in the New Testament. The first of the words is used by Aristotle and Polybius in the sense of flaming or firing. Hyacinth is a translation of a word that is rendered by various authorities as "red color bordering on black" (Thayer), "violet or dark blue" (Bailly), while ancient writers described it as "purple and iron colored" (cit. in Liddell and Scott). In the last half of this same verse and in the following verse three plagues are further described as fire, smoke and brimstone. Each of these words is different from the three used in the description of the breastplate. Coming from the mouths of the mounts are three things described by the common words for fire, smoke and brimstone. The word which is translated brimstone in the first instance, however, is to be found only in this verse. It is the common word in the Greek classics for "sulphur."

We are told that the third part of men were killed by the fire and smoke and the brimstone which issued from the mouths of the chargers upon which the army advanced.

If the main body of this passage is to be taken as referring to the supernatural, we can advance to the explanation with firmer tread. We have had frequent occasion to speak of the principalities which are under the leadership of Satan. These malicious forces, though led by Satan are under the restraining order of God.

If this vision in Revelation is of demon forces, there is no difficulty whatsoever in understanding the vast number. If a legion of demons could possess one man, and a Roman legion counted 6,000 men, then two hundred million might be but a small part of what the Holy Spirit calls "the spiritual hosts of wickedness in the heavenly places" (Eph. 6:12, RSV). It might be well to point out also that so far as Asia is concerned, demon religions are all east of the Euphrates. India is said

to have thirty-three million gods and we are told in the Bible that "all
the gods of the heathen are demons" (Ps. 96:5—LXX).

These myriads of horsemen seen in the present vision wounding by
"fire and smoke and brimstone" can easily represent demon hosts
which will move into the Holy Land with all restraint removed in
the days of the Antichrist. Naturally they would bring with them all
of the lasciviousness and corruption which brought the judgment of
God upon Sodom and which will bring once more the judgment of God
upon this earth. The reference to the poisoned tails "like unto serpents" has already been discussed under the fifth trumpet.

The closing verses of this chapter give us a woeful picture of the
heart of man, in its bitter hardness against God. Here is a picture of
the moral life of mankind into which the nations are already drifting.
It is to be noted in the first place that the great ills which were brought
upon mankind so that one-third of humanity dies has no effect upon
the rest. There is no evidence in the Bible; there is no evidence in
history; and now there is no evidence in prophecy which would indicate that men have ever been brought to God in great numbers through
tribulation. One-third of the race may die, but the other two-thirds
do not for that reason move toward God. Reluctantly we are forced
to accept the verdict, "There is none that understandeth, there is none
that seeketh after God" (Rom. 3:11).

The fact that this tribulation does not cause men to repent of the
works of their hands, gives us a picture of those works which are cata-
logued for us. We have been told in the Word of God that "evil men
and seducers shall wax worse and worse, deceiving, and being deceived" (II Tim. 3:13). In that same chapter the apostle emphasizes
the perilous times which will come in the last days.

Here in these verses, Revelation 9:20, 21, we are able to see the state
of society in the days of the Antichrist. It is to be noted first that
demon worship is rampant. Those who remain do not repent of their
demon worship, and they worship idols of gold and silver and brass
and stone and of wood which neither can see nor hear nor walk. The
fact that they refuse to repent, proves that they were doing it. With
the world worshiping demons and idols which, we have already seen,
are but the earthly front for demons, we can readily see that the state
of affairs, such as is described here, is the outcome of some of the
tendencies that are already visible in our day. During the last century
there has been a tremendous advance in what is called "spiritual" but
which is really spiritism or demonism. All this is to increase (until)
after the believers have been removed at the rapture of the Church.
It will be the predominating state of affairs after all believers have
been taken from the earth.

Works always follow doctrine and are developed from it. A man
becomes what he believes. Those who were false in creed, are false in

character. The men of these tribulations who worship demons or idols are seen to be guilty of the most terrible crimes. The bad state of the society of that day is seen by the pit into which the population sinks after the judgment of the sixth trumpet has passed. They did not repent of "their murders, nor of their sorceries, nor of their fornication, nor of their thefts." These four crimes are not repented of and even in our day they are looked upon far too lightly. Hearts become harder, human life is cheaper, public opinion makes no outcry even in the face of an ever-growing murder record.

The word which is translated sorceries is in the original, *pharmakeia,* and is the Greek word from which we get our English derivative, pharmacy. It comes from the root meaning drugs and this particular form has to do with the use or the administration of drugs. In a secondary sense it refers to poisoning, while the use of drugs as magic preparations by sorcerers gave the further idea of sorcery. The word in our present text cannot refer to poisoning which would be included in murders. It would appear that it must be limited to the use of drugs, most probably not in connection with magic or incantation but more likely to a craving, habit-forming addiction which destroys the will of its victims. I believe that the Bible teaches that drug addiction will indeed become very wide spread.

The list of crimes continues with an indictment of their lasciviousness. This has been one of the common sins of all ages. God has warned us of His hatred of all such uncleanness and though He now judges the world, it does not repent. We see the fulfillment of another passage of Scripture which describes men as "knowing the judgment of God, that they which commit such things are worthy of death, not only do the same, but have pleasure in them that do them" (Rom. 1:32). All that the world has known in the past of such lasciviousness is nothing in comparison to that which shall be in the future. We are living in the days of the increase of immoral tendencies. The invention of methods to cheat nature of the consequences of sin has given to man a false sense of security. Though the judgment of God sweeps over the earth because of sin, man does not repent.

The last crime in this category is that of theft. This is "the statement of general and abounding dishonesty, the obliteration of moral distinctions, the disregard of others' rights, and the practice of fraud, theft, and deceit wherever it is possible." In our day corruption in high places gives the example to all classes. The only wrong consists in getting caught. It has been written "let no man deceive you with vain words: for because of these things cometh the wrath of God upon the children of disobedience" (Eph. 5:6).

It is into a world such as we have just described that the messenger of God releases the judgment of the sixth trumpet. There is no repentance. Still further judgment will therefore follow.

CHAPTER 10

Verses 1–7

The End of God's Patience

¹*And I saw another mighty messenger coming down out of Heaven, arrayed with a cloud; and the rainbow upon his head, and his face as the sun, and his feet as pillars of fire;* ²*and having in his hand a little scroll open; he set his right foot upon the sea, and his left upon the earth;* ³*and he cried with a great voice, even as when a lion roars. And when he cried, the seven thunders spake their voices.*

⁴*And when the seven thunders had spoken, I was about to write; and I heard a voice from out of Heaven saying, Seal up at once those things which the seven thunders spake and write them not.*

⁵*And the messenger which I saw standing upon the sea and upon the earth lifted up his right hand toward Heaven,* ⁶*and sware by Him that liveth to the ages of the ages, Who created the Heaven and the things that therein are, and the earth, and the things that therein are, and the sea, and the things that therein are, that there shall be no more delay.* ⁷*But in the days of the voice of the seventh messenger, when he is about to sound, then is finished the mystery of God, according to the good tidings which he declared to his bondservants, the prophets.* (Rev. 10:1-7, Free Translation)

After the sixth trumpet, there is another parenthesis. The events recorded in Chapter 10 take place between the sounding of the sixth and seventh trumpet.

We have pointed out at various times that the word that appears in our King James Version as "angel" is the ordinary Greek word for messenger. We have kept to that word because we have believed that in some appearances in the book of Revelation, Christ Himself appears as a messenger. To call Him an angel would be the deepest error. Angels are created beings. The Lord Jesus is the creator of the angelic beings. There is no reason, however, that He cannot act in the capacity of a messenger as He already has acted in the capacity of a servant. There are commentators who believe that the "mighty messenger" who now appears is none other than the Lord Jesus Christ, and I so hold.

179

Another commentator says that the oath taken in verse 6 proves that this angel is not Christ. This latter objection may be dismissed by pointing out, for example that when God made a promise to Abraham, "because he could sware by no greater, he sware by himself" (Heb. 6:13). In all this matter "God, willing more abundantly to shew unto the heirs of promise the immutability of his counsel, confirmed it by an oath: so that by two immutable things, in which it was impossible for God to lie, we might have a strong consolation, who have fled for refuge to lay hold upon the hope set before us" (Heb. 6:17, 18). There can therefore be no objection to the identification of this messenger as Christ because of the fact that an oath is taken in the name of "him who liveth to the ages of the ages, who created the heaven and the things that therein are, and the earth, and the things that therein are, and the sea, and the things that therein are."

It is probably safest to say that we cannot be sure whether this mighty messenger is Christ or only an angelic being of high and exalted rank similar to that of the archangel or of the cherubim or seraphim. However, this is the third appearance of a messenger who has acted in a character quite different from that of the ordinary messengers who performed the work of judgment. The first appearance of this special messenger is in chapter 7, verse 2, where he holds back the sweeping judgments that are about to fall while God performs a special work of grace. Again in chapter 8, verse 5, he stands as the messenger of the covenant, pouring out the fire of judgment upon the earth. It should be noted that in the first instance, this messenger acts as prophet. In the second instance, he acts as priest. In this passage he acts as king. We are inclined to believe that no mere creature would be used of God in such high offices. Only the Lord Jesus Christ and those who have been redeemed by His death upon the cross can ever enter these sacred offices.

This identification is further enhanced by the details which follow. The mighty messenger comes forth from Heaven clothed with a cloud. This is the Lord's dwelling place in judgment. "Clouds and darkness are round about him: righteousness and judgment are the habitation of his throne" (Ps. 97:2). The cloud, of course, does not mean a rain cloud, but it is a reference to that which is called a cloud, for its appearance is such that a cloud is the nearest thing to it that we have in our vocabulary for identification.

This mighty one possesses another symbol of deity. The rainbow which was last seen around the throne of God (4:3) here encircles the head of the mighty messenger. We have already given its meaning in full and it is sufficient to state that it is a mark of God's faithfulness and the remembrance of His covenant promise. There is to be joy after the great storm breaks, so there is a rainbow.

His face was like the sun. What a symbol is to be found in this glorious word! One day I traveled by airplane between two cities. As we took off from the first airport, the sky was dark and lowering, there was a ceiling of about five hundred feet. Our plane rose rapidly and soon we pierced the clouds. For several minutes we were surrounded by a dark grey mist and could not even see the tips of our wings. A few moments later, however, the mist turned white and soon we sailed out above a sea of clouds where the sun was shining in splendor in a gorgeous blue sky that knew no clouds except those which billowed beneath us. So it is with our Lord Jesus Christ. If sinful earth is to know the dark clouds of judgment, Heaven can always see Him in His authority as the One to whom all power in Heaven and in earth has been committed. Earth does not see Him in that way as yet, though the believers on the earth can still look through this cloud by faith and see Him in His eternal glory.

Although His face was like the sun, His feet were as pillars of fire. When they are revealed beneath the clouds of judgment, the earth will know its darkest hour. "His feet shall stand in that day upon the mount of Olives . . . and the mount of Olives shall cleave in the midst thereof toward the east and toward the west, and there shall be a very great valley; and half of the mountain shall remove toward the north, and half of it toward the south. And ye shall flee to the valley of the mountains . . . ye shall flee like as ye fled from before the earthquake in the days of Uzziah, King of Judah: and the Lord my God shall come, and all the saints with thee. And it shall come to pass in that day, that the light shall not be clear, nor dark; But it shall be one day which shall be known to the Lord, not day, nor night: but it shall come to pass, that at evening time it shall be light" (Zech. 14:4-7). The day in which this mighty messenger speaks is not the day that Zechariah describes but symbolically it is seen in Heaven, the cloud of judgment with the feet of fire upon the earth and the glory of eternal authority in Heaven with the rainbow promise that God will never forget His own.

The messenger holds in his hands a small scroll that is unrolled. Commentators differ widely as to the significance of this scroll. We believe that we can best discover its meaning by the result of its presentation. The mighty messenger, whom we have almost certainly identified as the Lord, comes forth indeed for judgment. The sea and the land are well known Scriptural symbols for the Gentile nations and Israel. These feet as pillars of fire, the Scriptural symbol of judgment, come now upon Jew and Gentile alike.

The gospel of Christ "is the power of God unto salvation to everyone that believes; to the Jew first, and also to the Greek" (Rom. 1:16). We must not forget that God has also said, "Indignation and wrath, tribulation and anguish, upon every soul of man that doeth evil, of the Jew first, and also of the Gentile" (Rom. 2:8, 9). With God there is no such thing as a difference between race, religion or men. The little scroll, we believe, contains the record of that which God is going to perform against those who have been contentious and who after a hard and impenitent heart have treasured up unto themselves wrath against the day of wrath and revelation of the righteous judgment of God (Rom. 2:5).

A cry is now heard, for the mighty messenger "cried with a loud voice, as when a lion roareth." In the book of the Proverbs Solomon tells us that "the king's wrath is as the roaring of a lion" (19:12). Joel, describing the great and terrible day of the Lord, says, "The Lord also shall roar out of Zion, and utter his voice from Jerusalem; and the heavens and the earth shall shake; but the Lord will be the hope of his people, and the strength of the children of Israel" (Joel 3:16). The terrible moment has come when the Lord Jesus Christ will pray for the world. That may seem an astonishing statement, but nevertheless, it says that one day He will pray for the world that it might be judged. "We know that we are of God, and the whole world is in the power of the evil one" (I John 5:19, RSV). There is no record that our Lord ever prayed for this world in its evil state. There is a positive statement that He refused to pray for the world. The night that He was betrayed we have the true Lord's prayer. Talking with the Father in what in many ways is the holiest chapter of the Bible, He said, "I have manifested thy name unto the men which thou gavest me out of the world: thine they were, and thou gavest them me; and they have kept thy word . . . I pray for them: I pray not for the world, but for them which thou hast given me; for they are thine" (John 17:6, 9).

The Word of God tells us, however, that the day is to come when our Lord shall pray for the world, and a terrible moment it is, for His prayers are always answered. We forget in our thinking of Scriptural things that it is possible to pray for an enemy to be confounded as well as for a loved one to be blessed. Christ has prayed for us as we have just read in the record of His high priestly prayer. That prayer has been answered, and we can say, "Blessed be the God and Father of our Lord Jesus Christ, who hath blessed us with all spiritual blessings in heavenly places in Christ" (Eph. 1:3). But God has also promised Christ the answer to His prayer for the world, and a terrible answer it is.

In the second Psalm is the whole story. The nations have raged and the people have imagined a vain thing. The kings of the earth have set themselves, and the rulers have taken counsel together against the Lord Jehovah and against His Christ. But the Lord who sitteth in the Heavens shall laugh and shall have them in derision. Here we have the fulfillment of the psalm. "Then shall he speak unto them in his wrath, and vex them in his sore displeasure . . . Ask of me, and I shall give thee the nations for thine inheritance, and the uttermost parts of the earth for thy possession. Thou shalt break them with a rod of iron; thou shalt dash them to pieces like a potter's vessel" (Ps. 2:5, 8, 9). Here is the unprayed prayer of Christ. This is the future Lord's prayer. The patient Saviour has looked out over this world for ages. He has seen His love despised and His sacrifice trodden under foot. He has seen men exalting self and refusing to worship the Father. But, the day will come when, rising as the sun in His strength and with feet as judgment fire, He will come forth to receive the answer to His prayer.

Seven thunders are now heard. What do they represent? John saw something and was about to write down what he saw when a voice from Heaven said to him, "Seal up those things which the seven thunders uttered, and write them not." Here is a definite commandment from God that no indication shall be given as to the correct interpretation of the seven thunders. In spite of this, however, some commentators have attempted to do that which God forbade John to do. It seems that the reverent student of the Word of God can do nothing but pass on to that which follows.

There is one Old Testament light upon the seven thunders. David sang prophetically, "The voice of the Lord is upon the waters: the God of glory thundereth: the Lord is upon many waters" (Ps. 29:3). Immediately there follows a series of seven effects of the sounding of the voice of the Lord. The word, "voice," is to be found six times and is understood in the context of the seventh effect of the voice. "The voice of the Lord is powerful: the voice of the Lord is full of majesty. The voice of the Lord breaketh the cedars . . . The voice of the Lord divideth the flames of fire. The voice of the Lord shaketh the wilderness . . . The voice of the Lord maketh the hinds to calve, and [the voice of the Lord] discovereth the forests . . ." (Ps. 29:4-9).

There is undoubtedly some connection between the Psalm and the seven thunders of John's vision. It is a revelation of both God's power and majesty. Trees are broken, judgment flames apportioned, the wilderness shaken, fear comes on even the animal world in the forest, and the forests are stripped bare. All that this means we are not even allowed to guess. John was ordered to seal up the utterances of the seven thunders. A great grammarian says that the verb here is in the tense of urgency. "Seal up at once." Paul saw glory in Heaven that was not lawful to utter (II Cor. 12:4). John sees judgment as the power and majesty of God in action. We bow with reverence before the seal and pass on.

The mighty messenger now lifts his hand to Heaven and swears a great oath. The oath is by the eternal Creator, Author of Heaven, earth and sea, and all they contain. Tradition has given an unfortunate interpretation to the words of the oath. The messenger sware "that there should be time no longer." Some have imagined that this was

God's way of announcing that what we call time was to come to an
end and that eternity, as something separate from time, was about to
begin. Of all the commentators Robinson puts it most neatly. "This
does not mean that *chronos,* time, Einstein's 'fourth dimension,' added
to length, breadth, height, will cease to exist, but only that there will
be no more delay in the fulfillment of the seventh trumpet."

The souls under the altar had cried out to God, "How long, O Lord,
holy and true, dost thou not judge and avenge our blood on them that
dwell on the earth?" (6:10). They had been told by the Lord "that
they should rest yet for a little season" (vs. 11). Now the Lord swears
that there shall be no more delay. An oath is taken by the Creator,
and when the seventh messenger sounds his trumpet, the mystery of
God will be finished.

Several things should be noted in connection with this seventh verse.
First, the voice of the seventh messenger is heard for some considerable time, "In the days of the voice." It is not a sharp piercing cry,
but a long drawn out judgment. Secondly, the completion of the mystery is to take place "when he is about to sound." Robertson translates this, "Whenever he is about to begin to sound." Thirdly, the
completion of the mystery is something that has been declared by God
through the prophets. The word translated "declared" is literally "evan-
gelized." The sentence might be translated, "As he has announced
the good news to his servants, the prophets."

All of this is easily understood if we think of the structure of the
judgments we have studied thus far. It is to be remembered that the
seven seal judgments came first. Terrible as they were it was found
on the opening of the seventh seal that it was in reality seven trumpets.
Now we are approaching the seventh trumpet. Is this seventh judgment expansion to go on forever? God announces that there is to be
no more delay. The seventh trumpet is about to be blown. It will be
seen indeed that many judgments crowd forth from it. In particular,
"seven messengers having the seven last plagues; for in them is filled
up the wrath of God" (15:1). When the seventh of these bowls of
wrath is poured out, God will speak saying, "It is done" (16:17).

Verses 7–11

Bitter Honey

*7But in the days of the voice of the seventh messenger, when he is
about to sound, then is finished the mystery of God, according to the
good tidings which He declared to His bond servants, the prophets.*

*8And the voice which I heard from out of Heaven, I heard again
speaking with me and saying, Go, take the book which is open in the
hand of the messenger which standeth upon the sea and the earth.*

⁹*And I went to the messenger, saying to him that he should give me the little scroll. And he sayeth to me, Take it and eat it up; it shall make thy belly bitter, but in thy mouth it shall be sweet as honey.* ¹⁰*And I took the little scroll from the hand of the messenger and ate it up and it was in my mouth sweet as honey; and as soon as I had eaten it, my belly was bitter.*

¹¹*And they say to me, Thou must prophesy again concerning many peoples, and nations, and tongues, and kings.*
(Rev. 10:7-11, Free Translation)

When our Lord Jesus Christ first spoke in parables, He was immediately questioned by His disciples concerning His reasons for the use of this method of teaching. In the course of the 13th chapter of Matthew we have His answer which, if properly understood, will help us with this passage of Scripture.

The first part of our Lord's reply was, "Because it is given unto you to know the mysteries of the kingdom of heaven, but to them it is not given" (Matt. 13:11). The question arises as to the meaning of these mysteries. Some have argued in their attempt to explain this portion of Christ's revelation that there is a difference between the kingdom of God and the kingdom of Heaven. Others have argued that there is no difference between the two terms. Whichever way that matter may be decided, the answer to the question concerning the mysteries of the kingdom is found within the same chapter. The further reason which our Lord gave for speaking in parables was "that it might be fulfilled which was spoken by the prophet, saying, I will open my mouth in parables; I will utter things which have been kept secret from the foundation of the world" (Matt. 13:35). Therefore, the Lord is speaking of something that has not happened before in human history.

A kingdom was described and prophesied throughout the Old Testament. It was a literal, earthly kingdom. The Messiah was to rule over it. Jerusalem was to be its capital. The Jews were to be its chief citizens and the instrument of its rule over the Gentile world. When our Lord Jesus began to speak in parables, however, He spoke of "the mysteries of the kingdom" the secret aspect of the kingdom and He took the trouble to add that He was talking about something that was absolutely new, something that had been kept secret before then. One of the most important rules of New Testament interpretation, therefore, is that the kingdom of which the Lord Jesus Christ spoke was either not the same kingdom of which the Old Testament prophets spoke or it was a phase or aspect of that kingdom unknown before His time. In order to avoid confusion, let us speak of it as the kingdom in its mystery form.

The Jews had their eyes so filled with the picture of the literal earthly kingdom that they rejected Jesus Christ because He did not fit into their idea of what they thought the kingdom ought to be. To certain disciples our Lord revealed that this aspect of the kingdom would be rejected, and that many things would come to pass before the mystery aspect of the kingdom would be finished and the real earthly kingdom should be set up in glory.

Again, in the eleventh chapter of Romans, the Holy Spirit speaks to us of the mystery and its application to the time of Israel's blindness. Here it is revealed that a space of time would intervene during which Israel would be blind to the things of the Lord. More than 1900 years have passed and this blindness is still upon Israel. It has been revealed, however, that this blindness is to have an end and that Israel shall see when "the fulness of the Gentiles be come in," at which time "all Israel [then living] shall be saved" (Rom. 11:25, 26). To Isaiah it had been revealed that such blindness would come upon Israel (Isa. 6:9, 10), but only through Paul was it revealed that God had a purpose for the Gentiles during the blindness of Israel. Therefore the fact that this parenthesis is opened makes it possible for Gentiles ultimately to be in Heaven. There would be no chance apart from that, but the mass of the unsaved would be reserved for the judgment of God. When would their judgment be full, however? Even this was not revealed to Paul and the answer is in this passage.

To the Corinthian Church another phase of the divine secret was revealed. They learned that not all believers should pass through death but that there would be one generation, living at the coming of the Lord Jesus Christ which would be transformed, receiving bodies like the Lord's without passing through death (I Cor. 15:51).

Throughout this interval of Israel's blindness and the divine outcalling of Gentile believers into a new body, where God would reign only in human hearts upon this earth, as He does today, there would be another aspect of the mystery hard to understand. Lawlessness or iniquity would begin to work, God tells us, and that lawlessness and iniquity has been working for the last two thousand years. Satan, the prince of this world, would begin to be revealed as the god of this age. This lawlessness will run concurrently with the other events that were prophesied to take place during our Lord's absence from the world (II Thess. 2:7).

The principal secret that was revealed as a New Testament "mystery," however, is that which is outlined in the book of Ephesians. Paul had written to the Romans that this mystery had been "kept secret since the world began, but now is made manifest" (Rom. 16: 25, 26). We must realize that there was great truth "which in other ages was not made known to the sons of men" (Eph. 3:5). You and I can know much more about truth than Abraham and Moses knew; "which from the beginning of the world has been hid in God" (Eph. 3:9); which "had been hid from ages and generations, but now is made manifest" (Col. 1:26). When we have realized this great fact we shall not only understand much that is in the epistles but we shall also be ready to have the key of the parables and of this section of the book of Revelation. In other words God worked from the time of Abraham to Christ with the Jews, and then He opened a parenthesis. For the last 1900 years He has been working with the Church, the Gentiles and Jews together as believers. When He finishes with this period, He will go back once more, and will work with the Jews. It is just as though there were a great clock running, its pendulum ticking off time, Jewish time, because in the Bible, time is only in connection with God's people the Jews. Then when Christ died, God just took hold of the pendulum and stopped the clock. Today, you and I are living in a parenthesis of grace when anybody can be saved, not merely a Jew as in the Old Testament, but we who were dogs of Gentiles by nature. But when Jesus comes in the Second Coming, God will take us out and touch the pendulum and Jewish time will start ticking again and everything of greatness that was prophesied for that people will yet come to pass.

One or two commentators have imagined that the mystery to which John refers is the Church alone and that, therefore, the Church is on earth until this point in the revelation narrative. That this idea is utterly erroneous will be evident to those who have followed closely the position of the earlier chapters of this book. Beyond any shadow of a doubt the Church is away from the earth by the opening of the fourth chapter of Revelation, for we know that the Church will meet the Lord in the air before the tribulation begins. Moreover, not all phases of the mysteries, as revealed in the New Testament, began in the same instant, nor do they all end in the same instant. In the verse which we have before us, God is still gathering out tribulation saints; God is still judging Israel; lawlessness is still at work. Here the final phase of all the mysteries is completed.

"But in the days of the voice of the seventh messenger, when he is about to sound, then is finished the mystery of God, according to the good tidings which he declared to his bond servants, the prophets." The Lord Jesus Christ is about to come forth from Heaven and complete all of the work which remains for Him to do, as Messiah of the Jews, Bridegroom of His chosen one, the Church, and Lord of creation. Now the mystery aspect of the kingdom will come to an end and the Lord will take His throne and reign upon the earth according to the prophecies of the Old Testament. Now the blindness of Israel will come to an end and the fullness of the Gentiles will come up for judgment before God. Now "the first resurrection" (Rev. 20:5) will be completed. Now the mystery of lawlessness will come to an end and righteousness will be enforced upon the earth. Now will come the end of the Church age and "all Israel [then living upon the earth] shall be saved" (Rom. 11:26).

God never begins anything that He does not finish. "When I begin, I will also make an end" (I Sam. 3:12), and we can trust Him for that. The climax of God's judgments and blessings is now reached. He announces it as "good tidings" and surely it is just that. For whether it be of blessings for those who are God's or whether judgment upon those who have resisted Him, it is wonderful to know that evil is about to be curbed and that righteousness is about to break forth and dominate. The prophets, who are spoken of here as God's servants, are not those of the Old Testament. This has been clearly seen by James Moffat in his commentary, *The Expositor's Greek Testament*. He says, "The near approach of the end has been for years a matter of confidence and joy to the Christian prophets—for it is they and not their predecessors who are especially in view."

John now heard the voice again, telling him to take the little book from the hand of the messenger which stands upon the sea and the earth. When the book was received, the messenger said to John, "Take it and eat it up; it shall make thy belly bitter, but in thy mouth it shall be sweet as honey." John obeyed and the result was exactly as indicated. John was not the first of God's servants called to do such a thing, for Ezekiel, hundreds of years before John, had been commanded to eat the roll of the book.

We will understand the symbol of the honey that became bitter to John if we study the incident in the life of Ezekiel. The Lord spoke to Ezekiel as follows: "And thou, son of man, be not afraid of them, neither be afraid of their words, though briers and thorns be with thee, and thou dost dwell among scorpions; be not afraid of their words, nor be dismayed at their looks, though they be a rebellious house. And thou shalt speak my words unto them, if they will hear them, or if they will not hear them; for they are most rebellious. But thou, son of man, hear what I say unto thee; be not thou a rebel like that family of rebels! Open thy mouth, and eat that which I shall give to thee. And I looked, behold, a hand was stretched out toward me; and, lo, a scroll of a book was held therein; and he spread it before me; and it was written within and without; and written therein lamentations, and mourning, and woe. Moreover, he said unto me; Son of man, eat that which thou hast found; eat this scroll and, go speak unto the house of Israel. So I opened my mouth, and he caused me to eat that scroll. And he said unto me, Son of man, feed thy belly and fill thy bowels with this scroll that I give thee. Then did I eat it; and it was in my mouth as sweet as honey (Ezek. 2:6–3:3, Free Translation).

A careful study of the context in Ezekiel shows that the prophet was immediately commissioned as a watchman who was to speak to Israel. This fact, of course, would be honey to the mouth of any prophet.

But as soon as the message is known, it is discovered to be one of

bitterness. Let us take a parallel. Say to a young girl who faces her
bridal day that you have the power to reveal to her the life that lies
before her. In all eagerness as something greatly desirable she turns
toward the course of her own life. She is to know her future, but suddenly everything turns to bitterness. She sees the sickness and death
of her loved one, poverty and loneliness, misery and pain. Immediately
her life is filled with bitterness at the anticipation of all that lies before
her.

Lange, the German commentator, has said truly, "Apocalyptic things
have a wondrous charm. To the honeylike sweetness of the little book
in the mouth, that enormous mass of literature testifies, which is engaged in the eating of it. But whosoever has, with some degree of
understanding, appropriated the little book, is greatly pained within him
by its startling perspectives and images. A termination is then put to
all idyllic conceptions of the future and the end of the world."

The world has long dreamed of a golden age that could come to the
earth by man's own working, but it was announced at the time of
Christ's first coming that He would one day lay the axe to the root
of a tree, that His fan of judgment would be controlled by His hand,
that His winds would thoroughly purge His floor, gathering His wheat
into the barn but burning up the chaff with unquenchable fire (Matt.
3:12). This is the future of the world. The world crucified Christ and
its princes will turn against Him when He comes, but He shall break
them with a rod of iron and dash His enemies to pieces as a potter's
vessel (Ps. 2:9). Ottman well says, "The solemn truth has been rejected by men of all generations and is rejected today. The prophets
that proclaimed it were hated. Stephen reviews the history of Israel,
and brings in the solemn indictment: "Ye stiffnecked and uncircumcised in heart and ears, ye do always resist the Holy Spirit: as your
fathers did, so do ye. Which of the prophets have not your fathers
persecuted? and they have slain them which shewed before of the
coming of the Just One; of whom ye have been now the betrayers and
murderers: Who have received the law by the disposition of angels, and
have not kept it' " (Acts 7:51-53).

"This refusal of prophetic testimony bears witness to the moral unity
of the nation throughout its history. Jesus, in His denunciation of the
Pharisees, charges them with the same crime committed by their fathers, 'Woe unto you, scribes and Pharisees, hypocrites; because ye
build the tombs of the prophets, and garnish the sepulchres of the
righteous. And say, if we had been in the days of our fathers, we
would not have been partakers with them in the blood of the prophets.
Wherefore ye be witnesses unto yourselves, that ye are the children of
them which killed the prophets. Fill ye up then the measure of your
fathers. Ye serpents, ye generation of vipers, how can ye escape the
damnation of hell?' That was Christ speaking (Matt. 23:29-33). He

that speaks here is no mere prophet. He is the Lord God of the prophets, and that generation, as the fathers had rejected the prophets before Him, filled up the measure of iniquity by rejecting Him. But this rejection only thickened the gloom that hung over their future, alongside the prophecies of the past, he placed still another, 'Behold, I send unto you prophets, and wise men, and scribes: and some of them ye shall kill and crucify: and some of them shall ye scourge in your synagogues, and persecute them from city to city: That upon you may come all the righteous blood shed upon the earth, from the blood of righteous Abel unto the blood of Zacharias son of Barachias, whom ye slew between the temple and the altar. Verily I say unto you, all these things shall come upon this generation' " (Matt. 23:34-36).

The fearless denunciations of our Lord must still be emphasized if we are to be faithful to revealed truth. Rather than as a golden age of its own achievement, the glory of humanity is seen to be an open sore. Man, so proud, beholds himself in the dust. What he calls achievement and civilization is seen to be rebellion and apostasy crying out to God for judgment, and the answer from God is not delayed. Political life is to end, so far as man is concerned, with the Antichrist who shall be cast into the lake of fire. Ecclesiastical life, so far as man is concerned, is to end with Babylon the great, the mother of harlots, to be wasted by the political power. Commercial life, so far as man is concerned, is to end with the other Babylon which is destroyed in an hour, bringing forth the tears of the traitors who receive their life from its merchandise. All of the other works created by man, his museums and art treasures, his monuments and their magnificence, his universities, foundations, schools, churches, banks, buildings, homes are revealed to be a part of the elements that "shall melt with fervent heat, the earth also and the works that are therein shall be burned up" (II Pet. 3:10).

A knowledge of the future is sweet, but that the nature of what the immediate future holds is bitter. The true servant of God, however, will always find God's Word sweeter than honey to his mouth (Ps. 119:103). This has ever been the true experience of the servants of God. When Jeremiah found the words of the Lord, he ate them and said, "Thy word was unto me the joy and rejoicing of mine heart" (Jer. 15:16). We can readily understand that to John the little book was both sweetness and bitterness, for John soon learned that he was not only to assimilate the truth of God concerning the judgment to come, but that he was to prophesy concerning peoples, nations, tongues and kings.

John, having received the message from the Lord, now becomes qualified to go forth for further service. He is to be the instrumentality by which God is to give the exposition of His final wrath. He is to speak concerning peoples, nations, tongues and many kings. The re-

mainder of the book of Revelation comes through John as a result of
his commission in this verse. He is chosen and ordained for the purpose of speaking the word which will describe God's final wrath upon
all the doings of men. We will listen, though it be bitterness to us,
and as human beings will humble ourselves in the dust before our
God, but we will listen to the sweetness of it as we realize that he
vindicates our God from all the blasphemies of men, and causes us to
see that all our hope is in the Lord Jesus Christ.

CHAPTER 11

Verses 1, 2

The Measuring Rod

¹*And a reed was given unto me like unto a rod: the giver saying, Rise, and measure the inner temple of God, and the altar, and the ones worshipping therein.*

²*And the court, which is outside the inner temple, cast without; do not measure it, because it was given unto the nations; and the holy city they shall trample under foot forty-two months.*
(Rev. 11:1, 2, Free Translation)

Nowhere in the book of Revelation has there been more confusion among the commentators than in the verses which open the eleventh chapter. Dean Alford speaks of this chapter as "undoubtedly one of the most difficult in the whole Apocalypse." Ottman titles his chapter of the exposition, "Crux Interpretatorum" which means the very heart and crux of interpretation. There is a problem, that is certain, but whether or not this passage can be looked upon as the chief difficulty of the interpreters is another question. To my mind the Holy Spirit sheds a revealing light throughout the whole Book the moment we recognize, first its essential Jewishness and second, that, though it may prefigure certain tendencies that are present in the history of this age, it is entirely concerned with the future from the beginning of the fourth chapter.

One commentator has brought together on one page the interpretations of his fellows in a way that will explain much of the confusion that has arisen out of this passage. He points out that almost universally the commentators have tried to force the church into the picture that is painted here when, of course, the church is not in view at all. "The temple is here figuratively used of the faithful portion of the church of Christ." The command is given to John "to measure the temple of God" in order to call his attention to "the size of the church of God." The "altar" is again, in the mind of one commentator, "the church." The "outer court" signifies "a part of the church of Christ." The "Holy City," according to these expositors is "always in the Apocalypse the title of the church." The "two witnesses" represent "the elect church of God," says one (embracing both Jew and

Christian), "and the witness which she bears concerning God, especially in the Old and New Testaments." "The twelve hundred and sixty days" constitutes the period "during which the church, although trodden under foot, will not cease to prophesy." Concerning the war of the beast against them we are told, "The whole vision is symbolical, and the intention is to convey the idea that the church, in her witness for God, will experience opposition from the power of Satan" and so on and on and on. Now, still other commentators bring the church into this. Finally, "the elders," who worship God after the sounding of the seventh trumpet are said to be "the church."

Well does the commentator who has assembled these quotations say, "In every turn of the kaleidoscope we get the Church. There is an endless variety of color, but without any symmetrical form. What wonder, when such diverse expressions are forced to mean the same thing, if there be endless confusion. Literalism may not solve every perplexity, but it does not lead into any such inexplicable obscurity as this."

When John had received the renewal of his commission to go forth and prophesy after he had eaten the little book, he was given a measuring rod, presumably by the messenger who had spoken to him about the book. This measure was a reed, the word used being that for those reeds which grew in immense brakes in the Jordan Valley. This reed, however was like a rod. The word translated rod is the same as that which is used of the royal scepter, the "rod of iron" (2:27) with which the Lord shall rule.

With the rod came instructions from the messenger for the measurement of the inner temple, the altar, and the one worshiping therein. We are immediately carried back to the Old Testament where two or three different men with measuring rods are to be found. In one of Ezekiel's visions he was taken to the land of Israel and set upon a very high mountain near "the frame of a city on the south" (Ezek. 40:2ff). "And he brought me thither, and, behold, there was a man, whose appearance was like the appearance of brass, with a line of flax in his hand, and a measuring reed; and he stood in the gate. And the man said unto me, Son of man, behold with thine eyes, and hear with thine ears, and set thine heart upon all that I shall shew thee; for to the intent that I might shew them unto thee art thou brought hither: declare all that thou seest to the house of Israel." Then follow some two chapters of description of the measurements of the future temple, which is to be built upon the earth during the millennial kingdom reign of our Lord Jesus Christ. It is a measurement in preparation for the dwelling place of the Lord.

In Zechariah's fourth vision, he too saw a man who was measuring. "I lifted up mine eyes again, and looked, and behold a man with a measuring line in his hand. Then said I, Whither goest thou? And he said unto me, To measure Jerusalem to see what is the breadth thereof, and what is the length thereof" (Zech. 2:1, 2). In point of fulfillment this prophecy precedes the one in Ezekiel. This measurement is in preparation for the Lord's coming to dwell among His people. The context clearly shows that Israel is called unto separation from Babylon (vs. 7), and the reference concerns the Jerusalem of the future time of Antichrist's reign.

The measuring in both cases is in view of the Lord's coming to dwell upon the earth and is in preparation for that event. It must be understood, however, that this preparation for God's occupation and use may well be a preparation by judgment and cleansing as well as a preparation by building. There came a time, when as the result of Lucifer's first sin, he became Satan and his realm was judged. The earth became waste and desolate, and darkness covered the face of the deep. This time of judgment preceded the blessing that followed. The Spirit of God brooded upon the face of the water, then He called light into shining. Thus we see that judgment may be a part of preparation for God's operations among men. So this judgment measuring we are considering is symbolical. Jeremiah in his great lament is given knowledge of the same symbol. "The Lord hath cast off his altar, he hath abhorred his sanctuary, he hath given up into the hand of the enemy the walls of her palaces; they have made a noise in the house of the Lord, as in the day of a solemn feast. The Lord hath purposed to destroy the wall of the daughter of Zion: he hath stretched out a line, he hath not withdrawn his hand from destroying . . ." (Lam. 2:7, 8).

Let us sum this all up in simple language in answer to the question, What was John measuring? Here, John is measuring the Lord's own people, the Jews. They are yet in unbelief at the time of this measuring, but they are known to God with all their doings. In their stubborn rejection of Messiah in His first coming, they will continue to the very end of the tribulation period. A sealed remnant will be saved and others will be undoubtedly brought to the Lord, but it is not until they have looked upon Messiah whom they have pierced (Zech. 12:10) that their national salvation will come. Whether the measuring is of the literal temple, or symbolically of Israel, is beside the point.

Some have raised the objection that the God who has torn the veil in two from top to bottom in the old Temple at the time of our Lord's death, can have no interest in a Jewish temple built in rejection of His Son, and with blood sacrifices denying the validity of the atonement provided by the Father and the Son. Such objectors have missed the point in the book of Revelation. God does watch over His own. We know from other passages in the Scriptures, notably Romans 11:26, that "all Israel shall be saved." That is, all the Jews living at the time of the return of the Lord Jesus in that given cross section will come to know the Lord. So Israel at the moment we are considering in this prophecy is all an elect Israel. Multitudes have not yet come to the place where they have fully acknowledged the Lord. They are still in the midst of unbelief but the hand of God is upon them, even as Hosea loved his adulterous wife and watched over her and provided for her until she came back to him repentant, recognizing her previous folly, and acknowledging his abiding love.

This measuring of the temple and the worshipers, therefore, shows that the Father is watching over those whom He has separated unto Himself. His honor and His holiness will be vindicated in the perfect completeness of the judgment that shall come upon the followers of the Antichrist. This same honor and holiness will be vindicated in the terrible tribulation through which His suffering ones must pass. Not one of them will believe that He has in any wise compromised Himself by yearning over them when they were far from Him. So John measures the true Israel and their doings. They are separated unto God and their works are marked off for judgment.

A part of the temple, however, is cast out. The Greek word is a very strong one. It does not at all signify mere omission. The court which is outside the inner temple is to be cast without. John is distinctly forbidden to measure it. God will take no care of it. It is to be trodden in the winepress of His wrath. The followers of the Antichrist have profaned it and they shall be allowed to trample it under foot for a determined time. Then God will take charge in His own moment.

In the Temple which had been built by Herod, in which Jesus walked when He was here upon earth, the outer court was marked off from the inner one where Israel was permitted to go and it was separated by "the middle wall of partition" (Eph. 2:14). Beyond this no Gentile could go. Paul, accused of breaking this rule, and bringing Gentiles into the holy place, was almost destroyed by the angry Jews (Acts 21:28). As John measures the temple, however, this court is to be cast out. In the former Temple there was some degree of holiness attached even to the outer court. It might be thought, therefore, that this action is contrary to the principle, "Give not that which is holy unto the dogs" (Matt. 7:6), but these Gentiles have befouled all this with their worship of Antichrist. "Outside are dogs, and sorcerers, and whoremongers, and murderers, and idolators, and whosoever loveth and maketh a lie" (Rev. 22:15). Thus it is today, and thus it shall be then.

All this and the Holy City itself they will trample under foot. But there is a definite term to their profanation. It will last for forty-two months only.

Is this a literal duration of time, or is it figurative? Some may say that we have constantly pointed to the symbolism, and may claim that, to be consistent, we must demand symbolism in these figures.

This would be so were it not for the fact that God Himself marked this period of time as being literal. In fact, we believe that no statement in all the Bible is more definitely marked for literal interpretation than that which limits the time of future judgment upon the earth preceding the millennium. Daniel speaks of it as one heptad, or seven years; and the completion of the sixty-nine periods, or four hundred and eighty-three years, ending with Christ's triumphal entry into Jerusalem, is a sufficient guarantee of the literalness of the seven-year measurement. Daniel divides this into two parts by announcing that the abomination of desolation would take place in the midst of the heptad. This divides the seven years into two parts of three and one-half years each. Here the period is measured in forty-two months, as it is again in announcing the limitations of the reign of the beast out of the earth (13:5). In two others passages this time is measured in days (11:3; 12:6), one thousand two hundred and sixty days being the Jewish lunar reckoning for forty-two times thirty days. In addition to this, the protection of Israel in the wilderness was said to be "for a time, and times, and half a time" (12:14). This is an expression that is carried over from a double use in the book of Daniel (7:25; 12:7).

This seven-year period then lies in the future and covers the rise and the reign of Antichrist, his abomination and ultimate destruction. Our Lord Himself gave to that event which takes place in the middle of the seven-year period, the abomination of desolation, a definite significance which all of the faithful who live at that time will undoubtedly see in a most startling realism. These passages and the closing verses of Daniel's prophecy will be as dear to their memory as are the great salvation passages to our hearts. There will be no moment during these long months of tribulation that the believers will not be able to say to each other that so many days are past and but so many remain. Almost certainly the Lord will appear from Heaven as the true and faithful One, judging and making war in righteousness (Rev. 19:11), at the very end of the last half of the seven year period. By thirty days from that time (Dan. 12:11) it would appear that the works of Antichrist will have perished from the earth. By forty-five days still further (Dan. 12:12) it would appear that the judgment of the nations will have been completed and the millennial kingdom fully established. Some of these passages that measure these times refer to the first half and some to the last half.

One of the most interesting and revealing portions of the vision concerns the two witnesses who rise to speak and work for God. They are clothed with divine power, and stir the wrath of the enemy. Their work cannot be hindered until forty-two months have passed. Then they are killed, amidst the rejoicing of the wicked, and their bodies lie in the street of Jerusalem for three and a half days. Then they are resurrected by the Spirit of God and are taken up into Heaven amidst the consternation of the enemy. A great earthquake follows. And light as to the identity of the two witnesses is certainly not lacking in the Scriptures.

The order of the revelation will lead us to this identification. Let us note, first, that John is not given this information through a vision, but by the direct speech of the mighty messenger, whom we have seen to be, almost certainly, none other than the Lord Jesus Christ Himself. He begins by telling the limit of their work and describing their dress. They are to prophesy for one thousand two hundred and sixty days. Beyond question this refers to one of the two halves of the seventieth week. Is it to the first or the second half? I believe it to be the first half, though some say the second. These base their conclusion on verses fifteen to eighteen which speak of the transfer of the kingdom of this world to our Lord, and the time of the approach of the judgment of the dead. But as we will see when we reach the latter half of this chapter, the sounding of the seventh messenger is a prolonged blast which covers the announcement of events to take place in the distant future, even after the millennial reign of Christ has been completed. It seems much more logical, though this is not a point at which dogmatism is possible, that the two witnesses perform their task throughout the first half of the seven-year period. Rather would we note that the witnesses are killed by the beast that shall ascend out of the abyss. This, we will establish later, is at the time of the abomination of desolation, the event which divides the week into the two halves. If we are correct, then, the order of events is as follows. The Church is removed from the earth at the time of the rapture; the two witnesses are manifested and begin their work in Jerusalem; the power of the Roman dictator rises throughout three and a half years; Satan is cast out of Heaven and incarnates this dictator, thus making him the Antichrist; his associate in power does away with the two witnesses; the great tribulation, which most certainly occupies the second half of the prophetic period, is ushered in.

The burden of the message of the two witnesses will be one of judgment. That is why they are clothed in sackcloth. They have no rank or dignity upon earth, though it is declared that they stand in the presence of the Lord of the earth.

Verses 3–12

The Two Witnesses

³And I will give power unto my two witnesses, and they shall prophesy a thousand two hundred and sixty days clothed in sackcloth. ⁴These are the two olive trees, and the two lampstands which stand in the presence of the Lord of the earth.

⁵*And if any man desire to hurt them, fire goes forth out of their mouth, and devoureth their enemies; and if any man shall desire to hurt them, he must thus be killed.* ⁶*These have the authority to shut the heavens, so that it raineth not during the days of their prophecy; and they have authority upon the waters, to turn them into blood, and to smite the earth with every plague as often as they shall desire.*

⁷*And when they shall have finished their testimony, the wild beast that cometh up out of the abyss, he shall make war with them; he shall overcome them and kill them.* ⁸*And their dead bodies lie in the street of the great city, which is called spiritually Sodom and Egypt, where also their Lord was crucified.* ⁹*And men from among the peoples and tribes, tongues and nations, do look upon their dead bodies three days and a half, and suffer not their dead bodies to be laid in a tomb.* ¹⁰*And the ones dwelling on the earth rejoice over them, and make merry, and they shall send gifts to one another, because these two prophets tormented them that dwelt upon the earth.*

¹¹*And after the three days and a half, the breath of life from God entered into them; and they stood upon their feet, and great fear fell upon those who beheld them.* ¹²*And they heard a great voice from Heaven saying unto them, Come up hither. And they went up into Heaven in the cloud, and their enemies beheld them.*
(Rev. 11:3-12, Free Translation)

The next declaration of the Lord sends us immediately to the prophecy of Zechariah. He speaks of these men as two olive trees and two lampstands and they are a part of the vision that was revealed to Zechariah. We have discussed the meaning of the lampstand as a symbol of witness as revealed in the first chapter of the Apocalypse. We know that in the time of Zechariah, Zerubbabel began the restoration of the Temple, and did his work in the power of the Holy Spirit. The heart of Zechariah's vision is the declaration, "Not by might, nor by power, but by my Spirit, saith the Lord of hosts" (4:6). The Hebrew that is translated "olive trees," is literally "trees of oil," and the phrase that is given as "the two anointed ones" is literally, "the two sons of oil." It is not necessary, here, to bring forth all the proofs that oil, in the Bible, is always a symbol of the Holy Spirit. The teaching of the ancient prophet is that the two men, Joshua, the high priest, and Zerubbabel, the builder, were God's chosen men, and stood in His presence, even while doing their work upon the earth. They were continually supplied with the Holy Spirit for their work, even as the golden pipes poured a constant stream of oil into the lampstands (Zech. 4:12).

The reference to this Old Testament scene in the midst of the prophecy of future things tells us to look for the work of the Holy Spirit rather than for any power of men, although the human identification of the two witnesses is about to be furnished for our edification, and not for our curiosity.

Hundreds of commentators, ancient and modern, identify one of the two witnesses as Elijah. Seiss furnishes pages of quotations from the early fathers to show that the Church has a long and continuous tradition which is fully in accord with the Scriptures of both Testaments concerning the coming of Elijah. We shall confine ourselves to the Scriptures. Our text first speaks of a power that was peculiarly that of Elijah. The witnesses are given authority to shut the heavens, "so that it does not rain during the days of their prophecy." In the days of the great apostasy under Ahab, God sent Elijah the Tishbite to stand before the King and declare, "As the Lord God of Israel lives, before whom I stand, there shall not be dew nor rain these years, except according to my word" (I Kings 17:1). In the New Testament, the Holy Spirit causes James to say, "Elijah was a man subject to like passions as we are, and he prayed earnestly that it might not rain: and it rained not on the earth by the space of three years and six months" (James 5:17). The time element is most striking, for the three and a half years mentioned in James are the exact measure of the twelve hundred and sixty days during which the two witnesses are to bear their testimony.

There is another line of teaching, however, that is still more important in this connection. There was a firm tradition among the Jews that Elijah was to return to earth again. Hengstenberg, the great German scholar, in his *Christology of the Old Testament,* cites the passage from the Talmud and quotes the various scholars who have gathered masses of material on the subject of Elijah's reappearance. In the Apocrypha, which we reject as uncanonical, but which is to be found between the Testaments in many an edition of the Bible, there is a long reference to Elijah's coming recorded in the book of Ecclesiasticus (48: 1-11). All this will explain why the Pharisees sent their deputation to John the Baptist with the question, "Art thou Elijah?" (John 1:19, 20).

The Old Testament gives us the basis for this tradition, for this teaching is not an error of interpretation, but a definite prophecy, given by the Holy Spirit. The last book of the Old Testament, even the very last words, speak of this subject. Malachi writes, "Behold, I will send my messenger, and he shall prepare the way before me; and the Lord, whom ye seek, shall suddenly come to his temple, even the messenger of the covenant, whom ye delight in: behold, he shall come, saith the Lord of hosts. But who may abide the day of his coming? and who shall stand when he appeareth? for he is like a refiner's fire, and like fullers' soap; and he shall sit as a refiner and purifier of silver: and he shall purify the sons of Levi, and purge them as gold and silver . . . And I will come near to you to judgment; and I will be a swift witness against (them) . . . for I am the Lord, I change not . . . For, behold, the day cometh, that shall burn as an oven: and all the proud, yea, and all that do wickedly, shall be stubble:

and the day that cometh shall burn them up, saith the Lord of hosts, that it shall leave them neither root nor branch . . . Behold I will send you Elijah the prophet before the coming of the great and terrible day of the Lord: and he shall turn the heart of the fathers to the children, and the heart of the children to their fathers, lest I come and smite the earth with a curse" (Mal. 3:1-3, 5, 6; 4:1, 5, 6). So ends the Old Testament.

Here, then, is a definite prophecy that Elijah will return to earth before the great and dreadful day of the Lord. There are some who seek to say that all this was fulfilled in John the Baptist, but this is a strange idea in light of the definite words of Christ, and comes from the misreading of our Lord. The answer of John, himself, should have been sufficient. The Jews sent the delegation of "priests and Levites from Jerusalem to ask him, Who art thou? And he confessed and denied not; but confessed, I am not the Christ. And they asked him, What then? Are you Elijah? And he said, I am not. Art thou that prophet mentioned in Deuteronomy? And he answered, No" (John 1:19-21). These questions demonstrate that the people of his day believed that the Messiah, Elijah and the prophet that was to come were three separate and distinct persons. John the Baptist, then, did not consider himself to be the fulfillment of the prophecy made by Moses concerning the prophet that was to come (Deut. 18:15-18), and he distinctly denied that he was the reincarnation of Elijah for the fulfillment of Malachi's prophecy. The greatest proof that the prophecy is not fulfilled in John the Baptist is that he did not turn the hearts of the children to the fathers, as Malachi predicted, nor did he usher in the great and dreadful day of the Lord. The error of attributing the Malachi prophecy to John the Baptist has arisen from a misunderstanding of a word spoken by Christ after His transfiguration. The three disciples who were permitted to see that wonderful sight were stimulated in their thinking by the details of what had passed before them. Moses and Elijah had been seen and recognized. As they were walking down the mountain with the Lord one of the disciples, remembering the old tradition, asked Jesus, "Why then say the scribes that Elias must first come? And Jesus answered and said unto them, Elias truly shall first come, and restore all things. But I say unto you, that Elias is come already, and they knew him not, but have done unto him whatsoever they listed . . . Then the disciples understood that he spake unto them of John the Baptist" (Matt. 17: 10-13).

The declaration of Christ as to the future coming of Elijah is formal and definite. "Elijah truly shall come first and restore all things." But what of His statement, "Elias is come already"? Certainly He spoke of John the Baptist. The answer is found in an earlier statement of the Lord when John was in prison. "All the prophets and the law prophesied until John. And if ye will receive it, this is Elias which was for to come" (Matt. 11:13, 14). It is to be noticed that the word "it" is in italics. This means that it was not in the original Greek. The statement means then not that John the Baptist was Elijah, but that John the Baptist would have been considered by God as fulfilling the prophecy if the men of Christ's day had been willing to receive the ministry of John concerning the Messiah. The context clearly shows this. The Lord immediately likens that generation to the children playing in the market place who refuse the invitation of their fellows to play a sad game or a glad game. John came with a stern message of repentance and Christ came with a wide call to forgiveness. Both were refused. The failure of the men of Christ's day to receive the kingdom-offer as it was presented by John and by the Lord disqualified John the Baptist from being the Elijah who would restore all things. John the Baptist did his work in the spirit and power of Elijah (Luke 1:15-17), but the greater fulfillment is yet to be. It is this greater fulfillment which is seen in the revelation concerning the two witnesses.

The identification of Elijah is very clear. What can we say of the other witness? Here there are not as many details, but we believe, nevertheless, that the second witness can be clearly identified. Some very good commentators, however, have made a curious mistake. Seiss, for example, identifies the second witness as Enoch on the ground that Enoch is the other man in the Bible who did not die physically. He quotes the famous passage in Hebrews, "It is appointed unto men once to die . . ." (Heb. 9:27), and argues naively that it will therefore be necessary for Enoch to return to die! But at the moment when the two witnesses come forth there will be multitudes in Heaven who have never died. The whole of the generation living at the return of the Lord will escape death. "Behold, I shew you a mystery; we shall not all sleep, but we shall all be changed, In a moment, in the twinkling of an eye, at the last trump; for the trumpet shall sound, and the dead shall be raised incorruptible, and we shall be changed" (I Cor. 15:51, 52). And there are some men who have died twice, Lazarus and the others raised from the dead by our Lord and by Paul and in the Old Testament by Elijah and Elisha. The simple fact is that the famous text on death and judgment does not refer to physical death at all. In view of the fact that the context clearly speaks of salvation from eternal death, a paraphrase of the misapplied verse in Hebrews would, in my opinion, read as follows: As it is appointed unto men once, in Adam's sin, to die spiritually, as a result of which judgment passed upon all the race, because all have sinned, so Christ was once offered to bear the sins of many. There is no prophecy in either Old or New Testament which demands the return of Enoch. Further, Enoch is a type which had its fulfillment before the witnesses. For Enoch is a picture of the Church of Jesus Christ, taken out of the world before the tribulation shall come upon it. There are prophecies, on the contrary, which demand the appearance of another Old Testament figure.

The second witness, announced both in the Old Testament and in the New, is Moses. The phraseology of our text points to him first of all. The two witnesses are to have authority upon the waters to turn them into blood, and to smite the earth with every plague as often as they desire. Just as the prophecy concerning the drought pointed us to Elijah, so this prophecy concerning the plagues points us to Moses. But there are further means to certify this identification. Moses was given a prophecy concerning a prophet who was to be like himself. "The Lord thy God will raise up unto thee a Prophet from the midst of thee, of thy brethren, like unto me; unto him ye shall hearken . . . And the Lord said unto me, They have well spoken that which they have spoken. I will raise them up a Prophet from among their brethren, like unto thee, and will put my words in his mouth; and he shall speak unto them all that I shall command him. And it shall come to pass, that whosoever will not hearken unto my words which he shall speak in my name, I will require it of him" (Deut. 18:15, 17-19). There is a possible explanation of this passage which would refer it to Christ Himself, but there can be no doubt of the fact that the Jews of Christ's day made a difference between Messiah, Elijah and the prophet (John 1:25). We believe then that the Deuteronomy prophecy refers to the second of the two witnesses who are to precede the coming of the Lord.

There are still other passages that throw a great deal of light on this subject, namely, the accounts of the transfiguration of our Lord. There have been many explanations of this scene, but we believe that only one is tenable, that which is given by the Holy Spirit through Peter. We must not forget that this impetuous disciple was one of the three who was taken to the mount for this great occurrence and who fell asleep until after the transfiguration had begun (Luke 9:32). It was Peter who interrupted with words from the human spirit, "not knowing what he said" (Luke 9:33). The scene had a great effect on him, as may well be understood, and he wrote about it later in his life. He declares in connection with his preaching of a future kingdom of the Lord Jesus Christ, "We have not followed cunningly devised fables, when we made known unto you the power and coming of our Lord Jesus Christ, but were eyewitnesses of his majesty. For he received from God the Father honor and glory, when there came such a voice to him from the excellent glory, This is my beloved Son, in whom I am well pleased. And this voice which came from heaven we heard, when we were with him in the holy mount . . ." (II Pet. 1:16-18). This definitely refers to the transfiguration and connects it with the future reign of Christ. Therefore, Moses and Elijah are the two figures

who are most certainly connected with the inauguration of the coming
of the Lord in power to establish His earthly kingdom.

There is also an interesting line of teaching in connection with the
bodies of these two men. Elijah did not die. His body was carried up
from earth in what appeared to Elisha as a chariot of fire. That and
the whirlwind took Elijah to Heaven (II Kings 2:9-11). That Elijah
was thus preserved from physical death is most significant. There is
a similar mystery concerning the body of Moses. We read that he
"died there in the land of Moab, according to the word of the Lord.
And he buried him in a valley in the land of Moab, over against Beth-
peor; but no man knoweth of his sepulchre unto this day" (Deut. 34:
5, 6). In the course of my travels I have seen tombs that were supposed to be those of Abraham, Isaac and Jacob in Palestine; one that
natives near Nineveh claim to be that of Jonah; and still another that
is claimed by copper-seeking peasants to be that of Job. But though
we traveled through the country described in this passage, we found
no traces of a legend of Moses' sepulchre. The reason seems to be
found in the New Testament. Jude writes, "Michael the archangel,
when contending with the devil he disputed about the body of Moses,
dared not bring against him a railing accusation, but said, The Lord
rebuke thee" (Jude 9). We must certainly consider the possibility that
Michael was commissioned by God to secure the body of Moses and
that Satan resisted him in the performance of his commission. Certainly there need to be no difficulty in the thought that these bodies
could be kept in some special way by God for the fulfillment of His
purpose. The moment we admit any purpose in God, that moment
we must concede the power of God to perform that which He purposes.

Ottman has a good thought on this whole subject. "Peter recognized
them (Moses and Elijah) on the mount, which he could not have
done, if they had been disembodied spirits. Their conversation with
Christ had reference to His approaching death, literally the exodus
that He should accomplish at Jerusalem, and Peter affirms that the
entire transfiguration scene was a foregleam of the establishing of the
kingdom of Christ in power and glory. These two men are in some
manner definitely associated with Christ in the inauguration of His
kingdom. They represent the law and the prophets which unite in proclaiming the certainty of that coming kingdom. The reappearance of
them at the time of Israel's restoration can be conceived of without
much difficulty, and such a theory is not burdened with the obscurities
involved in any other. If objection be raised against the *literal* return
of these two men, then it can be shown from the statement of Jesus
concerning John, that another Elijah could fulfill the predictions concerning him. This is equally true of Moses. Therefore any two men
endowed with the power and spirit of Moses and Elijah might be

raised up for this period of testimony, and answer all the necessary demands of the prophecy."

One of the reasons why I believe the two witnesses perform their work in the first half of the seven year judgment period, is the statement that now occurs concerning their principal enemy. "When they shall have finished their testimony, the wild beast that cometh up out of the abyss, he shall make war with them; he shall overcome them and kill them." The narrative at this point introduces the rise of the beast merely to complete the revelation which the Lord is giving concerning these two witnesses, and to give us the end of their history. It is to be noticed, however, that Satan's power is not able to touch them until God is through with their witness.

The bodies of these two witnesses are said to lie in the street of the great city. Two symbolical names are given to the city, Sodom and Egypt, but it is immediately identified in reality as Jerusalem, the place where the Lord was crucified. To call it Sodom and Egypt is to indicate that it is utterly given over to the devil and to the vicious practices of sin which result where God takes His hand from a nation, people or city, and allows men to go to the extremes of their desire. Sodom is the name which ever presents God's estimate of moral corruption, while Egypt is the reminder of that great darkness which covered the land, out of which God took His people by a mighty act of His grace.

The verses which follow have been quoted by some as proof that the witnesses are not individuals. All of the earth seems interested in them and therefore, say some commentators, their testimony must be the worldwide testimony of a group of whom these individuals are symbols. But we cannot follow this interpretation. We believe that the men from among the peoples and tribes, tongues and nations are those who are in Jerusalem, just as such men were in Jerusalem on the day of Pentecost. We also believe that this passage was given by God with the clear knowledge that means of intercommunication and travel would be tremendously speeded up in the last days. Why should we hesitate to present the idea that radio and television will be so developed, by the time these two witnesses will perform their wonders and finally reach their death, and their doings will be known to earth-dwellers as a matter of common knowledge? Their death will be a matter of the triumph of the dictator, and those who surround him to glorify him will see that the news is spread.

A few years ago we went into a store at Christmas time and tried to find a greeting card which contained a Christian sentiment. Among the yulelogs and amidst the pictures of Santa Claus, was a card which contained the verse, "And they that dwell upon the earth shall rejoice, and make merry, and shall send gifts one to another." We recognized it immediately as a Satanic distortion. The rejoicing is over

God's martyrs. The gifts are thank offerings of relief that the judgments exercised by the two witnesses are now over. Men reckon without God. Worse judgments are yet to come. That which He calls the *great* tribulation is about to begin.

The consternation of men may be imagined as the sequel is brought out. Three days and a half pass by; suddenly the bodies of the witnesses are raised from the dead. A great voice is heard from Heaven. The faithful witnesses are called to Heaven, and in the sight of their enemies they leave the scene of their witness and are taken to Heaven in a cloud. We believe that this is the cloud of glory, the glory of God, which appears throughout the Bible.

And as the enemies see the risen witnesses ascend into Heaven, the city rocks with a great earthquake. The time of Jacob's trouble is upon them. This is the introduction to the great and dreadful day of the Lord.

Verses 13–18

The Great Panorama

[13] *And in that hour there was a great earthquake, and the tenth part of the city fell; and (the names of) seven thousand men were killed; and the rest became affrighted, and they gave glory to the God of Heaven.* [14] *The second Woe is past; behold, the third Woe is coming speedily.*

[15] *And the seventh messenger sounded; and there were great voices in Heaven saying, The kingdom of the World is become that of our Lord and of His Christ; and He shall reign unto the ages of the ages.* [16] *And the twenty-four elders which are sitting in the presence of God upon their thrones, fell upon their faces and worshipped God,* [17] *saying, We give thanks to Thee, O Lord, God, the Almighty, the One who is and who was, because Thou hast taken Thy great power and didst begin to reign.* [18] *And the nations were angry, and Thy wrath came, and the time of the dead to be judged and to give the reward to Thy bond slaves the prophets, and to the saints, and to them that fear Thy Name, the small and the great; and to destroy them which destroy the earth.*

(Rev. 11:13-18, Free Translation)

Some of God's judgments are very slow in appearing, others fall like His lightning. The judgment that follows the martyrdom and resurrection of the two witnesses is instantaneous. In the same hour there was a great earthquake, and the tenth part of the city fell; and seven thousand men were killed.

Is this a statement of literal earthquake and slaughter, or is there symbolism that must yield up its light from other portions of the

Word? If it is a literal earthquake, we have little to stop us in our study. The account is as definite as a cable dispatch from the far corners of the world, announcing succinctly, that a major disaster has taken place and that the loss of lives and property has reached a certain figure. It may be well that there is nothing more in view here than a trembling of the earth, with the falling of stone walls and the crushing of human bodies. There is, however, an alternative which must be given at least passing consideration.

Earthquakes are frequently found in the Scriptures as symbols of great upheavals in the realm of government as well as in the social and spiritual order. We have commented on this at length in the discussion of "the great earthquake" (6:12). In our present passage we have certain details, however, that need to be touched in passing. "The tenth part of the city fell." The Lord had expressly declared to Israel that the tenth belonged to Him (Lev. 27:30-34).

Any failure to pay that tithe involved heavy judgments from God. The fact that Israel had become lax in this matter, withholding that which had been set apart as God's own, is given as the reason for the curse that had fallen upon the people in the days of Malachi. "Will a man rob God? Yet ye have robbed me. But ye say, Wherein have we robbed thee? In tithes and offerings. Ye are cursed with a curse; for ye have robbed me, even this whole nation" (Mal. 3:8, 9). But God will always collect that which is His due. Men may refuse the tithe to Him, but they will lose ten-tenths as a result.

"The names of seven thousand men were killed." The use of the word "names" here in the original is most peculiar. Some have thought it to be merely a figure of speech to express the ordinary fact that seven thousand men were killed. We are wondering if it is not possible to find here a full explanation of the passage which has caused some difficulty to those who are not grounded in the sure word of the certainty of salvation for those who have been born again. In the letter to the church in Sardis, the Lord stated that He would not blot out of the scroll of life the names of the overcomers (Rev. 3:5). Is this not further proof that there is a book containing the record of every individual who is ever born into this lost world? God has a census of all human beings. The day comes when, in His sight, they have rejected Him beyond any hope of salvation. Spiritual judgment falls. Their names are blotted out of the book of life. Of course, they have never been written in the *Lamb's* book.

The great upheaval of this time, whether it be a literal earthquake or another major outbreak of anarchy, causes great fear to come into the hearts of those who escape. They are filled with terror and give glory to the God of Heaven. It is an awesome revelation to the human heart that men should kill the two witnesses sent by the God of Heaven to the earth, even while recognizing His existence in Heaven and while being filled with terror of Him. It is one more proof that the carnal mind is enmity against God. Their glorifying God does not come from repentant hearts. Rather is it like that glory given to God when Jesus raised the son of the widow of Nain. There came a fear on all, and they glorified God . . ." (Luke 7:16). The same thing is seen with a sharp contrast in the two types of glorifying after the Lord had healed a paralytic. The healed man "departed to his own house, glorifying God. And they were all amazed and they glorified God" (Luke 5:25, 26). How different the two!

This upheaval constitutes the second of the three woes announced under the fourth trumpet (8:13). The third is to follow speedily.

Handel has chosen the passage that follows as part of the text for his famous Hallelujah Chorus. We must recognize the necessity of the slight revision that is given to the translation in versions translated in modern times. The Lord recognized the right of the ruler He had placed over the world at the beginning, and clearly gave him his title— The Prince of this world (John 12:31; 14:30; 16:11). We shall never understand this passage and the chapter that follows unless we realize a little of his history. Lucifer, the anointed cherub that governed, was perfect in all his ways from the day he was created until iniquity was found in him (Ezek. 28:15). He was God's prophet, priest and king. He spoke for God to the universe as prophet. He took the worship of the universe to God as priest. He ruled over the universe as king. When he sinned he had aspired to be like the Most High, taking worship unto himself (Isa. 14:14). Thus he had lost the office of priest. God no longer spoke through him, a sinful channel. He therefore lost his office of prophet. But he still retained his office of king. His title was clearly recognized by the Lord Jesus. We know from many portions of Scripture that the father of lies was telling the truth for once at the time of the temptation of our Lord. "The devil said unto him, All this power will I give thee, and the glory of them: for that is delivered unto me; and whomsoever I will I give it" (Luke 4:6).

The Lord Jesus refused to take the power from Satan by some easy way. God was not going to snatch it back as though He had made a mistake and now saw better. He was going to proceed according to His eternal plan. By virtue of the death of the Lord Jesus He would provide the basis and ground work for the removal of the power from the usurper who had been made prince of this world and who had become "god of this age" (II Cor. 4:4). He would do this in His own good time. That time is now announced. The kingdom, singular, not plural, of this world is become that of our Lord and of His Christ.

Now appears the reason why we have entitled this chapter study, "The Great Panorama." This verse and those immediately following, all of which come under the sound of the seventh trumpet, contain the announcement of many events, in fact, the summary of all that will be studied down to the end of the book of Revelation. We can best describe it under the following analogy. The heralds of William of Normandy announced as they landed on the sands of England, that the kingdom of that island had become the possession of the Duke of Normandy. A historian might begin his account with the words of the herald, and continue in a sentence saying that the land was now given over to the followers of the Norman, and that the doom of those who resisted was sure. Then, after this panoramic view, the recital might turn to the battle of Hastings, and then at long length to the settling of the country, the division of the land, and the subsequent peace.

We have still another analogy from the Old Testament in a passage that is very similar in construction to this passage. The Heavenly messenger brought to Daniel the interpretation of the seventy periods of seven years which he had seen in the vision. In one brief verse the messenger, Gabriel, covered all the rest of world history. As a decade is ten years, a heptad is seven years. "Seventy heptads are determined upon thy people and upon thy holy city, to finish the transgression, and to make an end of sins, and to make reconciliation for iniquity, and to bring in everlasting righteousness, and to seal up the vision and prophecy, and to anoint the most Holy" (Dan. 9:24). It takes very little discernment to understand that there are vast periods of time between some of these events. Those clauses which speak of the death of the Saviour are readily identifiable. But, with no more than a comma in between, the following clause speaks of the bringing in of everlasting righteousness. That is still in the future. We, ourselves, are living in the time of the comma between the two phrases.

The words spoken by the great voices announce the taking over of the kingdom power. The details of the transfer of power will be seen when we come to the war in Heaven described in the next chapter (12:7ff).

Another great error is also eliminated by a clause in this verse. The reign of Christ is stated to be "for ever and ever." In the Greek it is literally, "unto the ages of the ages." Some, have claimed that there is no eternal punishment of sinners. They take the passages which speak of their torment as existing "for ever and ever" (Rev. 14:11; 20:10), to mean a limited time, with a definite terminus. We answer simply that the duration of the doom of the wicked is described in the same terms that are used here to depict the duration of the reign of Christ. That should settle the question.

The announcement by the great voices of the approaching sovereignty of Christ has a profound effect upon those who are in Heaven. We have examined at some length the identity of the twenty-four elders (Rev. 4:4), seeing in them the symbols of the Church and the elect of Israel. How long they have waited for this moment! The announcement of its coming now causes them to leave their thrones and to prostrate themselves before the Lord in worship. Now, after all these ages, the time of vindication of the Lord is about to take place! Is it any wonder that we join in this worship? "We give thanks to Thee, O Lord God, the Almighty, the One who is and who was, because Thou hast taken Thy great power and dost reign." It should be noted that the clause "and art to come" is not in the original. It was probably added by come copyist and thus crept into some of the later manuscripts, but the best authorities omit it. And certainly it should be omitted. Its absence in the oldest manuscripts is another proof of the detailed accuracy of the whole of the Bible revelation. He is now taking the power and is beginning to reign. Some have seen confusion in the change of tense that is so clearly seen in the Greek. For the text distinctly does not say what the King James Version says. The revisers, and other modern translators have all joined in showing the change of tense. We have rendered it "Thou hast taken thy great power and dost begin to reign." A. T. Robertson, one of the greatest Greek authorities, says of this sentence: " 'Thou hast taken' is the perfect active indicative emphasizing the permanence of God's rule, 'Thou hast assumed thy power.' 'Didst reign' is the ingressive first aorist active indicative 'didst begin to reign.' " This comment is strong evidence for the moment when the actual reigning of Christ begins. Not yet is the world under His kingship, but that day will come and is what is described here.

The eighteenth verse is composed of different clauses which describe events that are more than a thousand years apart. There are three lines of truth in the verse. There is God's dealing with the earth rebels, with the saints and with the invisible forces of Satan.

First we see the announcement of God's dealing with the unsaved. "The nations were angry, and thy wrath came, and the time of the dead to be judged." The first clause is the fulfillment of the second Psalm. "Why do the nations rage, and the people imagine a vain thing? The kings of the earth set themselves, and the rulers take counsel together, against the Lord, and against his anointed, saying, Let us break their bands asunder, and cast away their cords from us" (Ps. 2:1-3). There was a partial fulfillment of this at the first coming of our Lord, but the main anger of the nations now comes to its highest fermentation. Like the victims of depressive psychosis whose madness recurs with increasing frequency and intensity, the poor, insane world rages out its hate against its Creator. Heretofore He has been patient, but it has been written for thousands of years that His patience will come to its end. "He that sitteth in the heavens shall laugh; the Lord shall have them in derision. Then shall he speak to them in his wrath, and vex them in his sore displeasure" (Ps. 2:4, 5). All this is to be found in our phrase, "And thy wrath came." The utter simplicity of the

statement marks its divine origin. Only God could speak of such stupendous matters in a way that is not casual but powerful in its artless
reality.

The next phrase carries us over to the twentieth chapter of Revelation for its complete fulfillment. "The time of the dead to be judged"
is very definitely fixed in Scripture as coming after the thousand years
of the millennial kingdom. This means that the vision in the verse we
are studying covers the whole of the period of the "day of the Lord."
The millennium is in the comma between the two clauses. This is a
well-known biblical phenomenon. The whole of the age in which we
live is to be found in a comma between two clauses in Isaiah (61:2),
as our Lord demonstrated by stopping there when He read the passage
in the synagogue at Nazareth, as recorded in the gospel (Luke 4:19,
20). The same principle is observed in the passages which speak of
His comings in the same verse, and in the passage describing the order
of the resurrection.

"Every man in his own order: Christ the firstfruits; afterward [by
about 2,000 years!] they are Christ's at his coming. Then [after the
millennium] cometh the end . . ." (I Cor. 15:23, 24). So it is here.
The full scope of God's dealing with rebel man is spanned in one
sentence.

Those who are His own are next seen. "The time . . . to give the
reward to thy bondslaves the prophets, and to the saints, and to them
that fear thy name." These are believers, the saints are the recipients
of grace in our age, while those who fear His Name are the ones who
will believe on Him during the reign of Antichrist. We can readily
understand that the Old Testament saints have not yet received their
reward, "God having provided some better thing for us, that they without us should not be made perfect" (Heb. 11:40). The reward of the
tribulation saints is but a moment after.

There is one final phrase—"and to destroy them which destroy the
earth." This refers to those spirit beings who have followed the one
who is called the Destroyer. They are carefully separated from those
who are called the nations. The event is the fulfillment of the double
prophecy, "And it shall come to pass in that day, that the Lord shall
punish the host of the high ones that are on high, and the kings of the
earth upon the earth" (Isa. 24:21). There can be no doubt that here
is a division that recognizes Satan and his followers on the one side
and the earthlings on the other. Thus God's judgment will deal righteously with all beings.

PART VI
THE FALSE TRINITY

CHAPTER 12

Verses 11:19–12:6

The Eternal Plan

¹⁹And the sanctuary of God was opened in Heaven, and the ark of His covenant was seen in His sanctuary; and there were lightnings, and voices, and thunderings and an earthquake, and great hail.

¹And a great sign was seen in Heaven, a woman clothed with the sun, and the moon beneath her feet, and upon her head a crown of twelve stars; ²and she was with child, crying, travailing and in pain to be delivered.

³And there was seen another sign in Heaven, and behold, a great red dragon, having seven heads and ten horns, and upon his heads seven diadems; ⁴and his tail drew the third part of the stars of Heaven, and he cast them to the earth. And the dragon stood before the woman who was about to be delivered, so that when she was delivered he might devour her child. ⁵And she bore a son, a man child, Who is to rule all the nations with a rod of iron, and her child was caught up to God and to His throne. ⁶And the woman fled into the wilderness where she hath a place prepared of God, that there they may nourish her a thousand two hundred and sixty days.

(Rev. 11:19–12:6, Free Translation)

The Word of God tells us very plainly that the source of judgment is the same as the source of mercy. Both flow from the heart of God. Both are essential to His nature. Both can be understood only at the cross of Jesus Christ.

The last verse of the eleventh chapter gives the source of all the judgment messages that follow. After the summary He has just given, which covers the whole of the great and terrible day of the Lord, God reveals His innermost sanctuary, the symbol of His holiness, and shows us that judgment flows from there. To deny the reality of His judgments is to deny the reality of His holiness. To deny the essential nature of God, is in one sense to class oneself with the atheists.

The Old Testament again reveals the secret of the interpretation of this passage. By way of the epistle to the Hebrews we proceed back to the writings of Moses and all will become clear. The former temple and the tabernacle of Moses followed the pattern revealed by God, which was a definite pattern "of things in the heavens" (Heb. 9:23). Here we are suddenly given a vision of the inner sanctuary of Heaven, the Holy of Holies, and there we find the ark of God strikingly and startlingly revealed. To one who reads the whole Bible through for the first time, the ark of God must take a very important position. It is the center of much in the Old Testament. But there comes a time when it is taken from our view and we hear not one word of it. The New Testament opens and proceeds on its course. Here and there a little light is shed revealing some of the meanings of the ancient symbols. When we come to the last book in the Bible we are far removed from thoughts of the ark of God, until suddenly, when we have our mind set upon the completion of the great plan which has been announced, we are brought sharply before the ark of God once more.

We are convinced that the ark of God in Old Testament symbol represented the throne of God. One commentator whom we are seldom able to quote favorably because he has the Church and Israel so confused, is very clear on this one point. "The ark was the place of God's holy presence, of whom it was said that 'He dwelleth between the cherubim' (I Sam. 4:4). It is the throne of righteousness and judgment, for these are declared to be 'the habitation of his throne' (Ps. 97:2). But that throne becomes the 'throne of grace,' when the slain and risen Lamb occupies it, after having borne for us the just judgment of God, and having fulfilled all righteousness by His sacrificial death . . . Nothing more need be said in order to identify the ark of the covenant with the throne of God in Heaven."

With this paragraph we are in hearty accord. One reason that the throne is presented under its symbolical name is to remind us of the process by which it was revealed in the Old Testament. The ark was made of wood and covered with gold. In this double construction it is a picture of the nature of our Lord Jesus Christ who had the perfect human nature, perfectly clothed with the divine nature. He was and is man; He was and is God. He must be approached with reverence. Not everyone that says, "Lord, Lord," but he that does the will of the Father in Heaven, may come to that holy presence of Jesus Christ. To do the will of the Father, He has declared to us, is to believe in the Son (John 6:29). Therefore there can be no approach to the Father except by the cross where the redemption from sin has taken place. The high priest of Israel never approached the ark which was hidden behind the great veil of the temple, except he had first fulfilled all of God's appointed demands. A bullock had been slain for his sins, and a goat for the sins of the people. The blood was taken in God's appointed way and at His appointed moment and placed between the cherubim on the mercy seat (Lev. 16:14, 15). All this was given in order to impress upon the people, who at that period were still childish and ignorant, that which is expressed in the great charter of the holiness of God, "No MAN COMETH UNTO THE FATHER BUT BY ME" (John 14:6). Woe unto that religious person who thinks that he may approach God without the atoning work of the cross of Jesus Christ. Fire had gone out from the presence of God and had lighted the sacrifice on the altar which Aaron had dressed on the day of the opening of the tabernacle service. Fire went out from that same presence of the Lord and struck Nadab and Abihu who dared approach His presence without due regard for the conditions which He had laid down.

Here we are given one more indication that all these symbols of judgment, the lightnings, the thunders, the earthquake, and the great hail come from the throne of God. The Lord will judge sin. The Lord will condemn rebellion. The Lord's patience will come to its righteous end. The Lord will vindicate His name and the honor of those who have trusted in His Word. His throne is pledged to the fulfillment of His eternal purposes. Those who have trusted in the redemption He has provided are as secure as that throne is sure. "The foundation of God standeth sure, having this seal, The Lord knoweth them that are his . . ." (II Tim. 2:19). Here is the security of the saints. From this same throne of God, which bears the seal of the safety of His own, proceed the judgments which insure the doom of those who have refused to recognize His authority and who have announced that they would not have this man to reign over them.

Another reason why the throne of God is here presented to us under its symbol of the ark is because that symbol so surely reminds us of God's relationship with the children of Israel. The Church of Jesus Christ is not seen in this portion of the book of Revelation except enthroned in Heaven. The travail and pain of those who are to be purified in the tribulation, and the tortures of those who will be judged with no further mercy cannot point in any way to the redeemed host of the saints of this present age. All of this section of the book wherever concerned with any portion of the elect, shows us God's dealings with His earthly Israel.

At this point John is given another vision. Signs and wonders appear in Heaven. The first is that of a woman clothed with the sun, with the moon beneath her feet, and with a coronet of twelve stars upon her head. Some have applied this vision to the Virgin Mary. The great Spanish artist, Murillo, has given us painting after painting of this scene. It was one of his favorite subjects. Magnificent canvasses they are, showing the Virgin Mary, in her traditional robes of blue and white, her body great with child, most modestly portrayed, with the glory of the sun about her and the crescent moon under her feet, and the coronet of stars upon her head. No one who has looked on one of those great paintings will ever forget the gifts and powers of the artist; but this is not a vision of the Virgin Mary.

Nor can we follow the many commentators who see in this vision the representation of the Church. In spite of the fact that this woman is represented as the mother of the Lord, there have been those commentators who wish to bring every glory to the Church, and have attempted to see her here. Some have even gone so far as to declare that the "birth" described here is the return of the Lord in judgment, and that therefore the Church is portrayed. But other considerations force us to abandon any such view.

The symbols of the Old Testament inform us of the identity of this personage, made glorious by the gifts of God. Most expositors have seen clearly that this woman represents Israel, but have stopped with that simple identification. We believe that there is something more in view here. The rest of this chapter is going to reveal that there is war in the spiritual realm, and that this war is a great controversy, ages long, for the control of the universe. The war began with the fall of Satan, and will continue until the great and terrible day of the Lord shall bring this war to a close. The woman, then, represents not merely Israel "of whom, as concerning the flesh, Christ came" (Rom. 9:5), but is that spiritual body of the elect from the very beginning of the history of man, by whom God had eternally purposed to bring to naught the revolt of Satan. All of the symbols mentioned in these verses are found in the earliest chapters of the book of Genesis. The woman, the sun, the moon, the stars, the man-child, the seed, the dragon, "that old serpent which is the devil and Satan"; all of these are to be found in the opening paragraphs of the Bible.

Those who know the book of Genesis well, realize that Satan must have existed before he appeared in the third chapter. The rest of the Bible presents this malignant figure as having once been among the angels of God. When did he fall? There is evidence which demonstrates that there was a long interval between the first creation, described in the first sublime sentence of the Bible and the chaos of the second verse. It was during this interval that the war in Heaven was begun by Lucifer's rebellion. God's next revealed move was the creation of man to whom all of the symbols of authority were committed. God purposed eternally that all authority should be gathered together in Christ. He proceeds to this end, however, by way of the garden of Eden, the cross of Calvary and the return of the Lord in glory.

As soon as Satan had intruded into the new creation which God had made, thinking to have gained a great victory by accomplishing the fall of the man and the woman, God proceeded to announce in prophecy that which is here portrayed in Revelation. A great drama of spiritual warfare in the heavenly places. The great curse upon

Satan was announced in terms which included the promise of the
Redeemer and the triumph of God. "And the Lord God said unto
the serpent, Because thou hast done this, thou art cursed above all
cattle, and above every beast of the field; upon thy belly shalt thou
go, and dust shalt thou eat all the days of thy life. And I will put
enmity between thee and the woman, and between thy seed and her
seed; it shall bruise thy head, and thou shalt bruise his heel" (Gen.
3:14, 15).

The earthly struggle involving Adam, Eve and Satan, is presented
to us in the twelfth chapter of Revelation as being a part of the spiritual warfare which we shall some day realize is but a tiny corner of the
whole battlefield, though the scene of the decisive struggle and the victory of God. God created the woman who represents the elect of the
race in order that she might become the channel of His redemption.
We must look beyond mere Israel to the greater vision of the whole
plan of redemption. This is revealed in Galatians in a beautiful way.
Speaking of the inviolability of the covenants of God, St. Paul says,
"Now to Abraham and his seed were the promises made. He saith
not, And to seeds, as of many; but as of one, and to thy seed, which
is Christ" (Gal. 3:16). Here God definitely takes the promises out
of the realm of the mere literal progeny of Abraham and back to the
third chapter of Genesis where we see that Jesus Christ was in view.
Why was there a chosen people? In order that there might be a line
for the Lord Jesus Christ. Why was there a holy land? In order that
there might be a place to erect the cross to crucify the Lord Jesus.
These were the chief elements in the divine strategy.

So the identification of this woman, clothed with all the authority
of God, is certain. She represents that spiritual Israel that is more
than Israel. It goes backward through the line of the seed to Eve and
forward through the line of the seed to Mary and the Lord Jesus. The
enmity of Satan came against this people because they have been chosen
as the channel of the power and blessing of God. It may have seemed
for a moment that the fall of man caused the plans of God to be
frustrated, but the great promise which we have seen brought the
matter clearly out into the realm of a promise of victory. God has
promised, and what He has promised He will fulfill. Between the
second and third verses of our chapter we see that the woman who
was clothed with all authority presented as crying with great travail. The
entrance of sin into the human race, the fall, has taken place between
the two verses; nevertheless, the promises of God are sure and certain
in Christ, and He will bring His victory in His own time, even though
the following verse in Genesis announces that the woman shall bring
forth her children in sorrow. Many verses speak of the sorrows of
Israel under the figure of a woman in travail.

The identification of the dragon with Satan is made by the Lord

Himself in the ninth verse. We need not, therefore, pause to emphasize the fact. The red color is an interesting symbol. There are many
Greek words to describe varying shades of red, from pink through
scarlet and crimson. The particular word used in this passage is found
only here and in the description of the red horse (6:4). The word
comes from the Greek word for fire, and makes us think of his ferocity
and cruelty. The dragon has seven heads, each with a diadem, and
is pictured with ten horns. These symbols are easily determined in the
light of all that we have already seen. Satan has a kingdom, and God
put it into his hands, and has not yet taken it from him. When he
came to Christ at the temptation, he showed the kingdoms of the
world, and said, "All this power will I give thee, and the glory of them:
for that is delivered unto me; and to whomsoever I will I give it" (Luke
4:6). The figure seven is the symbol of that completeness of authority,
and the diadems are the crowns of power given by God, the ten horns
the universal nature of his earth-rule. These symbols bring into sharp
relief the power that is committed into the hands of Satan and which
he will use to the utmost of his strength in the last, desperate effort
which is described in verse 12, where Satan is spoken of as "having
great wrath, because he knoweth that he hath but a short time" (Rev.
12:12).

The next clause (Rev. 12:4) gives us one more glimpse of the beginning of that heavenly struggle in the time before the world was. His tail
drew the third part of the stars of Heaven, and he cast them to the earth.
Of all the verses where the stars are mentioned there are some which
point to a certain identification of this symbol. The demonized apostates
described by Jude are presented as "wandering stars, to whom is reserved the blackness of darkness for ever" (Jude 13). All of the angel
hosts were created by God, and creation by God implies perfection.
Some of them followed Satan in his rebellion, and of these he is still
the ruler. Satan's angelic hosts of verse 7 are evidently the stars of
verse 4. One commentator has said, "Remembering that he is 'a liar
and the father of it' (the lie), we get the thought that it was through
some falsehood that the devil drew the angels after him into rebellion
against God, even as by a lie he seduced the woman at the beginning.
The ground of this revolt of the angels may be inferred from Hebrews
1:6 where it is recorded of God the Father, that 'when he bringeth
the first begotten into the world, he saith, And let all the angels of
God worship him.'"

In casting them down to earth we have, perhaps, an indication that
Satan as a part of his strategy against God is now about to withdraw
his forces from the air, of whose power he is the prince (Eph. 2:2),
and marshal them upon the earth for the final conflict on this front.
Some may object that we speak of events that are yet to take place
in the same breath with events which took place when our Lord was

born into this world almost two thousand years ago. We must not forget that the present scene that we are looking at in Revelation is speaking of the whole age-long conflict, and the details are telescoped into one small picture. Between events that may seem far apart to us because we are living in them in time, there is but an instant so far as God is concerned. Speaking of Israel in another great passage under the same image as the one presented here, namely, a travailing woman, God says, "For the Lord hath called thee as a woman forsaken and grieved in spirit, and a wife of youth when thou wast refused, saith thy God. For a small moment have I forsaken thee; but with great mercies will I gather thee" (Isa. 54:6, 7). There has always been enmity between Satan and the woman, at every moment of her history, whether it be in the garden, or at the birth of Cain and Abel, or against the whole line of her sons from whom the Messiah was to be born. At His birth there was weeping in Ramah because of the slaughter of the innocents in Satan's effort to reach the Lord. The life of the Lord was sought many times before His hour came. Israel has borne the enmity of association with the promises of God, and Satan still seeks to destroy them. But God's purposes will not be foiled. It is Christ who shall rule the nations with a rod of iron (Ps. 2:9). He overcame the enemy and was caught up to the throne of God. The elect of God's purposes, and at this point it is Israel according to the flesh, is still hidden in the world as the hid treasure was found in the parable and then hidden again.

We are inclined to believe that it is definite, literal, future and limited to the thousand two hundred and sixty days. This number has appeared too often in this book and has been too well balanced by other teachings to attempt to find in it a symbol. In fact, we believe that this announcement in verse six is the first mention of that which is given in detail in the end of the chapter.

Verses 7–10

War in Heaven

⁷And there came to pass war in Heaven; Michael and his messengers going forth to war with the dragon; and the dragon warred with his messengers; ⁸and they prevailed not, neither was their place found any more in Heaven. ⁹And the great dragon was cast down, that old serpent, which is the slanderer, and Satan, the deceiver of the whole world, he was cast down to the earth; and his messengers were cast down with him.

¹⁰And I heard a great voice in the Heaven saying, Now is come the salvation, the power and the kingdom of our God, and the authority

of His Messiah; because the accuser of our brethren is cast down, who accuseth them by day and by night.
(Rev. 12:7-10, Free Translation)

That Satan should be in Heaven should not surprise anyone who is familiar with the general teaching of the Word of God. The twenty-eighth chapter of Ezekiel gives us the outline of the creation and fall of Satan. He was originally God's prophet, priest and king. As prophet he spoke for God to the universe, as priest he took the worship of the universe to God, as king he ruled for God. He was the cherub, anointed to govern, as we might well translate the verse that is usually rendered, "The anointed cherub that covereth" (Ezek. 28:14). The Eden that is mentioned by Ezekiel, is, as the context clearly shows, a perfect Eden, long before the time of Adam. It is in that great time which took place between the "beginning" when God created the heavens and the earth and when it became waste and desolate, without form and void. The picture in Ezekiel, in other words, must be seen as lying between the first two verses in Genesis.

Ezekiel concludes the picture of Satan in his unfallen state with the definite statement concerning the origin of sin, "Thou wast perfect in thy ways from the day that thou wast created, till iniquity was found in thee" (Ezek. 28:15). The next verses gave a definite prophecy which we are now seeing described in fulfillment. The casting out of Satan from Heaven described in our passage is an event, yet future, which is often seen in the Scriptures. Ezekiel says, "By the multitude of thy merchandise they have filled the midst of thee with violence, and thou hast sinned: therefore I will cast thee as profane out of the mountain of God: and I will destroy thee, O covering cherub, from the midst of the stones of fire. Thine heart was lifted up because of thy beauty, thou hast corrupted thy wisdom by reason of thy brightness: I will cast thee to the ground, I will lay thee before kings, that they may behold thee . . ." (Ezek. 28:16, 17).

Now Satan, the deceiver, has many devices, and we are told by the Holy Spirit that we should not be ignorant of these devices (II Cor. 2:11). One of his foremost devices is to cover his tracks and make people think that he is not what he really is. He has made multitudes seriously think that he is a joke for a masquerade costume. Other multitudes seriously think that he is already in Hell, and, furthermore, that he is there as ruler. Milton and Dante have given ideas that have entered into the literary consciousness of nations, and spread the plan of Satan to cover his ways and his being. The sculptors of the great cathedrals of the middle ages added to this error. One of the commonest scenes to be found carved on the walls of the churches of Europe represents Satan as he likes to be represented—out of this world and in Hell. Over the doors of many Gothic edifices there is a triangular space that needed some special motif to fill it properly. Christ, seated in the center, with Mary and the twelve apostles somewhere near in artistic proportion, has, over His head, the Holy Spirit in the form of a dove. Above this is a patriarchal old man, representing God the Father. Below Christ, the recording angel reads the record of the works of souls, another angel weighs the souls in balances. Those who are found to be worthy proceed to the lower right hand corner of the scene where angels are fastening wings upon them, while those who have been found wanting are being led to the lower left hand corner where imps with pitchforks lead them toward stony flames, where the head of Satan can be seen grimacing with pleasure at the idea that they are now his. But all of this is, of course, false.

When Satan finally reaches Hell he will be there as the chief victim of punishment and not in any sense as the ruler or the one who causes the torture. The important thing about Hell is that God runs it, and we must never forget that fact. There is not a line in the Bible that shows that the devil has ever been in Hell, and there is no line in the Bible that says that when he gets there he or his minions will have any authority.

The war that is going on in Heaven began with Satan's sin. Immediately other angels followed him in his desire for worship and power. These are the fallen angels. Pember distinguishes between these and the demons, the latter being, in his thought, the disembodied spirits of the earth-beings of the interval between the first two verses of the Bible. God did not immediately destroy these rebels, but moved in His own majestic way to perform His plan that would ultimately bring out His perfections, and show the utter defeat of Satan. This warfare is being carried on in many spheres. The result will always be the same, however. Every attack by Satan ends in defeat. At the beginning of human history this was announced in the curse upon him. "Upon thy belly shalt thou go, and dust shalt thou eat all the days of thy life" (Gen. 3:14). Let us present a parable which will show the meaning of this curse.

A certain man had a beautiful estate upon which were some 'magnificent trees in which he took great pride. It was his custom to walk among them and gaze upon their beauty. This man had an enemy who hated him sorely. This enemy was always seeking ways of annoying the master of the estate. At last the enemy conceived a plan which he thought would greatly wound the heart of the proprietor. He decided to go to the estate in the dark of night and cut down one of the most beautiful of the trees. He laid his plans well. He took with him axe and saw and began his work. All night he toiled till his muscles were sore and his hands were blistered. As morning dawned he saw the proprietor riding with a companion toward the trees where he had been toiling. He redoubled his efforts and the great tree began to creak and totter. As it gained momentum in the fall the enemy began to shout in triumph. One of the branches however, came toward him and pinned him to the ground in agony. His hatred, however, was strong, and he jeered at the proprietor who approached him. The owner of the estate called his companion to him and said to the enemy, "You thought to do me a great harm, but I want to show you what you have done. This man with me is the architect of the beautiful home that I intend to build here in the midst of these trees. In order to make room for the house it was necessary to cut down one of these trees. Look at this plan! The tree upon which you have toiled all night and which is the cause of your death is the tree which must be cut down to make way for my house. You have worked for me without knowing it, and your toil is for nothing and bitterness is your food in death."

So it is with the warfare that is being waged in the heavenly places. We are sure of the ultimate triumph of God, not only in the main struggle, but also in the final and eternal view of every skirmish in the whole conflict.

Those who, in this chapter, are fighting for God are presented under the title, "Michael and his messengers." The Bible indicates in many places that Satan's kingdom on this earth is divided into nations and that various powers are in control of the different sections. "We wrestle not against flesh and blood, but against principalities, against powers, against the world-rulers of this darkness, against the spiritual hosts of wickedness in the high places" (Eph. 6:12). In the book of Daniel we see behind the scenes in this heavenly warfare. Daniel had prayed to the Lord for further understanding. Day after day he waited and God seemed not to have answered. But the reason for the delay was going to be recorded, and this would give to many saints throughout the years, an insight into the spiritual conflict that is being fought, and would help to arm them, for the further defeat of Satan.

Finally, a messenger arrived and spoke to Daniel. The vision of this glorious one overwhelmed Daniel, but when he was helped and restored he heard the messenger say, "Fear not, Daniel; for from the first day that thou didst set thine heart to understand, and to chasten thyself before thy God, thy words were heard, and I am come, because of thy words. But the prince of the kingdom of Persia withstood me for twenty-one days . . ." (Dan. 10:12, 13). Who was this prince that could resist a mighty messenger of God? Certainly not a human being with an earthly authority in Persia. It was the invisible being, recognizing the power of Satan, and responsible for Satan's government in the land of Persia at that time. This angelic messenger of Satan had hastened to fight with the messenger who came from God with the answer to Daniel's prayer. For some time he had delayed the answer. But suddenly another mighty one came to the fight. "Lo, Michael, one of the chief princes, came to help me . . ." (Dan. 10:13). This, of course, was not a human being, but one of God's own mighty messengers. Indeed, this is the same one that has the honor of gaining the final battle over Satan.

The messenger who came to Daniel performed his duty and then announced that he was going back into the fray. "Now I will return to fight with the prince of Persia: and when I am gone forth, lo, the prince of Greece shall come" (Dan. 10:20). We are not told in this latter case whether the prince of Greece was on Satan's side and come to attack Daniel, or whether he was one of the faithful ones coming to his help. In the light of the whole passage the latter is more probable. At any rate, we see that the earthly nations have Satanic powers back of them, and that God has even mightier powers which are overruling all of Satan's desires. The Holy Spirit told John, "Greater is he that is in you than he that is in the world" (I John 4:4). Elisha's servant realized this when the vision came to him and he learned that "They that be with us are more than they that be with them" (II Kings 6:16).

The messenger that spoke to Daniel continued the revelation before he left by saying, "I will shew thee that which is noted in the scripture of truth: and there is none that holdeth with me in these things, but Michael your prince" (Dan. 10:21). This leads us to inquire into the special relationship that existed between this mighty messenger of God and Daniel, God's prophet, that should have led the other messenger to speak of Michael as Daniel's prince. This is answered further on in the narrative of Daniel's prophecy. In speaking of the great tribulation that is to come upon the children of Israel, the divine messenger announces to Daniel, "At that time shall Michael stand up, the great prince which stands for the children of thy people, and there shall be a time of trouble, such as never was since there was a nation even to that time: and at that time thy people shall be delivered, every one that shall be found written in the book" (Dan. 12:1).

The New Testament tells us that the angels study the Bible, in fact, that they are eager to look into prophetic matters (I Pet. 1:12). Here are two angels, at least, to whom God has been pleased to reveal His detailed purpose of end times. The one who brought the message to Daniel, and Michael, God's great messenger who is in authority over those spiritual forces which deal with the affairs of the children of Israel, are engaged in a great struggle, along with myriads of others. At least these two, however, know that the end is victory, and that they will have part in that victory.

The conflict we are studying here is not the first encounter between Satan and Michael. The book of Jude gives us another incident in this unseen warfare. In describing the lightness with which apostate teachers speak of spiritual powers, Jude is led to say, "Yet Michael the archangel, when contending with the devil, he disputed about the body of Moses, dared not bring against him a railing accusation, but said, Jehovah rebuke thee" (Jude 9). Who can tell how this mighty prince of angels, Michael, whose very name means "one like God," has been tried in the midst of conflict with this enemy who has no honor? But Michael's day is coming, as our day is coming, the day when the Lord Jesus Christ will take His power and reign. Jesus said, "The Son of man shall send forth his angels, and they shall gather out of his kingdom all things that offend, and them which do iniquity" (Matt. 13:41). This is the moment of the fulfillment of that prophecy.

Not only do Michael and his angels gain a complete victory, but there is something new in the age-long conflict. Heretofore there have been victories, but Satan has always retained his place in Heaven. Now he is cast forth. To some it seems amazing that we should speak of Satan in Heaven, but the Bible clearly teaches us that Satan has had and still has access to Heaven. He had access there as an unfallen angel. After his fall he still was forced to go back to report to the Creator. We see one such scene in the first chapter of Job. "Now there was a day when the sons of God [this phrase in the Old Testament always refers to angelic creatures] came to present themselves before the Lord, and Satan came also among them. And the Lord said unto Satan, Where do you come from? Then Satan answered the Lord, and said, From going to and fro in the earth, and from walking up and down in it" (Job 1:6, 7). This passage gives us an account of the spheres of the activity of Satan. No passage in the Bible speaks of Satan in his present activity as being in any other place than this earth and the air that surrounds it, with visits to the presence of God in Heaven. Since spiritual beings travel with the speed of thought there is no difficulty in this teaching.

The presence of Satan in Heaven is the explanation for the necessity of Heaven's destruction and the creation of a new Heaven at the same time that there will be the new earth. No other explanation would suffice. The moral cleansing of Heaven is by the death of the Lord Jesus Christ. When He announced that He would "go to prepare a place" (John 14:2, 3), it was not as a glorified carpenter engaged in heavenly building. All of material creation would come from Him who made all things by the expression of His Word. Creation is nothing more nor less than the materialization of the thought of God. The preparation of the place by the Lord Jesus is more fully described in the epistle to the Hebrews, "It was therefore necessary that the . . . heavenly things themselves should be purified with better sacrifices . . ." (Heb. 9:23).

What a glorious truth it is that Satan's place is to be found no more in Heaven. He had said in his heart, "I will ascend . . . I will . . . I will . . . I will be like the most High" (Isa. 14:13, 14). But he was to be brought down to Hell. The verse we are studying tells of Satan's first step toward Hell. From this prophetic moment he is out of Heaven; from the earth he is to be sent to the bottomless pit, the abyss (Rev. 20:3); from there he will be taken forth for judgment and will finally reach the lake of fire (Rev. 20:10), which was prepared for him and his angels (Matt. 25:41), and which he has not yet occupied. One commentator has well written, "God preserved His right of choice in act and process to the end of His dealings with Satan and his angels. Thus, though He has allowed him and them to exist and largely to have their own way for thousands of years past, He now deals with them in judgment, not in an instant of time, but gradually, in successive stages, and only finally, when He has accomplished through them great time-consuming events of judgment toward men which it is His purpose to bring to pass. Satan has pitched his throne high, but God has placed His higher. Satan is mighty, but God is Almighty. Satan can destroy, but God can destroy the destroyer. Satan is free, but God will shut him in, at last, so that he may never more harm or even touch His holy ones. In His own time, therefore, God will indisputably enthrone Himself by indisputably dethroning Satan. All this was the vision Christ had when He was on earth, when He said, 'I beheld Satan as lightning fall from heaven' (Luke 10:18); and again, 'Now shall the prince of this world be cast out' (John 12:31); and finally, 'The prince of this world is judged' (John 16:11). To the eternal Christ, Satan's downfall was already visible and accomplished. But for mortal men, time had to pass."

The name given to Satan at this moment which describe his ejection from Heaven are most significant. He is called first, "the great dragon," and under that name is frequently mentioned in the Bible as the great enemy of God. This takes us back to the third chapter of Genesis where he is identified as "that old serpent." The word that is translated "old" comes from another word meaning "beginning." How significant, since Jesus said that the devil was a murderer "from the beginning" (John 8:44). The word translated "devil" means "slanderer," and surely all of the lies which mankind has believed against God come from this source. How many people think that God is unjust, that He is unkind, that He is unwise, and so on! All of these slanders come from the one whose very name is "the slanderer."

One commentator has tried to show that Satan has been cast forth from Heaven since the time of the cross. He would teach that the presence of Satan at times in Heaven today would be denial of the power of the death of Christ. But that is not so. Satan's presence in Heaven at the time of Job's trial did not cause Job's defeat. Satan never had the upper hand. We can claim by simple faith the victory that is ours in Christ. Satan's power over the believers has been broken.

Christ is the present intercessor, now appearing in our behalf in Heaven. Why should we need an intercessor if there were no accuser? Much is made of the verse, "Who shall lay anything to the charge of God's elect?" But the answer of the New Testament is surely that though Satan is evil enough and stupid enough to go on rebelling against God, and to go on accusing God's elect, nevertheless, God has justified us, and that, therefore, "principalities and powers" are among those things which can never separate us from the love of God (Rom. 8:38).

We must not forget that there is not only salvation in the past tense, and in the present tense, but also a "salvation ready to be revealed in the last time" (I Pet. 1:5). The salvation in the future tense comes to this earth at the time of the return of the Lord Jesus Christ. As soon as Satan is fully upon the earth, cast out of Heaven, cast out of his dominating position in the air, the judgments of God are poured upon the earth. Salvation will now be revealed. Then will come the authority and the kingdom of our God. Satan has been the world's prince long enough. He has been the god of an age which is now closing, and with its close he ceases to be other than a mere creature, doomed to judgment for his rebellion.

Verses 11–17

Satan Rampant

¹¹And they overcame him because of the blood of the Lamb and because of the word of their testimony, and they loved not their life even unto death. ¹²For this reason, rejoice O Heaven, and they that tabernacle therein. Woe for the earth and for the sea, because the devil is gone down to you having boiling rage, knowing that he hath but a short time.

¹³And when the dragon saw that he was cast out into the earth, he pursued the woman who brought forth the manchild. ¹⁴And there were given to the woman the two wings of the great eagle, that she might fly into the desert, into her place, where she is nourished there for a time, and times, and half a time, from the face of the serpent. ¹⁵And the serpent cast out of his mouth water as a river after the woman, that he might cause her to be carried away by the stream. ¹⁶And the earth helped the woman, and the earth opened its mouth and drank down the stream which the dragon cast out of his mouth. ¹⁷And the dragon became enraged because of the woman, and went to make war with the remnant of her seed, which keep the commandments of God and hold the testimony of Jesus.

(Rev. 12:11-17, Free Translation)

Satan is a defeated enemy. Our Lord has won the victory, and that victory belongs to all who take their stand in Him. Steadily, through the ages, this enemy has been forced to give up his fortified positions,

the dust of retreat has ever been his food. All this is on the basis of
the death of our Lord Jesus Christ.

Victory, however, is not dependent upon the death of Christ in point
of time. There was victory over Satan before Christ had actually
died in point of time. There is victory today before the final expulsion
of Satan from Heaven in point of time. The important truth is that
all victory is on the basis of what the Lord Jesus Christ accomplished
at Calvary. There are many fruits of that victory which are certain,
though not yet accomplished. The redemption of our bodies we await
with groaning (Rom. 8:23), for much of our salvation is in hope
(Rom. 8:24). True faith, however, learns to stand with God and
look upon these struggles from the calm of His throne and the objective viewpoint of eternity.

All victory, then, has always been on the grounds of the victory
which Christ provided in dying upon the cross. This was the very
purpose of the incarnation. The Son of God was manifested that He
might destroy the works of the devil (I John 3:8), and He took a
human body in order that through the death of that body and the
shedding of His atoning blood, the Saviour might destroy the enemy
who had the power of death (Heb. 2:14). We must not go by this
text without seeing the practical truth that is to be found in it for
our own conflict today. The victory which Christ prepared is for His
people in all ages. The victory of Michael the archangel and his messengers in the future day will be because Christ has already died.
The victory of Israel in the land and in flight will be because Christ
has died. That which we so sorely need moment by moment today
is available for us when we enter into the fruit of that which Jesus
Christ accomplished in dying on the cross.

One commentator who attempts to place the expulsion of Satan
back in the days of Christ's earthly existence, claims that there would
be no victory today if Satan still had access to Heaven. A host of Old
Testament saints rise to claim that this is not true. They, too, overcame the enemy by the blood of the Lamb and the word of their testimony. The claim that, since Christ's death, "Satan no longer has the
upper hand" is most simply answered by the plain teaching of Scripture that Satan at no time had the upper hand. He may accuse the
brethren; he may even accuse them with truth on his side, but thanks
be to God, the victory is ours through the Lord Jesus Christ. Satan,
the author of sin, casts it upon us, and finds us, in our old natures,
eager to have it upon us, yet he is utterly foiled by the simple turning
in faith to the place of forgiveness. All of which we are accused, in
whole or in part justice, is washed away by the blood of the Lord Jesus
Christ, which cleanses from all sin.

There is a practical participation, however, in which the believer
experiences the victory only as he joins himself to it in an open testi-

mony. Mere resistance of the devil is not enough. The command, "Resist the devil and he will flee from you" (James 4:7), has long been proven untrue unless the place of resistance be the proper one. How many children of God have resisted the devil only to find that, instead of fleeing, he attacked all the more boldly? But the first half of that verse gives us the truth that brings victory. "Submit yourselves therefore, to God. Resist the devil and he will flee from you." The resistance must follow submission. The submission is our true testimony that we have no other hope and no other strength. Let the weakest believer submit to the life of God as it comes upon him in Christ, acknowledging his own utter nothingness, and taking, by faith, the bold stand of victory in Christ, and Satan will flee immediately.

> *Did we in our own strength confide,*
> *Our striving would be losing;*
> *Were not the Right Man on our side,*
> *The Man of God's own choosing.*

The Greek word that is used to describe the overcoming is the same that is used elsewhere to describe the victory of Christ Himself. "Be of good cheer, I have overcome the world" (John 16:33). This is the quality of the overcoming victory that is promised to us. How many there are, from Abel, down to the martyrs who have yet to die in the future, who have experienced, and will experience in all ages, the splendor of the conquest that Christ accomplished by dying for us on the cross. How humiliating to think that we do not avail ourselves of this victory as we might and as we should. What cause we have to glorify God for His patience and His faithfulness. These that are mentioned here were spendthrifts in their surrender to God. They did not count the price. Horrible death might be their lot; what matter? They had done their reckoning, counted themselves debtors, and had learned truly that the constraining love of Christ deserved their all. They had resisted the attacks of Satan "even unto blood" (Heb. 12: 4). They were, by His grace, true followers of Him who said, "He that hateth his life in this world shall keep it unto life eternal" (John 12: 25). It would seem that this verse speaks of those who are still alive and who are about to be the victims of the tremendous hatred of Satan. The great Greek scholar, Robertson, says that their future martyrdom is foreseen prophetically. They are to be the last of the company who during all ages, say:

> *Here, Lord, I give myself away,*
> *'Tis all that I can do . . .*

The great voice from Heaven now speaks its last word. We are taken back to the great picture of victory in verse ten. The downfall of Satan and the establishment of the empire of God through the authority of Christ gives the ground for rejoicing. Satan is no longer in the Heavens. Therefore, all the angelic hosts are bidden to rejoice. Their warfare with the enemy which has been waged over a wide front for so many ages is now restricted to the earth, the last battleground of the enemy. Satan, who was cast out of the Heaven of God into the heavens of which he is said to be the prince of the power of the air, now is on earth alone. Soon he will be still further restricted, but how wonderful for all the hosts of God, saints and angels, that the Satanic struggle is at that time so restricted.

On the other hand the earth and the sea will have reason to fear. The animal that was dangerous enough when he roamed through the whole forest is now limited to a stockade, where, mad with the restrictions which he sees around him, and raging because he feels the end near, he throws the insane strength of the death struggle into all of his movements. Seiss has well said in this connection, "We would think that so signal a defeat in Heaven would cure him of his malignity. at least induce him to refrain from any further attempts against God and His people. But he is hopelessly depraved, and nothing but absolute force can quell his devil nature. There is no cure for a being so totally perverted." This is true. And yet there are those who dare to teach that even the devil will be ultimately saved. There are those who assert that the day will come when all punishment will cease and all Satan's followers, together with himself, will be brought repentant to Heaven. The fact is that Satan's malignity grows with his continuing rebellion. So it is with those who reject Christ. Ye will not come unto me that ye might have life" (John 5:40), our Lord said to those who rejected Him, and it was necessary, also to say to them, "If ye die in your sins, whither I go ye cannot come" (John 8:21).

The Revised Versions properly translate the last half of the verse, "Woe to the earth and sea." These words are undoubtedly symbolical. The woe is not pronounced upon the ground and the water, nor the "inhabitants" of the sea, which would mean the fish. In the Bible the earth is used as a symbol of Israel and the sea as the symbol of the Gentile nations.

We now return to the continuation of events described in the first part of the chapter. The great voice has interrupted the narrative with the cry of victory in Heaven and woe to the earth. We now are to see the actions of Satan, cast to the earth. His first wrath was against the woman who had brought forth the manchild. This woman represents all the saved of God from the time of Eve who received the promise that her seed would bruise the serpent's head. Satan now realizes afresh that his defeat has been wrought through the instrumentality of feeble human beings. That God did the empowering he does not take into consideration, but turns his boiling rage against the faithful followers of God.

It should be remembered that the earthly people of God at this time is made up in a different manner from the Church of our day. We are a new people, formerly Jew or Gentile, but now one in Christ. Every member of this mystical body will have been removed from the earth at the time of the rapture. The saints of the tribulation period come from definite sources. First of all, there are the one hundred and forty-four thousand Israelites from all of the tribes, specially called of God for the great kingdom preaching of this time, and chosen from among the twelve tribes, twelve thousand from each tribe. These we have seen in our discussion of the seventh chapter and we will have occasion to refer to them again in the fourteenth chapter. These are those whom Christ calls "my brethren" in His famous phrase quoted of the judgment of the nations. "Inasmuch as you have done it unto one of the least of these, my brethren [my Jewish brethren of the tribulation period] you have done it unto me" (Matt. 25:40). From their preaching there comes a great Gentile host of believers, as well as many others who are Jews, but who are not the specially chosen messengers through whom the gospel of the kingdom is announced in all the world. These are the representatives of God, the line of the believers in all the ages, who draw the wrath of Satan. God is about to deal with Israel in a special way, and Satan, knowing the Bible well, and knowing that his time is short, now proceeds to pursue Israel with his greatest wrath.

God's people have never yet known persecutions like those that yet confront them. The Word of God is very clear on this subject. The time of Jacob's trouble (Jer. 30:7) is yet in the future, and the closing verses of this chapter announce the trouble that is yet to come, and at the same time announce God's care over His people.

"And there were given to the woman the two wings of the great eagle, that she might fly into the wilderness, into her place where she is nourished there for a time, and times, and half a time from the face of the serpent." There can be no doubt whatsoever that we have before us a phrase indicating one plus two plus one half, making a total of three and one half years, which is half of the final seven-year period and which is also the forty-two months and the one thousand two hundred sixty days (Rev. 11:2, 3). We have then, one more of the indications which God has given us concerning the length of the last half of the prophetic "week."

This verse, however, contains a promise that leads us to an Old Testament passage which gives us one of the most memorable views of the love and tenderness of the Father that we shall find in the whole of the Word of God. Remember that God's people of the future time will have this Word, and will know every line of it. What comfort, therefore, to learn that God will give them the two wings of the great eagle. The concordance takes us back to the eagle promises of the Old Testament. Once before, Israel was persecuted and led by God into the desert, in order that He might fulfill His Word to them. Pharaoh, who is a type of the Antichrist who is about to rage against God's people, and who is called "the great dragon that lieth between his rivers" (Ezek. 29:3) pursued them with his troops. God delivered them in a way that was memorable to them through the thousands of years of their history. They turn in their law today and read that God spoke from the very Mount Sinai from which the law was given, saying, "Ye have seen what I did to the Egyptians and how I bore you on eagles' wings, and brought you unto myself" (Exod. 19:4). Thus God worked for His people. For forty years He kept them in such a way that He was able to say to them, "I have led you forty years in the wilderness: your clothes are not waxen old upon you, and thy shoe is not waxen old upon thy foot" (Deut. 29:5; Neh. 9:21). There was not a feeble person in all of the tribes (Ps. 105:37).

Through this wilderness experience God bound His people to Himself, and through another wilderness experience He will bring them back to Himself. He spoke through Moses, when this faithful leader was about to die, and said, "The Lord's portion is his people; Jacob is the lot of his inheritance. He found him in a desert land, and in the waste howling wilderness; he led him about, he instructed him, he kept him as the apple of his eye. As an eagle stirreth up her nest, fluttereth over her young, spreadeth abroad her wings, taketh them, beareth them on her wings: So the Lord alone did lead him, and there was no strange god with him" (Deut. 32:9-12).

Here we see eagles' wings and a wilderness in the picture of Israel's birth. Israel was never allowed to forget this time. Even today in their wretched unbelief the Jews have their passover services and eat a feast remembering their deliverance from Egypt. Even though they have forgotten the God who delivered them. Scores of times, yes, hundreds of times throughout the Old Testament we find references to the redemption that lasted through the forty years from Egypt to Canaan. The Bible could not be understood if we took away all the references to God's power, love and mercy manifested to Israel under Moses. But Jeremiah says the day will come when they will not talk about these wonders any more. They talk about them today in their unbelief, but they will stop talking about them in the time of their return! The reason is that God will perform so much greater wonders in their behalf in the time to come that there will be no comparison. "Therefore, behold, the days come, saith the Lord, that it shall no more be said, The Lord liveth, that brought up the children of Israel out of the land of Egypt; but, The Lord liveth, that brought up the children of Israel from the land of the north, and from all the lands whither he had driven them . . ." (Jer. 16:14, 15). And now this time of wonder is upon them. Satan, with boiling rage, may fight against them, but God takes them into the wilderness on eagles' wings.

The failure of Satan's attack against those who have fled into the desert causes him to turn back to make war with "the remnant." Those who are thus described are further identified as keeping the commandments of God and holding the testimony of Jesus. It is our belief that this refers to the one hundred and forty-four thousand who have been witnessing throughout the earth. Those who have been in Palestine have fled into the wilderness in a flight which has been marked by God's miraculous care. The wrath of Satan now turns to the faithful band, scattered through many lands, and he hounds them with all his power. We have come to this opinion because they, indeed, keep the commandments of God and hold the testimony of Jesus. Further, after the parenthesis of the thirteenth chapter which will show us Satan's methods of warfare, we will return in the fourteenth chapter to a description of these faithful ones who are so evidently the object of the hatred of Satan and his counterfeit trinity.

CHAPTER 13

Verses 1–10

The Wild Beast Out of the Sea

¹*And I saw a wild beast coming up out of the sea, having seven heads and ten horns, and upon his horns ten diadems, and upon his heads names of blasphemy.* ²*And the wild beast which I saw was like unto a leopard, and his feet are like those of a bear, and his mouth like the mouth of a lion. And the dragon gave to him his power, and his throne and great authority.* ³*And one of his heads was as though slain to death, and his death stroke was healed; and the whole earth wondered at and followed after the wild beast.*

⁴*And they worshipped the dragon because he had given the authority to the wild beast; and they worshipped the wild beast, saying, Who is like unto the wild beast? and who is able to make war with him?* ⁵*And there was given unto him a mouth speaking great things and blasphemies; and authority was given unto him to act forty-two months.* ⁶*And he opened his mouth for blasphemies, against God, to blaspheme His Name, and His tabernacle and those dwelling in Heaven.* ⁷*And it was given unto him to make war with the saints and to overcome them; and authority was given to him over every tribe and people, and tongue and nation.*

⁸*And all that dwell upon the earth shall worship him, every one whose name hath not been written in the book of life of the Lamb, who hath been slain from the disruption of the world.* ⁹*If any one hath an ear, let him hear.* ¹⁰*If any man is for captivity, into captivity he goeth; if any man shall kill with a sword, he must be killed with the sword. Here is the endurance and faithfulness of the saints.*
(Rev. 13:1-10, Free Translation)

The opening clause of the thirteenth chapter really belongs to the close of the preceding chapter. The Bible divisions of chapter and verse are man-made conveniences to facilitate our finding passages in the Scriptures, and it is necessary to have them. But they must never be considered as being inspired. The original narrative runs along in great paragraphs, which in their earliest forms were not separated by any punctuation. If you could see an original manuscript of the New Testament you would see that such divisions did not occur.

There is no doubt that the early manuscripts all read, "And he stood upon the sand of the sea." The one who stood was not John, but the dragon. The whole of the previous verse would really read, "And the dragon became enraged because of the woman, and went to make war with the remnant of her seed, which keep the commandments of God and hold the testimony of Jesus; and he [the dragon] stood upon the sand of the sea."

This position of the dragon forms the connection between the war in Heaven and the war that is about to break forth upon the earth with increased fury. The dragon, that old serpent, the devil and Satan (12:9) is the first person of the Satanic trinity. We have seen how he hated God and how he had rebelled against God, warring in Heaven against the angels of God. Cast out of Heaven, he came down to earth, filled with wrath because he knew he had but a short time (12:12). How does he proceed upon his definite and final arrival upon the earth?

The answer to that question is now presented to us. Enraged with the woman, he stands upon the sand of the sea and immediately he enters into negotiations with one who is called a wild beast which was then rising out of the sea. The symbolism takes us back to the Old Testament. The sand of the sea does not mean the seashore in Scriptural language. The sand, always represents an innumerable company, as will be easily seen by a comparison of the passages from the time when God promised Abraham seed as the sand of the sea in multitude. The sea is clearly shown as a symbol of the restless nations of the earth. Further in this prophecy we will see that the "many waters" are "peoples, multitudes, nations, and tongues" (Rev. 17:15). To anyone who has traveled widely, in trains and ships and planes across the world or in books across the past, there can be no doubt that the nations are unceasingly restless, fitting perfectly the picture given by Isaiah, "The wicked are like the troubled sea, when it cannot rest, whose waters cast up mire and dirt. There is no peace, saith my God, to the wicked" (Isa. 57:20, 21).

The dragon, cast out of Heaven after his final defeat at the hands of Michael and his forces, comes to the earth looking for an instrument through whom he can carry on his warfare against his hated Creator and God. John, in the revelation that is given to him, sees a wild beast coming up out of the sea to whom Satan gives his power.

The identity of this wild beast and that of the second which appears later in the chapter are among the most interesting points in biblical prophecy. There have been many attempts by the commentators of the past to identify these beasts.

There have been intelligent commentators who have seen in this first wild beast an imperial nation or system, and others have seen an individual, the head of such a nation. I shall present the two views because I believe that both are true. After all, it was Louis XIV, the sun-king of France, who claimed that he, himself, was the state. The wild beast that is before us here is most certainly the final imperial power of a great nation arrayed against God and His people, but a nation incarnate in its leader, an individual through whom Satan will seek to rule and build his empire.

All commentators have pointed to the resemblance between this prophecy and one to be found in the book of Daniel. Our purpose is not so much to convince the unbeliever as to teach the believer. Every believer in the Word of God knows that no part of this inspired record contradicts any other part, and that a careful comparison will bring out the truth from the various parts. The difficulties that men have imagined in these passages arise from the minds of men and not from the Word of God.

Commentators of every school of thought have been forced to admit that Rome is envisaged in the prophecies. Of this there can be no doubt. To Daniel was given the interpretation of Nebuchadnezzar's dream of successive world empires. That of the Babylonian king was the first in the series; the last was to be an empire of iron, finally mixed with clay, and smitten by a stone cut out without hands, which in turn, after consuming the kingdoms of earth, filled the whole earth as a kingdom set up by God, a kingdom that will never be destroyed (Dan. 2:31-45). This kingdom of living stone is none other than the Messianic kingdom of our Lord Jesus Christ.

After Daniel had been given the interpretation of the dream of the Babylonian king, he was granted a further revelation in the matter of world empires. Four winds of Heaven broke upon the great sea and four wild beasts came up out of the sea. The details may be followed in the seventh chapter of Daniel. The first beast was like a lion, the second like a bear, the third like a leopard and the fourth a nondescript beast not to be found in nature, but "terrible and powerful, and strong, exceedingly," having ten horns, and later another. In John's vision which we have before us, one beast is seen with significant characteristics from each of Daniel's four beasts, but in reverse order. John mentions first the ten horns, then the leopard, bear and lion. There is one commentator who ingeniously suggests that Daniel was looking at the vision from past to future and John was looking back toward the past and that which was nearest to Daniel was farthest from John, and vice versa. Is it not more simple to state that John saw a future empire that was to have the characteristics of the great empires of the past? The Rome of tomorrow will have the rapaciousness of the lion, the crushing power of the bear and the swiftness of the leopard. When Daniel asked the truth concerning this vision, he was told, "These great beasts which are four, are four kings, which shall arise out of the earth . . . The fourth beast shall be a fourth kingdom upon earth . . ." (Dan. 7:17, 23). So we have definite Scripture warrant for saying that the beasts are both kingdom and king, or rather, as we have stated, the incarnation of the empire idea in some strong dictator.

When the beast of John's vision is described in a later chapter of the Revelation it is said very definitely that the seven heads are seven mountains (17:9), and, as we have already seen, a mountain in the Bible is the symbol of a nation. For these nations there are kings. "And there are seven kings; five are fallen, and one is, and the other is not yet come; and when he comes he must continue a short space" (Rev. 17:10). This definite statement of the existence of the sixth kingdom at the time of John's vision identifies it clearly as the Roman Empire of John's day. Of the five that preceded John's time, two are named by Daniel, that is, Babylon and Medo-Persia. The remaining three are easily found from history, as there were only three other world kingdoms which were enemies of God's people Israel. These three are Egypt, Assyria and Greece. These six, together with the future empire of the Antichrist, form the seven successive phases of Gentile world government from the time of the scattering of the peoples at Babel until the time of the end. Daniel had a vision only of those four powers which arose after God had set aside the governing authority of Israel. John sees the whole scope of Gentile history in his final vision. How sobering a thought that God sees the nations of the earth as wild beasts.

It is the seventh of the kingdoms that is yet future. It is this last kingdom which is to have the ten horns. The explanation of this feature is again given to John in a later portion of his vision. We read, "And the ten horns which thou sawest are ten kings, which have received no kingdom as yet; but receive power as kings one hour with the beast" (Rev. 17:12). It is absolutely impossible for us to follow all the weavings of the future minor kingdoms which will compose the realm of the Antichrist. Suffice it to say that the Scripture seems to indicate here and in Daniel that the realm of Antichrist will be in ten parts, each with a king reigning over it. He will receive power from the devil to govern for a short time just before the great battle of Armageddon, in which these nations will participate with the Antichrist (19:19), and in which they and their power will be destroyed. Those who live upon the earth after the taking out of the Church and the establishing of the rule of Antichrist will be able to trace these ten kingdoms with ease. Daniel even tells us that there will be some trouble among them, and that one shall arise who shall put down three others (Dan. 7:24), and that this little one shall be particularly blasphemous.

In fact, it would appear that it is this "little horn" which arises and subdues three of the ten kings, who is given the authority by Satan to be the very incarnation of his power in this phase of his rebellion against God. He it is who leads the war against the saints of that tribulation time (Dan. 7:25), and who is given authority by Satan for a stated period. It might be well to note that there are thirteen different titles given in the Scriptures to this sovereign of Gentile power. These titles are: "the king of Babylon" (Isa. 14:4), "Lucifer, son of the morning" (Isa. 14:12), "the Assyrian" (Isa. 14:25), "the little horn" (Dan. 7:8), "the king of fierce countenance" (Dan. 8:23), "the prince that shall come" (Dan. 9:26), "the vile person" (Dan. 11:21), "the willful king" (Dan. 11:36), "the one that shall come in his own name" (John 5:43), "the man of sin" (II Thess. 2:3), "the son of perdition" (II Thess. 2:3), "the lawless one" (II Thess. 2:8), "the beast" (Rev. 13:18). The spiritual wisdom of generations of believers is responsible for the prominence given to a fourteenth title, the Antichrist. In I John 2:18, the Holy Spirit distinguishes carefully between an antichrist and the Antichrist. This Satanic spirit, which is at work in the world today, is to come to its climax in the future, when Satan clothes the wild beast out of the sea with all his authority, becoming incarnate in him. This title is given to the beast because it is seen that he is indeed the second person of the Satanic trinity. Satan can never originate, he can only imitate. So, when Satan is cast out of Heaven he remembers that all of the victories which God has won have been on the ground of the divine incarnation of the Godhead in Jesus Christ. It was the man Christ Jesus who was responsible for Satan's defeat. So now Satan seeks to incarnate himself in a human power. At the time of the temptation of Jesus, Satan boasted truly that he had been given great authority and that this was his to give to whomsoever he desired (Luke 4:6). Christ, of course, refused to take back the rebel kingdom on Satan's terms so the battle continued. Now, in our prophecy, Satan has found a man to his liking, and in the willful king, the little horn who arises at this future time in the midst of the Roman empire that is then reviving, we find the incarnation of Satan. This will explain why some of the titles we have given refer to Satan as well as to this particular personage in whom he dwells at the time of the end. The power of Satan, the throne of Satan, and the authority of Satan all pass into the hands of one man.

We have seen that the seven heads are declared to be the seven successive kings leading up to the climax of Satanic audacity against the Most High. We now see that one of these heads passes through an experience which is described as being slain and then healed. I am frank to say that I have two different conceptions of the meaning of this wounding and healing. One of them is certainly true, the other may well be true also. The sixth head, the Roman Empire of the past, received its death stroke centuries ago. Many men have been haunted with the idea of the revival of this empire, but it has never yet been revived. Charlemagne attempted it, and the pope who crowned him Emperor on Christmas day of the year 800, no doubt saw a revival of Caesar's power. But at Charlemagne's death the dream vanished and the division of his kingdom at the treaty of Verdun in 843 laid the foundation for all the wars of Western Europe since that time. The Holy Roman Empire was then established, and it moved in spectral fashion across the history of the centuries that followed, never achieved, yet never forgotten. Napoleon found himself on an island in the South Atlantic after he had consolidated European power for a few brief moments and named his own little boy "the king of Rome." Mussolini added a worthless African plateau to the territory of Rome and immediately proclaimed a "Roman Empire," a haunting name, evoking thoughts of grandeur and glory that have never been forgotten since the Roman legions wrote their laws in letters of blood across the Mediterranean lands. But the death stroke of the Roman Empire most certainly will be healed. God's Word will never pass away. Every jot and tittle must be fulfilled.

There is another thought, however, which is ever in our mind as we read this passage. Is there to be a death and a healing of the literal Antichrist? Satan imitates God in an incarnation. Will he imitate him in a resurrection? It is certain that there will be "all power and signs and lying wonders" (II Thess. 2:9). Will there be an assassination and a resurrection? We have no evidence on this matter beyond the verses we have quoted, and we give it merely as a suggestion of what may well be one of Satan's tricks.

At all events, the world runs after the Antichrist, and in bowing before him they are really worshiping the dragon.

"Who is like unto the wild beast?" the world cries blasphemously. It was the Holy One of God who had said, "To whom then will ye liken me, or shall I be equal?" (Isa. 40:25), and the world thinks that the Satanic counterfeit is the true God! The Lord Jesus had announced this, "I am come in my Father's name, and ye receive me not: if another shall come in his own name, him ye will receive" (John 5:43).

"Who is able to make war with him?" How Satan is able to blind his followers! Heaven at that very moment is still echoing with the shout of triumph of Michael and his angels as the war in Heaven is brought to its final issue and the usurper is cast out forever. Yet the vicious enemy gathers his followers about his shattered power and is able to convince them that he is yet invincible. God allows his blasphemous mouth to speak for yet a moment before it will be silenced forever. But his authority is strictly limited to the end of the forty-two months.

Once more the mystery of the suffering of God's people is seen. There is to be a great persecution that shall include the saints of God. It is more than a persecution: it is war. Those who stand for Christ are

hated by Antichrist. They are a constant reminder that he is a conquered foe, that his master, Satan, has long since met his Master,
Christ, and that his time is short. This war against the saints takes us
back to the Heavenly scene in the sixth chapter where the early martyrs are told to be quiet until their full number will be completed,
"until their fellow-servants also and their brethren, that should be killed
as they were, should be fulfilled" (Rev. 6:11). It may be a hard lot
for those who must pass through these terrible experiences, but a
blessed lot it shall prove to be. Our God has never made a mistake,
and if He has called upon some to suffer for Himself, it is because
His hidden purposes demand it, and because He knows that even their
terrible suffering, like our lesser suffering, is not worthy to be compared with the glory that shall be revealed (Rom. 8:18).

But though Satan has power to make war on the saints of God,
he has no power to force them under his sway. The only ones who
will worship and follow him are those whose names are not found
written in the book of life of the Lamb. Those who are the redeemed
of God can never be touched by Satan.

The book in which the record of the saints is kept belongs to "the
Lamb who hath been slain from the disruption of the world." It will
be noticed, immediately, that we have not adopted the translation of
the King James Version which has been followed by others. The
justification of this translation will be found in the following quotation
from an English student: "A comparison of all the passages (in which
the Greek verb and cognate noun are found) will show that these
words are not the proper terms for founding and foundation, but the
correct meaning is *casting down,* or *overthrowing.* (The same verb is
used in II Cor. 4:9 and Rev. 12:10 in this sense.) Accordingly the
noun, derived from and cognate with the verb, ought to be translated
'disruption' or 'ruin.' The remarkable thing is that in all occurrences
the word is connected with the world and therefore the expression
should be rendered 'the disruption, or ruin, of the world,' clearly referring to the condition indicated in Genesis 1:2 where the earth was
wrecked and ruined. 'The disruption of the world' is an event forming
a great dividing line in the ages of God's testing of man. In Genesis
1:1 we have the founding of the world . . ." and this we have long
held to be one of the most important studies in the Word of God;
for without it much of the plan of God cannot be seen. Satan has
succeeded in hiding this truth from many, but there are those who
see clearly that this earth was once created perfect with Satan as its
ruler before his fall, and that the earth was overthrown and disrupted
in judgment upon him. The world which we know is quite different.
The truth here found, then, would be that the death of Christ was
ever known to God.

To those who dwell on earth there is a sharp warning given. The danger of worshiping Antichrist is a real danger. And so, as in the letters to the seven churches, the solemn admonition is given, "If any one has an ear, let him hear."

Verses 11–15

The Unholy Spirit

¹¹And I saw another [similar] wild beast coming up out of the earth; and he had two horns like a lamb, and he was speaking like a dragon, ¹²and he exerciseth all the authority of the first wild beast in his sight, and he causeth the earth and them that dwell in it that they shall worship the first wild beast whose death stroke was healed. ¹³And he doeth great signs so that he should even make fire come down out of Heaven into the earth in the sight of men. ¹⁴And he deceiveth the ones dwelling upon the earth because of the signs which it was given unto him to make in the sight of the wild beast, saying to them that dwell upon the earth that they should make an image to the beast which had the stroke of the sword and came to life. ¹⁵And it was given to him to give breath to the image of the wild beast, that the image of the wild beast should both speak and cause as many as would not worship the image of the wild beast that they should be killed.
(Rev. 13:11-15, Free Translation)

In the last half of chapter thirteen we see the third member of this Satanic trinity. The devil is making his last and greatest effort, a furious effort, to gain power and establish his kingdom upon the earth. He knows nothing better than to imitate God. Since God has succeeded by means of an incarnation and then by means of the work of the Holy Spirit, the devil will work by means of an incarnation in Antichrist and by an unholy spirit. After we had written this down, we discovered this same thought in a very old commentator, brilliantly expressed more than a century ago. "The full embodiment of all evil in our world comes out in an infernal trinity, the mimicry of eternal realities. First, is the unseen and hidden father, the dragon, the old serpent, the devil. The next is the seven-headed and ten-horned beast from the sea, 'the son of perdition,' begotten of the devil, his earthly manifestation, who dies, and revives again, and reappears on earth after having been in the invisible world, and is awarded the power and throne of his father, the devil. And to this comes a third, the two-horned beast from the earth, who proceeds from the dragon father and the dragon son, for his speech is the dragon's speech, and 'he exerciseth all the authority of the first beast in his presence,' carrying into living effect the Satanic will of both the father and the son. Thus we perceive three distinct personalities, the devil, the antichrist, and 'the False

Prophet'; and these three are one—one vital essence, one economy and one administration. The dragon sets up as anti-God; the beast, his son, is the anti-Christ; and the two-horned beast, proceeding from and operating in the interest of both, is the anti-Holy Spirit. And these three together are Hell's trinity in unity, the devil's unity in trinity, as revealed and operative in our world, when iniquity has once come to the full."

Now let us turn to the Word of God to examine the third person of this Satanic trinity, the wild beast out of the earth to whom the power of the first beast is given. We must turn to the Word of God, for the commentators are in the most dire confusion on the identification. Seiss gives us these various identifications: the Roman church, the Greek church, the French Republic, the Jesuits, the Roman theologians, the earthy, carnal wisdom, including the heathen philosophies, false doctrines and the like. Another thinks it to be "the evil that arises in the Church of Christ." Still others identify the second beast with the heathen priesthood, the principle of inductive philosophy, witchcraft and soothsaying, divination and magic. Seiss rightly concludes, "To get anything solid out of such presentations is simply impossible. We must therefore abandon entirely the whole system of interpretation which results in such confusion and uncertainty, or conclude, with some, that nothing definitely ascertainable is contained in these prophecies; in other words, that there is here no revelation at all. The fault has not been in the intentions, the learning, the earnestness, the diligence, or the candor of the men concerned, so much as in the unwarranted prejudices, misconceptions, and defective methods by which they have approached what God has thus commanded to be written."

If we remain within the bounds of the Word of God as we have done in all previous interpretations, we shall find ourselves in the midst of what is indeed a revelation and therefore, clarity. In the first place, it should be noticed that the second beast is like the first. In Greek there are two words for "another" which expresses the two radically different meanings which are to be found in that English word. We purchase a fountain pen and find that it leaks and is generally unsatisfactory. We return it saying, "I want another pen." This means we want one that is quite different from the one we have had. Then we find this to be the best pen we have ever had, and it is so much admired by a friend that we decide to give him a present. We go to the salesman and say, "This is the best pen I have ever had; I want another." In this case we mean that we want one exactly like the one we have. In the Greek language there are two different words which express these different ideas. Just as the Lord Jesus said, "I will send you another—absolutely alike—Comforter," so this passage says, "And I saw another — absolutely alike — wild beast coming up out of the earth." There can be no doubt that this beast is a Satanic representation.

He arises out of the earth, as the first beast arose out of the sea. We have seen that the sea represents the great restless body of the nations. The earth here is most evidently a symbol. The word occurs eighty times in the book of Revelation, and in most instances can be taken in the literal sense. Here, however, it is necessary to take it in the figurative sense, such as that which is manifestly used in Corinthians where Paul writes, "The first man is of the earth, earthy; the second man is the Lord from Heaven" (I Cor. 15:47). It should be remembered that the earth is also symbolical of Israel in certain instances in the Scripture. It might well be, therefore, though we would not press the point, that this anti-Spirit would be a Jew, and that he would be used of Satan to deceive Israel if possible. The great passage in the twenty-fourth chapter of Matthew that deals with the same epoch which is treated in this portion of the Apocalypse contains a prophecy of the coming of "false Christs and false prophets, and they shall show great signs and wonders; insomuch that, if it were possible, they shall deceive the very elect" (Matt. 24:24). Jesus Christ had to say to the people of His day, "Ye are from beneath; I am from above: ye are of this world; I am not of this world" (John 8:23). The same thing could be said of the counterfeit spirit. There are many false prophets gone out into the world (I John 4:1), but the wild beast out of the earth is called the false prophet in exactly the same way that though there are many antichrists, yet the wild beast out of the sea is the Antichrist. When a thing is of the earth, it cannot please God, who has said, "that which is highly esteemed among men is abomination in the sight of God" (Luke 16:15).

The spiritual character of the false prophet is again to be seen in the description which follows. It is said that "he had two horns like a lamb, and he spake as a dragon." There are three symbols to be explained here, horns, lamb and dragon. We have seen that the horn is a symbol of authority or power. The lamb is one of the scriptural symbols of Christ, the Saviour; the dragon is one of the names for the devil. Putting these three symbols together we find that the false prophet has an authority like that of Christ, that is, a spiritual authority, but that the voice that speaks is the voice of Satan.

As the Holy Spirit is the effective, working power of God in the Church, so the false prophet will be the effective, working power of Satan in the time of the end. His authority will be of a spiritual nature, but the voice and message will be Satanic.

It might be well to point out, once more, that all true believers in Christ will have been removed from the earth at the end of the age in which we live, which is the beginning of the period which will close with the destruction of the Antichrist and his power. We have seen that there is a political power which arises in Rome, bringing together the ancient Roman Empire under a new dictator, who at the time Satan is cast out of Heaven, becomes incarnated by Satan and is thus turned into the Antichrist. Corresponding with this Satanic political development, there is a Satanic religious development. God, of course, will be working in the world, even as He worked through the Holy Spirit from afar before the day of Pentecost. But there will be counterfeit religious development, at which we must look for a moment. Today we see a world that is filled with "religion" in addition to Christianity. True children of God are to be found in many varying shades of Christianity, sprinkled throughout Christendom. There are undoubtedly born-again individuals in the midst of all churches. They are saved in spite of the organizations and not because of the organizations. What is going to happen to all of these organizations when the true believers are removed from the world? Already, in our day, we see indications that much of the guiding force of these great organizations is in the hands of those who would deny essential truths of Scripture. This tendency will increase, and at the coming of Christ for the believers, the tares in the midst of the wheat will go on functioning as usual, all moving rapidly into one great church union, with one head of all. This religious leader will work together with the political dictator. Whether the religious power takes over the government in a time of crisis or not, we cannot be certain. Such a thing might well be the meaning of two portions of this chapter, the one speaking of the political power being wounded to death (vs. 3), and the other speaking of the religious power exercising all the power of the first wild beast before him (v. 12). At all events, we know that the two will work together, and that the political shall finally destroy the religious.

Here it is said that the false prophet exercises all the power of the Antichrist "before" or that is to say "in the presence of" the latter. His particular function is to lead the earth dwellers to worship the Antichrist, whose deadly wound is now healed. One of the greatest dangers of the totalitarian state is that religion is forced into the position of handmaiden to the government. In our generation we have seen a great state like Germany make every attempt to force the church into the role of state servant. The state is held to be lord of all, therefore the state concluded that the church must fall into line, training youth for state purposes and extolling all of the actions of the state, no matter how they may violate the principles of religious liberty. By the time of the tribulation, the church will have succumbed. The false prophet will force the earth and all that dwell therein to worship— acknowledge the worth of—the Antichrist.

For the pursuit of this task Satan has endowed this false prophet with a mighty power. He does great wonders, so that he makes fire to come down from Heaven on the earth in the sight of men. Here is a manifest imitation of the power which had been given by God to Elijah (Rev. 11:5). It is to be noted that Satan always imitates; he has no power to create. We are not to suppose that these wonders are counterfeit. They are real miracles. When Moses performed the wonders which preceded the exodus of the children of Israel from the land of Egypt, he was imitated by the priests of Pharaoh. In the midst of the countless number of frauds perpetrated by spiritualistic mediums, there has been a small number of genuine works that have been beyond the natural, and these have come from the devil. There has never been a total absence of Satanic power, but it comes to its full fruition under the false prophet.

All of this deceived many. The touchstone of deliverance from deceit is the love of the truth. It is worthwhile noting that it is not the truth itself, but the love of the truth which keeps men from being deceived by Satan (II Thess. 2:10). The love of an individual is spent on truth or on unrighteousness. If a man has pleasure in unrighteousness (II Thess. 2:12), he will not receive the love of the truth, and if he receives the love of the truth, he shall be saved from unrighteousness.

In this future time, Israel, especially, has been awaiting the coming of her Messiah. The Antichrist will be put forth by Satan to play that role. Israel also awaits a prophet, announced by Moses (Deut. 18: 15, 18). This is why John the Baptist and Jesus were both asked if they were "that prophet" (John 1:21; Luke 7:19). The false prophet arises to play the part expected of the prophet who had been announced for so long, and his role will be to tell Israel that their Messiah has come. Just as an oppressed Israel in the day of Jesus was looking for one who could deliver them from Rome, so Israel in this future day will be looking for someone who can deliver them from the bondage of their circumstances and give them the place of prominence which they have been taught to expect by the very promises of God.

The false prophet causes the earth dwellers to erect an image of the Antichrist. Robertson points out that this image could be his head upon a coin, an image painted or woven upon a standard, a bust in metal or stone, a statue or anything that people could be asked to bow down before and worship. Because of the vision of Nebuchadnezzar of the great image, we are inclined to believe that it is a giant statue. We have the record of giant images of the past. The pagan world is full of them. They are to be found in remote caves of China, openly in Japan, Indo-China and India, and on remote islands of the Pacific, even on lonely Easter Island. The colossus of Rhodes was one of the seven wonders of the ancient world. In our day, the great dictators were drawn by the same fanciful desire, and giant statues arose in Ethiopia and Rome, in Moscow and in other parts of the western lands. The image that the false prophet will cause to be built would seem, by all of the context of the central portion of the Revelation, to be in Rome. To it the false prophet has power to give the gift of speech. In addition, we see the beginning of another wave of persecution. The false prophet has the power to cause the death of those who refuse to worship the image, whatever it be, of the Antichrist.

Seiss has an excellent comment upon this image-worship of the future. "It is not difficult to trace what sort of arguments will be brought to bear for the making of this image. In the ages of great worldly glory and dominion statues were raised to the honor of the great of every class, but who of all the great ones of the earth is so great as the Antichrist! Statues have ever been common for the commemoration of great events; but what greater event and marvel has ever occurred than that in the history of this man, in that he was wounded to death, and yet is restored to life and activity, with far sublimer qualities than he possessed in his first life? How much more worthy of memorialization this than the scar of Scipio, or the appearance of a star supposed to be miraculous which Octavianus commemorated on the consecrated image of his imperial foster-father? If the grand old Romans thus honored their human emperors and benefactors, why withhold this veneration from one so evidently and eminently super-human? And who will there be among the proud sons of earth to stand out against such arguments? The leaders of the apostate world will cheerfully acquiesce in the preeminent propriety of such a memorial, and an image of the beast, and to his sacred honor, is made and set up, particularly emphasizing his great characteristic that he once was wounded to the death, and that he has come back to life again with his death-wound healed."

It is written of the idols of the heathen that they "are silver and gold; . . . they have mouths, but they speak not" (Ps. 135:15, 16). The Satanic powers are now permitted to give a living quality to this devilish image. And we must not forget that it is written, "Woe unto him that saith to the wood, Awake; to the dumb stone, Arise, it shall teach" (Hab. 2:19). And it is the false prophet who shall do that very thing.

The wild beast out of the sea is undoubtedly an individual personage. He cannot be identified as a system. There are too many distinguishing characteristics of individuality. It is *the* Antichrist. The same argument holds good for the false prophet. He is a man, as is the personal Antichrist. The pair are united in the source of the power. The pair shall be united in their doom, for they are both taken captive at the coming of the Lord in the midst of the battle of Armageddon (Rev. 19:20), and are cast together into the lake of fire forever (Rev. 20:10). All of this is sufficient to prove their personality and individuality, and to demonstrate that they are not governments, nations, religions or systems.

The Antichrist will appear suavely, swiftly, quietly. He will be a man, first of all, of quietness before he manifests himself in his Satanic form. He will be an anti-Christ, a counterfeit Jesus—not a counterfeit devil. When we understand this, we will understand what to look for. If there is some truth in a false religion, men will take it more easily. That is why we must receive the love of the truth and measure everything by the Word of God. When we do this, we cannot be deceived.

Verses 16–18
The Number of Man

16And he causeth all, the small and the great, and the rich and the poor, and the freemen and the bondmen, that they should give themselves a mark upon their right hand or upon their forehead; 17and that no man should be able to buy or to sell except he that hath the mark, the name of the wild beast, or the number of his name.

18Here is wisdom, He that understands, let him calculate the number of the wild beast; for it is a man's number, and the number of him is 666.

(Rev. 13:16-18, Free Translation)

The intolerance of Satan now reaches its peak. Power is in his hand, he uses it against all who will not acknowledge him and worship him. One commentator has written, "Thus, in the name of Democracy and popular rights, comes absolute Dictatorship and Imperialism; in the name of Freedom, comes complete and universal enslavement; in the name of the better Reason, which tramples on religion and revelation, comes a great consolidated system of gross idolatry; in the name of a charitable Liberalism, which disdains allegiance to any creed, comes a bloody Despotism, which compels men to worship the base image of a baser man, or die. Here is one star in the crown of this world's boasted Progress."

It is the purpose of the false prophet to bring every human being under this bondage of Satan, and to this end a monstrous procedure is followed. All people within the dominion of the Antichrist are forced to accept an outward and visible mark of their allegiance to this Satanic power. Hengstenberg points out that "the named are seven, the all at the beginning, then the three pairs, the small and the great, the rich and the poor, the free and the bond." Some commentators have spoken of this mark as a brand, and have explained it as referring to the common practice of branding slaves. But John in the apocalypse never refers to heathen practices; he always takes us back to the Old

Testament Scriptures. In the book of Deuteronomy God gave the summary of the law, "Hear, O Israel; the Lord our God is one Lord: And thou shalt love the Lord thy God with all thine heart, and with all thy soul, and with all thy might" (Deut. 6:4, 5). These words became the very center of Jewish thought. Even today, in their unbelief, the Jews repeat the first half of this summary as an oft recurring chant in their services. Through Moses, at the time of the giving of this summary, God gave definite commands concerning these truths in their most literal form. "And these words, which I command thee this day, shall be in thine heart: And thou shalt teach them diligently unto thy children, and shalt talk of them when thou sittest in thine house, and when thou walkest by the way, and when thou liest down, and when thou risest up. And thou shalt bind them for a sign upon thine hand, and they shall be as frontlets between thine eyes. . . . You shall not go after other gods . . ." (Deut. 6:6-8, 14).

Will this practice be re-established during the time of the rise of the Antichrist? Will the one hundred and forty-four thousand witnesses who go forth for God during this time wear such phylacteries? We do not know. It is possible. If so, it can readily be understood that the fanaticism of the followers of the Antichrist would lead them to give themselves a similar mark, denoting that they are utterly given over to the service of the Antichrist. The right hand, in the Bible, is the symbol of strength, the forehead is the most conspicuous part of the body. To bear the mark of the beast in those parts of the body is to confess one's self utterly given over to the service of the Antichrist. The strength and allegiance of body and mind are thus marked as belonging to the beast. The Greek word for the mark is not one of the common classical words for a brand (*puros, stigma*) which were used to describe the branding of cattle and slaves, but quite another word (*charagma*) which is used in the Scriptures in only one place outside the book of Revelation, and in that place it describes the idols of the heathen. Paul, on Mars' Hill, told the Athenians that they should not "think that the Godhead is like unto gold or silver, or stone, graven by art and man's device" (Acts 17:29). The word translated "graven" is the same Greek word as "mark" in this passage.

It should be pointed out, also, that the Greek here is quite different from the idea given in the English as to the application of this mark. Our versions might lead us to think that the mark was forced upon unwilling men. But the original is that the false prophet "causeth all . . . that they should give themselves a mark . . ." The picture behind these words is that of masses of people cutting or burning the mark upon themselves, or eagerly pressing forward to receive it at the place of worship.

The immediate effect of this wholesale marking of the population is the boycott upon all those who would stand out for God. There is no possibility of buying or selling. This would cause starvation to those who refused to give in. But those who refuse to receive the mark of the beast will find themselves more than conquerors through Christ. Famine, nakedness, peril, and the sword will never be able to separate them from the love of God which is in Christ Jesus.

So the people will flock to their eternal doom, and receive with gladness the mark which will ultimately brand them for the lake of fire. Out of Heaven we shall hear very distinctly in the next chapter of this prophecy, "If any man worship the beast and his image, and receive his mark in his forehead, or in his hand, the same shall drink of the wine of the wrath of God, which is poured out without mixture into the cup of his indignation; and he shall be tormented with fire and brimstone in the presence of the holy angels, and in the presence of the Lamb; and the smoke of their torment ascendeth up for ever and ever: and they have no rest day nor night, who worship the beast and his image, and whosoever receiveth the mark of his name" (Rev. 14: 9-11).

Just what is the character of this mark which people place upon their hands and their foreheads? The Scriptural statement is simple, but has probably given rise to more conjecture than any other single verse in the whole Bible. "Here is wisdom. He that understands, let him calculate the number of the wild beast: for it is man's number, and the number of him is 666."

Devout men and curious men have sought the answer to this symbol, and have ranged over the whole of the field of history and speculative imagination to find it. There have been many attempts to identify the number with historical personages. This is done by gematria. It should be understood that the letters of the alphabet were used for numbers in the ancient languages, and that the use of numerals distinct from letters is a comparatively recent achievement in man's progress. We are all familiar with the Latin inscriptions on public buildings in our own cities, and the dates are carved in what we know as Roman numerals. Almost every schoolboy is able to translate MDCCCLXXVI into our Arabic numerals, 1876. The same system of letters for numerals existed in Hebrew and Greek as well as in Latin. Two English authors, who published an anonymous book on the subject, claim that the same system held good in Sanskrit and other ancient languages. It can readily be seen, therefore, that every word containing the letters that were used as numbers would also have a numerical value. The last work mentioned even cites Groves in "Echoes from Egypt" as holding that many of the heathen gods had names whose number value is 666, as for example Amenoph and Baalzephon.

Since the passage we are studying speaks of the number of the beast as being the number of his name, and gives it as 666, there would appear to be an apparent justification for such identification.

If a name can be found of which the numerical value of the letters totals 666, it might be thought proof positive that the identification had been established beyond all doubt. But such is not the case, as we shall see.

The early fathers were almost unanimous in the opinion that the passage referred to Nero. When the Reformation came to pass, there were many Protestants who were eager to find every possible arm to use against the Pope. It was not long before he was called the Antichrist, and efforts were made to associate the names of individual popes with the number of Antichrist.

Some scholars have put forward the Greek word TEITAN, which totals 666 and which is a form of the name of the Emperor Titus. One of the most ingenious explanations comes from a French scholar, Bruston. We translate as follows, "The name of an emperor, that of the founder of an empire, can easily personify that empire . . . It is clear that if the name of Caesar, in Greek or in Hebrew, gave the desired result (i.e. 666), the problem would be resolved. But this is not the case. What, then, must we do? Let us consider the fact that in order to personify the empire that is spoken of in the Apocalypse, that of Babylon the great, we must not look for a Roman name but for that of a Babylonian. The Roman Empire is to Julius Caesar as that of Babylon is to the founder of the Empire of Babylon, who was, according to Genesis 10:8, Nimrod. The Hebrew form of the words, Nimrod, son of Cush (NMRD BN KSH) gives us the total of 666."

There have been many other attempts to discover the identity of the Antichrist on these principles, and some of them have been pretty sad attempts. Men have twisted the spelling of names and distorted grammar in order to get a result. One man discovered (!) the fact that the letters "TI" added to the name of the great emperor of the French, NAPOLEONTI, upon the basis of the Greek numerical values, would give 666. This, of course is more than senseless.

One further modern interpretation has been made which shows that the practice is not yet ended. Throughout Italy in the 1930's there were thousands of signs to be seen, painted on walls and monuments, reading in Italian, "Long Live Mussolini." The Italian word for the first part of the phrase is "viva." Almost universally the vowels are omitted. I, myself, have seen the interlocked letters, looking almost like a W, painted on the marble of the posts along the enclosure at Pisa where the famous tower leans. VV IL DUCE was painted on every one of the marble posts, and scrawled on the tower itself after the fashion of those who scribble their names in public places. My own mind would never lean toward gematria, and so I did not see that which another mind has found in those letters; for leaving out the E and counting the U as a V, we find the number 666 . . . !

Now, all of these "interpretations" have been quoted as typical examples and Seiss says of them, "The endless guesses and experiments with which expositors have occupied themselves and their readers on this point can be of very little practical worth to us. When the monster comes 'the righteous shall understand.' Our business is rather to reckon up the number of the beast as to his moral identification. It is here that the chief stress falls, and where the greatest exposure lies . . . The wisdom here, as required by us, is the wisdom to detect and discern the antichristian badness, the ill principles which lay men open to Antichrist's power, the subtle atheism and unfaith by which people are betrayed into his hands."

It is a remarkable fact that the numerical value of the ordinary Greek form of the name of Jesus is 888. This number is the number of perfection. Eight is the number of new things. It is the perfection of the octave. The children of the great composer, Bach, found that the easiest method of awakening their father was to play a few lines of music and leave off the last note. The musician would rise immediately and go to his piano to strike the final chord. I awoke early one morning and went to the piano in our home and played the well-known carol, "Silent Night." I purposely stopped just before playing the last note. I walked out into the hallway and listened to the sounds that came from upstairs. An eight year old had stopped his reading and was trying to sound the final note on his harmonica. Another child was singing the last note, lustily. An adult called down, "Did you do that purposely? What is the matter?" Our very nature demands the completion of the octave.

The whole universe cries out for the perfections of the Lord Jesus Christ. The groaning of the earth, travailing in pain, is awaiting His manifestation. There shall arise upon this earth a being who shall claim to satisfy the desire of the nations. But when he plays his tune it will be without any final chord. The name of Jesus adds up to all perfection, but the name of the Antichrist is the perfect symbol of imperfection and incompleteness. Seiss ends the paragraph, part of which we have quoted, with these words, "Six is the bad number, and when multiplied by tens and hundreds, it denotes evil in its greatest intensity and most disastrous manifestation. This number of the beast's name thus gives his standing in the estimate of Heaven, and fixes attention on that rather than on the numerical spelling of the name he bears on earth. If we can only know the principles pertaining to his badness; if we can only have understanding to detect his spirit which already works so powerfully in so many specious forms about us, we shall have accomplished the most useful reckoning of the number of his name. And without this we may be carrying his damning mark upon our souls, even while we think ourselves forearmed against his power by what we have discovered of the word by which his contemporaries designate him. The moral insight into his nature is the wisdom we require, rather than the spelling of the name by which he is called. In this, therefore, let us try to skill our souls, cleaving ever to our only Lord God, and His Son, Jesus Christ our Saviour in the meekness of a confiding faith and obedience, that no marks or stains of the beast, or his abominations, even in spirit, may ever be found upon our souls."

In conclusion, it is impossible to connect the number of the beast with any historical figure of the past, but it will perfectly delineate the Antichrist, a historical figure of the future. Those believers who live in his time will read this passage, now unknown to us, as clearly as we read the twenty-second Psalm, which was known to those of David's time. The first beast is the future Roman dictator who shall become the Antichrist by the incarnation of Satan; the second beast is the personal head of the religious system which will go along with the dictatorship and the Antichrist. But we who are in Christ know well that He will keep us from the tribulations that shall come upon this world.

PART VII
THE LAMB'S REDEEMED

CHAPTER 14

Verses 1–5

The Lamb Upon Mount Zion

¹And I looked, and behold, the Lamb, standing upon Mount Zion, and with him a hundred and forty-four thousand, having His Name and His Father's Name written upon their foreheads. ²And I heard a voice from out of Heaven as the voice of many waters and as the voice of great thunder; and the [accompanying] sound which I heard was as the sound of harpers harping with their harps. ³And they sang a new song in the presence of the throne and in the presence of the four living creatures and the elders; and no one could learn the song save the hundred and forty-four thousand which had been purchased from the earth.

⁴These are they which were not defiled with women; for they are virgins. These are they which follow the Lamb whithersoever He goeth. These were purchased from among men, to be the first fruits to God and to the Lamb. ⁵And in their mouth was not found the lie; for they are without blemish.

(Rev. 14:1-5, Free Translation)

Doubt looks at circumstances; faith looks to Christ. Here the beloved disciple is given another vision, and he looks through all of earth's misery and sees the Lord Jesus Christ enthroned. He has been listening to earth's groanings, but now the groaning is drowned by the songs of the redeemed.

The Lamb, of course, is the Lord Jesus Christ. This is one of the best known symbols in the Scripture. He is here seen standing upon Mount Zion. A careful study of this symbol gives us a rich reward.

The first mention of any word or place is generally very important, and it is especially so in this instance. David and his army came up to Jerusalem where the Jebusites were in control. The incident is found in II Samuel 5. It is necessary to revise the translation in order to catch the full meaning of the scorn of the enemy and the victory of David. "The king marched with his men against the Jebusites in Jerusalem, for they were the inhabitants of the land. And they said to David: Thou shalt not enter here, for even the blind and the lame shall repulse you; which really meant, David shall not enter here. But David captured the fortress in the citadel, and called it the city of David. . . ." (II Samuel 5:6, 7, 9, author's paraphrase). From this time on, Mount Zion was connected with David and associated with his name.

But David's choice of this place is not that which gives it its importance. We read in the Psalms, "The Lord hath chosen Zion; he hath desired it for his habitation. This is my rest forever: here will I dwell; for I have desired it. . . . There will I make the horn of David to bud; I have ordained a lamp for mine anointed. His enemies will I clothe with shame: but upon himself shall his crown flourish" (Ps. 132:13, 14, 17, 18).

These are the key passages with reference to Mount Zion, but there is much more truth connected with this place. There can be no doubt that God has definitely stated that He has chosen Mount Zion for the emplacement of the throne of the Messiah during the kingdom age when He shall rule in righteousness. The verse we are studying in Revelation is the only mention of this place which is to be found in this book, but it opens the door to a line of teaching which must not be disregarded. Just as the vision of the risen Christ in the first chapter brought together various passages throughout the Old Testament which reveal to us that the risen Christ is none other than the Jehovah of the Old Testament, so the mention of Mount Zion at this particular point takes us back through the corridors of prophecy, linking scores of passages of divine truth with the incidents that now lie in the path of our study.

The spiritual import of this verse is that the moment of God's triumph is now at hand. When we consider this verse with the one that precedes, the thought is as follows: The whole earth seems to be going after the Antichrist; the false prophet is leading multitudes to his worship, and with signs and lying wonders is causing almost the whole earth to go after him; but his number is a number of incompleteness. In spite of the raging of the people and the vain imaginings of the nations, God says, "I have set My King upon My holy hill of Zion." The kingdom which has so long been awaited is now to begin. The bitterest judgments are about to fall, but look up! The Lamb is taking His proper place in Heaven and He will soon come forth to take it on earth.

Mount Zion is to be found in scores of passages in the Scripture and it will be well for us to consider the more important of these. First, let us consider a few of the Psalms.

The righteous remnant of Israel is seen in the twentieth Psalm, and it is more than likely that there is a reference here to the one hundred and forty-four thousand and the other believers whom they symbolize.

It is a day of trouble, and the Lord alone can deliver. The cry goes forth, "The Lord hear thee in the day of trouble . . . Send thee help from the sanctuary and strengthen thee out of Zion" (vss. 1, 2). It is the Lord, once more as Priest and King delivering His people. No wonder they cry, "Some trust in chariots and some in horses, but we will remember the name of the Lord our God" (vs. 7).

In the forty-eighth Psalm, we find the kings of the earth gathered together. This is certainly symbolical, if not prophetic, of the gathering of the kings at Armageddon. Why are they troubled? Why do they fall? Why are they seized as a woman in travail? Once more we find that it is the appearance of the Lord in Zion. It then becomes, "Beautiful for situation, the joy of the whole earth. . . . Zion, the city of the great king" (vs. 2).

In the seventy-fourth Psalm there is another of the double pictures so frequent throughout the prophetic Word. An event that took place or a situation that existed in the time of the writer becomes like a stereopticon slide, through which light may be passed to reveal a similar image on a much larger scale, in the future. Here, there is sorrow over the desolations which an enemy has committed in the sanctuary. The people cry, "Remember thy congregation, which thou hast purchased of old . . . this mount Zion wherein thou hast dwelt" (vs. 2). But what a picture of the greater desolations, the abomination of desolations, and the corresponding cry of God's people for the deliverance that must come to Zion because of the promise of God! If we look at the third verse of Revelation 14, we will see that the singers are like those in the Psalms, "purchased" of old.

The seventy-sixth Psalm is another picture of the Lord on Mount Zion, bringing peace and joy after the battle. It describes this moment "When God arose to judgment, to save all the meek of the earth . . ." (vs. 9), cutting off the pride of princes, being terrible to the kings of the earth. "In Salem also is his tabernacle, and his dwelling place in Zion" (vs. 2). Note once more the Priesthood and Kingship of our Lord together.

Again, in Psalm 102 the great tribulation is in view. This is another of the double Psalms; for it is a partial description of the suffering of Christ on the cross, and also a description of the suffering of Israel in the time of Jacob's trouble. "Thou shalt arise, and have mercy upon Zion; for the time to favor her, yea, the set time, is come" (vs. 13). It is a "set time."

After all that we have shown of the various Psalms which precede the one hundred and tenth, it is almost superfluous to add a word. Here we find the moment of Christ's reign. The high priest after the order of Melchizedek comes to reign. "The Lord shall send the rod of thy strength out of Zion; rule thou in the midst of thine enemies" (vs. 2). "The Lord at thy right hand shall strike through kings in the day of his wrath" (vs. 5). Here, again, is Armageddon.

Psalm 133 sees Judah and Israel united. Hermon in the north and Zion in the south are encompassed by the same dew from God. All strife and divisions are past. The anointing oil which set apart God's high priest, flows over all His people and they are a kingdom of priests before Him. That blessing unspeakable is commanded in Zion, when He is manifested.

In Psalm 137 we find how inseparably God has linked His people to His land. They cannot sing the songs of Zion when they are out of His will, but the implication is that the confusion of the world— Babylon in which Israel has been scattered—will be brought to an end. It is announced prophetically that Babylon is to be destroyed, and the same announcement appears in fulfillment in our passage (Rev. 14:8), as soon as the Lamb appears in Zion.

In Psalm 146, we see Israel once more in the midst of the great tribulation. There is a warning, "Put not your trust in princes, nor in the son of man" (vs. 3). The princes we know; they are the rulers who "take counsel together against the Lord and against his anointed" (Ps. 2:2). But who is this son of man against whom they are warned? Is he not the one of whom Christ warned when He said, "I am come in my Father's name, and ye received me not: if another shall come in his own name, him ye will receive?" (John 5:43). In the time of Jacob's trouble, "Happy is he that hath the God of Jacob for his help" (Ps. 146:5); for the God of Zion shall come to reign. This is what will turn the way of the wicked one upside down.

The last of the Zion Psalms is the one hundred forty-ninth. The King is now on the throne. "Let Israel rejoice in him that made him; Let the children of Zion be joyful in their king" (vs. 2). In the Psalm that is next to the beginning, the nations are in tumult and the people are filled with vain imaginings. In this Psalm which is next to the end, worship is in the mouth of God's people, and His Word is in their hand. The result is that there is "vengeance upon the nations, punishments upon the people" (vs. 7). In that second Psalm the kings and the rulers are in rebellion. Here we read, "To bind their kings with chains, and their nobles with fetters of iron; to execute upon them the judgment written; this honor have all his saints" (vss. 8, 9).

The picture is complete. I must testify that no study in this book brought more personal joy than this realization that from the single word "Zion" in Revelation 14:1, it was possible to go back through thirty different Psalms and find that each of them fits into the book of Revelation at this point, and sheds its light upon the great vision of the end. Is this chance? Is this coincidence? The very laws of mathematics cry out against such a possibility. This is God's Word.

The whole of the Zion Psalms are summarized by a passage in Isaiah, "And it shall come to pass in the last days, that the mountain of the Lord's house shall be established in the top of the mountains, and shall be exalted above the hills; and all nations shall flow unto it. And many people shall go and say, Come ye, and let us go up to the mountain of the Lord, to the house of the God of Jacob; and he will teach us of his ways, and we will walk in his paths: for out of Zion shall go forth the law, and the word of the law from Jerusalem. And he shall judge among the nations, and shall rebuke many people: and they shall beat their swords into plowshares, and their spears into pruninghooks; nation shall not lift up sword against nation, neither shall they learn war any more" (Isa. 2:2-4). The same prophecy is repeated in almost identical terms in the book of Micah (4:1-4).

With the lamb on Mount Zion are seen the one hundred and forty-four thousand. We have already studied in detail the significance of this company. Just before the final bowls of judgment are poured upon the earth, the Lord stops to reassure His own that He is already taking the place of government, and that His own are safe in Him. They have refused the name and the mark of Antichrist upon their foreheads; He has written His name and His Father's name upon their foreheads. It is to be noted that the Greek text speaks of the names of both the Father and the Son. We remember that in the upper room, the Lord said to His disciples, "If a man love me, he will keep my words: and my Father will love him, and we will come unto him, and make our abode with him" (John 14:23). Here the Son and the Father have placed Their name upon the forehead of those in whom They dwell.

John, who has been given the vision of the approaching kingdom with the Lamb reigning and His blessed people with Him, now hears the first strains of the heavenly song and the accompanying glory of the divine, eternal symphonies. Beethoven wrote nine symphonies, and when Brahms composed his first symphony there were those who saw it as a completion of the work of the former master, and who called it the tenth symphony. And here in Revelation we catch, through John, the faint echo of the completion of all of earth's praise and the beginning of the eternal song.

Under all the laws of interpretation which we have been following, we must look upon this company of one hundred and forty-four thousand as the same group which we have studied in some detail in chapter seven. While it may be true that they include "a multitude which no man can number, of all nations, and kindreds, and people and tongues" (Rev. 7:9), since these were associated with them in the former description, we have no right to speak of them as the Church. It is to be noted that this group is composed of those who are *learning* the new song. The singers are already in Heaven, another definite proof that the Church is caught away before the tribulation period begins. Only the redeemed can sing the song. The redeemed of this age are singing the song in Heaven as we come back with the Lamb to Mount Zion. Here the saints of the tribulation period join in the chorus. They, too, were purchased by His blood, so they can sing the songs of redemption.

They are presented to us as being free from the Satanic defilements which accompanied the worship of the image of the Antichrist. In the Middle Ages, there were those who took this passage as a condemnation of marriage and as a support of the doctrine of celibacy. Even one of the greatest Roman Catholic commentators, the Abbot Crampon, takes this point of view. "The *woman* with which these were not defiled," he writes, "are those impious doctrines and that guilty lasciviousness symbolized in the Apocalypse itself by Jezebel and the great whore (Rev. 2:20, 22; 17:1ff). The virgins represent here all those purified souls which, taken together, form the mystic body of the Church, the Lamb's wife (Rev. 21:9). It is in this same sense that St. Paul wrote to the Corinthians, 'I have espoused you to one husband, that I might present you as a chaste virgin to Christ' (II Cor. 11:2)." We would change that in only one way. The virgins here represent the one hundred and forty-four thousand, which thus are seen to have a position similiar to that of the Church.

They follow the Lamb, whithersoever He goeth. It would appear that they are given a special place of honor, similar, we might say to the royal bodyguard of a reigning monarch. We have seen that they are to be the instruments for the salvation of a great multitude which no man can number. They, themselves, are called the firstfruits of this harvest which is gathered in the rebel province of the great enemy of souls at the time of his greatest wrath. They are trophies of the last great phase of the fighting in the invisible warfare in the spiritual realm.

While the Antichrist is about his work, he is given the ability to work with "all power and signs and lying wonders, And with all deceivableness of unrighteousness in them that perish . . . And for this cause God shall send them strong delusion that they should believe *the* lie" (II Thess. 2:9-11). It is important that a particular lie is spoken of as "the" lie. The one hundred and forty-four thousand, who have been called out while "the" lie has been having its great circulation, are found to have mouths that are free from this lie. Here, also, these firstfruits of the tribulation period are seen in all the unblemished glory of their imputed righteousness in Christ. Like the three who came through the fiery furnace without even the smell of fire, they have known the breath of Satan in its last and most violent gasps, yet they stand in the sight of God without blemish. Oh! the grace of God!

Verses 6–8
The Everlasting Gospel

⁶And I saw another messenger flying in midheaven, having an eternal Gospel to proclaim to those dwelling upon the earth, and to every nation, tribe, tongue and people; ⁷saying with a great voice, Fear God and give glory to Him; for the hour of His judgment is come; and worship Him who made the Heaven, the earth, the sea and the fountains of waters.

⁸And another, a second messenger, followed, saying, Fallen, fallen is Babylon the great, which hath made all nations drink of the wine of the wrath of her fornication.

(Rev. 14:6-8, Free Translation)

The vision of the Lamb on Mount Zion was but a momentary glimpse of the coming triumph of God's government on earth. The whole of the fourteenth chapter might be likened to a moment in the midst of bitter warfare. The troops reach a summit after heavy fighting. From that summit they survey the valley that now lies before them, before they dash down into the forests which cover the scene of the great battle which they are about to undertake. First of all, they see the towers of Mount Zion, their objective in the battle. The flag of victory waves there and they know that strong forces are about to proceed from its gates to attack the enemy which lies between them and it. The victory is assuredly theirs, but the steps by which they must proceed are clearly shown to them from the summit before they go down into the valley to fight through to the end of the warfare and the sure triumph. Soldiers might see before them a wood to be passed, a stream to cross, a village to be captured, an artillery post to be destroyed. So in this fourteenth chapter of Revelation is Mount Zion across the valley and the conquering hosts on her battlements. Down in the valley what is called Babylon the great, already tumbling, though the fall will not be complete until the eighteenth chapter. In the plain by the city, the host has bowed to the Antichrist, and the defeat of this host is announced. Some of the army of the righteous will fall; but their blessedness is foreseen; and finally, the hand-to-hand struggle of Armageddon at the very gates of Mount Zion is seen as a triumph for the forces of the Lord of Hosts, though the details will not be seen until the twentieth chapter.

First of all, an angel messenger comes forth from God, flying in mid-Heaven, proclaiming the everlasting gospel. This gospel must be distinguished from the gospel of the grace of God which is the theme of our preaching in this twentieth century. The word "Gospel" is a translation of the Greek word from which we derive our word "evangel" and means, simply, "good news." It was a common word in the Greek tongue long before the time of Christ. It should be noticed that the word "angel" is to be found in the word "evangel." The first was the messenger who brought the second, the good message. In classical Greek it is possible to find the word "angel" applied to men, women, children, birds, the morning star, slaves, ambassadors, and anything or anybody capable of bringing a message, literally or figuratively. In like manner the word "evangel" was applied to almost any type of good news. Indeed, first of all it was applied to the pagan sacrifices offered at the time the good news was received, or to the crown of leaves placed on the brow of a messenger who brought good news, and only later did the word come to mean the good news itself. The runner who brought the tidings of the defeat of the Persians at Marathon to the city of Athens is called an "angel" and the news he brought is called the "evangel" or gospel in ancient classical Greek.

We point this out because there have been some who deemed that every time the word "gospel" was to be found in the New Testament it applied only to that which is defined by Paul in his first epistle to the Corinthians. "I declare unto you the gospel which I preached unto you . . . how that Christ died for our sins according to the scriptures, And that he was buried, and that he arose again on the third day, according to the scriptures" (I Cor. 15:1, 3, 4). As a matter of fact, there are other matters of good news which are also called "gospel" in the Scriptures. False doctrine is called "another gospel" (II Cor. 11:4; Gal. 1:6). But many different items of good news from God are called "gospel" in the New Testament narrative. The noun or the verb is used in all the following instances: the message of Gabriel announcing the birth of John the Baptist (Luke 1:19), the announcement of Christ's birth by the angelic hosts to the shepherds (Luke 2:10), the news of the spiritual growth of the Thessalonian church (I Thess. 3:6), the announcement of the seventh angel in the book of Revelation that the "mystery of God is finished" (Rev. 10:7), the preaching of the nearness of the literal phase of the kingdom of our Lord (Matt. 24:14, etc.), as well as scores of instances where the words are used to describe salvation flowing from the atoning work of the Saviour.

We have every right, therefore to examine the message of this angel who preaches "an eternal gospel," to see exactly what good news it is. We have seen at length in previous studies the gospel of the kingdom as preached by the hundred and forty-four thousand messengers in the early part of the tribulation period. This is, of course, all that the gospel of grace contains, plus the announcement that the actual reign of the Lord Jesus Christ is about to begin. It should go without saying, to anyone who knows the scriptures, that the only method of salvation, in any age—law, Church, kingdom—is by the sovereign grace of God, on the basis of the work that was accomplished by our Lord's atoning death.

The eternal gospel is a proclamation to all who dwell upon the earth and to every nation, tribe, tongue, and people. It is the good news that the judgment of God, so long awaited, is about to be consummated, and that the groaning earth will be brought back from the reign of the rebel prince, under the sway of the Son of God. The rod which Satan has held over the earth has been heavy because it has been held by Satan. The rod which the Lord Jesus is about to hold over the earth is an iron rod, but it is held in the hand of the One who has said, "My yoke is easy, and my burden is light" (Matt. 11:30).

There are those who seek to escape the plain implications of the text before us. How can we follow interpreters who admit that this messenger preaches an everlasting gospel, but who yet deny that what is recorded of his preaching is the gospel that is announced? But let us examine the Scriptures and find the true answer. When God plainly says, "another messenger . . . having an eternal gospel . . . saying with a great voice, Fear God and give glory to him; for the hour of his judgment is come . . ." let us admit the plain fact and see that is what God is pleased to call "the gospel everlasting."

Once more, we repeat that men are saved only by the redemptive work of the Lord Jesus Christ. We believe that Adam and Eve were saved through believing God's Word concerning the Seed of the woman who would bruise the serpent's head (Gen. 3:15), and that in token of that salvation the Lord God made coats of skins (after having slain some sacrificial victim) and clothed them (Gen. 3:21). So much for the past. We believe that every blessing that will ever come to this earth or to any individual or group of individuals on it will come on the ground of Christ's death on the cross. But the open preaching of salvation to all who will come on the simple basis of trusting God's Word about the work that was accomplished on Calvary, is a phenomenon which begins with Pentecost.

The gospel has always had an element of judgment in it. When it was first preached in Eden, it contained the thunder of judgment. "The seed of the woman shall bruise the serpent's head." That is bad news to the serpent, but it is good news to all who refuse to follow him. So the gospel goes on down through the ages. At times the bad news has more emphasis than the good news; that is to say, at times God proclaims the judgment side of the gospel more than He proclaims the theme of mercy. John the Baptist preached the gospel of the imminence of the kingdom of Christ. His wilderness cry was, "Repent ye: for the kingdom of heaven is at hand" (Matt. 3:2). What judgment there was in all of his gospel preaching! "O generation of vipers, who hath warned you to flee from the wrath to come? Bring forth, therefore, fruits meet for repentance . . . the axe is laid to the root of the trees: therefore, every tree that bringeth not forth good fruit is hewn down, and cast into the fire . . . he that cometh after me is mightier than I . . . Whose fan is in his hand, and he will throughly purge his floor, and gather his wheat into the garner; but he will burn up the chaff with unquenchable fire" (Matt. 3:7, 8, 10-12).

Isaiah had announced that the Messiah would "purge Jerusalem from the blood that was in the midst of her" (Isa. 4:4, Heb.) and that this would be done by "the spirit of burning." Thus John the Baptist introduces Him. One commentator has described it thus: ". . . the inauguration of the Messianic kingdom was the gospel that John proclaimed. The King had come, and He would thoroughly purge His floor, and gather His wheat into the garner, but burn the chaff with unquenchable fire. Such a message has been the burden of all past prophecies and could justly be termed *the everlasting gospel.*"

Before the time of Christ, there was a period when for hundreds of years there had been no gospel at all proclaimed to the Gentiles. In fact, a Gentile woman who asked a boon from the Saviour Himself, heard Him answer, "It is not fit to take the children's bread and cast it to the dogs" (Mark 7:27). It was only when she stopped addressing Him as "Son of David," a title to which she had no right at all, and approached Him as "Lord" of the universe, that she was able to receive a few crumbs of grace from the table that was then spread for those who had the priesthood, the altar of sacrifice, the blood, the promises, and, in short, the whole covenant. It was only with the death of Christ that the Gospel became universal. The commentator whom we have last quoted says, "The gospel entrusted to Paul is a very different one from that proclaimed by John the Baptist. Paul's commission was of far wider import." On the road to Damascus he was commissioned to go to the Gentiles (Acts 26:16-18). "This commission drives Paul beyond the boundaries of Judaism, and enjoins upon him the proclamation of a world-wide gospel. We have long since seen that Israel's history as the elect people of God was suspended when Christ was refused; and during the time of that suspension, there comes in this world-wide proclamation of salvation by grace through faith in Christ. This is not the theme of the Old Testament preachers. This is not the announcement of the king standing at the door; it is not the declaration of impending judgments to purge the earth and prepare it for the establishing of the Messianic kingdom; it is not confined to the Jewish people; it is a message for all men, in all conditions and in every clime; and it gives assurance of salvation by grace; and joint-heirship with Christ to an inheritance incorruptible, undefiled, and that fadeth not away. This is the gospel proclaimed by Paul, and by the multitude of evangelical preachers since his day. This is *not* 'the everlasting gospel,' which John the Baptist preached, and which shall be preached again when the Church has been taken up out of the world, and Israel's history once more resumed."

There are others who teach along the same line, and speaking of the form of this everlasting gospel as it is preached by this angel messenger, Grant says, "This is the gospel which has been ringing through the ages since, which may well be called the everlasting one. Its form is only altered by the fact that now at last its promise is to be fulfilled. 'Judgment' is to 'return to righteousness' . . . Man's day is past; the day of the Lord is come, and every blow inflicted shall be upon the head of evil, the smiting down of sorrow and all that brings it. What can he be but rebel-hearted who shall refuse to join the anthem when the King-Creator comes into His own again? The angel gospel is thus a claim for worship from all people, and to Him that cometh, every knee shall bow."

The second angelic messenger announces the doom of Babylon. This is the third of the series of seven events announced in this fourteenth chapter. (1) The Lamb on Mount Zion with the 144,000 (1-5); (2) The messenger with the eternal gospel (6, 7); (3) The second messenger announcing the doom of Babylon (8); (4) The third messenger with the announcement of the fury of God upon the worshipers of the wild-beast (9-12); (5) The heavenly voice announcing the happiness of the righteous dead from henceforth (13); (6) The harvest of the righteous (14-16); (7) The gathering of the unrighteous for judgment (17-20).

The first messenger announces the hour of God's judgment. The second messenger announces that Babylon is fallen. In the Bible, Babylon stands for all that is the world, as over against the call of the heart of God. God has given to man the capability of loving Him. Therefore, if our love is spent on any object which in any wise detracts from the love of the Father, we are sinning. Anything which draws the love of men away from God is necessarily Satanic and shall be judged. There is a form of Babylon which is political, and there is a form which is religious. Both shall be judged, and God has deemed the matter of sufficient importance to devote two entire chapters of this revelation to the detailed description of the fall of these great systems which have drawn away the minds of men from the worship of Him who is the perfect One. There are some minds which are drawn to the woman Babylon, the mother of harlots. There are others who think nothing of the religious forms of earth who are nevertheless drawn away by the pomp and circumstances of this life. Rightly does one commentator state, "The city, Babylon the great, has strong attractions, not for the religiously minded only, but also for the many who are irreligious. And it is this power of allurement, this fascinating attractiveness of the world, its power to seduce the hearts of men from God, who has a just claim to their undivided affections, that is emphasized by this vision."

Several passages in the Scripture illustrate this allurement of the world and God's judgment upon it. "Ye adulterers and adulteresses, know ye not that the friendship of the world is enmity with God? Whosoever therefore will be a friend of the world is the enemy of God" (James 4:4). "Love not the world, neither the things that are in the world. If any man love the world, the love of the Father is not in him. For all that is in the world, the lust of the flesh, and the lust of the eyes, and the pride of life, is not of the Father, but is of the world. And the world passeth away and the lust thereof; but he that doeth the will of God abideth for ever" (I John 2:15-17). Here in this passage we see the announcement of the condemnation and destruction of that which the Scripture elsewhere calls "the world." Here it is Babylon the great, and the reason that is given is that she has caused men to be seduced from God by the wine of her fornications.

This symbol of the drunkenness of the nations is one that is found frequently in the Old Testament. If men are drunken they are no longer themselves. They are turned into something less than human and their drunkenness brings in its train misery, sorrow, poverty, degradation, and shame. It is very interesting to note that in Japanese they have, to describe different types of drunkenness, the different names of animals, If a man is just filthy drunk, the Japanese call him pig-drunk; if he's just so drunk that he wants to cut capers, they call him monkey-drunk; if he's just so drunk that he wants to make love to every woman he sees, they call him rooster-drunk; if he wants to fight everyone he sees, they call him lion-drunk; and so on. This symbol of bestiality of drunkenness is found throughout the whole of the Bible. The reference that is the most apt is one which uses this same symbol in speaking of the Babylon of the Old Testament. "Flee out of the midst of Babylon, and deliver every man his soul; be not cut off in her iniquity; for this is the time of the Lord's vengeance; he will render unto her a recompense. Babylon hath been a golden cup in the Lord's hand, that made all the earth drunken; the nations have drunken of her wine; therefore the nations are mad." Immediately, there follows the declaration of God's intention to destroy such a monstrous thing. "Babylon is suddenly fallen and destroyed; howl for her . . . her judgment reacheth unto heaven, and is lifted up even to the skies" (Jer. 51:6-9).

There is a verse in the Old Testament which explains the repetition in this prophecy. "Fallen, fallen is Babylon the great." Pharaoh had a dream and it was doubled. Joseph explained this to Pharaoh, "And for that the dream was doubled unto Pharaoh twice; it is because the thing is established by God, and God will shortly bring it to pass" (Gen. 41:32). So it is with the prophecies of the chapter we are studying. Just as the Lord Jesus put a "verily, verily" before some of His great promises as a mark that they were indeed established and certain, so God announces the doom of all that offends in His Kingdom. Babylon is fallen, is fallen. This is established; it is certain; it is *shortly* to come to pass.

Verses 9–13

Vintage Wine

⁹And another, a third messenger, followed them, saying with a great voice, If any man worshippeth the wild beast and his image, and receiveth a mark upon his forehead or upon his hand, ¹⁰he also shall drink of the wine of God's fury, which is prepared unmixed in the cup of his wrath, and he shall be tortured with fire and brimstone in the presence of the holy messengers and in the presence of the Lamb. ¹¹And the smoke of their torment rises unto ages of ages; and they have no rest day and night for those who worship the wild beast and his image, or receive the mark of his name. ¹²Here is the endurance of the saints, they that keep the commandments of God and the faith of Jesus.

¹³And I heard a voice out of Heaven saying, Write: Happy are the dead who are dying in the Lord from now on; yea saith the Spirit, that they may rest from their labors and their works follow with them.
(Rev. 14:9-13, Free Translation)

The third messenger announces the doom of those who will worship the Antichrist and his image, receiving the mark on the forehead or hand. First, it is said that they are to drink of the wine of God's fury, which is prepared unmixed in the cup of his wrath. An interesting description in the writings of one of Europe's foremost liberals will throw some light on this.

Thomas Mann, noted German writer, exiled because he would not bow to a dictatorship, saw Europe's greatest danger in the late 1930's to be that of mass-drunkenness. As a result of this intoxication, "virtue sets aside her shield, the mind drops its scepter, the indestructible union of beings makes death more distant and their eternal youth gives beauty and felicity to the world. This describes the Dionysiac fervor of which collective drunkenness is a humiliating parody. The youth that marches in step, singing the watchwords and popular tunes, experiences a purely selfish and sterile enjoyment. . . . The end of the march is of little importance . . . . Mass-drunkenness, which relieves the individual of responsibility, is an end in itself. The ideology which it exalts, such as the State, or Socialism, or the greatness of the country, is not essential to it. They are only pretexts. The one aim is drunkenness. One must get rid of his own self, his own thoughts—or, more precisely, of morality and reason in general." This describes, of course, the mass-drunkenness under fascist dictatorships and also that under Soviet dictatorship.

If we analyze this closely, and under the light that falls from the Word of God, we note that one of the world's foremost thinkers saw that great sections of humanity are drunk. How else could nations act as they were acting. Yet he did not know that the wine with which they are drunken comes from Satan.

Now our passage announces that there is to be another drunkenness, far worse, that is to come upon men because they have not been willing to go God's way. The mass hysteria, or drunkenness which permitted mobs to give themselves to such men as Hitler, Stalin and Mussolini, will head up in that mass-drunkenness which will bow to the image of the Antichrist and accept a brand upon the forehead or hand as a sign of subservience to him. To all such, God will give another wine to drink.

Figure is added to figure to describe the terror of the judgment of God. Like a bitter drink, the wrath of God will be forced down the throats of those who have failed to recognize that He who created them has a right to demand their subjection; and that if this subjection is not given, He has the right to judge and punish them. There are two judgments, one in this world, and one in the world to come. The first is the tribulation wrath which is about to be poured out in its fullness. The undiluted wine of God's fury must be taken by those who worship the Antichrist, and it must be taken from the cup of God's wrath. We remember that God has said, "I am the Lord; I will not give my glory to another" (Isa. 42:8). When the nations, intoxicated with Satan's brew, turn away from the one true God and ascribe worth to the Antichrist, the anger of God, which has been patiently restrained through these centuries of His grace, is poured out upon the world, well deserving all that comes upon it.

The passage that follows easily disposes of the common statement that "all the Hell we will ever get will be in this world." That could be said in a restricted sense, of the one who is a believer in the Lord Jesus Christ. For Jesus Christ bore our eternal punishment upon the cross, and we shall never bear it. Therefore, all that there is of sorrow, trouble, and pain for us, we receive in this world. But let us not forget that none of these things that fall upon the believer ever come from the cup of God's wrath. In His love He may chastise, but He will never forsake. It is literally correct, then, to say of the believer, that he has no Hell in this world nor in the world to come. It is just as correct, therefore, to say of the unbeliever, that he has no Heaven in this world nor in the world to come, and that as believers truly know a foretaste of Heaven while yet living on earth, so the unbeliever knows a foretaste of eternal punishment here, and the full consciousness of it hereafter.

As we are about to consider the doctrine of eternal punishment rather fully, I wish to present a paragraph or two from one of my teachers, Dr. R. A. Torrey. I sat in class as a boy of eighteen and heard Dr. Torrey lecture on the future destiny of unbelievers. I never could forget it. He said, "In conclusion, two things are certain. First, the more closely men walk with God and the more devoted they become to His service, the more likely they are to believe this doctrine. Many men tell us they love their fellow men too much to believe this doctrine; but the men who show their love in more practical ways than sentimental protestations about it, the men who show their love for their fellow men as Jesus Christ showed His, by laying down their lives for them, *they* believe it, even as Jesus Christ Himself believed it.

"Second, men who accept a loose doctrine regarding the ultimate penalty of sin (Restorationism or Universalism or Annihilationism) lose their power for God. They may be very clever at argument and zealous in proselytizing, but they are poor at soul-saving. They are seldom found beseeching men to be reconciled to God. They are more likely to be found trying to upset the faith of those already won by the efforts of others, than winning men who have no faith at all. If you really believe the doctrine of the endless, conscious torment of the impenitent, and the doctrine really gets hold of you, you will work as you never worked before for the salvation of the lost. If you in any wise abate this doctrine, it will abate your zeal.

"Finally: Do not believe this doctrine in a cold, intellectual, merely argumentative way. If you do, and try to teach it, you will repel men from it. But meditate upon it in its practical, personal bearings, until your heart is burdened by the awful peril of the wicked and you rush out to spend the last dollar, if need be, and the last ounce of strength you have, in saving those imperiled men from the certain, awful Hell of conscious agony and shame to which they are fast hurrying."

This passage now gives some of the details of the eternal torment of the condemned. The first is that they shall be tortured with fire and brimstone. We are not going to avoid any of the questions that are raised by unbelievers, or by those who seek to deny the doctrine of eternal punishment. Such questions will arise frequently in the remainder of the Apocalypse, and we shall attempt to meet them fairly and completely. First, then, Is the fire spoken of in this and similar passages literal fire? First, of all, the expression is a common one, especially throughout the New Testament. For the doctrine of eternal punishment may be said to be a doctrine that is peculiar to the personal teachings of the Lord Jesus Christ, and the disciple who was closest to Him during His earthly ministry. We must consider the word "fire," as we would any other word used by the Lord Jesus. The word is literal or it is symbolic. Is there anything that would tend to teach that it is literal fire? In the parable of the wheat and the tares, the

Lord gives certain teaching under symbols and then interprets those symbols. The wheat represents the children of the Kingdom; the tares represent the children of the wicked one; the harvest is the end of the age; the reapers are the angels; the gathering of the wheat into the barn is the gathering of the righteous into the kingdom; *but the gathering of the tares to be burned in the fire is the gathering out of offensive things and iniquitous persons to be cast into the furnace of fire* (Matt. 13:36-42). Realize the importance of this. Every symbol in Jesus' parable is given a meaning by him, except the word fire. But fire in the parable is also fire in the interpretation. We are forced to conclude that the fire is literal fire, or else, under the well-known law of biblical interpretation, that it is so much more terrible than literal fire that there is no word in human language to explain it. Therefore, the Lord has given to our little human minds the nearest thing to the explanation of a divine fact that our human minds can take in.

Immediately there arises another question. Fire on earth consumes. Would not this fire consume its victims and thus end the consciousness of their torment? In other words, must we not look upon the moment of being cast into the lake of fire as a moment of annihilation? The Word of God will not permit that interpretation for a moment. He who raises the bodies of the believers so that they may be like unto the body of His glory by the power that He has to subdue all things unto Himself (Phil. 3:21) will most certainly give to the unsaved the body that He desires (I Cor. 15:38).

Another objection is raised by some that may best be met here. Our passage says that the torment of the beast worshipers will take place in the presence of the holy messengers and the Lamb. Some find a moral difficulty in this. They know that there have been monsters in human form who permitted torture. They cite the chambers of the Inquisition or the secret dungeons of the police in Communist countries today. We admit, immediately, that such tormentors are fiends. Then, says the objector, why is not your God a fiend, who would torment people forever in much worse torment? The answer lies in the nature of sin and in the nature of God. The Creator has chosen, in His infinite wisdom, to give eternal existence to all of His creatures. He is absolutely holy, with a holiness that not only manifests itself in a positive delight in righteousness, but in a positive and unchanging hatred of sin.

Now the creatures that make up the human race have rebelled against God, falling into sin, which God hates with perfect hatred. His loving-kindness caused Him to come into the world in Jesus Christ and accomplish a redemption which reconciled to Him all who will turn away from sin and receive the pardon offered by His grace, on the ground of the blood shed by the Lord Jesus Christ in dying on the cross. He now invites men to be reconciled to Him. If they will come and receive the pardon which He offers to them, He will give them eternal life with Himself. But if they refuse to accept that gift of His grace, then they must remain in their lost condition, eternally deserving, eternally provoking, and eternally receiving the holy wrath of God. The wrath of God is greater toward the smallest infraction that could go by the name of sin than is our wrath toward the greatest villainy that could come from a dictator who would bomb cities, destroy civil and religious liberties, and plunge nations into warfare. When we have this view of the holiness of God, we will begin to understand why God must punish the sinner who remains in his sin. There is a startling contrast between the two kinds of physical death mentioned in the Bible. Compare "ye die in your sins" (John 8:21), with "they which are fallen asleep in Christ" (I Cor. 15:18).

We should not be surprised at the announcement that the eternal punishment is carried out by holy messengers of God. They speed to do His bidding whatever it may be, and with a perfect comprehension of His holiness, before which the noblest of their ranks must cover their faces and their feet. That the presence of God should be somehow manifested in the place of punishment will add an impressiveness that could not be obtained otherwise. And this is not a new thought. David cried out, "Though I make my bed in hell, thou art there" (Ps. 139:8). Perhaps indelibly stamped upon the minds of the lost will be the presence of the Redeemer. This goes to show how the issues of eternity are settled in this life. Let no man think that he will repent after death. Not only is there no opportunity for such repentance even dimly taught in Scripture, but the contrary is definitely taught. "The carnal mind is enmity against God; for it is not subject to the law of God, neither indeed can be" (Rom. 8:7).

A great illustration of this is seen in the actions of Judas. He was in the most intimate personal contact with the Lord Jesus during the three years of His earthly ministry. He saw Christ moved with compassion, saw His love for souls continually pouring itself out in the abandon of love that was manifest throughout the life of our Lord. Yet Judas was unmoved. He saw no beauty in Christ after all he had witnessed in Him. At the end, caring only for gain, dominated by self, he was ready to sell the Lord for the price of a slave. So it is with all men who reject Christ. And that formidable bent away from righteousness and God is eternally fixed with the end of this human existence. The man who dies in a state of enmity against God will never change, though the fires or torment be his forever. His heart hates holiness; his heart hates God. This is the paramount reason, why eternal punishment is a divine necessity.

Another writer has attempted to get around the truth by explaining away the eternity of the phrase "for ever and ever." In the Greek it is, literally, unto ages of ages, although in a dozen other passages the article occurs and it is literally, unto the ages of the ages. Now, it is conceivable that after ages of ages a period of punishment might come to an end, and were this the only passage where the phrase were to be found we would not be permitted such absolute certainty as we have from the study of the rest of the book. Twelve times in the book of Revelation do we find this phrase. Eight times it refers to the duration of the reign and glory of God the Father and the Lord Jesus Christ. Three times it refers to the duration of the punishment of the devil and his beastly incarnations. The other instance is the one here, referring, most certainly, to human beings who have refused to follow God, but who have followed Satan and accepted his leadership. There can be no doubt of the fact that the phrase is the strongest possible for the expression of the idea of having no end. One commentator has well said, "It is a picture not merely of years tumbling upon years, but of ages tumbling upon ages in endless succession. It is never in a single instance used of a limited period. Nothing could more plainly or graphically picture absolute endlessness."

One last objection must be met here. There have been those who claimed that this passage could not speak of eternal punishment since there was a reference to "day and night." We have only to turn back through the Apocalypse, however, to find that this is a common figure for the word "unceasingly." The four living creatures before the throne of God rested not *"day and night,* saying, Holy, holy, holy, Lord God Almighty, which was, and is, and is to come" (Rev. 4:8). It is even more striking in the original language, as the entire clause is repeated letter for letter describing the restlessness of the living creatures to worship and the restlessness of the wicked in torment. It speaks of an intense activity of torment, best described, perhaps, in the words of Isaiah, "for their worm shall not die, neither shall their fire be quenched" (Isa. 66:24).

The followers of God know these facts in advance. This is why the Holy Spirit can say to them, "Here is the endurance of the saints, they that keep the commandments of God and the faith of Jesus." The earthly torment may be painful, and the earthly fires hot, but they can last only as long as the thread of physical life. Endure, therefore, in the faithful obedience to the commandments of God and the faith that is our Lord's. For though "weeping may endure for a night, but joy cometh in the morning" (Ps. 30:5).

Now in the text, another voice comes out of Heaven. We are not told whether it is the voice of a messenger, or the voice of the Lord Himself. John hears the order to write, and obeys. "Happy are the dead who are dying in the Lord from now on; yea, saith the Spirit, that they may rest from their labors, and their works follow with them." This is true of all believers in all ages in one sense, but it is especially true of those who die at this moment in the tribulation for their faith in the Lord and their obedience to His Word. We must not forget that our Saviour said that this tribulation would be more terrible than any the earth has ever seen and more terrible than earth would ever see again.

There are two words for work used in the next clause. "They rest from their labours and their works follow with them." They rest from the toils, the wearinesses, the hardships of life, but not from their activity. This passage has generally been taken to mean that the reward of their labors would go with them into Heaven, and that there they would find a recompense for the toils of life as they entered into "heavenly rest." From this there has grown up the idea, widely spread and in many circles, that Heaven will be a place of idleness. Some of our hymns have strengthened this idea.

> *Where congregations ne'er break up*
> *And Sabbaths have no end . . .*

Such ideas are certainly not in harmony with the Word of God. There is rest from the weariness of work but there will be the joy of continuing activity without the accompanying fatigue that we now know. Heaven will be a place of great growth, development, and increase in knowledge and service.

Verses 14–20

The Winepress of God

[14]And I saw, and behold, a white cloud, and upon the cloud I saw one sitting like unto a Son of man, having upon His head a crown of gold, and in His hand a sharp sickle. [15]And another messenger came out of the inner temple, crying with a great voice to Him that sat on the cloud, Send forth Thy sickle and reap; because the hour to reap is come; for the harvest of the earth is overripe. [16]And He that sat upon the cloud cast His sickle upon the earth, and the earth was reaped.

[17]And another messenger came out of the inner temple which is in Heaven, he also having a sharp sickle. [18]And another messenger came out from the altar, having authority over fire; and cried with a great cry to him that had the sharp sickle, saying, Send forth thy sharp sickle and gather the clusters of the vine of the earth, because her grapes are fully ripe. [19]And the messenger cast his sickle into the earth and gathered the vintage of the earth, and cast it into the winepress, the great winepress of the wrath of God. [20]And the winepress was trodden outside of the city, and blood came forth from the winepress, even to the bridles of the horses, as far as a thousand six hundred furlongs.

(Rev. 14:14-20, Free Translation)

For an understanding of the verses which follow, we must study briefly the significance of the word "cloud" in the Scriptures. There is one particular cloud which follows the Lord Jesus Christ from eternity to eternity. It is the cloud of the glory of God, the Shekinah. The Lord came down to dwell in the midst of His people, appearing before them at night as a pillar of fire and in the day as a pillar of cloud. This cloud went before them as they journeyed through the wilderness (Exod. 13:21, 22; 14:19-24). When the Lord gave the manna, which is certainly a type of Christ, the living Bread from Heaven, the glory of the Lord appeared in the cloud (Exod. 16:10). It was the same at the giving of the law (Exod. 19:9, 16; 24:15-18). This glory was again manifested at the second giving of the law (Exod. 34:5).

When the tabernacle was finished, "a cloud covered the tent of the congregation, and the glory of the Lord filled the tabernacle. And Moses was not able to enter into the tent of the congregation, because the cloud abode thereon, and the glory of the Lord filled the tabernacle" (Exod. 40:34, 35). This cloud of glory abode at all times in the tabernacle within the Holy of Holies upon the mercy seat which was, of course, the place of the atonement. "So it was always: the cloud covered it by day, and the appearance of fire by night" (Num. 9:16-22). When the seventy elders were chosen to help Moses, "the Lord came down in a cloud, and spake unto him" (Num. 11:25). Other like appearances are to be found elsewhere in the Old Testament. Now this is not a cloud in the ordinary sense of a rain cloud. They used the word "cloud" because the thing that appeared was describable only in terms of something that they knew. We have a similar illustration when people speak of the mushroom cloud that appears at the time of the explosion of an atomic bomb. It is not a mushroom, and it is not a cloud, but it is something that is shaped like a mushroom and looks like a cloud.

When Solomon had finished the Temple, we find that this cloud of the glory of God came in with the bringing of the ark. When the priests had withdrawn after the ark had been placed in the Holy of Holies, "the cloud filled the house of the Lord, So that the priests could not stand to minister because of the cloud: for the glory of the Lord had filled the house of the Lord" (I Kings 8:10, 11).

One of the saddest passages in the Word of God describes the departure of this cloud from the Temple. The glory of the God of Israel had been dwelling upon the mercy seat which was overshadowed by the cherubim. Then we read "The glory of the Lord of Israel was gone up from the cherub, whereupon he was, to the threshold of the house . . . then the glory of the Lord went up from the cherub, and stood over the threshold of the house; and the house was filled with the cloud, and the court was full of the brightness of the Lord's glory" . . . The great cherubim then appeared above the temple and "Then the glory of the Lord departed from off the threshold of the house, and stood over the cherubim. And the cherubim lifted up their wings, and mounted up from the earth in my sight . . . and the glory of the God of Israel was over them above . . . And the glory of the Lord went up from the midst of the city . . . which is on the east side of the city" (Ezek. 9:3; 10:4, 18, 19; 11:22, 23). The next time the glory is mentioned by Ezekiel, it is seen in the vision of the future where it shall be taken from man no longer (Ezek. 43:2ff). Daniel 7:13, 14 is a picture of the scene in Heaven which we studied in Revelation 5. There the coming King is seen arrayed in the glory which He shall bring with Him.

In the New Testament, this cloud is to be found at many points in the narrative. Dr. A. T. Robertson, the noted Greek scholar, speaks of Luke's account of the virgin birth in a way that leads us to believe that the cloud of glory was present at the supernatural conception of the baby Jesus in the womb of Mary. Luke describes the scene, "And the angel answered and said unto her, The Holy Spirit shall come upon thee, and the power of the Highest shall overshadow thee" (Luke 1:35). Dr. Robertson says that the words, "shall overshadow thee," are "a figure of a cloud coming upon her . . . Here it is like the she-kinah glory which suggests it, where the cloud of glory represents the presence and power of God."

It was the shining of this same glory round about the shepherds who were watching over their flocks in the fields that caused them to be sore afraid (Luke 2:9). It was certainly this glory in which the Lord Jesus Christ was transfigured, which the Holy Spirit gave to Peter as a guarantee of the truth of Christ's literal return to reign (Matt. 17:5; II Pet. 1:17-19). When the Lord ascended into Heaven, it was this same cloud that received Him out of their sight (Acts 1:9). When the Lord Jesus Christ comes again to take His own to be with Himself, the dead in Christ and those who live shall be caught up together with them into this same glory (I Thess. 4:17). At the close of the great tribulation period, He will come with clouds and every eye shall see Him (Matt. 24:30; 26:64; Rev. 1:7).

It is immaterial whether this being, seated upon the white cloud, having on his head the wreath of gold and carrying in his hand a sharp sickle, is the Lord Jesus Christ in person or a mighty angelic ambassador, clothed for the moment with the authority of the Lord in carrying out the task that this messenger is to fulfill. Commentators see the Lord in person, others an angelic messenger.

We are inclined to believe, personally, that this is the Lord Jesus Christ, Himself, fulfilling the prophecy of Luke, "They shall see the Son of Man coming in a cloud with power and great glory" (Luke 21:27). If it be objected that this being is said to be *like* a Son of Man, and that, therefore, it cannot be the Son of Man Himself, we would simply point to John's first vision of Christ as recorded in the first chapter of Revelation. "In the midst of the seven lampstands" John saw "One like unto the Son of Man" and this One was most clearly, the Lord Jesus Christ. He said to John, "Fear not; I am the first and the last; I am he that liveth and was dead; and behold I am alive for evermore" (Rev. 1:13, 17, 18).

The commentators have been clearly divided as to the meaning of the reaping which now takes place.

We are quite in accord with Frost who says that "the whole portrayal of the fourteenth chapter is a foreview of what comes afterwards." If we read through the remaining portion of the Apocalypse, we find that there are two great judgments to take place after this announcement of reaping and vintage. There is the judgment of the seven last bowls of the wrath of God which sweeps away "Babylon the great," and there is the judgment of Armageddon. It should be noted immediately that the first of these is an ecclesiastical judgment and the second a judgment of the nations. How in keeping with the prophecy we are now studying: the first is a reaping, the second is a vintage.

The Lord administers much of His government by means of angel powers. Daniel tells us that the angel of God who represents the affairs of Israel, is Michael the Archangel (Dan. 12:1). This passage goes even so far as to state that Michael, the great prince which standeth for the children of Israel, shall "stand up" for Israel in the time of the end under the reign of the Antichrist. Is it inconceivable, therefore, that this messenger of verse fifteen is Michael calling unto the Lord to bring the long awaited judgment upon those who have oppressed His people? At all events, the angel messenger cries out, "Send forth thy sickle and reap; because the hour to reap is come; for the harvest of the earth is overripe."

Judgment has long been overdue. Only the patience of God can account for the delay. But now the time has surely come. The harvest is overripe. A. T. Robertson discusses the meaning of this last word, and while pointing out that it might possibly mean nothing more than ripeness, nevertheless concludes that it means dead ripeness, overripeness. The word in the Greek really means to wither, to dry up, and is used in James with that meaning, "For the sun is no sooner risen with a burning heat, but it withereth the grass, and the flower thereof falleth" (James 1:11).

So the Lord heeds the cry of His angels. The sickle is cast upon the earth. The preposition is most revealing. The sickle is cast *epi,* upon or against the earth. Most clearly it is a judgment. The spiritual powers are reaped, as the national powers will be trodden down in the vintage.

But certainly it is only one phase of the destruction that is to come upon the world at this time; for after the harvest comes the gathering of the grapes.

Another messenger comes forth, this time from the inner temple which is in Heaven. We are inclined to believe that this is another representation of the Lord Jesus Christ. It does not harm the interpretation if it be insisted that this is a representative of His. But we know from the nineteenth chapter that the Lord comes forth with the judgment that is described here in anticipation. This fifth messenger has been described by Swete as a minister of vengeance. He answers to the call of the sixth messenger in the eighteenth verse, as the Son of man answered to the call of the fourth messenger in the fifteenth verse. The angelic messenger who calls out to the Lord to complete the judgment is none other than the messenger of God who has authority over the judgment fires of God. We saw, when we considered Revelation 8:5, that the judgment that fell upon the earth was on the basis of the righteousness of God as manifested at the cross of Christ. The altar not only bore the body of the lamb; the altar also contained the fire which consumed the lamb. Each individual must have either the lamb or the fire. If we do not take the Lord Jesus Christ as our Saviour, we must have Him as our Judge. Sin is either taken from us and borne by the Substitute or it is borne by us and must crush us as it receives the fires of God.

As the first harvest is declared to be overripe, so the grapes are said to be fully ripe. They call out for judgment. We remember an incident that occurred during our early school days. A boy in the school who was a bully had mistreated many of his smaller schoolmates and bore the enmity of many. It was tersely described one day by one boy who said of the bully, "He is certainly nursing a black eye." At the time the boy spoke the bully had no black eye. He meant that evil actions were preparing the way for one, inviting one, and in due time it was applied much to the delight of his other victims. So the holy angels, properly jealous of the righteousness of God, know that the world has long been the breeding place for sin and rebellion, calling out for punishment. When the moment arrives, their pent-up feelings cry out to God for precipitate action. Send forth the sickle and reap. Harvest is overdue.

There are two phrases in the following scene which link it, unquestionably, with the battle of Armageddon which is yet to come upon this earth. One phrase carries us on in the Apocalypse and the other takes us back to the Old Testament. Our last verse speaks of the treading of the winepress. We turn over to the nineteenth chapter and read, "Out of his mouth goeth a sharp sword, that with it he should smite the nations: and he shall rule them with a rod of iron; and he treadeth the winepress of the fierceness and wrath of Almighty God" (Rev. 19:15). This should have been enough to keep some commentators from the error of thinking that this judgment applied to Israel only, since Israel is spoken of in certain passages as the Lord's vine. Very clearly this application is to the Gentile nations and not to Israel at all. This becomes even clearer in the Old Testament description of the judgment of the nations at the battle of Armageddon. The wonderful prophecy of Joel gives us the detailed account of this judgment.

"For, behold, in those days, and in that time, when I shall bring again the captivity of Judah and Jerusalem, I will also gather all nations, and will bring them down into the valley of Jehoshaphat; and I will plead with them there for my people and for my heritage Israel, whom they have scattered among the nations, and parted my land" (Joel 3:1, 2). Here the time is clearly indicated. This judgment is to be at the time when the captivity of Israel is over. That time is, of course, yet future, and we know it to be the time of the great tribulation, described in Matthew 24, and the judgment of the nations, described in Matthew 25. There can be no doubt of the unity of all of these passages.

Joel describes the vintage judgment as follows: "Proclaim ye this among the nations; Prepare war; stir up the mighty men; let all the men of war draw near; let them come up. Beat your plowshares into swords, and your pruning hooks into spears: let the weak say, I am a strong warrior. Hasten and come, all you nations round about, and gather yourselves there: bring down thy warriors, O Lord." These mighty ones are none other than the angels who are the instruments of judgment which we now see at work in the book of Revelation. "Let the nations bestir themselves, and come up to the valley of Jehoshaphat: for there will I sit to judge all the nations round about. Put in the sickle, for the harvest is ripe: Go in, tread, for the winepress is full, the vats overflow; for their wickedness is great. Multitudes, multitudes in the valley of decision!" Note that this is not a text for evangelistic meetings. Some have used it to describe the decisions which individuals should be making for Christ. The reality, of course, is that it is the rendering of the divine court decision, the decision of final destruction from the face of the earth. "For the day of the Lord is near in the valley of decision. The sun and the moon are darkened, and the stars withdraw their shining. And the Lord roars from Zion, and utters his voice from Jerusalem; and the heavens and the earth shake; but the Lord is a refuge to his people, and a stronghold to the people of Israel." It should be noted that the winepress does not include Israel at all. They are clearly eliminated from the picture of judgment. "So shall you know that I am the Lord your God, who dwell in Zion, my holy mountain: and Jerusalem shall be holy, and strangers shall never again pass through it" (Joel 3:9-17, RSV).

In the Mediterranean countries it is a common sight at the time of the grape harvest to see the grapes cast into a large vat in order that the juice should be pressed by the naked feet of the vintners. Macaulay, in his famous poem, "Horatius at the Bridge," describes the countryside from which all the men have departed as soldiers so that the work has to be done by the women.

> *This year the must shall foam*
> *Round the white feet of laughing girls*
> *Whose sires have marched to Rome.*

But there will be no laughing when the winepress of the wrath of God is trodden. The Hebrew of Nahum 1:2 calls our God "the Lord of wrath." He is absolute master of His judgments and will give them according to the measure of His plan. The Lord Jesus Christ Himself will do the treading of the winepress. The wrath of the Lamb, which some men foolishly thought to be upon them as early as the time of the seal judgments (Rev. 6:16, 17), is about to be poured out upon the earth. All judgments up to this point have been introductory. All judgments up to this point have been samples. All judgments up to this point have been rehearsals. *The* judgments of God are about to take place.

Armageddon is in the north of Palestine, the valley of Jehoshaphat is in the south. Bozrah is named by Isaiah as the place where the Lord treads the winepress. And the distance between the farthest points of this "front" is 1600 furlongs. We shall discuss this great battle in detail when we come to the consideration of the nineteenth chapter.

PART VIII
THE BOWLS

PART VIII
THE BOWLS

CHAPTER 15

Verses 1–8

The Beginning of the End

¹And I saw another sign in Heaven, great and marvelous, seven messengers having seven plagues which are the last, because in them the wrath of God is finished. ²And I saw, as it were, a glassy sea, mingled with fire, and them that come off victorious from the wild beast and from his image and from the number of his name, standing upon the glassy sea having the harps of God. ³And they sing the song of Moses, the bondslave of God, and the song of the Lamb, saying, Great and marvelous are Thy works, O Lord God, the Almighty; just and true are Thy ways, Thou King of the ages; ⁴Who shall not fear, O Lord, and glorify Thy Name? because Thou alone art holy; for all the nations shall come and worship in Thy presence, for Thy righteous sentences have been made manifest.

⁵And after these things I saw, and the inner temple of the tabernacle of the testimony was opened in Heaven: ⁶And there came forth the seven messengers from the inner Temple, having the seven plagues, arrayed with precious stone, pure and bright, and girt about the breasts with golden girdles. ⁷And one from among the four living creatures gave to the seven messengers seven golden bowls full of the wrath of God Who liveth for ever and ever. ⁸And the inner temple was filled with smoke from out of the glory of God and from out of His power; and no one was able to enter into the inner temple until the seven plagues of the seven messengers should be finished.
(Rev. 15:1-8, Free Translation)

The third sign is called "another" sign. It is so wonderful that John calls it "great and marvelous." We may well wonder if this is not "the sign of the Son of Man in heaven" (Matt. 24:30), at which all the tribes of the earth will mourn. If it is, they would have good reason to wail. Zephaniah writes of this day, "Wait ye upon me, saith the Lord, until that day that I rise up to the prey; for my determination is to gather the nations, that I may assemble the kingdoms, to pour upon them mine indignation, even all my fierce anger: for all the earth shall be devoured with the fire of my jealousy" (Zeph. 3:8). All God's anger is here poured out. The seven messengers are seen in

283

Heaven, having the seven last plagues. The idea of finality is uppermost. In the pouring out of these bowls of judgment, the wrath of God is finished; comes to its final end against the sin of the earth.

In the early history of the people of God, they were led out of Egypt and through the Red Sea, in which their enemies were destroyed. The people, victorious by the power of God, sang with Moses, the great song of victory. "I will sing unto the Lord, for he hath triumphed gloriously: the horse and his rider hath he thrown into the sea. The Lord is my strength and song, and he is become my salvation" (Exod. 15:1, 2). Now, in the tribulation period, the people of God are kept safely through the sea of persecution and martyr-death, while their Pharaoh, the Antichrist, is destroyed behind them. They come victoriously to the safe shore of eternity and sing the song of redemption after the seven last plagues, even as Moses and the people sang it after the ten first plagues. Both of those numbers have spiritual significance, seven representing divine perfection and finality, and ten standing for numerical perfection. The twe series of events, both ending in triumph for God's people, call forth worship and praise to Him who deals so bountifully in His great grace.

The glassy sea recalls, of course, the sea of glass like unto crystal, before which the four and twenty elders sat (4:6). There are many commentators who have noted the similarity between the two and then, speaking of the dissimilarity, one says, "If it is the same, it has become ominously commingled now; for there it was 'like unto crystal' in clearness, but here it is 'mingled with fire.'" The difference is indeed striking and can teach us much.

When the believers of the Church period are removed at the beginning of the tribulation period their laver is seen as a sea of crystal. Some of them may have suffered martyrdom, but the maintenance of their fellowship was by the Word alone. In the tribulation period, the Lord has seen fit to demand, for His honor and glory, that they maintain their fellowship at the price of their sufferings. Their laver is crystal, mingled with fire. In the time immediately preceding the overthrow of the Antichrist and his power, there will be a sore trial of faith. Peter writes of the symbol of fire in this connection, "That the trial of your faith, being much more precious than of gold that perisheth, though it be tried with fire, might be found unto praise and honor and glory at the appearing of Jesus Christ" (I Pet. 1:7). In sea mingled with fire the Lord recognizes these sufferings and commemorates the faithfulness of this martyr group in this beautiful way. It would seem that this company of martyrs is kept distinct from all other groups of believers spoken of in the book of Revelation, as they are the ones who have come off victorious in the conflict with the devilish trinity of Satan, the dragon; the beast, the Antichrist; and the false prophet—the devil, the Antichrist, and the unholy spirit. Satan's counterfeit of the trinity.

This group of believers is seen to be standing upon the sea of glass mingled with fire. The preposition in Greek may be translated *by, upon,* or *over.* At all events, their labors are done, and they are now seen in full praise and worship. They have the harps of God and they sing the song of Moses and the Lamb. This does not mean that they sang the same words which Moses and the children of Israel sang when they stood on the victory side of the Red Sea. The words of this song are given to us, and they can be sung by this group irrespective of their race and background. We call attention to this because some commentators have sought to teach that this group were only Jewish saints of the tribulation period, because they sang the song of Moses, which was a song under the law. As a matter of fact, the song of Moses was sung before the giving of the law, but the question has no point here because the words of the song are given to us. To sing the song of Moses and the Lamb means to sing the song of physical deliverance and spiritual redemption.

"Great and marvellous," they sing, "are Thy works, O Lord God, the Almighty; just and true are Thy ways, Thou king of the ages; who shall not fear, O Lord, and glorify Thy name? because Thou alone art holy; for all the nations shall come and worship in Thy presence, for Thy righteous sentences have been made manifest" (vss. 3, 4).

As Moses and the children of Israel were drawn to praise because of the works of God displayed in their behalf, so these saints are drawn to praise because of the marvels which God works in their behalf. The prophet Micah, writing of these days, says, "The land shall be desolate because of them that dwell therein, for the fruit of their doings. Feed thy people with thy rod, the flock of thine heritage, which dwell solitarily in the wood, in the midst of Carmel: let them feed in Bashan and Gilead, as in the days of old. According to the days of thy coming out of the land of Egypt will I shew unto him marvelous things (Heb., new marvels). The nations shall see and be confounded at all their might: they shall lay their hand upon their mouth, their ears shall be deaf. They shall lick the dust like a serpent, they shall move out of their holes like worms of the earth: they shall be afraid because of the Lord our God, and shall fear because of thee. Who is a God like unto thee, that pardoneth iniquity, and passeth by the transgression of the remnant of his heritage? He retaineth not his anger for ever, because he delighteth in mercy . . ." (Mic. 7:13-18).

Here is a prophecy of "new marvels" which the Lord is going to perform in behalf of His people Israel. In Egypt there was a marvel of grace in passing over the bloodstained houses of His people. There was a marvel of power in opening a way through the Red Sea. There was a marvel of judgment in destroying the pursuing Egyptians in the sea. There was a marvel of guidance in supplying the cloud and the fire to lead the people by day and by night. There was a marvel of goodness in giving them manna and quails for their daily food. There was a marvel of condescension in pitching His tabernacle to dwell among them. There was a marvel of patience in enduring their murmurings and rebellion. There was a marvel of faithfulness in the constant remembrance of His covenant. Yet God says that He is going to show His people new marvels! What will they be? How infinite is our God! Jeremiah tells us that the works of the Lord on behalf of His people will be so great that "the days come, saith the Lord, that it shall no more be said, The Lord liveth, that brought up the children of Israel out of the land of Egypt; But, the Lord liveth, that brought up the children of Israel from the land of the north, and from all the lands whither he had driven them: and I will bring them again into their land that I gave unto their fathers" (Jer. 16:14, 15). These new marvels of grace and deliverance are hidden from our eyes, yet they are certain.

Micah says that the sight of these wonders will confound the nations at the might of God's people. They will be astounded at the work of God. This passage in Revelation teaches that all of the nations shall be brought to bow in the presence of the Lord as a result of these marvels. His righteous judgments are manifest, and all shall see God in His workings in behalf of His people.

The different ancient manuscripts of the New Testament have three different readings for one of the phrases in verse three. The text from which our King James Version was made names the Lord as "the king of saints." The revision and most commentators take the reading which describes Him as "the king of the nations." A. T. Robertson holds to "the king of the ages," corresponding to Jeremiah, where He is called "the living God, and an everlasting king" (Jer. 10:10), and to Timothy where He is called "the king eternal, immortal, invisible, the only wise God" (I Tim. 1:17). We may be sure that one of the last two is correct. The context would justify His being called "king of the nations" (as in Jer. 10:7), or "King of the ages." He is announcing the final judgments upon the nations, and is showing Himself to be the Lord of eternity. Either, therefore, is acceptable in place of the authorized rendering.

Now that the saints, victorious in their struggle with the enemy, are seen to have overcome the Antichrist and to be safely in glory, the seven messengers are allowed to proceed to the fulfilling of their mandate. They go forth from the inner temple of Heaven, that is, from the very presence of God, to pour out the bowls of wrath with the last plagues that are to come upon the nations. Once more, it should be observed, the judgment of God proceeds from the very heart of His holiness. Time and again, we have seen that judgment is based on the righteousness displayed at the cross. The inner temple which is mentioned here, was the holy of holies in the earthly tabernacle, the place in which the ark, with its mercy seat, received the drops of blood in the propitiation on the day of atonement. In the heavenly temple, the inner temple is the very presence of God Himself. Judgment proceeds, therefore, from all that God reveals Himself to be, the holy and righteous One. The vision that John saw under the seventh trumpet (11:19) is here expanded to its fullness. We are about to see further details of the judgment that was there announced (11:18).

One of the four living creatures now hands the seven bowls of wrath to the seven messengers. Our King James Version renders this word as though the vessel were some sort of a bottle. It is most certainly the common Greek word for a rather flat bowl, almost a saucer in which incense was carried into the Temple. It is the same vessel as that which was carried by the living creatures and the four and twenty elders in their worship before the Lamb (5:8). The Antichrist and the nations would not bring the censers of worship, therefore they must have these censers filled with the wrath of God.

From the glory and power of God came a smoke, filling the inner temple. Smoke is frequently a symbol of the presence of the Lord in His holiness. When He came down to give the law, "Mount Sinai was altogether on a smoke, because the Lord descended upon it in fire: and the smoke thereof ascended as the smoke of a furnace, and the whole mount quaked greatly" (Exod. 19:18). Before Isaiah was cleansed from his sin, he saw the vision of the Lord, high and lifted up, His train filling the Temple, with the attendant seraphim veiling their faces and their feet, crying to one another of the holiness of the Lord of hosts (Isa. 6:1-4). "The posts of the door moved at the voice of him that cried, and the house was filled with smoke." When Aaron and his successors offered the sacrifice on the day of atonement, the Lord ordered that "he shall take a censer full of burning coals of fire from off the altar before the Lord . . . that the cloud of the incense may cover the mercy seat that is upon the testimony, *that he die not*" (Lev. 16:12, 13).

But though Aaron could not approach the mercy seat without hiding it with the smoke of the incense, and though we can never come to God except through the Lord Jesus Christ, it should be noted that not even the redeemed children of God are permitted to enter into the inner temple during the pouring out of the seven bowls containing the last plagues, the fullness of the wrath of God. What insight we should have here of the holiness of God, and may we not be allowed to think that behind this hiding smoke the heart of God is weeping, even as the Lord Jesus wept over Jerusalem, as He acknowledged that all the efforts of His mercy had been in vain, and that the city refused all of His offers of pardon and love? And as we shall be in Heaven at that moment, yet outside of the presence of God, shall we not know that He suffers alone for the horror of the sin that separates men from Himself and forces Him to send them away to outer darkness forever?

CHAPTER 16

Verses 1–7

Bowls of Wrath

¹And I heard a great voice out of the inner temple saying to the seven messengers, Go forth and pour out the seven bowls of the wrath of God into the earth. ²And the first went and poured out his bowl into the earth; and there came a bad and malignant sore upon the men who had the mark of the wild beast, and which worshipped his image. ³And the second poured out his bowl into the sea; and it became as the blood of a dead person, and every living soul died in the sea. ⁴And the third poured out his bowl into the rivers, and the fountains of waters; and they became blood. ⁵And I heard the messenger of the waters saying, Righteous art Thou, O Lord, the existing One, the One Who was, Thou holy One, because Thou didst thus judge. ⁶For they poured out the blood of saints and prophets, and Thou hast given them blood to drink; they deserved it. ⁷And I heard (the messenger of) the altar saying, Even so, Lord God, the Almighty; true and righteous are Thy judgments.

(Rev. 16:1-7, Free Translation)

The voice that now speaks is the voice of God Himself. No angelic messenger is in His presence in this awful instant. The messengers bearing the bowls stand outside; the living creatures have there handed them the bowls of wrath; the smoke excludes all, yes, all from the divine presence. And then God, whose patience has lasted throughout the centuries, comes to the final end. He speaks. The great voice from the inner temple is the voice of the long-offended God. The messengers receive His direct orders: Go forth and pour out the seven bowls of wrath into the earth. The end of all earth judgment has come. The mills of God grind slowly, but they grind exceeding fine, and the last of the grist is now to go through. The machinery of judgment has been set in motion, and the Creator Himself has said that it shall not be arrested until the last plagues of His wrath are finished.

If any be disposed to ask why we look upon the present chapter as literal when we have given rules for understanding previous chapters as symbolical, we would answer that the symbols always point to passages in the Old Testament which clarify them. The concordance takes us back to literal judgments, whether we look at "plague," "sore," "blood," "darkness," or other words in the passage while there will be two or three words which will take us back to symbolism. The unfolding of the chapter will make this clear.

Ezekiel, the prophet, saw the terrible abomination of devil worship within the very Temple of God. God spoke to Ezekiel, saying, "Hast thou seen this, O son of man? Is it a light thing to the house of Judah that they commit the abominations which they commit here? For they have filled the land with violence, and have returned to provoke me to anger; and lo, they put the branch (cut like a phallus) to my (Heb.) nose. Therefore will I also deal in fury: mine eye shall not spare, neither will I have pity: and though they cry in mine ears with a loud voice, yet will I not hear them" (Ezek. 8:17, 18). Immediately Ezekiel adds, "He cried also in my ears with a loud voice" (9:1). So it is with the order from God for the pouring out of the golden bowls of wrath. The abominations of humanity have filled up the sum. The devilish rebellion has reached its climax. God, who cried out to Ezekiel with a loud voice for judgment, now cries out with a loud voice for His angelic messengers to proceed to their appointed tasks. The wrath of God falls upon the earth.

A noisome and grievous sore breaks out upon all who had worshiped the image of the Antichrist and had received his mark upon them. Now we see the importance of the mention of the company of the faithful who sing the song of Moses and the Lamb (15:2, 3). The believers who pass through the tribulation time have a divine immunity from the judgments of God, even though they suffer from Satan. These latter sufferings purchase a good reward for those who are so honored, but those upon whom the wrath of God falls, are merely experiencing, as it were, the first of the eternal torments, as though, standing upon the brink of the lake of fire, a few high tongues of its flame had leaped up to torture them.

How appropriate that a grievous sore should be the first of these judgments. Medically speaking, a sore is the outward sign of some inner corruption, and it would, therefore, be entirely fitting that the corruption of the hearts of these rebels should be manifest before all men. When the first golden bowl of wrath is poured out, there comes upon men a literal sore, which symbolizes all that they are in the abomination of their rebellion against God and in their worship of Satan. In the days of the Lord Jesus, there were children of the devil to whom the Lord spoke sharply and revealingly. "Woe unto you, scribes and Pharisees, hypocrites! for ye are like unto whited sepulchres, which indeed appear beautiful outward, but are within full of dead men's bones, and of all uncleanness. Even so ye also outwardly appear righteous unto men, but within ye are full of hypocrisy and iniquity" (Matt. 23:27, 28). Here, under the first bowl of wrath, no such outward appearance will be permitted to any of the worshipers of Satan. All will be outwardly what they are inwardly.

There are two outstanding instances of sores in the Bible. The first, of course, is the sixth plague upon the Egyptians under Moses (Exod. 9:8-11). Ashes were thrown into the air, became dust, which was blown throughout the land of Egypt, and became "a boil breaking forth with blains, upon man and upon beast." Here, indeed, is the type which must be fulfilled literally in the antitype. In addition to this there is a prophecy, also given by Moses, concerning another plague of boils which has not yet been fulfilled. When the law was repeated before the people, certain curses were pronounced upon those who would fail to follow after the Lord, but who would depart after strange gods. "The Lord will smite thee with the botch of Egypt, and with hemorrhoids, and with the scab, and with the itch, whereof thou canst not be healed . . . . The Lord shall smite thee in the knees and in the legs, with a sore botch that cannot be healed, from the sole of thy foot unto the crown of thy head" (Deut. 28:27, 35). Here is a prophecy which has never been fulfilled, and it would appear that a part of the first bowl of wrath takes care of this prophecy. Those who have refused to worship the Lord, but who worship the Antichrist, receive the incurable sores that mark the judgment of God upon the bodies which have been defiled with the mark of the beast. Those who insist on a figurative interpretation of this plague, describe it as "an eruption of a moral character, breaking forth upon the surface of human society."

Satan has afflicted untold numbers of God's saints through the ages, and they have glorified God; but the hearts of Satan's followers speak out the abundance of the blasphemy. The judgment, then, is just and significant, since it reflects a scene of the invisible conflict and shows the humiliation of the enemy.

The second golden bowl is poured out upon the sea, which became as the blood of a dead person, and every soul of life died in the sea. If it be attempted to symbolize a judgment upon the nations in general, typified by the sea, then it must mean the annihilation of these nations, for it leaves no survivors. Rather take it as a literal judgment. In one of the plagues of Egypt, all the waters of the river were turned to blood, and the fish that were in the river died. One commentator demands a figurative fulfillment because, says he, the literal ocean could not be the scene of a visitation of God. But most certainly the turning of the seas to a pestilential marsh of death, with all of the fish killed, would have a swift repercussion upon mankind, as it did when "He turned their waters into blood, and slew their fish" (Ps. 105:29). "Mortality by violence upon an enormous scale" is the interpretation suggested by one who interprets this passage figuratively. Some may object to calling fish "living souls," or, as it is in the Greek, "every soul of life." Of the 754 instances in which the Hebrew word, *nephesh,* occurs in the Old Testament, 22 can be applied only to the lower orders of animals (creature, Gen. 1:21, 24; 2:19; 9:10, 12; Lev. 11:46, twice; beast, Lev. 24:18, thrice; fish, Isa. 19:10; etc.).

There is a deep spiritual significance attached to blood. In the verse which might be called the John 3:16 of the Old Testament, God lays down the principle of salvation by blood which runs through all the succeeding dispensations of His grace and government. "For the life of the flesh is in the blood: and I have given it to you upon the altar to make an atonement for your souls: for it is the blood that maketh an atonement for the soul" (Lev. 17:11). That, then, which has always been the symbol of salvation in the midst of life, becomes the symbol of condemnation in the midst of death. But now, the seas are turned to blood; the fish die; the winds of God blow death over all the earth. They had refused the salvation that would have come to them from the blood of the One who is Life; they now receive condemnation from the blood that symbolizes death.

The third of the messengers pours out his golden bowl of the wrath of God, upon the rivers and fountains of water; and they, too, become blood.

The symbolical interpretation of the rivers and springs was covered in the eighth chapter where the third part of the symbolical waters became wormwood, the crazing *absinthe,* which drug the spiritual streams of earth.

In line with the correspondence between these last plagues and those of Moses' day, which were the first, we would hold that these are literal. Upon the command of God, Moses took his rod, stretched out his hand over the waters of Egypt. When this was done, "all the waters that were in the river were turned to blood; And the fish that was in the river died; and the river stank, and the Egyptians could not drink of the water of the river; and there was blood throughout all the land of Egypt" (Exod. 7:20, 21). Now, upon the pouring out of the wrath of the third golden bowl, that which once happened to the waters and springs of one land, takes place in all the waters and all the springs of all lands. The followers of the Beast can find nothing to drink but blood. The impression that this makes upon the third messenger who has been the instrument of the judgment, is indeed amazing. It is as though he, himself, were astonished at the wide-spread effect of his work. But the factor that brings forth his cry, is the rightness of the judgment and the holiness of the Lord who thus judged. Those upon whom the judgment falls are receiving a recompense in kind, for they have shed the blood of saints and prophets, and they now receive blood to drink. They have received just what they deserved. God had long since announced that "Whoso sheddeth man's blood, by man shall his blood be shed" (Gen. 9:6). The principle of retribution in kind is established.

A voice is heard from one who is called "the messenger of the waters." He is undoubtedly a creature of the order of angels, and it is interesting to note that he has a title that would indicate that he had been placed in charge of the flowing waters of earth. Here we have an angel who is master of the waters. He is not necessarily the messenger who pours out the third bowl. The fact of an angelic being having control of the running waters was evidently known in the dawn of the race when the Lord spoke to His people directly, as there was no written revelation in existence. This truth, passed down through the distortions which came from those who were scattered at Babel, has given rise to the perversions of mythology, which speak of the spirits of the waters. Practically all Satanic teachings may be traced to germs of truth in the revelation of God.

The angel speaks of the Lord as the One "which art and wast." The Greek definition leaves out the words which have been added in the King James Version. There is no point in speaking of the One who shall come. He has already come at the time this prophecy is fulfilled. Instead of any phrase which speaks of the future work of God, the Greek gives Him a title here which points to His holiness. He is, in fact, called the Holy One. The whole phrase reads, "the existing One, the One who was, the Holy One." The choice of holiness among all the attributes of God is indicative of the effect these judgments produce upon the Heavenly beings who observe them. Let sinful men talk against God because the Bible teaches that there is to be an eternal punishment, and because He speaks of judgment in terms of fire and tribulation. The angelic beings who cover their faces in the presence of God, and who hasten to do His will, have long known that the world is ripe for judgment. When it comes at long last, they are the first to acknowledge that it was deserved, and that the holiness of God is now manifested, just as the death of the Lord Jesus was the highest manifestation of the justice and righteousness of God.

To the cry of the angel of the waters comes the answering cry from the altar. The Greek states simply that the altar speaks. We are possibly to understand an ellipsis here and think of the voice as coming from another of these mighty beings, who might be called the angel of the altar, as the other is called the angel of the waters. But on the other hand, there are other thoughts that arise if we consider the altar itself speaking. Remember that the altar stands for the cross of Christ. In the symbolism of the tabernacle, the altar represents the sacrifice and the fire that consumed the sacrifice. We must also remember that under the judgment of the fifth seal (Rev. 6:9-11), the souls of the first sheaf of the tribulation saints were seen under the altar, crying out to God for judgment upon His enemies who had caused their martyrdom. How significant, then, that the altar which was their shelter, should now cry out the holiness of God because He had heard the cry for vengeance and had answered from the heart of His holiness. "At the mouth of two witnesses shall a thing be established" (Deut. 19:15). The voice of the altar is the supporting witness to the words of the angel of the waters. "Even so, Lord God Almighty, true and righteous are Thy judgments." Every voice that has ever derided God for the prophecy of judgment is now stilled. This is the moment when the prophecy of Habakkuk is fulfilled: "The Lord is in his holy temple [for judgment]; let all the earth keep silence before him" (Hab. 2:20). What can sinful man say? Every mouth is stopped. All the world is brought guilty before God (Rom. 3:19). No one dare speak when God's two angelic witnesses speak from Heaven.

Verses 8, 9

Judgment Upon the Sun

⁸And the fourth poured out his bowl upon the sun; and it was given unto him to scorch men with fire. ⁹And the men were scorched with great heat, and they blasphemed the Name of God Who hath the power over these plagues; and they repented not to give Him glory. (Rev. 16:8, 9, Free Translation)

The fourth messenger poured out his bowl of wrath upon the sun. The immediate result was that men were burned, scorched with great fire. If this is looked upon as symbolical, it would mean that human government was overturned and that men were in calamity as the result of the upheaval. If it be looked upon as literal it would seem to need no explanation, a child being able to understand what it would mean by men being scorched with heat from the sun. Behind this literal explanation, however, there lies a most important line of teaching with regard to the sun.

The origin of sun worship comes directly from the plain of Shinar and takes us back to the book of Genesis, where we have the account of its origin.

When the posterity of Noah began to multiply upon the earth, there arose one man, Nimrod, son of Cush, who "began to be a mighty one in the earth. He was a mighty hunter before the Lord: wherefore it is said, Even as Nimrod the mighty hunter before the Lord. And the beginning of his kingdom was Babel . . ." (Gen. 10:8-10). The name Nimrod comes from the Hebrew *marad,* "to rebel." In its biblical form it is in the form and tense which might be translated, "We will rebel," or "Come, let us rebel." The word "before" the Lord might well be rendered "in defiance of the Lord." That this is no new idea is easily seen from the ancient Jewish sources themselves. Josephus (*Ant. Jud.* i. c. 4. 2) says, "Nimrod persuaded mankind not to ascribe their happiness to God, but to think that his own excellency was the source of it. And he soon changed things into a tyranny, thinking that there was no other way to wean men from the fear of God, than by making them rely upon his own power." The Targum of Jonathan says, "From the foundation of the world none was ever found like Nimrod, powerful in hunting, and in rebellions against the Lord." The Jerusalem Targum says, "He was powerful in hunting and in wickedness before the Lord, for he was a hunter of the sons of men, and he said to them, 'Depart from the judgment of the Lord, and adhere to the judgment of Nimrod!' Therefore is it said, 'As Nimrod is the strong one, strong in hunting, and in wickedness before the Lord.'" The Chaldee paraphrase of I Chronicles 1:10 says, "Cush begat Nimrod, who began to prevail in wickedness, for he shed innocent blood, and rebelled against Jehovah."

This reference to the judgment of the sun, which was first worshiped on the plain of Shinar is highly significant. As Satan in Revelation is called "that old serpent" (Rev. 12:9), with certain reference to the third chapter of Genesis, so we believe that the announced judgment on the sun refers to this sinister chief of the demons who "changed the truth of God into a lie, and worshipped and served the creation [Gk.] more than the Creator, who is blessed for ever" (Rom. 1:25). The sun was first worshiped by Nimrod and his followers on the plains of Shinar, and Babylon was the site of the first temple to the sun. This was the apostasy which led to the confusion of tongues and the scattering of mankind over the face of the earth. The people, gathered in the plain of Shinar, "said one to another, Go to, let us make brick, and burn them thoroughly. And they had brick for stone, and bitumen [Heb.] had they for mortar" (Gen. 11:3). The following verse is the key to the incident, and the correct translation must be established before the truth can be discerned. The King James Version renders it, "Go to, let us build us a city and a tower, whose top *may reach* unto Heaven . . ." It should be noted that the words *may reach* are in italics in the King James Version. This means that they are not in the Hebrew, but were added by the translators, who failed to sense the great truth that was hidden in the verse. The Hebrew reads literally, "Let us build us a city and a tower, whose top . . . the Heavens." This is not fully comprehensible until we understand the nature of a temple dedicated to the worship of the sun, moon, and stars. At the top of the tower of the temple there is representation of the sun, moon, and stars, or what is known as the zodiac. The followers of Nimrod, then, decided to build such a temple. The worship of the devil under these forms had begun. The scattering of the nations at the confusion of tongues carried these ideas throughout the world, and all paganism is derived from this beginning. They all had a certain knowledge of the truth of God as it had been revealed to the patriarchs, and in a greater or less measure they mixed truth with Satanic error to originate the various forms of paganism. This accounts for the parallelism in the pagan myths in all parts of the world.

It is easily understandable, therefore, that sun worship becomes the rallying point of Satan's attack upon the truth of God, and we can the more readily understand why God announces the judgment upon the sun, and upon Satan behind the idea of sun worship, before the utter destruction of the Babylon which grew out of Satan's ideas.

Further, we have in this fact the explanation of a score of texts which are scattered throughout the Old Testament. When Moses repeated the law to the people, as recorded in the book of Deuteronomy, he reminded the people that God had given them a commandment with respect to the host of Heaven. There were to be no graven images for reasons that included the following: "And lest thou lift up thine eyes unto Heaven, and when thou seest the sun, and the moon, and the stars, even all the host of Heaven, shouldst be driven to worship them, and serve them . . ." (Deut. 4:19). Such worship is again forbidden and is given as the illustration of "working wickedness in the sight of the Lord thy God, in transgressing His covenant (Deut. 17:2, 3).

By the time of the kings, the children of Israel had completely departed from the commandments of God, and their principal sin lay in the fact that they had departed from the true God and had gone a whoring after strange gods, which means, the sun, moon, and stars. This is specifically stated: "And the children of Israel did secretly those things that were not right against the Lord their God, and they built them high places [sun-altars] in all their cities . . . . and they set them up images and groves in every high hill, and under every green tree: And there they burnt incense in all the high places . . . . and wrought wicked things to provoke the Lord to anger . . . . And they left all the commandments of the Lord their God, and made them molten images, even two calves, and made a grove [i.e. a phallus, symbol of sex worship], and worshipped all the host of heaven, and served Baal [the sun god]; And they caused their sons and their daughters to pass through the fire, and used divination and enchantments, and sold themselves to do evil in the sight of the Lord, to provoke him to anger" (II Kings 17:9-11, 16, 17).

This passage is most revealing, it is the background to the understanding of the prophets in their preaching to Israel of repentance from these very things.

With all this in mind, it is easy for the discerning mind to understand why there should be a judgment upon men that should include the sun. This is the final stage in the battle which began as a result of the rebellion of Satan. Men are to be taught that the very things in which they have trusted or to which they have given their worship are to be the sources of their most terrible punishments. The first three bowls of wrath when poured out affected men at the level of the earth; the last four have to do, in some way, with men as they are linked with Babylon. To put it another way, the first three have to do with the earthly scene of the conflict, the last four seem more to be in the realm of the prince of the power of the air. The final group begins with the sun, passes to the throne of the Satan-incarnate Antichrist, to the demon forces, and finally, the last bowl is poured out into the air.

Many commentators have seen nothing more here than the judgment upon mankind through the cruel oppression administered by the governmental powers of earth. We must see something more here. Two prophecies in the Old Testament speak of the last days as including plagues of heat upon mankind. Moses wrote that among the judgments which would come upon the unbelieving and disobedient would be one like that which is under consideration here. "For a fire is kindled in mine anger, and shall burn unto the lowest hell, and shall consume the earth with her increase, and set on fire the foundations of the mountains . . . . They shall be burnt with hunger and devoured with burning heat . . ." (Deut. 32:22, 24). At the mouth of two witnesses shall a thing be established, and we find the second witness in Malachi. "For, behold, the day cometh, that shall burn as an oven; and all the proud, yea, and all that do wickedly, shall be stubble: and the day that cometh shall burn them up, saith the Lord of hosts, that it shall leave them neither root nor branch" (Mal. 4:1). Isaiah has also given a prophecy which applies to this day, "The earth mourneth and fadeth away, the world languisheth and fadeth away, the haughty people of the earth do languish . . . . because they have transgressed the laws, changed the ordinance, broken the everlasting covenant, Therefore hath the curse devoured the earth, and they that dwell therein are desolate: therefore the inhabitants of the earth are burned, and few men left" (Isa. 24:4-6).

It will not be long now. God has dealt with the nature behind which Satan has hidden to deceive the nations of the world. He now presses the attack to the very throne of Satan, and soon all will be over.

Verses 10, 11

The Throne of the Beast

[10] And the fifth poured out his bowl upon the throne of the beast. And his kingdom became darkened; and they gnawed their tongues for

*pain, ¹¹And they blasphemed the God of Heaven because of their
pains and their sores, and they repented not of their deeds.*
(Rev. 16:10, 11, Free Translation)

Now is the moment when the Lord, after proceeding against Satan
in Heaven and in the air, proceeds against his power on earth. The
battle is pressed to the gates of his earthly citadel.

Is there, then, a place on earth where Satan has his authority
centered? The Scripture does not leave us in doubt upon this subject.
At the time when the Lord left the earth and the apostolic age was
drawing to a close, we are told that Satan's throne was in Pergamos
(Rev. 2:13). Where it is today, we are not told. That it was once
in Babylon, before coming to Pergamos, seems evident to those who
have studied Hislop's *The Two Babylons.* If the literal Babylon is to
be rebuilt, it may already have become the place of the throne of
Satan by the time that is in view here under the fifth bowl.

At all events, the Lord now presses the conflict to the very center
of Satan's rule on earth. When he had come to indwell the beast, thus
producing the Antichrist, it had been announced that his power would
endure for forty and two months. His mouth had become full of blasphemies, and his boast had been, "Who is like unto the beast? Who
is able to make war with him?" The answer is not slow in coming.
God is able to make war with him though He is in no whit like him.
The outpouring of the fifth bowl brings the conflict to the very center
of Satan's rule; his whole kingdom is immediately full of darkness.

The Scriptures are filled with teaching concerning darkness, and
we find that both literal and spiritual darkness are described at length
throughout the Word. In the land of Egypt, God had manifested His
power against the enemy by smiting the land with darkness. "And
the Lord said unto Moses, Stretch out thine hand toward heaven, that
there may be darkness over the land of Egypt, even darkness which
may be felt. And Moses stretched forth his hand toward heaven; and
there was a thick darkness in all the land of Egypt three days: they
saw not one another, neither rose any from his place for three days:
but all the children of Israel had light in their dwellings" (Exod.
10:21-23). The ancient conflict with Satan had seen the use of darkness as an arm in the struggle. It is not astonishing that it appears
again.

And it should also be remarked that there are several passages in
the prophecies which speak of darkness that is to come upon the
earth. "For, behold, the darkness shall cover the earth, and gross darkness the people" (Isa. 60:2). "A day of darkness and of gloominess,
a day of clouds and of thick darkness, as the morning spread upon
the mountains; a great people and a strong; there hath not been ever
the like, neither shall be any more after it, even to the years of many

generations" (Joel 2:2). "But with an overrunning flood he will make an utter end of the place thereof, and darkness shall pursue his enemies" (Nah. 1:8). The Lord Himself called attention to these prophecies by announcing, "But in those days, after that tribulation, the sun shall be darkened and the moon shall not give her light. And the stars of heaven shall fall, and the powers that are in the heaven shall be shaken" (Mark 13:24, 25).

It would seem, with such evidence drawn from witnesses scattered throughout the whole of God's revelation, that we are forced to conclude that there will be a time of literal darkness upon the earth or upon that portion of it where the Antichrist is reigning. The transition from the fourth to the fifth bowls is most striking. The one had been the fiery, scorching, blinding brightness of the sun; the next is an impenetrable darkness. Astronomers have observed phenomena in star-suns outside of our solar systems, where, within a few days time, a star has increased from the fifteenth magnitude, for example, to third or fourth magnitude. Then, after this great flare-up, the star has been dimmed far beneath its earlier brightness. So it may well be that God touches our sun and causes it to flare forth with an intensity that sears and then dims it until there is gross darkness upon the earth, as the diminishing of the sun would cause a thickening of the clouds of our atmosphere until little light could come through.

But just as the noisome and grievous sore under the first bowl was the outward symbol of an inward work of corruption, so the darkness that falls upon the kingdom of the Antichrist is the symbol of the even greater spiritual darkness which falls upon those who worship him. The false prophet had allured multitudes to the worship of Antichrist by the exercise of power which caused men to see great wonders, miracles, or signs (Rev. 13:13, 14). Now this light vanishes away, and the people that walked in this light are in great darkness. When our Lord came to the earth, the people that walked (Isa. 9:2) and then sat (Matt. 4:16) in darkness saw a great Light. The situation is reversed with the coming of the Antichrist. He came with great pomp and show and with the light of great deeds. Men received him because of the light of his doings, and Satan who is called the angel of light (II Cor. 11:14) succeeds in clothing him with all the brilliance and brightness of the power that has been delivered to him to give to whomsoever he desires (Luke 4:6). That light is now turned to darkness by God, and the multitudes who had hastened to its deceptive rays now find themselves in groping bewilderment. They had received this emissary of light and he has failed them. They had turned away from dull truth in order to believe in brilliant error, and they now discover the light to be like the poisonous rays of radium which have the power to kill. All of their hopes vanish and they fall back into the despair of their unchangeable position; they gnaw their tongues with pain.

It should be noted that the judgments of the bowls overlap. They come with such swiftness, one upon the heels of the other, that the effects of the first bowl are still present at the time of the judgment of the fifth. We wonder if some of the men who, under the sixth seal, called unto the rocks and the mountains to fall upon them (Rev. 6:16) because they thought those little judgments were the great day of wrath, can remember back to those days of little distress and compare them with the horror of what they are now going through. Their bodies are covered with sores, the stench of death in seas and rivers fills their nostrils with the odor of corruption, their bodies are scorched with fire, and then suddenly they are precipitated into the utmost darkness.

The blasphemy against the God of Heaven that is heard in the time of this judgment is because of the judgment pains from the previous bowls. This proves beyond any doubt that these prophecies are not spread over centuries, but that they are all fulfilled in one and the same generation. The Antichrist had been given power to continue for forty-two months only (Rev. 13:5). The greatness of the brilliant phase of his reign must last for several months, the events of the very end, the destruction of the two Babylons and the preparation for the battle of Armageddon, all must take up months at the end, so that the bowl judgments, greatest of all, can occupy but a comparatively short space of time. The manifestation of Satan as Antichrist is described by Christ as "the abomination of desolation" (Matt. 24:15) and this is followed by warnings of a short time of great and devastating judgment. "Then shall be great tribulation, such as was not since the beginning of the world to this time, no, nor ever shall be. And except those days should be shortened, there should no flesh be saved; but for the elect's sake those days shall be shortened" (Matt. 24:21, 22). This can apply to nothing but the period that is now under our consideration.

The object of men's blasphemy is "the God of Heaven." There are many false gods, or, to be more accurate, the devil manifests himself under many different aspects, some of them being in light and some of them being in darkness. The one, true God, is the God of Heaven, or, to give Him the title He receives in Ephesians, "The God and Father of our Lord Jesus Christ" (Eph. 1:3). This title which we have before us is taken out of the book of Daniel. In the dream which Daniel revealed and explained to Nebuchadnezzar, the ten toes of the feet of the image were said to be ten kings. "And in the days of these kings shall the God of Heaven set up a kingdom, which shall never be destroyed: and the kingdom shall not be left to other people, but it shall break in pieces and consume all these kingdoms, and it shall stand for ever" (Dan. 2:44). Five times in the prophecy of

Daniel, He is spoken of as the God of Heaven, once as the King of Heaven and once as the Lord of Heaven (Dan. 2:18, 19, 28, 37, 44; 4:37; 5:23). He now vindicates Himself. Men may blaspheme Him, but His sovereign will will be brought to pass. All that He has promised to do, He will perform.

What a picture this gives us of the heart of man. Put it alongside the revelation of the heart of man as found in Judas when confronted with the tenderness of Christ, and we see that nothing can change man. Christ called Iscariot His own familiar friend (Ps. 41:9), and gave him the sop which was the mark of honor, fellowship, and esteem (John 13:26), and when love, such as this, was rejected by Judas, then Satan entered into him (John 13:27). Infinite love or eternal punishment, neither of these can change the unregenerate heart. For the carnal mind is *enmity* against God (Rom. 8:7), and enmity means hatred. Truly, God proved that He knows the heart of man (John 2:25), and He has said, "The heart is deceitful above all things and desperately corrupt" (Jer. 17:9, RSV).

Verses 12–16

Preparation for Armageddon

¹²And the sixth poured out his bowl upon the great river, the Euphrates; and the water of it was dried up, so that the way of the kings from the rising of the sun might be prepared. ¹³And I saw, coming out of the mouth of the dragon, and out of the mouth of the wild beast, and out of the mouth of the false prophet, three unclean spirits, as it were frogs. ¹⁴For they are the spirits of demons, working signs; which go forth to the kings of the whole inhabited earth, to gather them for the war of the great day of God the Almighty. ¹⁵Behold, I come as a thief. Blessed is he that watcheth, and keepeth his garments, lest he walk naked and they see his shame. ¹⁶And they gathered them together into a place, called in the Hebrew, Harmaggedon.
(Rev. 16:12-16, Free Translation)

Under the sixth trumpet the four messengers which had been prepared for that very instant were freed from their place of binding at the Euphrates, and a mighty invasion of demon forces was loosed upon the western world.

The messenger of the sixth bowl poured his judgment upon the river Euphrates and its waters were dried up. We have no reason for believing that this is other than a literal picture. In the context of the other bowls of wrath it would seem that every detail has been a prophecy of reality. Zechariah tells us that "He shall pass through the sea with affliction, and shall smite the waves in the sea, and all the deeps of the river shall dry up: and the pride of Assyria shall be brought down, and the sceptre of Egypt shall depart away" (Zech. 10:11).

There are two factors in the prophecy from the Old Testament that
are similar to what appears in our passage. The deeps of the river are
dried up and the pride of Assyria is brought down, for the judgment
of the sixth bowl is most clearly in anticipation of the fall of Babylon,
the pride of Assyria. Isaiah has a similar prophecy. "With His mighty
wind shall he shake his hand over the river, and shall smite it in the
seven streams, and make men go over dryshod. And there shall be
a highway for the remnant of His people, which shall be left, from
Assyria; like as it was to Israel in the day that he came up out of
the land of Egypt" (Isa. 11:15, 16).

The drying up of a passage through the Red Sea in order to free
the children of Israel and bring judgment upon the Egyptians was
literal in the time of the Exodus. The Jordan river was stopped by
a dry passage to let Joshua and his hosts through to the promised
land, where they were used of God to destroy Jericho and the Ca-
naanites.

Throughout all history the Euphrates has played the part of a
boundary. Seiss writes of it as follows: "From time immemorial the
Euphrates, with its tributaries, has been a great and formidable boundary between the peoples east of it and those west of it. It runs a
distance of 1800 miles, and is scarcely fordable anywhere or at any
time. It is from three to twelve hundred yards wide, and from ten
to thirty feet in depth; and most of the time it is still deeper and
wider. It was the boundary of the dominion of Solomon, and is repeatedly spoken of as the northeast limit of the lands promised to
Israel. . . . History frequently refers to the great hindrance the Euphrates has been to military movements; and it has always been a line
of separation between the peoples living east of it and those living
west of it."

This barrier is to be divinely removed. The sixth messenger ac-
complishes this so that the way may be prepared for the coming of
the kings of the rising of the sun. This phrase is very interesting when
it is examined in detail. The King James Version translates it merely
as one of the points of the compass, the east. But there is more to it
than that. The common word for the east in the Greek is *anatole,*
from which has come the geographical name Anatolia. The word
means, literally, the rising, and it occurs ten times in the New Testament. It usually refers to the east, though once it refers to Christ
Who is called the "rising" from on high, translated "the dayspring
from on high" (Luke 1:78). This usage was brought in from the
Septuagint where the word, used many times as a compass point, is
used three times in the Old Testament to speak of Christ the "branch,"
as someone Who rises from the stem (Jer. 23:5; Zech. 3:8; 6:12).
The reason we enlarge upon the phrase here is because, apart from
all ordinary usage (Rev. 7:2 being the only other exception), the word

for "sun" is added in this instance. The literal translation, then, is "that the way of the kings from the rising of the sun might be prepared." In classical Greek the word is used without a noun to describe the rising of sun, moon, and stars. Polybius even uses it to describe the source of a stream. But in instances when the word is used for the compass point, the word for sun is never added, just as in modern Italian, "levante" means "rising" and is the common word for "east."

Now the Satanic trinity combines in a special effort to carry on its work. From the counterfeit god—the devil, the counterfeit son—the Antichrist, and the counterfeit spirit—the unholy spirit, come three unclean spirits, said to be like frogs.

The unclean spirits are described in a symbol. They are "as it were, frogs." Multitudes of frogs were sent as the second plague upon the Egyptians. "And if thou refuse to let them go, behold, I will smite all thy borders with frogs: And the river shall bring forth frogs abundantly, which shall go up and come into thine house, and into thy bedchamber, and upon thy bed, and into the house of thy servants, and upon thy people, and into thine ovens, and into thy kneading-troughs: And the frogs shall come up both on thee, and upon thy people, and upon all thy servants. And the Lord spake unto Moses, Say unto Aaron, Stretch forth thine hand with thy rod over the streams, over the rivers, and over the ponds, and cause frogs to come up upon the land of Egypt" (Exod. 8:2-5). All this came to pass, and when the Lord finally revoked the plague there were so many frogs that the people gathered them together in heaps and the land stank (Exod. 8:14).

The point that is particularly noticed here is the uncleanness, and it is possible to trace the cause through a reference to frogs in classical literature. Aristophanes tells of a special costume worn on the Greek stage, and never worn elsewhere, that was called the frog-garment, the *batrachis*. It was frog-green in color and undoubtedly caused a lewd laugh when it was seen on the Greek stage as the frog was a sex symbol, representing the idea of fecundity. This unclean animal, then, is a symbol of the loathsomeness of the power that now comes forth from Satan, still acting in great wrath because he knows that his time is so short (12:12).

Here there are said to be three evil spirits. It may be that this is a literal number, in which case it needs no explanation. If, on the other hand, the number is symbolical, rather than definite, it would stand for the indefinite multitude of Satan's forces that now proceed to do this work of gathering the hosts together for the judgment that will come upon them. The three spirits of Satan go forth to make ready the company of the rebels for the slaughter of the Lord. And they go in all the infernal power of Satan, working miracles in accordance with the New Testament prophecy that the Antichrist should come "after the working of Satan, with all power and signs and lying wonders, And with all deceivableness of unrighteousness in them that perish; because they received not the love of the truth, that they might be saved" (II Thess. 2:9, 10). Thus are the unbelieving rebel chiefs brought to the place of judgment.

Just here a voice from Heaven speaks. The Lord Jesus Christ says, "Behold, I come as a thief." It is the announcement of the suddenness of the next phase of His work.

By the time the final days of Antichrist's power draw on there are very few believers left. "And shall not God avenge his own elect, which cry day and night unto him, though he bear long with them? I tell you that he will avenge them speedily (Gk. shortly, quickly). Nevertheless, when the Son of man cometh, shall he find faith on the earth?" (Luke 18:7, 8). We have a picture of the earth almost rid of believers. Seiss believes that this verse fifteen is the calling out of the whole group of believers before the final crushing judgment. "Somewhere about this time," he writes, "Christ comes for this last band of the children of the resurrection, whether dead or yet living. Of course, it is a coming for those saints who were taken earlier, for it is the completion of that one coming for His people which is everywhere set forth." While agreeing that there is a coming for His people which is everywhere set forth, we can not follow Seiss in believing that this final removal of the believers of the Tribulation period takes place this early. We will discuss that final removal when we come to it after the battle of Armageddon. Daniel tells us that there will be one thousand two hundred and ninety days from the time that the abomination of desolation is set up until the end (Dan. 12:11), and adds, "Blessed is he that waiteth, and cometh to the thousand three hundred five and thirty days" (Dan. 12:12). This will be as plain as a sign post to those who live in that time, though the meaning may not be perfectly clear to us today. Yet it most certainly indicates that some, at least, of the believers will not receive their eternal bodies until forty-five days after the destruction of the Antichrist. We can well imagine that those days will be filled with judgments upon the earth that flow from the main destruction of the forces of Antichrist at Armageddon, though we cannot speak with certainty.

Verse 15 constitutes a wonderful promise and a solemn warning. Those who are hounded in the midst of the Satanic persecutions devised by the one whose very name, the Beast—the wild-beast—gives an indication of his methods, will rejoice to hear the promise, "Behold I come." Yet there is a warning: "I come as a thief," that is, suddenly, unexpectedly. And there is this word of encouragement to the believers to whip up their flagging courage, to cause them to hold out for just a little longer. "Blessed is he that watcheth, and keepeth his garments, lest he walk naked and they see his shame."

There are two words here, which because of their use in the same passage, give the key to its understanding. "Watch" and "garment" point to a picture of drowsiness. The common dress in Christ's day was one voluminous, all-covering garment which was laid aside as one went to sleep. As soon as one awakened the garment was donned. Bengel says, "Now, if something suddenly happens, such as the arrival of the Lord, one who is asleep does not readily get himself clothed; but he who is in a wakeful attitude is safe also in respect to his clothing." The garment in the Scripture is always a symbol of righteousness. It first appears in the garden of Eden where Adam and Eve lost the light that had been their covering and sought to replace it with fig-leaves, symbols of righteousness of their own providing. This must certainly be rejected since they did no more than call attention to their efforts to clothe their nakedness. In this beautiful scene the Lord Himself shed the blood of a sacrifice in order to provide garments of skins for the man and woman who had just believed His word about the Seed of the woman, the Redeemer. From these beginnings the Bible gives a consistent series of pictures of garments as symbols of righteousness, whether it be the white robes of His providing or the filthy rags of man's righteousness (Isa. 64:6). Keeping the garment, then, has nothing whatsoever to do with attempting to keep saved, for we are kept by the power of God through His faith, unto the completion of our salvation which shall be revealed at the return of the Lord. But the believer must ever look to his habits lest in his walk he should expose his nakedness. It is interesting to note that the word "habit," which in English retains its older meaning of a manner of living, has a developed meaning in French, where the exact same word designates one's clothing. The two meanings are certainly combined in this passage.

Hengstenberg says, "The nakedness here is not the guilt, but the punishment: by means of the judgment the nakedness, which existed already, becomes a matter of public shame. It is not the being naked but the walking naked, that is mentioned: and the clause, 'and that they may not see his shame,' serves as an explanation of the walking naked." It is a warning similar to that admonition which is given to us for this age, wherein we are told to be on guard lest we be ashamed before Him at His coming (I John 2:28). We can draw the deepest lesson for ourselves from this similar warning which is addressed to those of the tribulation saints whose zeal and diligence may be flagging under the great provocation of the tribulation miseries.

Suddenly the scene changes again. The Lord announces that the preparation for judgment is complete. The nations are all gathered at Armageddon. It is to be noticed that the record clearly states that it is He who has gathered them there. The three unclean spirits may have done the actual driving, but it is the Lord, the righteous Judge who has done the ordering and the planning, and they are there in accordance to His plan.

The Hebrew form of the word Armageddon is *Har meghiddo,* "mount of Megiddo." It is the only mention of this place in the Bible, but most surely it refers to the mount or city of Megiddo, or the great plain of Esdraelon which is known as the valley of Megiddo (II Chron. 35:22; Zech. 12:11). Seiss says, "That has ever been one of God's great battle grounds for the judging of the armies of the wicked. There Jabin's hosts with their 900 chariots of iron were utterly overwhelmed by Jehovah's special interference. There the Midianites, and Amalekites, and children of the East were routed before Gideon's 300 men with pitchers and lamps. There Samson triumphed with his crude instrument over the might of the Philistines. There the ruddy son of Jesse met and slew the great Goliath, and opened a breach of destruction upon those who defied Israel's God. And it is but fitting that here should be the seat of the winepress for the final crushing out of the mightier Jabin and Goliath of the last evil days."

Verses 17–21

The Seventh Bowl

17And the seventh poured out his bowl upon the air; and a great voice came from out of the sanctuary, from the throne, saying, It is done. 18And there came to be lightnings and voices and thunders, and there was a great earthquake, such as came not since the time that men came upon the earth, so great an earthquake, so mighty. 19And the great city came into three parts; and the cities of the nations fell; and Babylon the great, was remembered before God, to give unto her the cup of the wine of the fierceness of His wrath; 20and every island fled away, and the mountains were not found; 21And there fell upon men a great hail from out of Heaven, of about the weight of a talent; and men blasphemed God because of the plague of the hail; for the plague thereof was great, exceedingly.
(Rev. 16:17-21, Free Translation)

There remains one last sphere of Satan's influence. He has long been the "prince of the power of the air" (Eph. 2:2), and he is now to be judged in the last sphere of his power.

The powers of Satan at present infest the "high places" (Eph. 6:12). This term is the same as that elsewhere translated "the heavenly places" or "the heavenlies" (Eph. 1:20; 3:10). The last of these references, in fact, states that God is even now making His wisdom known to Satan's hosts by means of the body of believers, and that this is being done in the Heavenly places. This is the sphere where Satan's hosts have so long wrestled with the believers as they sought to realize the access that had been provided through Christ. It is, therefore, very significant that Satan is to be judged in this sphere where he has so long usurped the place of authority.

The results of this seventh and last judgment are immediately manifest. It is the falling of the stone from Heaven, foreseen by Daniel (Dan. 2:44, 45), and it now does its terrible work of smiting. Satan, stricken in every part of his kingdom, is in confusion and disaster, and his earthly strongholds immediately capitulate. These are three in number, Mystery, Babylon, which is the apostate church; the civil Babylon which is commercialism, the city of the Antichrist; and, finally, the power of the nations which are gathered together against each other and then against the Lord at Harmageddon.

A great voice now speaks from the very throne of Heaven. This can be none other than the voice of the Lord God of Hosts. Christ has been off the throne since the early part of this judgment period (5:7), working as the active agent in the judgments that have been poured out. Here, then, God the Father speaks in words of awful import, and of supreme triumph. The voice comes from out of the sanctuary, from the throne of God's presence. The words are brief and wonderful. In the original tongue there is but one word which, though not the same word, has no other comparison than the word spoken from the cross of Jesus Christ by the dying Saviour. "It is finished," He said as He completed the sacrifice for sin (John 19:30). "It is done," cries God the Most High, possessor of heaven and earth (Gen. 14:19), against whom Satan had first rebelled (Isa. 14:14). The word from the Cross had come as a word of comfort, hope and salvation. There was nothing more to be feared from God because the price had been paid in full and there could be no further condemnation upon those who put their trust in their Saviour. This word from the throne comes as a word of Judgment, doom, and condemnation. For those who refuse to put their trust in the Man who died for them, there is the end of earthly torment, but no hope for eternity, no second chance, no further help. The issues of eternity are settled in this life and they have passed the day of settlement. Their die is cast. Their doom is sealed.

Following the voice from the throne come lesser voices which echo the divine commands. The consequences of this final judgment will be fully described in the chapters which follow. The preliminary disasters are here portrayed in some detail, and they are seen to be without parallel in the long history of mankind. When Christ was here on earth, He announced that there would be judgments greater than any which had ever fallen upon this world, greater even than any which would ever fall thereafter (Matt. 24:21), and we now see the accomplishment of His sure word of prophecy.

Great electrical storms cleave the sky while cosmic disturbances grip the earth. There does now come to pass that judgment upon Jerusalem and upon all the nations of which Isaiah prophesied, saying, "Thou shalt be visited of the Lord of hosts with thunder, and with earthquake, and great noise, with storm and tempest, and the flame of devouring fire" (Isa. 29:6). Here, too, is that of which the Psalmist sang, "Our God shall come, and shall not keep silence: a fire shall devour before him, and it shall be very tempestuous round about him. He shall call to the heavens from above, and to the earth, that he may judge his people" (Ps. 50:3, 4).

At the same time there is a great, a mighty earthquake, "such as was not since men were upon the earth." The catastrophe that is here announced is not the slip of a geological fault. It is a mighty phenomenon which engages the very bowels of the earth and which causes the whole surface of the globe to slip around on its foundations.

First of all, the effects of the earthquake upon the great city, Jerusalem, are seen. It is not mentioned by name, but it is so clearly distinguished from "the cities of the nations," that there can be no doubt. Here is the moment of the fulfillment of several prophecies concerning geographical changes in Jerusalem. The Lord has been working in the midst of the city for some time before this moment. The temple area was first possessed by His messengers (11:1). This would seem to indicate the first exclusion of Satan from any area of the earth. Then there occurred an earthquake at the time of the ascension of the two witnesses (11:13), and the tenth part of the city fell. But now, in this greater calamity the city is divided into three parts. That this is a literal and physical division is indicated by the detail of the prophecy of Zechariah, "The mount of Olives shall cleave in the midst thereof toward the east and toward the west, and there shall be a very great valley; and half of the mountain shall remove toward the north and half of it toward the south" (Zech. 14:4). This makes possible the flow of the stream that is later to come forth from the sanctuary and which is to change the whole of the Dead Sea valley (Ezek. 47). It is a division analogous to that of the land (Zech. 13:8), and we would judge that two parts of the city are destroyed while the Lord reserves the third part as a refuge for those who stand firmly for Him in the midst of these last frightful moments of the power of the Antichrist. "And I will bring the third part through the fire, and will refine them as silver is refined, and will try them as gold is tried: they shall call on my name, and I will hear them: I will say, It is my people: and they shall say, The Lord is my God . . . . And ye shall flee to the valley of the mountains . . . . and the Lord my God shall come, and all the saints with thee" (Zech. 13:9; 14:5).

Then we read that the cities of the nations fell. It is interesting to note that the devil's prophets, through the ages, have frequently re-

ferred to such a judgment. The most famous of all the astrologers,
Nostradamus, foretelling the doom of Paris, wrote,

> *A driving great flame will leap and scatter everywhere;*
> *Then they will be unable to extinguish the great flame.*
> *The grand city will be utterly waste,*
> *Not one of its dwellers will be left.*

And similar prophecies exist among the devil's followers which point
to the destruction of Rome and of cities in the Far East. We, of
course, do not need this extraneous testimony to bolster our belief, for
our faith is in the living Word of God, but it is curious, to say the
least, to note that the demon forces are aware of their coming defeat,
even as one of them asked the Lord if they were to be tormented
before "the time" (Matt. 8:29). Man has a proverb that God made
the country and man made the town. Truly these great cities of the
earth are heartless and cruel, and those who have lived close enough
to their hearts to hear their poisonous beats, know how much evil is
hid behind the great lights of the world's great agglomerations. They
are all to fall. This is the judgment of God. He has spoken, and says
that "It is done." We may rest assured of it. The corruption, the
graft, the buying and selling of justice, the deification of money, the
exaltation of lust, the exploitation of the masses in their lightless and
half-starved lives, all this, and much more, is to come to an end. We
believe, beyond any shadow of a doubt, that this prophecy covers
Peking and Philadelphia, Moscow and Melbourne, Berlin and Buenos
Aires, Cairo and the Cape, Bombay and Boston, Istanbul and Chicago,
Naples and New York. In short, all of the cities shall be destroyed.
It cannot be otherwise. The very nature of the cities and the nature
of God cry out that they should come into conflict, and this prophecy
calls forth an acknowledgment of its essential rightness from every
renewed heart. And God has said it, "Thus saith the Lord of hosts;
Yet once, it is a little while, and I will shake the heavens, and the
earth, and the sea, and the dry land; and I will shake all nations, and
the desire of all nations shall come . . ." (Hag. 2:6, 7). This is clearly
not the end of the world, for there is a thousand year kingdom that is
to follow, but it is, just as clearly, the end of the present civilization
and all that it stands for, no matter in what quarter of the world it
will be established.

Especially singled out is "great Babylon" which now comes into remembrance before God to receive the special wrath of the just Judge.
We shall soon study the locality and the identity of this metroplis and
shall see why it calls for the special attention of God in the dealing
out of the judgment catastrophes of the seventh bowl. It should be
noticed that there is a gradation in the judgments here meted out to
the cities of the world. Just as the Lord announced that some would

be beaten with few stripes and some with many, so there is a progress
in the devastation that falls upon the habitations of men. Two parts
of Jerusalem seem to be destroyed, all of the Gentile cities, but the
greatest of all the judgments is kept for Babylon, seat of Satan's power.

And at the same time the very topography of the earth is changed.
After the chaos of the first judgment upon Satan (Gen. 1:2), God
moved to restore the earth, and on the second of these days, brought
the dry land into one place and the seas were all together (Gen. 1:9).
Not until the days of Peleg did there begin what geographers and geologists have called "continental drift" which divided the lands of the
earth as they are found today (Gen. 10:25). Now all is changed. It
does not follow from a close reading of the text that the islands disappear into the sea, as islands have been known to do, but this may
well be the case. At all events, they are moved from their present
locations. The mountain ranges disappear. Scientists cannot laugh at
this idea because they, themselves, teach most earnestly that the mountains once rose to their present heights, and furnish us with an abundance of geological data to prove their points. We agree, although
we believe it was done, not by any slow process of evolution, but by
the catastrophe of judgment, just as God pours out his final wrath
upon this earth.

There is a passage in Jeremiah that is of great interest in this connection. It has been considered to be a description in retrospect of
the judgment that turned earth's first fair creation into the chaos out
of which the Lord later brought the reformation earth of which Adam
was the made the head. This need not in anywise disturb us, for
there are many passages of Scripture which serve a double purpose,
and this may well be one of them. At all events, we believe that it
is a most apt description of what we now see before us. "I beheld
the earth, and, lo, it was without form, and void [ARV waste and deso-
late]; and the heavens, and they had no light. I beheld the mountains,
and, lo, they trembled, and all the hills moved lightly. I beheld, and,
lo, there was no man, and all the birds of the heavens were fled. I
beheld, and, lo, the fruitful place was a wilderness, and all the cities
thereof were broken down at the presence of the Lord, and by His
fierce anger. For thus hath the Lord said, The whole land shall be
desolate; yet will I not make a full end" (Jer. 4:23-27).

The final portion of this cosmic disturbance is a great and disastrous precipitation of hail. Each stone is about the weight of a talent.
What is the weight of a talent? Just as there are long and short tons
of differing weights, so there are various talents. That with which the
Jews weighed silver was about 120 pounds Troy, or 96 pounds avoir-
dupois. That for weighing other materials was about 135 pounds. The
Baylonian talent was even heavier while the Greek talent was about
86 pounds. The lightest of all was the Attic talent which weighed 57.7

pounds. In biblical usage it would be the silver talent of 96 pounds that would almost certainly be designated. However, even if we take the smaller Attic talent, we have a weight that is considerable.

Hail is caused by rising convection currents of air, caused by some instability in the atmosphere. Heavy clouds result and the raindrops are carried upward by the currents, freezing in the cooling air. The Encyclopedia Britannica says that two or more such stones may be cemented together until they assume large properties and may reach 3 or 4 inches in diameter and a pound or more in weight, and states that such masses are capable of inflicting considerable damage.

It should be kept in mind, even if we wish to explain these without any recourse to the special, creative power of God, that the verses which precede this announcement, tell of disturbances which could readily account for such a phenomenon. With islands drifting or disappearing, with mountain ranges sinking into the earth, there would be released, most probably, currents of rising air which would bear such masses of condensing clouds aloft that stones of this size would easily become possible. But we do not have to stop to consider the natural possibilities of the judgment phenomena, for the Word of the Lord, by which the creation was made, and by which it is upheld, is sufficient explanation for all of these wonders.

Once more the picture is of a tortured, blaspheming humanity, that holds to its devilish allegiance and refuses to recognize the authority of God that it might come to Him and be blessed. And since the law of God provided that blasphemers should be stoned with stones until they died, so we see in the last moments of earth's civilization, God Himself upholds His law and stones blasphemers with hailstones.

PART IX
BABYLON

CHAPTER 17

Verses 1, 2

The Great Whore

¹*And one of the seven messengers which had the seven bowls, came and talked with me, saying, Come hither, I will show to thee the judgment of the great harlot, that sitteth upon many waters;* ²*with whom the kings of the earth committed fornication, and the inhabitants of the earth were made drunken with the wine of her fornication.*
(Rev. 17:1, 2, Free Translation)

There is a great godless system in this world, and it is now brought into view as claiming the special attention of God in a final destruction that will be in keeping with the nature and character of its organization and rebellion against God. The whole devilish system is summed up by our Lord under the name "the world," in His final address to the disciples. "If the world hate you, ye know that it hated me before it hated you. If ye were of the world, the world would love his own; but because ye are not of the world, but I have chosen you out of the world, therefore the world hateth you" (John 15:18, 19). He considered this great and monstrous system so terrible that as long as nineteen hundred years ago He refused to pray for it. "I pray not for the world," He said, "but for them which thou hast given me" (John 17:9). This whole godless system was foreseen throughout the Old Testament, and in one of the prophetic psalms we find a dialogue between the members of the Trinity in which They discuss the rebellion of the world and the judgment that shall come upon it. In that psalm it is announced that the day will come when the Lord Jesus will pray for the world—not for its conversion, which He has consistently refused to do, but for its judgment.

This Psalm, the second, opens with a statement by the Holy Spirit concerning the rebellion of the world system. The kings of the earth speak against the Father, Son and Holy Spirit, saying, "Let us break their bands asunder, and cast away their cords from us." The Holy Spirit announces the laughter of God at the puny might of the devil's

313

strongest efforts, and God the Father speaks from Heaven, "Yet have I set my king upon my holy hill of Zion." The Lord Jesus now takes up the message, announcing that He is to declare the decree which has been determined by God, the Father. The decree declares the deity of the Lord Jesus Christ, and proclaims the fact that the Father will give the world rebellion over to the Son for destruction as soon as He asks for it. In the seventeenth chapter of John we have the refusal of the Lord Jesus to pray for the world at that time, evidently on the ground that He has a company of "his own" who are yet in the midst of the world. If He should pray for the world before His own were removed from it, they would come under the necessary wrath that will flow forth from God the moment that prayer for the world is offered.

Now, in the seven bowls, we find the answer to that prayer. He has asked the Father for the nations and for the uttermost parts of the earth as a possession. He proceeds immediately to fulfill the prophecy of the Psalms, to break them with a rod of iron and dash them to pieces like a potter's vessel. It is interesting to note how the whole system, "the world," is divided in the mind of God in the closing chapters of the Bible. First of all, there comes a judgment on ecclesiasticism, described under the symbol of "the great whore." Commercialism is next under the rod and is broken under the symbol of "the city." Politics or government then follows, as the rulers of the nations are brought to the bar at Armageddon, while the Satanic trinity, the devil, the Antichrist and the False Prophet, sinister backers of all the earthly manifestations of "the world," come to their doom.

Many commentators have called attention to the contrast between this woman and the one who is described in the twelfth chapter of the Apocalypse. The best delineation of this contrast comes from Seiss. "There, in the twelfth chapter, 'a great sign was seen in the Heaven, a Woman'; here, it is remarked, 'he bore me away in spirit into a wilderness, and I saw a Woman.' Both these women are mothers; the first brought forth a son, a male (neuter, embracing either sex), who is to 'rule all the nations'; the second 'is the mother of harlots and of the abominations of the earth.' Both are splendidly dressed; the first is 'clothed with the sun.' Her raiment is light from Heaven. The second is 'clothed in purple, and scarlet, decked with gold, and precious stones, and pearls.' All her ornaments are from below, made up of things out of the earth and the sea. Both are very influential in their position; the first 'has the moon,' the empress of night, the powers of darkness, 'under her feet'; the second 'hath rule, or kingdom, upon the kings of the earth.' Both are sufferers; against the first is the Dragon, who stands ready to devour her child, and persecutes and pursues her, and drives her into the wilderness, and sends out a river to overwhelm her, and is at war with all her seed that he can find;

against the second are the ten kings, who ultimately hate her, and make her desolate and naked and eat her flesh, and burn her with fire, whilst God in His strength judges her, and visits her with plague, death, and utter destruction. Both are very conspicuous, and fill a large space in the history of the world, and in all the administrations of divine providence and judgment. That they are counterparts of each other, there can hardly be a reasonable doubt. The one is a pure woman; the other is a harlot. The first is hated by the powers on earth; the second is loved, flattered, and caressed by them. Where the one has sway, things are heavenly; where the other lives, it is 'wilderness.' The one produces masculine nobility, which is ultimately caught away to God and to His throne; the other produces effeminate impurity, which calls down the fierceness of the divine wrath. The one is sustained and helped by celestial wings; the other is supported and carried by the Dragon power—the Beast with the seven heads and ten horns. The one has a crown of twelve stars, wearing the patriarchs and apostles as her royal diadem; the other has upon her forehead the name of the greatest destroyer and oppressor of the holy people, and is drunken with 'the blood of prophets and the saints, and of all that have been slain upon the earth.' The one finally comes out in a heavenly city, the New Jerusalem, made up of imperishable jewels, and arrayed in all the glory of God and the Lamb; the other finally comes out in a city of this world's superlative admiration, which suddenly goes down forever under the intense wrath of Heaven, and becomes the habitation of demons, and a hold of every unclean spirit. These two Women, thus related, and set over one against the other as opposites and rivals, must necessarily be interpreted in the same way. As the Antichrist corresponds to Christ as a rival and antagonist of Christ, so Great Babylon corresponds to the Woman that bears the Man-child, as her rival and antagonist."

The first woman is none other than the spiritual Israel—all who in every age have been the redeemed of the Lord. From righteous Abel through to the last believer, we have the great company of "his own" represented by the woman clothed with the sun. So here in this evil woman we have the opposite company, those who are the children of Satan throughout all generations, but culminating in the group that triumphs under the reign of the Antichrist.

One of the seven messengers of the seven bowls of wrath comes to speak with John, inviting him to witness the judgment of the great whore. This fact ties this judgment to the seven bowls which complete the wrath of God, and it would seem that the repetition of the idea of "blood" in the sixth verse would point to the third of the bowl judgments which is the judgment of blood. It is her name that gives us the positive identification and which leads us, therefore, to a consideration, first of all, of the words "Mystery Babylon the great."

There are several mysteries spoken of in the Book, and in every case there is the revelation of something which had previously been hidden. It would be possible, in every instance, to translate the Greek word *mustërion* by our English word *secret*. "Behold, I show you a mystery . . . ." will be best understood this way, "Behold, I reveal unto you a secret . . . ." A revealed secret is no longer a mystery in the modern sense.

Mystery Babylon is the exact opposite of the Mystery Kingdom. It is in the thirteenth chapter of Matthew that we have the revelation concerning this truth. The Lord Jesus began to speak in parables. The disciples came to Him with the question, "Why speakest thou unto them in parables?" (vs. 10). His answer was most illuminating. "Because it is given unto you to know the mysteries of the kingdom of heaven, but to them it is not given" (vs. 11). This passage is one of the key portions of Scripture and the ignorance concerning it is widespread. Nevertheless, the true explanation is to be found in the same chapter. It was, of course, well known that the Old Testament was filled with prophecies concerning Messiah's kingdom. That fact was known to every disciple, and, indeed, to every Jew. That kingdom was so well outlined that all could see it clearly. It was the triumph of Israel, the transformation of the earth, the rule of righteousness, and the glory of God manifested throughout the earth. The Lord was carrying on His ministry according to a pattern that did not fit in with the well-known idea of the kingdom. Even John the Baptist, in prison, was confused and sent his disciples to ask, "Art thou he that should come, or do we look for another?" (Matt. 11:3). The parables were a part of the larger answer to that query. A few short paragraphs after the disciples asked the reason for the parabolic method in teaching, the Holy Spirit returned to the question and gave an enlarged answer. "All these things spake Jesus unto the multitude in parables; and without a parable spake he not unto them: That it might be fulfilled which was spoken by the prophet, saying, I will open my mouth in parables; I will utter things which have been keep secret from the foundation of the world" (Matt. 13:34, 35).

We gather from these definite statements that, whatever the explanation one may advance concerning the meaning of the parables of the kingdom, we have no right whatsoever to refer them to the kingdom that was so well outlined in the Old Testament and so eagerly awaited by Israel. For the visible kingdom was well known, but that which is presented in the parables had been kept secret from the foundation of the world. But the secret is now to be told. There is to be a Mystery Kingdom. It is to be formed by the scattering of the seed of the Word; it will grow even in the midst of the tares of iniquity, and the growth will continue parallel with evil until the time of the harvest. It is to have outward forms of rapid, abnormal growth (the mustard-seed), and the devil will accompany it with false teaching (the leaven). But, in the midst of all the outward forms, the Lord has His own for whom He left Heaven, and gave all that He had that He might purchase them, the treasure and the pearl, for Himself. The treasure, Israel, He has hidden again for a time, but the pearl is manifest at present. Together, Old Testament saints and New Testament saints, form the Mystery Kingdom. This is the woman revealed in the twelfth of Revelation, the true people of God of all ages and times.

Over against Mystery Kingdom we now see Mystery Babylon.

That sentence needs to be read several times, whereupon this passage will become clearer to our understanding. Just as there has always been a people in the midst of the world, called of God and faithful, the elect, the saints, the children of God; so there has always been a people in the midst of the masses, preeminently belonging to Satan, faithful to him, more damned than the sodden currents of humanity, the active agents of Satan's plan, the true children of the devil. In the early chapters of Genesis the Lord pronounced a judgment upon Satan in which He said that He was now putting enmity between the serpent and the woman and between the seed of the serpent and the seed of the woman. Three of these four personalities may be identified easily. The serpent is clearly Satan (Rev 12:9), while Eve was the woman mentioned in the passage (Gen. 3:15, 16). The seed of the woman is none other than the Lord Jesus (Gal. 3:16). But how are we to identify the seed of the serpent? Our Lord called the ecclesiastical leaders of the people, "generation of vipers" (Matt. 12:34)—brood of the serpent. No such epithet was ever applied to the masses of the people, upon whom the Lord looked with weeping because they were sheep without a shepherd. The Gentiles were called children of wrath and children of disobedience (Eph. 2:2, 3), but never children of the devil. It would appear that out of the masses of the lost some are translated into the kingdom of God's dear Son (Col. 1:13), becoming thereby the children of God through faith in Christ Jesus (Gal. 3:26). From those same masses come those who, through definite rejection of God's truth, give themselves over to be Satan's special followers, the children of the devil (John 8:44), through the acceptance of the principles of the rule of the spirit of Antichrist (I John 4:1-3).

The tares get ripe at harvest time and are gathered for burning. The mystery Babylon has been ripening through the ages, but the full fruition takes place when the whole ecclesiastical system is joined to the definite work of advancing the kingdom of the Antichrist. All true believers will have been called out of the world at the time of the rapture, and the saints of the tribulation period have been sealed so that the judgments of God will not touch them. Now ecclesiasticism is ripe for plucking.

First we read that the great whore sitteth upon many waters. Verse fifteen gives us all the commentary we need on this phrase. The waters are peoples, and multitudes, and nations, and tongues. The sinister influence of organized religion without Christ has leavened the whole world by this time, and judgment falls.

In order to explain the next clause, "with whom the kings of the earth have committed fornication," it would be necesary to recount the history of much of the world since the time of the so-called "conversion" of Constantine. The church which had been meant to be a persecuted body now took the throne of the Caesars. Little by little the church lost the vision of her heavenly calling and began to seek an earthly kingdom. A Charlemagne receives the crown of empire at the hands of a pope. The Holy Spirit who had been given to govern the church, was dethroned from His rightful place and men exalted themselves.

Lenin was not speaking an original thought when he said that religion was the opiate of the people. The thought that we have before us now is exactly that thought. Mystery Babylon is said to have made the inhabitants of the earth drunk with the wine of her fornication. An opiate puts people to sleep; wine puts them into a stupor. It is only the gospel which causes people to awake from their sleep and rise from their death that they may receive the light of Christ. In all the world—in the whole earth—the people are made drunken by the ecclesiasticism of a counterfeit church or by the religious paganism of which the ecclesiasticism is but one of the varied forms.

The one feature that stands out above all others in this passage is the idea of impurity and harlotry. The angelic messenger calls her the great whore, and the name on her diadem proclaims her to be the mother of the harlots and the abominations of the earth. It has been well put by one commentator, "Harlotry is the standing symbol in the Word of God for a debauched worship, idolatry, and false devotion. When people worship for God what is not God, or give their hearts to idols, or institute systems, doctrines, rites or administrations, to take the place of what God has revealed and appointed, the Scriptures call it whoredom, adultery, fornication (Jer. 3:6, 8, 9; Ezek. 16:32; Hos. 1 and 2; Rev. 2:22). . . . All false religions are associated with lewdness, even in connection with their most honored rites. . . . The very essence of the divine law is, that we love God our Lord with all the heart, mind, soul, and strength. This is Jehovah's due and requirement of all that live. Hence the bestowal of worshipful affection on any other object, or the putting of anything whatever in the place of the true God, is, in the very nature of the case, a great spiritual harlotry; for it is the turning of the soul from the only legitimate object of its adoration, to take into its embrace that which has no right to such room and place. And as this woman is a harlot, the great harlot, and the mother of the harlots and the abominations of the earth, she must

needs be the great embodiment, source, and representative of all idolatry, false worship, and perversion of the word and institutes of God.
This helps to determine her character as the rival and antagonist of
the Woman clothed with the sun, and makes her the symbol of the
universal body of the faithless, just as the sun-clad woman is the symbol of the universal body and congregation of believers. There were
believers and saints in the 4,000 years before the Christian era, and
so there were idolaters and perverters of the institutes of God in
plentiful abundance. And as the pure Woman is made up of the
whole congregation of the faithful from the beginning, so must this
great Harlot be made up of all the faithless from the beginning."

Verses 3–6a

The Whore Rides the Beast

*³And he carried me away in the Spirit into a wilderness: and I saw
a woman sitting upon a scarlet beast, full of names of blasphemy, having seven heads and ten horns. ⁴And the woman was arrayed in purple
and scarlet, and gilded with gold and precious stones and pearls,
having a golden cup in her hand full of abominations, even the unclean things of her fornication. ⁵And upon her forehead she had a
name written, a secret symbol,* Babylon the Great, the mother of the
harlots, and of the abominations of the earth. *⁶And I saw the woman
drunken with the blood of the saints, and with the blood of the martyrs of Jesus . . .*
(Rev. 17:3-6a, Free Translation)

The writer of the Apocalypse is now carried away by the Spirit into
the wilderness in order that he may truly understand the nature of the
fiendish system against which he is called to prophesy. John had already been carried in the spirit to Heaven (4:2), and later he was
taken to a great and high mountain (21:10). This was not a strange
thing to those who were the channels of inspiration. Among such instances those in connection with Ezekiel stand out, since he was taken
up—lifted up between the earth and Heaven—and brought to Jerusalem (Ezek. 8:3) on one occasion, and, on another, was brought by
the Spirit into Chaldea (11:24). Also Philip was caught away by the
Spirit after the baptism of the Ethiopian eunuch (Acts 8:39).

In order to understand the deeper things of God it is necessary to
get away from close association with the things of evil in order to view
the world from the standpoint of the holiness of God. It was in the
backside of the desert that Moses learned his most important lessons
(Exod. 3:1). The believer today takes his place by faith on the very
throne of God where he is seen to be seated in the Heavenlies with
Christ (Eph. 2:6). Only from such a detached place is it possible

to view the works of Satan and to see them in their proper perspective. While we are closely associated with evil on earth, it is impossible to learn about its true nature; the glare of its deceptions can too easily blind the eyes, or at least cast a false light upon it. But when we get alone with God, and look upon the world systems as He sees them in His Word, we can understand more of His eternal purposes. To those dwelling in Babylon, the place would seem like anything but a wilderness. " 'The vine of the earth' might flourish there, but fruit for God could not grow in such soil. To the anointed eye there is a moral and spiritual desert encircling far and wide this 'mother of harlots.' "

The woman is now seen seated upon a scarlet colored beast. At this epoch of the vision, then, the woman is clearly in control. Since we know that the woman represents the culmination of the whole godless religious system, and since the prophecies clearly represent the beast as the political power of the earth, the passage before us speaks of a time when the religious system shall dominate the political. We have frequently pointed out that every believing element will have been removed from all the churches before the tribulation breaks forth. At this time, as we have reached the end of the tribulation period, the system of ecclesiasticism without the saving salt of the presence of any born again ones, will have come to its putrifying end. The woman, then, represents the faithless in their moment of final power and control of the world, just before they are flung to earth by the civil power which, in turn is to be destroyed shortly thereafter.

It would amount to sheer repetition should we attempt to trace the tendencies within ecclesiasticism towards domination of the state by the church. The mystery of iniquity is, indeed, at work in the world today, and the leaven of false doctrine, malice, and corruption is at work within the church organization. But we are not here concerned with the course of this present age. At the time of the last judgments, the end of this age will have come, and the end of the tribulation also.

The beast is once more brought into view as the steed ridden by the woman. There can be no doubt that this portion of the vision refers to the political power. Indeed, throughout the whole of the Apocalypse there is but one political beast in evidence. We have examined this power in our study of his first appearance as he arises out of the sea (13:1). It is thoroughly identified by the seven heads and ten horns, and is the revived Roman Empire. At times the symbol speaks of the empire and at times of the imperial head of that empire, the Antichrist. The context determines whether the monarch or the power is in view. For example, when the beast is cast into the lake of fire, it is obvious that the reference is to an individual, the emperor (19:20). In our present reference, it would appear that the whole of the imperial power is in view.

The beast is scarlet in color. Ottman has said that this scarlet is the symbol of the glory of the world, characterizing the only glory possessed by the beast. Most other commentators have taken the color to be a symbol of the blood shed by the imperial power. Seiss says, "No color was noticed on his first rise; but by this time he has developed his bloody hue by his slaughter of the saints. Then he had names of blasphemy on his heads; by this time he is full of them all over. There his infernal origin did not so fully appear; by this time, he has demonstrated that he comes up out of the abyss. His seven heads were there left in mystery; here they are explained, and his true history and relations indicated. There his ten horns were noted; but only here is it told that they are ten kings, who rise contemporaneously with the beast. The two great beasts set up an entirely new religion upon earth, a religion which they insist on making as universal as their own dominion, and so must needs make war on all existing religions, true or false." The tendencies to this type of hatred of all religions is manifest in Communist lands, but it will become the prime characteristic of the revived Roman power under the man of sin who will come in his own name to be received by the world.

That the beast should be seen as filled with the names of blasphemy is readily understood by those who have studied the Old Testament prophecies of the powers that arise against God. The vision of the beast as given by Daniel presents a little horn with a mouth speaking great things (Dan. 7:8), while later in that same chapter the word is repeated for greater emphasis, as a mouth that spake very great things, and the power was said to possess a look that was more stout than his fellows (Dan. 7:20). This is still further amplified in a statement that "he shall speak great words against the most High, and shall wear out the saints of the most High (Dan. 7:25). It should be remembered, in passing, that Satan's conflict with God has, from the beginning, been with that phase of His being which is revealed under the title of the Most High God (Isa. 14:14), who is the possessor of Heaven and earth (Gen. 14:19). This king-beast, as the incarnation of Satan, plays the character true to the form revealed in the prophecies. He "shall do according to his will; and he shall exalt himself, and magnify himself above every god, and shall speak marvellous things against the God of gods, and shall prosper till the indignation be accomplished" (Dan. 11:36). Paul tells us that he "opposeth and exalteth himself above all that is called God, or that is worshipped; so that he as God sitteth in the temple of God, shewing himself that he is God" (II Thess. 2:4).

It should be noted that church organizations have frequently been guilty of blasphemy. One of the marks of false religions is to usurp the glory that belongs to God alone. Systems of salvation by works take the glory from God and are thus blasphemous. To do wrong, moral wrong even, in the Name of Jesus Christ is a blasphemy that is often committed by church courts which act in the Name of the Lord Jesus Christ to carry out selfish and fleshly motives of ecclesiastical politicians. All this may be expected in the culmination of the beast whose very name is blasphemy, but there is something more intended here. Perhaps the best illustration is that which is to be found in Ezekiel's lament against the prince of Tyre. "Thus saith the Lord GOD; Because thine heart is lifted up, and thou hast said, I am a God, I sit in the seat of God, in the midst of the seas; yet thou art a man, and not God, though thou set thine heart as the heart of God" (Ezek. 28:2). This whole passage is strangely prophetic of this beast we are studying, and the doom of the one is like the doom of the other. "Therefore thus saith the Lord GOD; Because thou hast set thine heart as the heart of God; Behold, therefore I will bring strangers upon thee, the terrible of the nations: and they shall draw their swords against the beauty of thy wisdom, and they shall defile thy brightness. They shall bring thee down to the pit, and thou shalt die the deaths of them that are slain in the midst of the seas. Wilt thou yet say before him that slayeth thee, I am God? but thou shalt be a man, and no God, in the hand of him that slayeth thee. Thou shalt die the death of the uncircumcised by the hand of strangers: for I have spoken it, saith the Lord GOD" (Ezek. 28:6-10).

The description of the woman's dress and ornament is most revealing. The fact that she was arrayed in the garments of imperial power shows the age-long desire of ecclesiastical leaders to have temporal authority. Purple and scarlet are the colors of rule. The Church was never meant to reign here upon earth until after her rejected Lord returns in power. That day is not yet. Nevertheless, we find in the course of church history, that one of the deadliest marks of ecclesiastical corruption is the lust for temporal power. In the earliest chapters we discovered that the deeds of the clerical party were already manifest in the Ephesian group among the seven churches of Asia. That which was a deed had become a doctrine by the time the Pergamos period was reached. Throughout the centuries Catholic and Protestant groups alike have struggled for earthly power and influence. Many have spent their time seeking to reform a condemned world rather than telling forth the glorious news that salvation was available to sinners out of every kingdom, tongue, and nation.

Christ had said that the part of Caesar was to be rendered to Caesar and that the part of God was to be given to God. But the carnal successors of the early Spirit-filled leaders were more interested in increasing their own part than in living as instruments of self-sacrifice, called to the service of the One who was born in a manger and buried in another man's tomb, and who, in between, had not a place where He might lay His head. The age-old struggle between church and state

went on. Our passage proves that the day will come, when the great
englobing church organization, bereft of all the true believers, will ride
high on political power, clothed with all of the accouterments of temporal reign. So has the mighty fallen. In addition to these marks of
government, there is a description which betokens vast riches. After
all believers are removed from the world and all religious organizations
have flowed into one, the property values and endowments that will
come under the single control of the great ecclesiastical organization
will be unbelievably great. This woman is seen as decked with gold
and precious stones and pearls. This great wealth is undoubtedly one
of the contributing causes of the hatred which the secular power de-
velops toward the woman (v. 16); for she will be stripped of all her
wealth in one moment, even as Russia in the revolution stripped the
Eastern Church of all her properties. "How much she hath glorified
herself, and lived deliciously, so much torment and sorrow give her . . ."
(18:7).

The height of hypocrisy is that abominations and filthiness should
be poured from a golden cup. A careful study of the word "abominations" throughout the Bible is very revealing. It is virtually synonymous with "idol" or "idolatry." An idol, as symbolical of something
that is put in place of the true God, is detested by the holy God who
is jealous for His people, though not jealous of the idol. The following quotations are instances where idols are directly called "abominations." "The high places that were before Jerusalem, which were on
the right hand of the mount of corruption, which Solomon the king
of Israel had builded for Ashtoreth, the abomination of the Zidonians,
and for Chemosh, the abomination of the Moabites, and for Milcom,
the abomination of the children of Ammon, did the king defile" (II
Kings 23:13). Here we see that the Mount of Olives was called "the
mount of corruption" because of idols—abominations—which were
built thereon. There are few statements that could be more striking.
Isaiah, also, speaks of idols as abominations. "None considereth in his
heart, neither is there knowledge nor understanding to say, I have
burned part of it in the fire; yea, also I have baked bread upon the
coals thereof; I have roasted flesh and eaten it; and shall I make the
residue thereof an abomination? shall I fall down to the stock of a tree?"
(Isa. 44:19). The picture is of a man who has cut down a tree, using
part of it to make a fire on which he bakes bread and roasts flesh, and
with the trunk of the tree makes an idol—an abomination. One more
passage, this time in Daniel, makes the matter conclusive. The famous
"abomination of desolation" to which our Lord referred as being the
central point of the great tribulation, is distinctly stated to be the
setting up of an idol: "the daily sacrifice shall be taken away, and
the abomination that maketh desolate set up" (Dan. 12:11).

We have all authority, therefore (and there are many other verses that could be used for the same proof), to say that the abominations of the ecclesiastical organization of the last days announce a large return to idolatry. The tendency is already firmly established both in ecclesiasticism and in political life.

It is also highly significant that the abominations and filthiness should be spoken of as coming from a golden cup. "Babylon hath been a golden cup in the LORD's hand, that made all the earth drunken: the nations have drunken of her wine; therefore the nations are mad" (Jer. 51:7). To those who are acquainted with the history of ancient religions this significance is heightened by comparisons with the rites of the pagan religious mysteries. A French scholar, Salverte, writing on *The Occult Sciences,* tells of the drinking in connection with these demon ceremonies. "To drink of mysterious beverages," he says, "was indispensable on the part of all who sought initiation in these mysteries. These mysterious beverages were composed of wine, honey, water, and flour, with various other ingredients used locally. From the nature of the ingredients avowedly used, and from the nature of others not avowed, but certainly used, there can be no doubt that they were of an intoxicating nature; and till the aspirants had come under their power, till their understandings had been dimmed, and their passions excited by the medicated draught, they were not duly prepared for what they were either to hear or see."

Upon the forehead of this woman there is the fearful inscription, *"Mystery, Babylon the Great, the mother of harlots and abominations of the earth."*

This woman is called the mother of harlots. There is the mother harlot and there are the daughter harlots. The course of history has revealed the development of the mother system of idolatry which has spawned many a lesser system. During the Reformation times, the Protestant commentators always identified the great harlot as the Roman Church. The Bible includes the Protestant organizations as the harlot daughters. Yet, most certainly, the time for separation has not yet come. It is impossible to have a perfect organization during this present age. God has true witnesses today in every denomination. They are saved, not because of the systems, but in spite of them. To the church that had a name to live and yet was seen by the Lord to be dead, the order was yet given to the faithful messenger that he should be watchful and strengthen the things that remain that are ready to die (Rev. 3:2). When God removes the believers from this world, the harlot organizations will go on functioning, but then without even the presence of believers, all of whom will then be called to leave. But today the Lord who founded the organizations, is not yet through with them. The wheat and the tares are to grow together until the day of the harvest, which is the end of the age (Matt. 13:40). The Lord will send divine messengers to do the separating in His own time.

The divine title given to this woman also announces that she is the mother of the abominations of the earth. Out of ecclesiasticism comes idolatry. Where Christ is not honored as the Head, and where the Holy Spirit is not acknowledged as the divine leader and guide, there can be nothing but idolatry as the result. And with the idolatries of ancient Babylon, the daughters inherit the hatred of God's true people, though here it is not Israel, but the tribulation saints of God who are persecuted.

The woman is drunk with the blood of the saints and with the blood of the martyrs of Jesus. From ancient times the people of God have been hated. The reason why Israel was set aside nationally was that multitudes had joined the system of false religions which were adopted from the surrounding tribes and that they thus came to hate the prophets who spoke against their abominations. Thus it has been through the centuries: the persecutions of the early Christians by pagan Rome and the persecutions of later Christians. The true believers will become the prey of the Satanic system, and will thus testify before the unseen hosts who war in the Heavenly places, so that Satan cannot turn all men's hearts to himself.

Verses 6b–18

The Last Kingdom

6b And when I saw her, I wondered with a great wonder. 7 And the messenger said to me, Wherefore didst thou wonder? I will tell thee the mystery of the woman, and of the wild beast that beareth her, which hath the seven heads and the ten horns. 8 The wild beast which thou sawest, was, and is not, and is about to come up out of the abyss, and to go into perdition: and they that dwell on the earth shall wonder, whose name hath not been written upon the scroll of life from the casting down of the world, when they behold the wild beast because it was, and is not, and shall be manifested. 9 Here is the understanding that hath wisdom. The seven heads are seven mountains on which the woman sitteth. 10 And they are seven kings; the five are fallen, the one is, the other is not yet come; and when he comes he must continue a little while. 11 And the wild beast, which was and is not, he also is an eighth, and is of the seven, and he goeth into perdition. 12 And the ten horns which thou sawest, are ten kings, which have received no kingdom as yet, but they receive authority, as kings for one hour with the wild beast. 13 These have one mind, and they give their power and authority unto the wild beast. 14 These shall war against the Lamb, and the Lamb shall overcome them: for He is Lord of lords and King of kings: and they that are with Him shall also overcome: called, elect and faithful. 15 And he saith to me, The waters which thou sawest where the harlot sits, are peoples and multitudes, and nations and

tongues. [16] *And the ten horns which thou sawest, and the wild beast, these shall hate the harlot, and shall make her desolate and naked, and shall eat her flesh, and shall burn her utterly with fire.* [17] *For God did put in their hearts to do His purpose, and to do one purpose, and to give their kingdom to the wild beast, till the Words of God should be accomplished.* [18] *And the woman which thou sawest is the great city, which reigneth over the kings of the earth.*
(Rev. 17:6b-18, Free Translation)

John, when he saw the harlot, drunk with the blood of the saints, "wondered with a great wonder." This, of course, is proof that ecclesiasticism is in view. It would have been no cause for wonderment that pagan Rome should persecute the believers. John, at the moment of writing, was in prison on Patmos because of the hatred of pagan Rome. But that ecclesiasticism should turn into a hating harlot is cause for wonderment. The following is a statement of the case which shows insight. "The love of a harlot is a *feigned* love; and its hatefulness consists largely in the fact that it is put in the place of the true love of a wife. The harlot's aim is to secure favors for herself. To that end she not only prostitutes whatever she may have of womanly charm, but she brings into play all manner of seductive arts, and adorns her person with whatever may increase her attractions in the eyes of men. But specially reprehensible is her *pretended affection* for those she seeks to ensnare in the web of her fascination and enchantments. Such is the false religion that feigns a deep solicitude for the spiritual good of the great ones of the earth, and exerts a mysterious and intoxicating influence over the inhabitants of the earth, making them, as it were, 'drunk with the wine of her fornication'; the religion that conceals the basest of motives behind the mask of pretended affection and fondness. This is the chief feature, according to the figures here used, of the guilt of which this woman is about to be judged." It is no marvel, therefore, that John "wondered with a great wonder."

The divine messenger is not astonished, except at the fact that John is wondering. "Wherefore didst thou wonder?" is the question asked by the angel, and the very form of it shows that the character of the religious organization is so clearly understood to be basically Satanic that no one should be deceived for a moment by the fact that the outward resemblances of religion have been retained. The messenger then announces that John is to learn the secret of this woman and of the beast which carries her, this beast with the seven heads and the ten horns.

"The wild beast which thou sawest, was, and is not, and is about to ascend out of the abyss, and to go into perdition: and the earth dwellers will wonder, whose names have not been written on the scroll of life from the disruption of the world, when they see the wild beast how that he was, and is not, and shall be present." The wild beast, is the personification of imperial power. Rome had its great rise and then its fall. For centuries it was, then for centuries it has not been. But it is to rise again, and the revival of the Roman Empire is the climax of Satan's power on earth. When it rises, it rises out of the abyss, that prison house of demons, which we have previously studied (Rev. 9:1, 2, 11; 11:7) and which we will yet see (20:1, 3) as the prison of Satan during the thousand years. We are not to look, therefore, for the mere revival of earthly power in a sphere that once was great and then was eclipsed. There have been many such revivals. The power of Germany under what was known as the Holy Roman Empire, fell into nothingness and has now risen during the past decades. The power of France which was great under Charlemagne, fell and was revived under Louis XIV, fell again in the Revolution, rose and fell again. This passage of Scripture is not leading us to contemplate any such natural phenomenon. Here is the rise of a power, once great and then low, which rises to preeminent heights, but rises by the power of Satan. This is clearly understood when we remember all that has been written on the incarnation of Satan in the Antichrist (Rev. 13:2).

The rise of imperial power is to have much of the supernatural about it. Most clearly it will be beyond any human possibilities of greatness. The world will have recognized that it is not human. Unfortunately, the world has accepted the devil's subterfuge that he does not exist. Therefore, the world has come to look upon everything that is more than human as being truly from God. The Christian should always suspect everything that is more than human as being demoniacal. We are not ignorant of the devices of Satan (II Cor. 2:11). So when the world sees this supernatural power tumble suddenly into perdition, the world will wonder. It will have the idea of divinity so firmly fixed in its mind that it will be difficult to root up that idea and to plant in its place the truth. To accept the truth about this sudden upheaval and overthrow will be to call its god the devil when it has thought all along that its god was God. Only those who have the divine wisdom of the new birth will be able to understand the truth. The tribulation saints are possessors of the life of Christ. To them is given the divine wisdom. They, therefore, will recognize the enemy as an enemy. The Lord's sheep "know his voice . . . a stranger will they not follow, but will flee from him: for they know not the voice of strangers" (John 10:4, 5). Thus it is that the unsaved wonder at the fall of Satan's power, while those whose names have been written in the book of life, from the foundation of the world are not astonished at the turn of events.

The believers have true understanding. For whosoever hath (new life in Christ) to him shall be given (understanding of spiritual matters) and he shall have more abundance; but whosoever hath not (new life in Christ), from him shall be taken away even that (common sense in ordinary matters) which he hath" (Matt. 13:12). Here is the understanding that hath wisdom.

Verse nine should be divided in two, for the last half of it clearly belongs with the following verse. There is a double identification of the beast under different symbols. First of all, there is the statement that the seven heads of verse three are seven mountains upon which the woman sitteth. Virgil, Horace, Ovid, Cicero and a host of lesser writers of ancient times have spoken of Rome as being the city on the seven hills. Here it is that the ecclesiastical power has its throne. All of this gives a clear picture of the ecclesiastical Rome governing, by means of her place in Rome over the political power of Rome. We have said elsewhere, in writing on certain phases of current events in the light of Bible truth, that imperial and ecclesiastical Rome were like two thieves, helping each other over a wall. The one aids the other to rise and in turn is pulled up by the first to scale the height.

The figure is now changed and our attention is called to seven kings. The verb form is such that we must translate the tenth verse not as "there are seven kings," but "they are seven kings." That is to say, the seven heads of the beast are also to be looked at as seven kings. This verse has given rise to more interpretations than almost any other in the book of Revelation. Let us see exactly what the Bible says before we attempt to discern the meaning. We read that of the seven kings, five have already reigned and are fallen, the sixth "is," the seventh is not yet come, but upon his rise to rule he shall remain but a short time. The Antichrist that was, and is not, is also an eighth, and is from out of the seven, and he goes into destruction.

It should be noted that this verse which has been called "one of the puzzles of the book" is preceded by the statement in verse nine with reference to the understanding which has wisdom. Most evidently this is a warning . . . special attention is called by the Holy Spirit to the need of spiritual discernment in explaining the passage. We believe that this is similar to saying: Do not be deceived by appearances. The obvious may not be the true explanation.

Perhaps if we digress for a moment to clear up one or two points, the explanation of the whole may be more simple. In the first place, we should note that the *beast* is sometimes the empire and at other times the emperor, or king. Each time the word is used in the Revelation, the context makes it clear, as to the identification. When the beast is taken alive and cast into the lake of fire, it is, of course, the individual. When it is spoken of as the steed upon which the woman rides to power, it is clearly the empire. Here, in verse 8, it is the empire and in verse 11 the emperor. In the second place, we must not think of the reference to the seven mountains as being exhausted by the classical symbolism of the city on the seven hills. Just here, we believe, many a commentator has erred. If we stop with that idea, even though it may contain an important germ of truth, we shall fall short of the full explanation. Instead of turning to Virgil and Horace for the explanation of the seven mountains, let us look at the meaning in the light of the Old Testament. A mountain, in Scripture, is the symbol of government. Let us apply this symbol. In Jeremiah, Babylon is called a mountain: "Behold, I am against thee, O destroying mountain, saith the Lord, which destroyeth all the earth: and I will stretch out my hand upon thee, and roll thee down from the rocks, and will make thee a burnt mountain" (51:25). Then, since we know that Babylon was one of a series, crushed by the stone which became a great mountain (Dan. 2:35), we can be sure that all these Gentile powers are part of this series.

With this in mind we return to our text and note that John says that five were fallen and the sixth was then in existence. If we look upon Rome, most certainly the existing power in the day of John, as being the sixth "mountain," or kingdom that partakes of the nature of Satan's rule, we can easily count back through Daniel's prophecies to Greece as the fifth, Medo-Persia as the fourth and Babylon as the third. It is very simple, with the characteristics of these powers in mind, to discover from the Old Testament that two earlier powers were the great enemies of God's people. At the moment John wrote, Israel was in subjection to Rome. It had been in subjection to Greece, Persia and Babylon. But in its still earlier history, Israel had been in slavery to Assyria, and, in its beginnings was in slavery in Egypt. So Isaiah writes, "For thus saith the Lord God, My people went down aforetime into Egypt to sojourn there; and the Assyrian oppressed them without cause" (Isa. 52:4). This passage goes on to describe the liberation of Israel from all her captors and comes to the glorious climax, "How beautiful upon the mountains are the feet of him that bringeth good tidings, that publisheth peace; that bringeth good tidings of good, that publisheth salvation, that saith unto Zion, Thy God reigneth" (Isa. 52:7). Truly those who realize the Satanic character of all these powers will find the feet of the Lord beautiful when they stand upon these nations in judgment. In many places, too, the oppression of Israel in Egypt and Assyria are linked together and made typical of that last oppression of Israel under the Antichrist (see, esp., Isa. 10:24; 27:13; Hos. 9:3; 11:11), while Zechariah tells us, "I will bring them again also out of the land of Egypt, and gather them out of Assyria . . . and the pride of Assyria shall be brought down, and the sceptre of Egypt shall depart away" (10:10, 11).

Throughout the centuries the Satanic power that has ever arrayed in government against God has been the same. Six various forms had appeared by the time John wrote. A seventh is announced that is to endure but for a short space. This, of course, is the Roman Empire in its revived form.

The eleventh verse introduces some of the details of that last empire revival. Many have found this to be an enigma, but if we remember what we studied in the thirteenth chapter, it will be simple. There we saw that the power rising out of the nations was the last dictator who would arise with Rome. To him Satan appears and to him the Satanic rule is committed. The dragon endows him with his power, his throne and with great authority (13:3). If we look upon the Roman dictator as being the seventh, he becomes the eighth, the Antichrist at the time of the Satanic incarnation, and thereby becomes an eighth (note that the Greek is not *the* eighth), who is thus out of the seven, since Satan is the cause of all of the others. He now comes to his judgment, going down to perdition. The details of this will be noted in the last verses of chapter nineteen.

We have seen, in several instances, that a horn represents government, or rule. Here, it is definitely stated, the ten horns are ten kings, which had not, in John's time (nor, indeed in ours), received their power. They are to receive this power and to reign for "one hour," with the Antichrist. All of this can be understood in the light of Daniel's prophecies. It is strongly indicated in Scripture that the revived Roman Empire shall rise in the form of ten kingdoms. The image seen in Nebuchadnezzar's dream had feet of iron and clay, and the ten toes are said to be ten kings (2:44). It is definitely stated that they are ruling at the time the Lord destroys the power of Antichrist. In the beast vision (Dan. 7), the ten are seen as ten horns, even as in our passage in Revelation (cf. Dan. 7:7, 8, 20). Putting these passages together, we judge that in the time of the end, ten kings will dominate in the area of the Roman Empire. Out of one of these kingdoms shall rise a king who will come to the control of that kingdom and two others, three in all (Dan. 7:8, 20, 25). It would appear that this is the king who then becomes the head of the ten kings, the Antichrist. Verse thirteen would indicate that they invite him to be their head. His hour will be short. He is to reign but three and a half years, as we have seen. We can readily imagine what would cause the ten kings to give their power to this one who shall rise from the East.

These ten kings will live and reign until the very end of the tribulation period. For it is written that they shall make war with the Lamb, and the Lamb shall overcome them. There is only one answer to this. The nineteenth chapter is in view where the battle of Armageddon is fought and where the Lord comes forth from Heaven to make war on the nations. It is interesting to note that already the shadow of the Lord Jesus Christ falls across the narrative of Satan's declining powers. A glimpse of Heaven is vouchsafed to us. The hosts are arming. The Lord of lords and King of kings is about to come forth with all His mighty power. His host is composed of those who are called, chosen, and faithful.

The fifteenth verse is one of simple explanation that needs no comment. "And he saith to me, The waters which thou sawest, where the harlot sitteth, are peoples and multitudes and nations and tongues."

The sixteenth verse announces the war to the death of which the next chapter will furnish the details. The civil power carries the religious power, but at a given moment will turn and rend her. To return to our earlier figure, the two thieves help each other over the wall, but when they are both on top, the civil power destroys the religious. This has been well described by one commentator, "Before that final overthrow of world power in the hands of men, the ten kings will completely change their attitude toward the great harlot; their fondness will be turned to extremest enmity; for they will hate her, and 'make her desolate and naked, and shall eat her flesh, and burn her with fire.' Her end will be like that of Jezebel, who typifies her both in life, and in death (II Kings 9:30-37). The terrible end of this enchantress will appear to proceed from natural causes. It will seem as if the ten kings were simply accomplishing their own mind, and were turned against this monstrous system of duplicity and covetousness by some more than usually arrogant assumption of authority, or usurpation of power. But it is given to us to know that *God's* hand will be the active agent in it; that He will 'put in their hearts to fulfil *His* will, and to agree, and give their kingdom unto the beast until the words of God shall be fulfilled.' "

CHAPTER 18

Verses 1–3

Commercial Babylon

¹After these things I saw another angel coming down out of Heaven, having great authority; and the earth was lightened with his glory. ²And he cried out with a mighty voice, saying, Fallen, fallen is Babylon the great, and is become the habitation of demons, and a hold of every unclean spirit and a hold of every unclean and hateful bird. ³For all the nations have fallen by the furious wine of her fornication, and the kings of the earth committed fornication with her, and the merchants of the earth waxed rich through the power of her wantonness.
(Rev. 18:1-3, Free Translation)

After the destruction of the woman—religious Babylon—comes the destruction of the mighty city—commercial Babylon. Some may point out resemblances between the harlot Babylon of chapter seventeen and the city Babylon of chapter eighteen. But there are also distinct differences between the two. They are alike in that they both are under the rule of the Antichrist and at the same time (17:3, 7-14; 16:10, 17-21; 18:1); they are both ruling like queens, and filled with blasphemy (17:3; 18:7); they both hate the saints and shed their blood (17:6; 18:24); they are both associated with the kings of the earth in what is called "fornication" (17:2; 18:3); they both come under the definite judgment of God and are destroyed (17:1, 16, 17; 18:2, 6-8). But here the similarity ends, and there are marked differences which distinguish them. Religious Babylon is called "Mystery Babylon, the Great, the mother of harlots, and abominations of the earth" (17:5), while commercial Babylon is called "great Babylon," and "Babylon the great" (17:5; 16:19; 18:2). The one is described under the symbol of a harlot woman, seated upon the beast of government, the other is presented as a mighty city. The seventeenth chapter presents ecclesiastical Babylon as a "woman," a "whore," a "mother"; the eighteenth chapter presents commercial Babylon as a "habitation," a "great city," a "mighty city," a market place, a burning city. The one is identified

332

with the city on the seven hills, Rome (17:9, 18); the other is a port city, visible from the sea (18:17, 21). The woman is described as guilty of religious abominations (17:4), the city is abominable because of its system of commerce (18:3, 11-19). The manner of their destruction is quite different. The woman is destroyed by the political power through which she has come to reign so arrogantly (17:16); the city is destroyed by an act of God (18:8-10, 19, 21).

Is this city a literal city, or is it symbolical of commercialism as a whole? Bible teachers—and here we speak only of those who are faithful to the Bible as being the inspired word of God—have been divided at this point between two interpretations. Many think that literal Babylon on the Euphrates is to be rebuilt, while others look upon this as figurative.

Ottman has gone over the whole field and presents the case for those who believe that the city of Babylon on the Euphrates will be rebuilt. "We must insist that the *city,* and not the woman, is before us in the eighteenth chapter. Moreover, the city, with which the woman is identified, is not Babylon, but Rome. Rome has neither answered, nor could she do so, to the terms employed in this prophecy . . . It cannot be forced to apply to something other than the Holy Spirit intended. The terms of the prophecy must of necessity be in harmony with the Old Testament predictions. Babylon of old never had any fall commensurate with the language announcing it. Dean Stanley admits that the facts of history do not justify the language of the prophets in reference to Babylon. There is certainly no obscurity in the following prophetic statements: 'It shall be no more inhabited forever; neither shall it be dwelt in from generation to generation. . . . No man shall abide there, neither shall any son of man dwell therein' (Jer. 50:39-40). 'Babylon, the glory of kingdoms, the beauty of the Chaldees' excellency, shall be as when God overthrew Sodom and Gomorrah. It shall never be inhabited, neither shall it be dwelt in from generation to generation: neither shall the Arabian pitch tent there; neither shall the shepherds make their fold there' (Isa. 13:19, 20)."

Ottman then quotes Stanley who describes the history of the decline of the city of Babylon. By the fourth century of our era it had become the hunting park of the Persian Kings, but by the Middle Ages, "when a Jewish traveler (Benjamin of Tudela) once more visited the ruins, it was seen in the state in which it has been ever since—a wide desert tract, interrupted only by the huge masses of indestructible brick, its canals broken, its rich vegetation gone; the habitation of the lions, the jackals, the antelopes of the surrounding desert. In detail of time and place the predicted destruction did not literally come to pass. It was neither so early nor so complete in all its parts, as might have been inferred, and as has been sometimes represented. But it is remarkable that, alone of the many pictures of ruin which the Prophets foreshadowed for the enemies of their country, this has, after a delay of sixteen centuries, and now for a period of seven centuries, been almost literally accomplished."

Ottman says, "This representation is in strict accord with the facts of history, and we are obliged therefore either to accuse both Isaiah and Jeremiah of having given us an overdrawn prophecy, if not an inaccurate one, or else admit the possibility of a future Babylon whose doom shall fully vindicate the terms of the Old Testament prophecies, and that shall tally in the last detail, item by item, with what is given us by John in the Apocalypse . . . Let man think what he will, Babylon must be restored in order that she may fall in a manner to fulfill to the last letter the predictions concerning her. Before judgment overwhelms her, a voice from Heaven is heard, saying, 'Come out of her, My people, that ye partake not of her sins, and that ye receive not of her plagues: for her sins have been heaped up to Heaven, and God hath remembered her unrighteous deeds.' In her there may be those of whom God can say 'My people' and they are called to come out of her before the judgment falls. The stroke that annihilates the apostate church . . . is one that involves the overthrow of literal Rome. Babylon, the great metropolitan city resurrected for the doom that awaits her, will naturally be an asylum for the refugees from Rome. The good and bad alike shall flock there when Rome falls, and the call to come out of Babylon is to God's people before the judgment descends . . . Jeremiah and John have under contemplation one and the same judgment. No such utter annihilation of Babylon took place when the city was captured by the Persians. Jeremiah and John have before them the same divine judgment and it is a *future* one."

There is a fair presentation of the interpretation of the group which believes that the literal Babylon on the Euphrates will be rebuilt. *It may be so.* We do not say that it will not be so. But there are certain difficulties that arise which should be pointed out. Ottman, and the others of his school, say that the description in Revelation 18 cannot be of Rome because Rome is not a seaport, nor is her influence on business great enough to cause the disruption of the commerce of the earth. If Rome, Italy, should sink into the sea tomorrow, the commerce of the rest of the world would go on as though very little had happened. The same things may be said of Babylon on the Euphrates. It is nowhere near the sea, in fact there is a ride of about eighteen hours in the train from Basra, the port near the Persian Gulf, to the site of ancient Babylon. And to look upon a city in the valley of the Euphrates as being the center of the commerce of the world is to envisage the prior fall of all Europe and America. Certainly, such a city would have to become—and in the short space of the few years of Antichrist's reign—the greatest city on earth. Proponents of this school may answer that "With God all things are possible," and

of course we agree to that. But we are inclined to believe that there
are other facts which can much more readily account for the fulfillment of this prophecy.

In the first place, what we have seen of the state of the ruins of
literal Babylon satisfies us that the prophecies of Isaiah and Jeremiah
have been fulfilled. That of John is future, certainly, but why is it
necessary to think of Babylon on the Euphrates in this connection? Let
us remember that early Babylon was composed of three interrelated
parts: religion, commerce and government. All three were united
against God and God pronounced a curse upon them. In the seventeenth chapter of Revelation God speaks of religious Babylon and
identifies it with the Roman ecclesiastical system. By the teaching of
the last verse in that chapter the woman—religious Babylon—is linked
with the city—political Babylon—which, because it is the seat of the
Antichrist as head of the revived Roman Empire, comes under the
judgment of God. Now if religious Babylon is not on the Euphrates,
and if political Babylon is not on the Euphrates, why must commercial
Babylon be on the Euphrates? We see no reason for such an interpretation, and, in fact, we believe that the definite symbolism of the
first two points to a symbolism for the commercial Babylon also.

When the Lord was here on earth He spoke of the great hatred that
"the world" had for Him and His own (John 15:18, 19). What is this
world but a combination of religion, government and commerce? In
other words, *Babylon* in all its parts stands for that which Christ called
"the world."

There remains one further prophecy to be considered with reference
to the identity of the city. There is a picture in Zechariah of a woman
who is transported "to her own place," "in the land of Shinar" (Zech.
5:5-11, see RSV). This woman is represented as seated in a large
measure, the ephah, and she, together with a weight of lead, which is
called wickedness, or the lawless (one), is carried away by two women
with wings like a stork, and the wind is in their wings. They take her
to the plain of Shinar, which is synonymous with Babylon. One commentator says, "When the time comes it will be marked by commerce
(the ephah), false religion (the woman), speedy accomplishment (the
wings of a stork), and a (demon) spirit in their wings."

During the past few years the relationships of commerce among the
nations have been disturbed by a new factor. There has been the continued "flight of gold," or "flight of capital" from one nation to another. As far as we are concerned, the "city" that represents commercial Babylon could be any great port city in the world to which the
commerce of the world should be transferred, and which should thus
head up the whole idea of commerce to be brought into judgment and
sudden destruction. It may be that Babylon on the Euphrates shall

be rebuilt. We do not say the contrary, but we expect that the commercial Babylon of Revelation eighteen will be far from the Euphrates.

Now, opposed to the idea of a literal Babylon, is the interpretation that sees a symbolism of commerce in the great city, and little more. One commentator has put it thus: "That which great Babylon typifies is a thing that is monstrously evil in the sight of God. It represents *the world*, of course; but particularly the world in the aspect of a gigantic system for the pursuit of wealth and pleasure. There is no one word that fully expresses what is here symbolized. It represents *commercialism*, or *industrialism;* but neither of those words adequately defines the symbol, though they help to convey the idea embodied in it."

We find this symbolism perfectly satisfying, and, if it be added that a certain city, the exact location of which we cannot be sure, will embody the climax and culmination of these tendencies, and will be destroyed in an hour at the time of the end, bringing down the commercial structure of the world, the chapter will be fully understood.

Verses 4–19

The Fallen City

⁴*And I heard another voice from out of Heaven, saying, Come forth my people, out of her, that ye have no fellowship with her sins, and that ye receive not of her plagues.* ⁵*For her sins have reached up to Heaven, and God remembered her iniquities.* ⁶*Render as she rendered, and double the double according to her works: in the cup which she mingled, mingle unto her double.* ⁷*How much soever she hath glorified herself and waxed wanton, so much give her of torment and mourning: for she saith in her heart, I sit a queen, and am not a widow, and shall in no wise see mourning;* ⁸*Therefore shall her plagues come in one day, death, and mourning and famine, and she shall be utterly burned in fire; for mighty is the Lord God which judged her.* ⁹*And the kings of the earth who committed fornication and lived wantonly with her shall weep and wail over her, when they see the smoke of her burning,* ¹⁰*standing afar off on account of the fear of her torment, saying, Woe, woe, the great city, Babylon, the mighty city, for in one hour is thy judgment come.* ¹¹*And the merchants of the earth weep and mourn over her, for no one buyeth their merchandise any more;* ¹²*merchandise of gold, and of silver, and of precious stones, and of pearls and fine linen, and purple, and silk and scarlet and all thyine wood, and every vessel of ivory, and every vessel of most precious wood, and of brass, and iron and marble,* ¹³*and spices and perfumes and ointments and frankincense, and wine and oil; and fine flour, and wheat, and cattle and sheep, and of horses and chariots, and bodies and souls of men.* ¹⁴*And the fruits which thy soul lusteth after are gone from thee, and all the dainty and the gorgeous things are perished from thee, and in no wise shall men find them any more at all.* ¹⁵*The merchants of these things, who were made rich by her, shall*

stand afar off because of the fear of her torment, weeping and mourn-
ing, ¹⁶and saying, Woe, woe, the great city, that was arrayed in fine
linen, purple, and scarlet, and bedecked with gold and precious stones,
and pearls! ¹⁷For in one hour so great wealth is made desolate. And
every helmsman, and anyone that saileth any place, and mariners, and
as many as work at the sea, stood afar off, ¹⁸and cried as they looked
upon the smoke of her burning, saying, What city is like the great
city? ¹⁹and they cast dust upon their heads, and cried out weeping and
mourning, saying, Woe, woe, the great city, by which all those who
have the ships at sea waxed rich from her costliness, for in one hour
was she brought to nought.
(Rev. 18:4-19, Free Translation)

Another "messenger" comes down from Heaven, different from those
that have immediately preceded. This messenger is one of glory, and
may well be the Lord Jesus Christ Himself, for He can act as the
messenger of God as well as one of the spirit beings who are mere
creatures, just as I can send either my son or my servant on an errand.
At all events, the coming of this messenger lightens the earth, and His
voice cries out that Babylon the great is fallen, is fallen. This double
announcement is significant and marks the utter speed and finality of
the judgment. Some of God's judgments have been lingering. The
days of His patience are now at an end and we see the growing speed
of His thrusts. This commercial metropolis has become, He says, the
abode of demons, and the hold of every foul spirit, and a cage of every
unclean and hateful bird. One has only to walk down the main streets
of a great city like New York or London to see the aptness of such
a description. Lust is unbridled and tens of thousands of girls each
year go on their way to prostitution. A murderer can be hired for
a comparatively small sum. Justice can be bought and corruption
flourishes. Sensuous pleasures attract the multitudes and hundreds of
millions of dollars pour into the hands of the gamblers who cheat the
crowds day by day. Sharp practices abound and lawyer fights lawyer
to discover new loop-holes that will benefit self, and each one is at the
other's throat. Stop on a street corner and listen to the few phrases
that can be caught from the stream of passersby. Nine out of ten
speak of money or pleasure. So the city is made up of these devilish
elements, and when we say "Broadway," "Wall Street," and "Park
Avenue," we have summed up the diverse elements which come under
the hatred of God.

It is not astonishing that God calls upon His people to come out
of her. In the accomplishment of the prophecy there will be the need
for a literal, physical flight from an individual city which is about to
be destroyed. In the meantime there is need for a spiritual separation
from all that is summed up in the one word, the "world."

Commenting on this, one writer has said, that the call to depart from

Babylon is first heard in the prophecy of Isaiah, and is heard seven times in all, the last being in Revelation 18:4. It is a significant fact also, that in each of these seven instances, the city of God, Jerusalem (or Zion) is in the context. Thus the Scriptures remind us repeatedly of the rivalry between the city of man and the city of God. The passages are these:

> 1. Isaiah 48:20, *Go ye forth of Babylon,* flee ye from the Chaldeans, with a voice of singing declare ye, tell this, utter it even to the end of the earth; say ye, the Lord hath redeemed his servant Jacob.

Even in this first passage the note of exultation is heard, as God contemplates the redemption of His people, and their deliverance from Babylon. In the context we read that "He will do his pleasure on Babylon, and his arm shall be on the Chaldeans" (vs. 14). Also, we find in verse 2 a reference to "the holy city."

> 2. Isaiah 52:11, *Depart ye, depart ye, go ye out from thence;* touch no unclean thing; go ye out of the midst of her; be ye clean that bear the vessels of the Lord.

Babylon is not mentioned here by name; but she is the subject of the passage. In verse 4 God speaks of the sojourn of His people aforetime in Egypt, and of the subsequent oppression by the Assyrian; and then He asks, "Now therefore, what have I *here,* that My people is taken away for nought?" This refers to the coming captivity in Babylon, which is the general subject of this part of the prophecy. Zion is named in verse 8, and Jerusalem in verse 9.

> 3. Jeremiah 50:8, 9, *Remove out of the midst of Babylon,* and go forth out of the land of the Chaldeans, and be as the goats before the flocks. For lo, I will raise, and cause to come up against Babylon, an assembly of great nations from the north country; and they shall set themselves in array against her; from thence she shall be taken.

In verse 5 it is said concerning the people of God, "They shall ask the way to Zion with their faces thitherward." The punishment of Babylon is told in later verses.

> 4. Jeremiah 51:6, 8, *Flee out of the midst of Babylon,* and deliver every man his soul; *be not cut off in her iniquity:* for this is the time of the Lord's vengeance; He will render unto her a recompense . . . . Babylon is *suddenly* fallen and destroyed.

The call here is very urgent, and the similarity of the language to that of Revelation 18:2-4 will be noted. In verse 10 Zion is named.

> 5. Zechariah 2:6, 7, *Ho, ho, come forth and flee from the land of the north,* saith the Lord; for I have spread you abroad as the four winds of the heaven, saith the Lord. Deliver thyself, O Zion, that dwellest with the daughter of Babylon . . .
>
> 6. II Corinthians 6:17, 18, Wherefore, *come out from among them,* and be ye separate, saith the Lord, and touch not the unclean thing; and I will

receive you, And will be a Father unto you, and ye shall be my sons and daughters, saith the Lord Almighty.

Babylon is not named in this passage, but it is implied in the confusion and mixture of believers and unbelievers, Christianity and paganism, described in verses 14-16. Moreover, the first part of the passage is a direct quotation from Isaiah 52:11, cited above. Neither is the holy city of God mentioned by name; but that, too, is implied in the words, "And I will receive you, and be a Father unto you." The family relation implies the family home.

> 7. Revelation 18:4, And I heard another voice from heaven, saying, *Come out of her*, My people, that ye be not partakers of her sins, and that ye receive not of her plagues.

This sevenfold call of God to His people to come out of great Babylon is most impressive. The call to come out implies that the way is open for them to depart. And such is the case, for Christ "gave himself for our sins that he might deliver us out of this present evil world, according to the will of God and our Father" (Gal. 1:4). The door of escape has been set open by Him who openeth and no man shutteth. But it should be remembered that whereas God brought His people out of Egypt in a body, with a strong hand and an outstretched arm, it was otherwise with respect to their deliverance from Babylon; for there He simply opened the way, and only those came out who were minded to do so.

It is consistent with all that the Bible teaches of the nature of God. He hates sin, and He will never forget a sin that is not covered by the blood of Jesus Christ. The sins of this whole system, therefore, come into remembrance before Him. When He says that she is to receive "double," or, more correctly, that the double is to be doubled, it is a reference to the common punishment of the law (Exod. 22:4, 7, 9). This is what Israel received from the Lord's hand (Isa. 40:2; Jer. 16: 18; 17:18); how much more then, shall He not say to Babylon, "double the double."

The seventh verse reminds us of the great prophecy against capitalism in the epistle of James. The fifth chapter begins, "Go to now, ye rich men, weep and howl for your miseries that shall come upon you. Your riches are corrupted, and your garments are motheaten. Your gold and silver is cankered; and the rust of them shall be a witness against you, and shall eat your flesh as it were fire. Ye have heaped treasure together for the last days. Behold, the hire of the laborers who have reaped down your fields, which is of you kept back by fraud, crieth: and the cries of them which have reaped are entered into the ears of the Lord of sabaoth. Ye have lived in pleasure on the earth, and been wanton; ye have nourished your hearts, as in a day of slaughter. Ye have condemned and killed the just; and he doth not resist you" (James 5:1-6).

Because of this passage and what we believe is its relationship to the destruction of commercial Babylon, we are firmly convinced that the Bible teaches that capitalism will endure in the lands of the west, where the Roman Empire is to be revived, until the very time of the end. Those Christians, therefore, who spend their time hunting "reds" and looking for the rise of Communism in our lands, are merely howling into the wind. The tendencies which they see undoubtedly exist, but we know that they will not come to fruition, for the rich are to be richer, and are to exploit the laborers, and are to gather their riches together for the last days. It is then that they will be destroyed, and that most suddenly. We have seen how all business and commerce was destroyed in Russia in a few brief months. The prophecy that we are considering would seem to indicate that commercialism, industrialism, capitalism, all that is characterized by the city, Babylon, will be destroyed in one sudden stroke. Whether this takes place by a real earthquake, or by a shaking of the common people makes no difference. The language covers both. The earthquake, followed by fire, could be the destruction of a literal London or New York, or a rebuilt Babylon for that matter, or it could be the sudden rise of the masses in a great shaking that would be followed by the fires of anarchy. At all events, the one who sits with all the glory of a queen, enthroned, shall receive her plagues "in one hour" (vss. 10, 19). In direct defiance of the Word which says she shall come to sorrow, she proclaims that she will see no sorrow. It is the same old word that was spoken in Eden, "Ye shall not surely die" (Gen. 3:4).

Naturally, with the destruction of commercialism will go the kings of the earth who have maintained their power by maintaining the power of the rulers of money. They will have cause to say, "Alas, alas." And the merchants will have every cause to weep and mourn, for their days of profiting are over. It should be understood that this picture is of the future, and we should never try to advance a radicalism that would seek to destroy commercialism before God's time. For liberalism's attempt to destroy capitalism is Satan fighting against Satan. God will use this divided power of the enemy to bring him down at last, but in the meantime, we are told, "Be patient, therefore, brethren, unto the coming of the Lord" (James 5:7).

It is very interesting to note the union of the merchants and the kings in the wailing over the destruction of Babylon. In ancient times, government and business were not united as they are now. Kings ruled apart from the "bourgeois" who carried on the business of the world. Business began to move into government at the time of the French Revolution and the upheaval in industry that followed the invention of the steam engine and the growth of modern commerce, put the merchants into the government as never before, where they stand, to-day, alongside the politicians, and with common interests. It is to be noted that the wailing is for the luxuries of humanity. No necessities are mentioned. "In the list of the merchandise wherewith men engaged in traffic in the marts of the great city, gold and silver and precious stones come first—earthly treasure which surely has the first place in the affections of men, and which was never so highly prized and so eagerly sought as at the present time. Then come things for show and personal adornment; and then choice articles of rare and precious wood, metal and ivory. Then come perfumes and other luxuries, which speak of the sensuousness of modern living; and then the more substantial commodities, including horses and chariots, which bring to mind the extraordinary development in our days of conveyances for travel and moving about. Most significantly this remarkable list of the wares of the great Babylon ends with the bodies and souls of men. The word translated *slaves* is literally *bodies*. For here is where men and women barter their bodies and souls for some trifle, something that at best can afford but a momentary satisfaction. Here is where the multitude of the Esaus of our day exchange their birthright for a mere mess of pottage. How pertinent and how impressive in this con-nection are the words of the Lord Jesus Christ, 'For what is a man profited, if he shall gain the whole world and lose his own soul? . . . For the Son of man shall come in the glory of his Father, with his angels, and then he shall reward every man according to his works' (Matt. 16:26, 27). Those who make the shrewdest bargains in the markets of the great city, who get the greatest return in exchange for their souls, must part forever with what they received, and be losers for eternity, when Christ shall come. But they that lose their lives in this world for His sake, waiting for their wealth, honors and pleasures until He shall return in power and glory, with the angels of His strength, will have enduring riches; they will enter upon pleasures forevermore, and will receive an inheritance that is 'incorruptible, and undefiled, and that fadeth not away' (I Pet. 1:4)."

The fourteenth verse is one of the most impressive pictures of eter-nal torment that is to be found in the Scripture. Here we have a de-scription in language that only the Holy Spirit could give, of the bitter-ness of soul and the anguish of the poverty-stricken souls who have lost everything they loved. "They shall find them no more at all." The unsaved man has lusted after certain things that are now gone from him forever. They were his life here on earth and he had no other life. Now he has lost them and has nothing else forever. A. T. Robert-son applies the word dainty to foods and the word sumptuous to clothing. People who have lived for the flesh suddenly find that they will nevermore be able to satisfy their desires.

One time, on a transatlantic steamship, we were in the midst of a chess game surrounded by a group of ungodly men who were watching. Something was said that caused us to speak a word of witness and the conversation immediately changed to a religious topic. We said something about hell and one of the men started to tell a funny story. A man died and went to hell and a good friend met him and started to show him around. They had been great golfers and the newcomer suddenly saw a golf course. His eyes lighted up but he noted that his friend who had been there a long time did not seem to be happy. They walked out on the course and the newcomer exclaimed with delight at the beauty of the course, the greens, the fairways— earth had never, never had anything like this. They came to a beautiful clubhouse and there were golf sticks so finely balanced that the newcomer was sure he would be able to drive four hundred yards with one of them. He turned with a glowing smile and asked his friend for some balls. The friend answered "That is the hell of it; there are no balls." The group around the chess table laughed, and then we answered, "But in all seriousness, gentlemen, that is a good and a scriptural story. For no matter how you wish to express it, the place of eternal torment is a place of unfulfilled desires. The drunkard will have his consuming thirst with nothing to slake it. The one who has lived for riches, fame, honor, and all that these could bring will find himself cut off from them forever and ever.

The description of the wailing of the shipmasters is an earthly wailing as they see all that has made up their life disappear before their eyes. But they do not know then that their wailing is but the prelude to an eternal sob that shall never be away from their lips. They could have had life and they have refused it for Babylon, and now that is taken from them. And, worst of all, their hatred of God is all-consuming, so that even were there a second chance for salvation after death — and of this Scripture not only gives no hint, but definitely teaches the contrary—there would be no desire for God in the hearts of those who are lost. This is the final fruit of sin. God's Word is vindicated, and all those who have preached, "The wages of sin is death" are vindicated. They have had their sin; they now have their death.

Verses 20–24

The End of the World

²⁰*Rejoice over her, O Heaven, and the saints, and apostles and prophets, because God hath judged your judgment upon her.* ²¹*And a strong messenger took up a stone, as it were a great millstone, and cast it into the sea, saying, Thus with a mighty fall will the great city Babylon be cast down, and she shall be found no more at all.* ²²*And*

*the voice of harpers, and of musicians, and of fluteplayers, and of
trumpeters shall be heard no more at all in thee; and no craftsman of
any craft shall in any wise be found in thee any more; and the sound
of a millstone shall in no wise be heard in thee any more; ²³And the
light of a lamp shall shine no more at all in thee; and the voice of the
bridegroom and of the bride shall be heard no more at all in thee; for
thy merchants were the great men of the earth; for with thy sorcery
all the nations were deceived. ²⁴And in her was found the blood of
prophets and of saints, and of all that have been slain upon the earth.*
(Rev. 18:20-24, Free Translation)

Heaven now rejoices at the end of "the world." Do not misunder-
stand. It is not the end of the earth. That does not come for another
thousand years. Babylon is the name that is given to it. It is the
world of politics, governmental Babylon—the world of ecclesiasticism,
the harlot Babylon—and the world of business, commercial Babylon.
All three come to a final doom. All are destroyed in a day.

Is it any wonder that Heaven, the saints, the apostles and the
prophets are called upon to rejoice over her? Here is the final triumph
of the kingdom of Heaven over the kingdom of Satan. The Heavens
include all the hosts of Heaven, cherubim, seraphim, angels and the
archangel, a company innumerable that would fill us with amazement
upon arriving in Heaven were it not for the fact that we will have
such a vision of the glory and power of God that all things will seem
simple and natural to us, when explained by the majesty of the source
of all things.

Our common version speaks of "the holy apostles," but the first of
the words, "holy," should be taken as a noun, "the holy ones," commonly translated "the saints." We must not forget that the richness
of our English language frequently gives us two words for the same
thing, and then with time the two words take on a distinction of their
own. The one word comes to us from the German and the other from
the Latin by way of the French. The Germans, today, speak of a
"Holy Bible" but also of "Holy Matthew," "Holy John"; the French
speak of "Saint Matthew," "Saint John," but they also call their Bible
the "Saint Bible." Both languages have only one word for our idea
that has now become a double one. We have learned to distinguish
holy things from holy persons, and to call the latter "saints." The Bible
has one word for the two. If we are saints, we are holy in God's sight.
Our position is one of perfect holiness.

Is it any wonder that all the saints rejoice at the destruction of "the
world." Our three great enemies have been "the world, the flesh
and the devil." How often we were buffeted by the blows of the
world. Did not the Lord say, "If the world hate you, ye know that it
hated me before it hated you. If ye were of the world, the world would
love his own: but because ye are not of the world, but I have chosen

you out of the world, therefore the world hateth you. Remember the word that I said unto you, The servant is not greater than his Lord. If they have persecuted me, they will also persecute you . . ." (John 15:18-20). What has the world not done to the saints? Why should not the saints rejoice when the whole world-system comes to an end? The Bible gives us a summary of some of the things the world has done to the saints: ". . . tortured . . . others had trial of cruel mockings and scourgings, yea, moreover of bonds and imprisonment: They were stoned, they were sawn asunder, were tested, were slain with the sword; they wandered about in sheepskins and goatskins; being destitute, afflicted, evil treated (Of whom the world was not worthy); they wandered in deserts and in mountains, and in dens and caves of the earth . . ." (Heb. 11:35-38). And now the world-system is utterly destroyed, and the saints are called upon to rejoice. Is it any wonder?

The apostles and prophets, leaders of the saints of all ages, who have, themselves, borne the brunt of the world's hatred, are given special prominence in the rejoicing. There is an interesting thought to be found in this fact. They are included in the grouping of the saints, but they are mentioned specially as though their special sufferings give them a special right to rejoice. Take Paul for an example. He pointed out that he and the other apostles had been chosen by God for special sufferings. "For I think that God hath set forth us the apostles last, as it were appointed to death: for we are made a spectacle unto the world, and to angels, and to men. We are fools for Christ's sake, but ye are wise in Christ; we are weak, but ye are strong; ye are honorable, but we are despised. Even unto this present hour we both hunger, and thirst, and are naked, and are buffeted, and have no certain dwellingplace; And labor, working with our own hands; being reviled, we bless; being persecuted, we suffer it; Being defamed, we intreat; we are made as the filth of the world, and are the offscouring of all things unto this day" (I Cor. 4:9-13). But God had revealed to him that this was but for a time, and he is able to write to the Romans, "I reckon that the sufferings of this present time are not worthy to be compared with the glory which shall be revealed in us" (Rom. 8:18).

It is the first time in this book of tears that the command to rejoice is given. The saints are in Heaven from the time of the fourth chapter, and there is worship, and honor and glory and power given by them to God who is indeed worthy to receive this praise. But here —as though the saints now had their eyes adjusted to the glories of Heaven—the command of rejoicing is given. The saints are called to look down upon the world they have left. They see that the vile Babylon against which they struggled and which poured out its scorn upon them, has come to a complete and final doom, and they know that this world-system will never rise again. There is full cause for rejoicing.

The King James Version gives this cause for rejoicing: "for God hath avenged you on her." The Greek is much stronger: "For God hath judged your judgment upon her."

The action of the mighty angel in verse twenty-one refers back, inevitably, to an incident in the life of Jeremiah. Great judgments are pronounced upon Babylon by the Lord God of recompenses (Jer. 51: 56), a title of God that needs to be brought into more frequent consideration. Babylon the city is in view, and Babylon, the world-system, is of course, in the prophetic view. Then we read, "The word which Jeremiah the prophet commanded Seraiah the son of Neriah, . . . when he went with Zedekiah the king of Judah into Babylon in the fourth year of his reign. And this Seraiah was a quiet prince. So Jeremiah wrote in a book all the evil that should come upon Babylon, even all these words that are written against Babylon. And Jeremiah said to Seraiah, When thou comest to Babylon and shalt see, and shalt read all these words; Then shalt thou say, O Lord, thou hast spoken against this place, to cut it off, that none shall remain in it, neither man nor beast, but that it shall be desolate for ever. And it shall be, when thou hast made an end of reading this book, that thou shalt bind a stone to it, and cast it into the midst of Euphrates; And thou shalt say: Thus shall Babylon sink, and shall not rise from the evil that I will bring upon her: and they shall be weary" (Jer. 51:59-64).

How wonderful are God's ways! In the midst of Babylon's splendor, he has Seraiah, "a quiet prince," tie a stone to a parchment in which the prophecy of destruction has been written and throw it into a river. Now he has a mighty angel cast a millstone into the sea, saying, "Thus, with a mighty fall will the great city of Babylon be cast down, and she shall be found no more at all." And all that men have called "civilization" will disappear in the judgment of God. God speaks truth through quiet princes, and if He is unheeded, God must speak through the mighty angels.

Commentators have argued whether this is a literally revived Babylon or a "spiritual" Babylon. To us it makes no difference. There may be a literal Babylon; of that we are not sure. But most certainly both Jeremiah and John are talking about the end of something much greater than a city. Here is the end of "the world" that hated the Lord first, and His saints afterwards.

One writer has well written: "The angel's words announce most impressively the vanishing forever of all the joys and delights of the great city, the music and the song, the hum of industry, the brightness of its illumination, and above all, the rejoicings of the bridegroom and bride, which in the Bible stand for the highest of all human joys." In another of Jeremiah's prophecies we have doom foretold, and in almost the same terms. Babylon came against the land of Israel, a land that is beloved of God, the Word tells us, and Babylon caused this land to be desolate. "I will take from them the voice of mirth, and the voice of gladness, the voice of the bridegroom, and the voice of the bride, the sound of the millstones, and the light of the candle" (Jer. 25:10). It was God who permitted Babylon to treat His land thus, nay! It was God who used Babylon as a scourge upon His sinning people. But now the Lord of recompenses gives back more than double. Babylon's lights go out forever.

The reason for this judgment is most revealing. "Because thy merchants were the great men of the earth; for with thy sorcery all the nations were deceived." Christ should have been acknowledged as the King and ruler of the earth. Instead, the men who became rich in the commerce of goods and souls (vss. 12, 13) thought more of their merchandise than they did of the Saviour of the world. They wept when their merchandise was destroyed (vs. 11), but they had never wept because they grieved the Lord.

A sidelight on the methods of the world is to be found in the declaration that these merchants used "sorcery" to deceive the world, and succeeded in the deception. The Greek word for sorcery is *pharmakia,* from which we get our word "pharmacy." It comes from an earlier word meaning "to prepare drugs." Roberston says, "If one is puzzled over the connection between medicine and sorcery as illustrated by this word (our pharmacy), he has only to recall quackery today in medicine (patent medicines and cure-alls), witch-doctors, professional faith-healers, medicine-men in Africa. True medical science has had a hard fight to shake off chicanery and charlatanry." But just as a pharmacist mixes his drugs to provide his various remedies, so we see the leaders of the earth mixing their designs—rewards, blandishments, promises and propaganda, war scares to force tax-raises to increase armaments, and all the thousand and one ingredients of their Pharmacopoeia, in order to drug the world into insensibility that they might keep and strengthen their hold upon the masses of men.

That they should have slain their own kind might have passed without judgment, for the devil's own are "taken captive by him at his will" (II Tim. 2:26). But they touched God's children, hidden in the midst of the world, in that world but not of it. And for this they have been brought in this final judgment upon their civilization, to the utter destruction of their world-system, which shall never rise again. The blood of prophets, and of saints, and of all that were slain upon the earth is now avenged upon the system that lived by the blood of its victims.

PART X
LORD OF LORDS

CHAPTER 19

Verses 1–10

The Hallelujah Chorus

¹After these things I heard as it were a great voice of a large multitude in Heaven, saying, Hallelujah, the salvation, and the glory and the power of our God: ²Because true and righteous are His judgments, because He has judged the great harlot which did corrupt the earth with her fornication, and He hath avenged the blood of His bondslaves from her hand. ³And a second time, they say, Hallelujah; and her smoke keeps on going up unto the ages of the ages. ⁴And the twenty-four elders and the four living creatures fell down and worshipped God, Who sitteth upon the throne, saying, Amen, Hallelujah. ⁵And a voice came from the throne, saying, Give praise to our God, all His bondslaves, those that fear Him, the small and the great.

⁶And I heard as it were the voice of a great multitude, and as the voice of many waters, and as the voice of mighty thunders, saying, Hallelujah; for the Lord our God, the Almighty, reigneth. ⁷Let us rejoice and be exceeding glad, and let us give the glory unto Him; for the marriage of the Lamb is come, and His wife has made herself ready. ⁸And it was given to her that she should array herself with fine linen, bright and pure, for the fine linen is the righteous acts of the saints. ⁹And he saith to me, Write; Blessed are they which are bidden unto the supper of the marriage of the Lamb. And he saith to me, These are true words of God. ¹⁰And I fell before his feet to worship him; and he saith to me, Take heed not; I am thy fellow bondslave, and of thy brethren who have the testimony of Jesus; worship God; for the witness of Jesus is the spirit of prophecy.

(Rev. 19:1-10, Free Translation)

The heavenly host breaks forth. It is responsive praise as chorus answers chorus. It would seem that this is the great company of angelic beings, for the redeemed are seen later. The Greek is literally, as Robertson translates it, "the great voice of much multitude," and it is this host that breaks forth into Hallelujahs—the only Hallelujahs in the whole of the New Testament.

Hallelujah is a Hebrew word, composed of two words, and meaning, literally, "Praise Jehovah." The first time the word is found in the Bible is in connection with the installation of the ark of God in the midst of Zion. David decided to have a choir in the midst of the worship of God and we read that "he appointed certain of the Levites to minister before the ark of Lord, and to celebrate and to thank and *hallelujah* the God of Israel" (I Chron. 16:4, Heb.). The ark of God was the symbol of His presence among His people. Christ, of course, is the true ark, and when the forces of the enemy are overthrown, Babylon destroyed, and Christ comes forth to take His rightful place in the world, Heaven breaks forth in glad Hallelujahs.

The punishment of sinners is a matter of praise on the part of the believers, and the Hallelujah chorus is sung when the forces of the enemy are dispersed and the righteouness of God is manifest. One commentator has well said, "Thus the thought of the destruction of the wicked out of the earth evokes a Hallelujah from one who is in accord with the mind and purposes of God. For just as in this day of salvation, His people rejoice with Him in the salvation of sinners, even so, in the coming day of judgment they will rejoice with Him in the judgment of the wicked."

And it is to be noticed that the second verse of our chapter distinctly shows that such righteous worship and praise is on the basis of the truth and righteousness of the judgments of God. The redeemed have long known that salvation from sin is by the work of the Lord; they have been redeemed from the penalty and power of sin. But now they see that they are to be redeemed from the presence of sin. The corruption of sin is to be rooted out of the earth, put down forever, cast off into outer darkness. Truly salvation, glory and power are from our God. The enemy is judged and we are freed from the great harlot forever.

The great Hallelujah burst forth a second time. And the hosts of Heaven add that the enemy is completely vanquished. "Her smoke keeps on going up unto the ages of the ages." And so long as the Godhead is to endure and so long as the believers are to reign with Him in glory, so long must the wrath of God be poured upon those who know not God and obey not the Gospel of our Lord Jesus Christ. There is not the shadow of evidence in the Bible that the lake of fire will ever turn one heart toward God or cause one guilty sinner to relax in the slightest the enmity against God that characterizes the carnal mind.

And now we read that the saints join in the praise of Heaven. The four and twenty elders who are the leaders of the church and Israel, join in the chorus which the angel hosts have started. The company of the cherubim join in this worship. It is interesting to note that these two groups fall down and worship before they take up the Hallelujah. For us, the believers out of this world, it is understandable

that the destruction of "the world" that hated us because it hated
Christ, calls forth the deepest praise and devotion from redeemed
hearts. Perhaps the worship of the cherubim can be better understood
when it is realized that Lucifer was originally of their number and that
he fell, dragging down a great number of the hosts of Heaven. Surely
these cherubim who remained faithful to God will have every cause
to be thankful that they did not follow the deceiver, but that they remained forever as the symbols of God's power and authority.

And it is to be noticed that in the praise of the church there is another word added which speaks volumes. For their word is not merely
Hallelujah, but Amen, Hallelujah. These are both Hebrew words
which have become universal. *Amen* is the word that was so frequently
and so solemnly upon the lips of the Lord Jesus when He was here
on earth. Every time we read that Christ said, "Verily, verily, I say
unto you," it is in the original tongue, "Amen, Amen, I say unto you."
This solemn asseveration of truth is most striking. And the church
now takes the word in praise to God. I wonder if there is not in this
brief word on the lips of the believers in Heaven the triumphant testimony to the Word of God in all its power and truth.

The throne itself then takes up the cry. A voice comes out from
the throne, which can be none other, we believe, than the voice of
God Himself. All in the universe who fear Him, both small and great
are called upon to praise Him. God tells us that His ways are not our
ways and His thoughts are not our thoughts (Isa. 55:8). God is
absolutely perfect. This perfection is such that God could never de-
teriorate nor could He improve. He could never learn anything new
for He is all knowledge. He is the eternal, absolute God. For this
reason it would be wrong for Him not to call for universal worship.
Every gifted human being is aware of the gifts he possesses. It would
have been impossible for Caruso not to have known that he was a
great singer. It would be impossible for a champion runner not to
know that he was always first at the tape. If this be so with human
beings, how much more is it so with God who knows that all fullness
dwells in Himself. He knows that for any creature to be satisfied with
anything other than God or for a creature not to praise Him is a mark
of imperfection in the creature. And imperfection is sin, and all sin
is to be removed from the universe. Now that Babylon is destroyed
and Satan is in full retreat and about to go into the bottomless pit,
God calls upon all Heaven from which every sinning angel has now
been banished and from which all sin will be removed forever, to join
in the Hallelujah.

The call is addressed to all His bondslaves, those that fear Him,
the small and great. Bondslaves are very different from ordinary
slaves. When, through difficulties, a Hebrew became a bondman of another, this slavery was not permitted by the law of God to endure

more than six years. In the seventh year the bondman was to be freed. The Lord made provision, however, for those who were so kindly treated that they did not wish their freedom. We read, "And it shall be, if he say unto thee, I will not go away from thee; because he loveth thee and thine house, because he is well with thee: Then thou shalt take an awl, and thrust it through his ear unto the door, and he shall be thy servant for ever. And also unto thy maidservant thou shalt do likewise" (Deut. 15:16, 17). So the call of God that is addressed to the universe reaches the ears of all the hosts of Heaven, angels and saints, all of them bondslaves, who delight in their submission to God, and who rejoice that now there is to be but one will in all the universe, the will of God, and that the will of rebellion is about to be broken forever.

Thus the voice of praise breaks forth, and it is as the voice of many waters, and as the voice of mighty thunders. This is the fourth and last of the Hallelujahs. It comes from hearts that are delighted to be at one with the divine will. The Lord our God, the Almighty, reigneth. The Lord Jesus sat at the right hand of the Father *until* the moment came to make the enemies His footstool; now the time of victory is here (Ps. 110:1).

A further reason for the glory and praise is the announcement that the marriage of the Lamb has come and that His wife has made herself ready. There has been a great deal of discussion among the commentators as to the identity of this one who is called the Lamb's wife. This discussion has been all the more involved because there is another company seen in the ninth verse who is evidently distinct from the bride. For there we find mention of those who are bidden to the wedding. Who are these, the bride and the guests? Let us quote one commentator: "Are we to regard the whole company of the called as constituting the bride? Or, do these called ones refer, in distinction from her, to guests at the wedding? Alford thinks the bride is the same as 'the sum of the guests.' Lange says, 'The Church in its unitous form is the Bride; in its individual members, it consists of wedding guests.'

"A double consciousness would be needed to get any meaning out of such a statement. There is nothing whatever to warrant or even to suggest such an identity. On the other hand, the words 'bride,' 'guests,' as ordinarily used, would seem to indicate a designed distinction between them. Christ has other relationships than that to the Church. The figure of marriage is a familiar one in Old Testament Scripture, and is there, without question, used in references to Christ and *Israel*. We surely cannot press the figure of marriage to mean more than the unity implied therein between Christ and the redeemed, whether they be Israel or the Church. If Israel, as distinct from the Church, *is* to be brought into such unity with Christ, then there is every justification for the use of such figurative language in reference to Israel. In view of this we cannot be positive of the identity of the company that here constitutes the bride. The Church, unquestionably, is the body of *guests* at the great supper (Luke 14). This is true also of her at the marriage feast (Matt. 22), where the bride is not in view; but this, however, does not imply that she is to be identified with 'the sum of the guests' . . .

"This relationship, according to Scriptural testimony, is to exist between the Lord and Israel as well as between the Lord and the Church. In all ages past there have been true Israelites that cannot be righteously identified and condemned with the nation in the rejection of the Messiah. They are 'the spirits of just men made perfect,' distinct from the Church, but eternally united to Christ in glory as much as the firstborn ones whose names are written in Heaven (Heb. 12:23). The relation is just as much *bridal* for Israel as it is for the Church. The thought of a double marriage, one between Jehovah and Israel, and the other between Christ and the Church, need not confuse us. In this event, the company that constitutes the bride of the one marriage would constitute the guests at the other. When Christ shall take Israel into eternal union with Himself, the Church shall be there as 'the called.' When Christ shall take the Church into a like eternal union, Israel shall be there as 'the guests.' In either case, 'Blessed are they who are called unto the marriage supper of the Lamb.' "

We know from many passages of Scripture that Israel is to be brought into eternal relationship with the Lord which is prefigured by the symbol of marriage. This is the heart of the message of Hosea (see especially Hos. 2:14-23), and Isaiah joins him in the use of this same symbol. Israel is to be called Hephzibah, My delight is in her, and thy land Beulah, married; "For as a young man marrieth a virgin, so shall thy sons marry thee; and as the bridegroom rejoiceth over the bride, so shall thy God rejoice over thee" (Isa. 62:5).

On the other hand, the Spirit of God yearned in Paul with a godly jealousy for the Church, "for I have espoused you to one husband, that I may present you as a chaste virgin to Christ" (II Cor. 11:2), and the union between Christ and the Church is presented as the great mystery of the bride and the bridegroom in their most intimate union (Eph. 5). If both Israel and the Church are seen in this relationship with each other as the delighted guests, the symbolism will be complete and all the passages on this subject will be understood without difficulty.

The angelic messenger who had spoken to John now added his own important witness. These are the true sayings of God. There has evidently been an impressive solemnity in this revelation concerning the marriage supper of the Lamb and the blessedness of those who are called thereto. For John, moved to the depths of his being, falls at the feet of the messenger to worship him. The reaction on the part of

the messenger is most significant. It must be seen as one of three instances in the New Testament where various beings receive worship
from human beings. In the book of the Acts we have the account of
an attempt by human beings to worship Paul and Barnabas. These
latter rent their clothes and running in among the people cried out
with horror against the blasphemy of receiving worship which belongs
to God alone. Here in our present passage we have one of the apostles
who mistakes a glorious angelic being for the deity and falls before
him to worship. The angel, also, refuses this worship. The Greek
words are much more staccato than the English. See thou do it not
is a formal statement. The Greek is two short words with only six
letters, *hora me*. The mighty angel knew well the peril that lurked in
any desire for worship. Here was a part of Satan's original sin, "I
will be like the most High God." This being was not to be ensnared
thus. The one other Being in the New Testament to whom worship is
offered is the Lord Jesus Christ. Thomas called Him, "My Lord and
my God" (John 20:28), and was gently rebuked for not having understood and worshiped sooner. Simon Peter fell at Jesus' knees, "saying, Depart from me; for I am a sinful man, O Lord" (Luke 5:8).
He is dealt with gently, and is told that he is to leave his work and
follow the Lord, in order to catch men. Jesus knew Himself to be
God and was glorified when men petitioned Him under the authority
of His Name. His attitude was in keeping with His words, "He that
hath seen me hath seen the Father" (John 14:9-11).

The final word of the angel must be paraphrased in order to be
understood fully. The angel has refused worship, and has pointed
John to God, that is to Jesus Christ; and thus he adds, "for the witness
of Jesus is the spirit of prophecy." This will be understood if expanded as follows: The possession of the prophetic spirit will always
manifest itself in a witness to Jesus. The angel has been the bearer
of a wonderful prophecy which John has recognized as divine and
which has brought him to the point of worship as he sees and understands the blessedness that is in store for those who are bidden to the
marriage supper of the Lamb. When the worship has been attempted
by John and rejected by the angel, the latter explains that worship
of the Lord Jesus Christ is the mark of the prophetic spirit and that the
two must go together. Thus, in a simple sentence, the Book does away
with all false prophets whose main object is always to draw men away
from the witness of Christ. Alford comments on the other side of this
saying as follows: "There is no real difficulty in this saying: no reason
for destroying its force by making 'of Jesus' subjective, and 'the testimony of Jesus' to mean 'the witness which proceeds from Jesus.'
What the angel says is this: Thou and I and our brethren are all 'those
who have the testimony of Jesus,' i.e., are witnesses to Jesus; and the
way in which we bear this witness, the substance and essence of this

testimony, is the spirit of prophecy; 'we have all been made to drink into one Spirit.' This Spirit, given to me in that I shew thee these things, given to thee in that thou seest and art to write them, is the token that we are fellow-servants and brethren. It does not follow that every one of those 'who have the testimony of Jesus' has, in the same distinguished degree, the Spirit of prophecy; but every such one *has* the same Spirit, and that one Spirit, and no other, is the Spirit of Prophecy."

Verses 11–16

The Coming King of Glory

[11]And I saw the Heaven opened, and, behold, a white horse; and He that sat upon him is called Faithful and True; and in righteousness He doth judge and make war. [12]His eyes are as a flame of fire; and on His head are many diadems; and He hath a name written, which no one knows but He Himself. [13]And He is arrayed in a garment sprinkled with blood: and His name is called The Word of God. [14]And the armies which are in Heaven were following Him upon white horses, clothed in fine linen, white and clean. [15]And out of His mouth goeth a sharp sword, so that He may smite the nations with it; and He shall rule them with a rod of iron; and He treadeth the winepress of the wine of the wrath of the anger of God the Almighty. [16]And He hath on His garment and on His thigh, a name written, King of Kings and Lord of Lords.

(Rev. 19:11-16, Free Translation)

Now from the opened Heavens, comes forth the Lord Jesus Christ, in all the glory and majesty that have been ascribed to Him throughout the Bible. He is seen riding upon a white horse, the familiar figure of war and victory. In an earlier passage (6:2) we saw the rise of the dictator who was to become the Antichrist, riding on a white horse, and we saw that many commentators had attempted to identify the former rider with this glorious Rider who now appears. But as Swete says, though "It is tempting to identify him with the Rider on the white horse whose name is 'the Word of God' . . . the two riders have nothing in common beyond the white horse."

That this final Rider is the Lord Jesus there can be no doubt. Earlier in the Revelation He is called the Faithful (1:5), and the True (3:7), and to the last of the seven churches, "the Faithful and True Witness" (3:14). His sayings are "faithful and true sayings" (22:6). There is more in this ascription than the mere joining together of two adjectives. This comes out from a consideration of the word "faithful" in other parts of the Scripture. Such a study reveals that when the Lord reminds us that He is faithful, He means that He is keeping

His promises, and insuring the fulfillment of every part of His covenant. "If we confess our sins he is faithful and just to forgive us our sins" (I John 1:9), means that He is looking back to the cross, and in faithfulness to all that was accomplished there, is maintaining His own in fellowship with Himself. So throughout the Word of God. He is the One who keeps His Word. "If we believe not, yet he abideth faithful; he cannot deny himself" (II Tim. 2:13). That He is the One who is True, is yet another lesson in the certainty of His Word. He has magnified that Word above His name (Ps. 138:2) because without the truth of His Word His name would stand for uncertainty and lying. This truth has been seized by the Old Scotch lady who, on her death bed, was glorying in the assurance of a certain salvation. The young minister had never seen anyone quite so sure and thought he should warn the dear soul against the possibility of a mistake on her part. She answered him well, "If I should awake in eternity to find myself among the lost the Lord would lose more than I would; for all that I could lose would be my immortal soul, but He would have lost His good name." Faithfulness to promises and woes that are true — this is the nature of our Lord in all ages. It is especially significant here as He leaves Heaven to come to earth for the last battle, and the accomplishment of the eternal plan which was announced throughout the Word, and which has been held in derision by that world which is now to know its truth and His faithfulness in a terrible way.

The work of the Heavenly Rider is a double work. He comes forth as Judge and Warrior. The combination of these two is especially significant, and also terrible. "Shall not the Judge of all the earth do right?" (Gen. 18:25). This judgment had been promised and prophesied throughout the Word of God. The very resurrection of Christ is bound up with the accomplishment of this fact. Paul, on Mars' Hill, gave forth the words of doom: "God now commandeth all men everywhere to repent; because he hath appointed a day, in the which he will judge the world in righteousness by that man whom he hath ordained; whereof he hath given assurance unto all men, in that he hath raised him from the dead" (Acts 17:30, 31).

The second work of the Conqueror is that of Maker of War. This is an important teaching because there has been such maudlin pacifism, attempting to teach that war was wrong in itself. War is not wrong in itself. If it were, Christ would not come, making war. The unbeliever has attempted to get around the dilemma by saying that this prophecy is false, and that He will not come as the avenging Judge. But the truth is that war is not wrong in itself. It is the sin which makes the war necessary that is wrong. The judge who sentences an assassin to the electric chair is taking life, but he is not violating the sixth commandment. It is the murderous heart of the assassin that is wrong, and not the judgment upon it. "Thou shalt not kill" has been woefully misinterpreted by the pacifists. The verse should be rendered, "Thou shalt do no murder." What is forbidden is the self-appointed killing of a personal enemy. The official destruction of a criminal, or the national attack on unrighteous enemies is never forbidden in the Word of God. "God is light, and in him dwelleth no darkness at all" (I John 1:5); and He "cannot be tempted with evil" (James 1:13). The war that He comes to bring upon this earth has waited overlong. He has not delayed because of any timid appeasement, but because of divine patience. But now the moment is ended. The final war is on, and it shall be carried speedily to a victorious consummation.

His eyes are as a flame of fire, seeing all, missing nothing. "Neither is there any creature that is not manifest in his sight; but all things are naked and opened unto the eyes of him with whom we have to do" (Heb. 4:13).

On His head are many diadems. When He was here upon earth men, mockingly, put a crown of thorns upon His brow. Those thorns were emblems of the curse, put upon the ground in Eden. He, becoming a curse for us (Gal. 3:13), felt those thorns for us, that we might be redeemed and given crowns of righteousness which we will gladly lay at His feet. And there are many diadems, since He is Lord of Lords and has many sovereignties. All this is more wonderful when we realize that through past ages He has been the despised and rejected of men, but now He is manifested by God, vindicated before all the universe. Now it is that every eye shall see Him, soon every knee shall bow and every tongue confess that this glorious One is none other than He who was the meek and lowly Jesus. He has been pronounced worthy, and He wears the diadems of that worth. He is the Nobleman who went into a far country to get a kingdom, even as He said (Luke 19:12), and now He returns with it.

Here all power is gathered together in Christ. The many diadems are symbols of the fact that no rule, might or authority can now stand against Him. Satan may have boasted that He had the power to give the rule to whomsoever he desired (Luke 4:6), and he was not lying for he had been "set" thus as the cherub that was anointed for governing (Ezek. 28:14). But now his power is revoked, not by an arbitrary thrust of superior power, but by the lengthy and involved process that vindicates the holiness and the justice of God, the destruction of Satan and his usurped power on the basis of the death of Christ, who by that death destroyed the power (Heb. 2:14) that is now, in all righteousness and justice, taken away forever. "All power is given unto me . . ." (Matt. 28:18).

He has a name written which no one knows but He, Himself. One commentator, describing the glory of the scene, the triumphant King with the many diadems, adds, "He has a glory and a character of His own, incommunicable and incomprehensible, 'a name written that no man knew, but He Himself.' Man as He is, He is also the Son of God, and thus a fullness resides in Him which no mere creature intelligence can fathom."

He is arrayed in a garment sprinkled with blood, for already many enemies have fallen before Him. This symbolism is awful, but understandable in the light of human depravity and the unchanging enmity of the carnal mind against God (Rom. 8:7). We follow A. T. Robertson here in his correction of the Greek text, accepting the word which speaks of the garment as sprinkled, rather than dipped in blood. The phrase takes us inevitably back to one of the great prophetic scenes. Isaiah, in one of his later visions, sees a figure approaching him, dressed in blood-stained garments, and asks, "Who is this that cometh from Edom, with dyed garments from Bozrah? this that is glorious in his apparel, travelling in the greatness of his strength?" An answer comes which shows Isaiah that He is seeing the Saviour in some phase of His work: "I that speak in righteousness, mighty to save." Immediately realizing that this is the Saviour, he asks again, "Wherefore art thou red in thine apparel, and thy garments like him that treadeth the winefat?" The Lord gives an answer to which our verse is a reference, and the two prophecies are thus linked together in certain manner. "I have trodden the winepress alone; and of the people there was none with me: for I will tread them in mine anger, and trample them in my fury; and their blood shall be sprinkled upon my garments, and I will stain all my raiment. For the day of vengeance is in mine heart, and the year of my redeemed is come" (Isa. 63:1-4).

And His name is called the Word of God. Thus it was when first He came. "In the beginning was the Word, and the Word was with God and the Word was God . . . and the Word was made flesh and dwelt among us . . . full of grace and truth" (John 1:1, 14). When first the Word of God came, He was full of grace and truth, but His own received Him not. He chose a people to bear His name and they continued the beseeching message of grace and truth, drawing upon themselves the same treatment which their Lord had received. "If the world hate you," Christ had told His followers, "ye know that it hated me before it hated you" (John 15:18). This hatred of grace and truth by the lost world was met with patience through the centuries, but only because God's justice knew that a day had been appointed to judge this hatred. Now the Word of God, who came in grace and truth, comes in power and great glory. It is His vesture which is sprinkled with blood. All the hatred of the carnal mind finds, at last, its rich reward.

Following the divine Leader come the armies of Heaven. The symbols have been examined previously. The white linen, clean and fine, identifies this host as the believers of all ages. We can wear the divine righteousness because He, first of all, wore the blood-stained garment.

And when we see Him in His triumph there will be these double marks of His suffering and His glory, the robe and the crown. These armies are not angelic hosts, for though there will be multitudes of angels surrounding Him when He comes, they are not spoken of here. We can be assured, in perfect faith, that we shall be in that ransomed throng. Enoch was the first to tell of this moment, "Behold the Lord cometh with myriads of his saints to execute judgment" (Jude 14). Zechariah saw it in connection with the return of Christ to the land where He had once lived, "and the Lord my God shall come, and all the saints with thee" (Zech. 14:5). It will take the entire company of the redeemed to reflect in any adequate way, the glory of the Lord Jesus Christ. He shall bring the many sons to glory (Heb. 2:10), fulfilling the promise, "When Christ, who is our life, shall appear, then shall ye also appear with him in glory" (Col. 3:4). The purpose of this is that we might be "to the praise of His glory . . . the fulness of him that filleth all in all" (Eph. 1:12, 23). And as He comes to judge this world we are not to forget that He has announced that we are to be associated with Him in that judgment, judging both the world and the angels (I Cor. 6:2, 3).

The sharp sword out of His mouth we have studied in the first vision of the ascended Lord (1:16). In the same manner we have seen the great promise of the second Psalm repeated in one of the letters to the seven churches (2:27). Nor is there anything hidden in the figure of the treading of the winepress of the wrath of God. The only thing to be noticed in that phrase here is the manner in which four genitives are made to depend one upon another as though to add an utterly solemn touch to that pouring out of the very last drop of the wine, of the wrath, of the anger, of God the Almighty. There is an ominous ring to the phrase. It reminds us that God has said, "When I begin I will also make an end" (I Sam. 3:12).

The final detail of this portion of the picture is the revelation of the third name to be considered in this paragraph. There is the name that He alone knows, there is the revelation of Himself as the Word of God and there is this proclamation of His position as King of Kings and Lord of Lords. Is there a hint of the Trinity in this threefold revelation? At all events three is the number of the Godhead, and we have here the unknown name that speaks of what He is within Himself, known only to Himself in all His perfections; the name of the Word in the expression and manifestation of the invisible God, since He, as the Word, is the image of the invisible God (Heb. 1:3). And finally, His glorious title shows Him as the ruler over all the universe, restoring the single will of the Father where first there was that one will, challenged by the rebel, Lucifer, making two wills, and then by a fallen race in which every last son of Adam turned to his own sinful will (Isa. 53:6). But now all other wills are to be put down. The one problem of the world, how to have only one will, God's will, is to be solved. The Lord of glory will bring that will into full play and all other wills fall before it.

Verses 17–20

The Battle of Armageddon

¹⁷*And I saw a messenger, standing in the sun, and he cried with a great voice, saying to all the fowls flying in mid-Heaven, Come and be gathered together unto the great supper of God, ¹⁸that ye may eat the flesh of kings, and the flesh of captains, and the flesh of mighty men, and the flesh of horses, and of them that sit on them, and the flesh of all, free and bond, and small and great. ¹⁹And I saw the wild beast, and the kings of the earth, and their armies, gathered together to make war against Him that sat on the horse, and against His army. ²⁰And the wild beast was seized, and with him the false prophet that wrought the signs in his sight, wherewith he deceived them that had received the mark of the wild beast, and them that worshipped his image. The two were cast alive into the lake of fire that burneth with brimstone.*

(Rev. 19:17-20, Free Translation)

When our Lord was on earth the first time, He told His disciples of a great feast to which all men were bidden to come freely. Love set the table and compassion was there to serve; grace sat as host and joy poured the wine. For almost two thousand years the Lord has sent out His servants, crying the invitation to one and all, and for almost two thousand years men, for the most part, have flouted the love that invited them and despised the grace that pleaded with them. Still they bring forth the flimsy excuses of a newly-married wife, of an unseen field, of an unproven yoke of oxen. Still the carnal mind thus proves itself at enmity against God. The Lord is the God of patience, but patience will not be mocked forever. The day of wrath must come. Those who have refused the call of grace to the banquet of love must be, themselves, the victims at another great supper, where their flesh will be picked clean by the fowls of the air.

The vision is introduced by the sight of a messenger in mid-Heaven, standing in the sun, crying out with a great voice to all the birds of the earth. Only the faithless will find this beyond the power of our God. For the messenger is the messenger of God, and who can withstand His power?

The banquet of flesh to which the fowls are called is indeed a banquet of flesh. The repetition of the word flesh, occurring five times over, flesh, flesh, is very revealing. The race has walked in carnal enmity against God, living after the flesh, and now the day of His patience is at an end.

In order for us to understand the scene that now takes place we must go back through the Bible and gather together certain passages so that we may see how earth's forces are arrayed at the moment of the triumph of the Lord. For the birds of prey are summoned by the angelic messenger in anticipation of the battle of Armageddon and the judgment of the nations, both of which are now to take place. The verses that we have before us at the close of this nineteenth chapter are merely index lines to great prophecies throughout the Scriptures, and by gathering them together we can see the details of this closing moment of earth's bitterness.

Before the Antichrist and his armies and the armies of the kings of the earth are at war against the Lord from Heaven, they are at war with each other. It is His visible presence, manifest in all the world, that turns their enmity into a speedy alliance, even as it was the presence of the Lord Jesus Christ at the time of His first coming that united former enemies in the one great hatred of the carnal mind, enmity against God, for when the Lord Jesus Christ was shuttled between the rulers, we read that "the same day Pilate and Herod were made friends together: for before they were at enmity between themselves" (Luke 23:12).

The scene of the triumphant coming forth from Heaven of the Lord of Hosts and the armies of Heaven is preceded by signs and portents clearly visible on earth. From the general knowledge of the Bible that is the common lot of Christendom, that knowledge that knows vaguely that there is to be an "end of the world," or something that they call by this name, the enemies know assuredly that this time has now come. Satan, too, cast forth from Heaven, has "great wrath, for he knoweth that he hath but a short time" (Rev. 12:12). The Lord Jesus, standing before the high priest of the Jews, refused to answer the futile questions, but announced the moment that is now to take place. "Thou hast said (i.e., It is true, that I am the Son of God): nevertheless I say unto you, Hereafter ye shall see the Son of Man sitting on the right hand of power, and coming in the clouds of heaven" (Matt. 26:64). On the day of Pentecost, the Spirit, through Peter, announced the same event: "And I will show wonders in heaven above, and signs in the earth beneath; blood, and fire, and vapor of smoke; The sun shall be turned into darkness, and the moon into blood, before the great and notable day of the Lord come" (Acts 2:19, 20).

What has been happening on earth just before these signs are seen in Heaven? The Antichrist is the ruler of the revived Roman Empire, and the rise of this power is one of the central themes of the prophecy of Daniel. Over against the forces of the Antichrist will be arrayed the power of the great confederation of Northern peoples, outside the bounds of the old Roman Empire. This force is outlined in the thirty-eighth chapter of Ezekiel.

At the time of the end it would appear that the Antichrist has centered his forces in Egypt, "But tidings out of the east and out of the north shall trouble him: therefore he shall go forth with great fury to destroy, and utterly to take away many" (Dan. 11:44). He plants his headquarters in Palestine (11:45), and waits the thrust from the East and the North.

The great motorized, mechanized army (Nahum 3:2), of the North (Ezek. 38:15), a "red" army (Nahum 2:3), swings down into Palestine where the force of the Antichrist awaits the shock. The vast air forces "ascend," "come like a storm" and are "like a cloud to cover the land" (Ezek. 38:9, 16). It is not quite clear whether the Lord strikes first, or whether He uses the Antichrist to crush the armies of the North before he, himself, is crushed in turn, by the Host of the Lord, or whether the two forces unite against the Lord and are crushed together. It is possibly a combination of the latter elements. The crushing of the Northern army is described by Ezekiel, referring in part, probably, to an earlier invasion long since past and to the great invasion of the last day. "I will turn thee back, and leave but the sixth part of thee, and will cause thee to come up from the north parts, and will bring thee upon the mountains of Israel: And I will smite thy bow out of thy left hand, and will cause thine arrows to fall out of thy right hand. Thou shalt fall upon the mountains of Israel, thou, and all thy bands, and thy people that is with thee: I will give thee unto the ravenous birds of every sort, and to the beasts of the field to be devoured. Thou shalt fall upon the open field: for I have spoken it, saith the Lord God . . . And, thou son of man, . . . Speak unto every feathered fowl, and to every beast of the field, Assemble yourselves, and come; gather yourselves on every side to my sacrifice that I do sacrifice for you, even a great sacrifice upon the mountains of Israel, that ye may eat flesh, and drink blood. Ye shall eat the flesh of the mighty, and drink the blood of the princes of the earth . . . Thus shall ye be filled at my table with horses and chariots, with mighty men, and with all men of war, saith the Lord God. And I will set my glory among the nations, and all the nations shall see my judgment that I have executed, and my hand that I have laid upon them" (Ezek. 39:2-5, 17-21).

In an early psalm one of the great conversations between the members of the Trinity is recorded. If the second Psalm is written out, as a passage of Shakespeare might be presented in print, we find that there are some verses spoken by God the Father, others by God the Son, others by the God the Holy Spirit. The whole great revelation is called forth by the arrogance of men in fighting against God. The second Psalm is a divine commentary on the events that are before us in the book of Revelation. The confederation of the Antichrist with the kings of the earth and their hosts is the literal fulfillment of that which was revealed to David. "Why do the nations rage, and the people imagine a vain thing? The kings of the earth . . . take counsel together, against the Lord, and against his anointed, saying, Let us break their bands asunder, and cast away their cords from us" (Ps. 2: 1-3). The Spirit announces, "He that sitteth in the heavens shall laugh: the Lord shall have them in derision. Then shall he speak unto them in his wrath, and vex them in his sore displeasure" (Ps. 2:4, 5).

According to this prophecy, the battle of Armageddon is the laughter of God against the climax of man's arrogance. The carnal mind is enmity against God. That carnal enmity crucified Christ. That carnal enmity will dare take up arms against the visible power of God. Newspapers tell us that thirty seconds of earthquake in Rumania did more damage than months of the bombing of England. What can man's puny weapons do against God? Yet the pride of man is so blind, when pushed by the Satanic powers, that he will dare to lift up his hand against God. The Lord shall have them in derision.

In the invisible world there is a simultaneous defeat of the forces of Satan that is not recorded here. Isaiah writes of it, "And it shall come to pass in that day, that the Lord shall punish the host of the high ones that are on high, and the kings of the earth upon the earth" (Isa. 24:21). The demon forces shall come to their doom as well as the earth forces whom they have prodded to their destruction. God will bring an end to all at the same time. There can be no doubt of the fact that the powers of Satan know that they are fighting directly against God; there can be little doubt that the kings of the earth are animated with this same knowledge. The signs in Heaven can have left no doubt of the fact. The array is a matter of conscious choice. It is to be noted that the Devil, who was not able to prevail against Michael (Rev. 13:7-9), has now put this trust in the arm of flesh, seeking to defy, not Michael, but Christ. This has well been called "the incurable insanity of sin, which wars away in spite of defeat after defeat, against a holy God."

There is not the slightest mention of any struggle. In no prophecy of the Bible is the thought of struggle found. The contrary is more than intimated. It would appear that such phrases as that of the Spirit through Paul speak of an instantaneous and catastrophic end of the Antichrist, the Wicked One, "whom the Lord shall consume with the spirit of his mouth, and shall destroy with the brightness of his coming" (II Thess. 2:8).

The Antichrist is seized, and with him the false prophet. These are the second and third members of the Satanic, counterfeit trinity. The seizure of the first member of that trinity, who is evidently not present in person, will not tarry long. The two who are seized are cast alive into the lake of fire.

Two men, Enoch and Elijah, are recorded in the Scriptures as passing from earth to Heaven without dying. The Satanic two are now seen as going to the lake of fire without passing through death. The two were cast "alive" into the lake of fire. The word might well be translated, "living." We are not to imagine that this word is used in the sense in which it commonly occurs when we speak of someone being buried alive, or burned alive. When we use the word in that sense we mean that life was extinguished by earth or by fire. When the Bible uses the word it means something far different. This passage teaches that the Antichrist and the false prophet, passed in their human bodies into a continued state of conscious existence in these bodies. It is not possible to interpret this passage as teaching the annihilation of the spirits or bodies of these two.

The battle of Armageddon is over. The leaders, hellish and earthly, are judged. The Lord now proceeds to judge the nations of the earth.

Verse 21

The Judgment of the Nations

²¹*And the rest were killed with the sword of Him that sat upon the horse, the sword which went forth out of His mouth: and all the fowls were gorged with their flesh.*
(Rev. 19:21, Free Translation)

A few verses before the end of this chapter we find a definite statement that the army of earth is gathered together under "kings . . . captains . . . and mighty men . . ." (19:18). "The kings of the earth, and their armies" are "gathered together to make war" against the Lord and they are associated with the Antichrist in their wicked enterprise. We saw how God deals with the supernatural powers, and now we see how God deals with the men who remain. A perfect outline of the closing verses of chapter nineteen and the opening verses of chapter twenty is indicated back in the prophecy of Isaiah: "And it shall come to pass in that day, that the Lord shall punish the host of the high ones that are on high, and the kings of the earth upon the earth" (Isa. 24:21). In the invisible realm God has dealt with the host of the high ones that are on high, whom Paul described as principalities and powers, "the rulers of the darkness of this age . . . the spiritual host of wickedness in the Heavenlies" (Eph. 6:12, Gk.).

The visible representatives of Satan's power have been dealt with in the destruction of the wild beast and the false prophet. The human beings who were in charge of government and who led men astray, and their followers are now to be dealt with. The whole matter is compressed into the single statement, "And the rest were killed with the sword of Him that sat upon the horse; the sword which went forth out of His mouth; and all the fowls were gorged with their flesh."

The most important passage which must be brought in to expand this scene to its larger proportions is the great statement of the Lord Jesus Christ, spoken upon the Mount of Olives in His prophetic discourse at the end of His ministry. "When the Son of man shall come in his glory, and all the holy angels with him, then shall he sit upon the throne of his glory: And before him shall be gathered all nations" (Matt. 25:31, 32).

This verse very definitely dates the scene of this judgment of the nations. It is not at the coming of the Lord Jesus Christ for His believers: that is not His coming in glory. It is not the judgment scene of the Great White Throne, in Revelation 20. That scene is before the throne of God the Father. This present scene brings us to the close of the Great Tribulation period when the Heavens open and the One who is called Faithful and True comes forth clothed for judgment, and accompanied by the Host of Heaven (Rev. 19:11-16). It should be noted, further, that this is the moment that was prophesied to the overcomers of the church at Laodicea. To them it was said, "To him that overcometh will I grant to sit with me in my throne, even as I also overcame, and am set down with my Father in his throne" (Rev. 3:21).

Today the Lord Jesus Christ is still seated upon the Father's throne, completing the work of mediation. At the close of this age He rises from the Father's throne, gathers all of His own out of this world taking them to Heaven before He pours out His wrath upon the world and its enmity. Having sealed those who are to be called out in the midst of the judgment, the company of the tribulation saints, He pours out the divine wrath upon this world which was long over-ripe for judgment, and then comes forth in glory at the head of the armies of Heaven. He deals with the spiritual heads of the rebellion, and then gathers the nations before Him for a special judgment.

Some little confusion will be spared the student if he realizes that this is a judgment with respect to earth power, and with respect to the treatment of His ambassadors by these rulers of the earth. This is not the judgment of any of the rulers of the past. Wicked men of the past, from Cain on down, including all of the usurpers of power, such as Ahab, will not appear at this judgment. There is no resurrection here. This is a judgment of those living rulers who shall be on earth at the time of the great tribulation. These are the men who followed the rule of the Antichrist and they now receive their judgment, not so much as individuals but as men of power, as those to whom government has been committed at this time and who have abused it, taking it for themselves and for Satan and not wielding it for God.

There were one hundred and forty-four thousand special ambassadors of the Lord Jesus Christ who went forth at the beginning of the seven-year judgment period to preach the Gospel of the Kingdom in all the world for a witness. These were Jews, and the result of their preaching was very great. Tens of millions of people believed in their word of grace and were given to be joined to Christ for the suffering of the final hour. They are "a multitude which no man could number, of all nations, and kindreds and people, and tongues" (Rev. 7:9).

The basis of our present judgment scene is the breaking of the powers who opposed these ambassadors of Christ and who tortured those who followed their word believing in the Saviour.

It may be helpful to give the following analogy which will explain the apparent differences in the various passages of Scripture describing a single scene such as this. Suppose a blind man should go to an opera in order to hear the music. The curtain rises and a friend, seated on his left, begins to describe to him in a whisper, the scene that is before them. The friend begins with the heroine, the hero, the villain, and then proceeds on to a description of the decor and the other occupants of the scene. Another friend on the right may describe the scene to him, in a quite different way. This friend, mathematically minded, may begin at the far left and go across the scene in careful detail, ending at the extreme right. An intelligent person could take the two accounts and superimpose them. Immediately he would see that there was no discrepancy whatsoever in the two descriptions. This is the method that God has used in the Scriptures. He has done it for a double purpose. He wishes to keep the detailed knowledge of His plan from those who refuse to know Him and follow Him, and He wishes the joy of the fellowship with His children as the Holy Spirit opens the eyes of their understanding in order to fit all parts of the Word together into the full picture of the glorious whole.

Through the whole of the Bible it is possible to see how all the little pieces of prophecy fit in perfectly, giving us the whole picture of God's great plan.

The multitudes who are in the valley of decision are the nations at this time of judgment which we are studying. The valley is that of Armageddon where the scene takes place. They are not there to make a decision but to listen to one. The judge has made the decision and is about to administer it. The Supreme Court of the United States holds a public audience on Mondays in order to announce its decisions. There is no appeal from their judgment. Now the Lord Jesus Christ the Chief Justice of all the universe holds court for the nations. He renders the decision. From it there will be no appeal.

There are three classes of people at the judgment of the nations.

They are called by the Lord Jesus, "sheep," "goats" and "my brethren." Perhaps the whole picture will fall into better focus if we discuss the third of these first. The brethren of the Lord are, most certainly, the Jews. During the seven-year period from the rapture of the Church to the coming of Christ in glory, the Lord has been dealing with them in a very special way. First of all, He called out from each of the tribes twelve thousand men to be His special agents for the work that was to follow, one hundred and forty-four thousand in all. These went out, divinely equipped, to work on behalf of the Lord throughout all the world. They were variously received. Multitudes accepted their message and believed in the Lord Jesus Christ, and among these there were multitudes from all of the nations of the Gentiles. But the Lord was doing a very special work in behalf of Israel at the same time. In Revelation twelve we have the presentation of Israel as the woman who is hated of Satan and protected by God. Very definite promises are made to Israel which must be fulfilled. God said that His covenant with Israel could not be broken until first of all His covenant with the sun, the moon and the stars could be broken (Jer. 33:20, 21). There is no exaggeration whatsoever in saying that there are several hundred prophecies in the Old Testament concerning Israel which have a primary or a secondary application to the dealings of God with His people at this time of fulfillment.

The children of Israel were once God's chosen people. This implies that there is a period in which they are no longer His chosen people. That is correct. The people of Israel have been set aside for the accomplishment of God's purpose in the Church during this present age. While this purpose is being accomplished, Israel is in the period of dispersion. The matter is stated with great clarity in the first portion of the book of Hosea. The Lord called upon Hosea to take the principal part in a pageant describing the faithfulness of God and the unfaithfulness of His people. Hosea was to marry a wife of whoredoms and was to have three children by her. She was to be unfaithful to Hosea but he was to love her in spite of all, even going so far as to give gifts to her lovers that she might not be in want and ultimately coming to the place where he went into the slave market and purchased her out of her low-fallen position. No clearer picture of the love of God could be given to man.

The whole teaching revolves around the naming of the three children of this faithful husband and the unfaithful wife. The first child was called Jezreel. In the Hebrew there are two meanings for this word. If you take a handful of material and throw it from you, you may be doing one of two things. You may be casting the matter away or you may be sowing seed for planting and harvest. The Lord told Hosea to name the first child Jezreel and explains which of the meanings He had in mind when He says, "I will cause to cease the kingdom of the house of Israel" (Hos. 1:4). We are at present living in that period.

The second child was named Loruhamah, which means "unpitied" or "without mercy." God said that He would have no more mercy upon the house of Israel but He would utterly take them away (Hos. 1:6). The third child was named Lo-ammi, "not my people," "for ye are not my people and I will not be your God" (Hos. 1:9).

Today, in this twentieth century, we are living in this period. God has not cast away His people (Rom. 11:1). He has set them aside for a certain period and in that period we are now living. But the time is to come, at the end of the Great Tribulation period, at the coming of the Lord Jesus Christ in glory, when He will gather His people back into the land again, and will change His relationship to them once more. The other meaning of Jezreel is now brought to the fore. "Then shall the children of Judah and the children of Israel be gathered together . . . great shall be the day of (their planting) Jezreel" (Hos. 1:11); "I will sow her unto me in the earth" (2:23). The other names are also changed. The first verse of the second chapter of Hosea belongs, definitely, with the first chapter. "Say ye unto your brethren, Ammi; and to your sisters, Ruhamah" (Hos. 2:1). The negative "Lo" is taken from their names. They are now called "objects of mercy" or "pitied," and they are called "My people."

This change is to come to Israel through the Great Tribulation. God says, "I will allure her, and bring her into the wilderness, and speak comfortably unto her. And I will give her her vineyards from thence, and the valley of Achor [trouble] for a door of hope" (Hos. 2:14, 15).

The theme of the ninth, tenth and eleventh chapters of Romans lies in this question of the setting aside of Israel so that blessing might come to the Gentiles, and the restoration of Israel so that blessing might come upon all the world. God says of Israel, nationally, "Have they stumbled that they should fall? God forbid: but rather through their fall salvation is come unto the Gentiles, for to provoke them to jealousy. Now if the fall of them be the riches of the world [i.e., by the coming of the Gospel to all], and the diminishing of them the riches of the Gentiles (i.e., by the calling out of the body of believers into the Church); how much more their fulness? . . . For if the casting away of them [at the end of the age of law] be the reconciling of the world [Gk. *kosmos,* mankind; i.e., by the preaching of the Gospel], what shall the receiving of them be [i.e., God's receiving of them once more] but life from the dead [i.e., all millennial blessings]?" (Rom. 11:11, 12, 15).

Before the Lord Jesus Christ, at the moment when He establishes His throne upon the earth at this time of His coming in glory, are gathered these, His brethren. They have come to the day of which it is written, "And I will pour upon the house of David, and upon the inhabitants of Jerusalem, the spirit of grace and of supplications: and they shall look upon me whom they have pierced, and they shall mourn for him, as one mourneth for his only son, and shall be in bitterness for him, as one is in bitterness for his firstborn" (Zech. 12: 10). A nation shall be born in a day.

This throne of the Lord upon the earth is not only the throne of His glory, it is also, in a very special way, the throne of David. All of the passages of the Bible which speak of Messiah ruling on this throne are to be applied here. The two comings were seen by Isaiah in one view, the Babe and the King, and the throne of His power was announced. "Unto us a child is born, unto us a son is given; and the government shall be upon his shoulder . . . Of the increase of His government and peace there shall be no end, upon the throne of David, and upon his kingdom . . ." (Isa. 9:6, 7). This promise was repeated when the Lord Jesus came into this world the first time, "The Lord God shall give unto him the throne of his father David; And he shall reign over the house of Jacob for ever; and of his kingdom there shall be no end" (Luke 1:32, 33).

We now have established a most important fact. The Lord Jesus Christ as His second coming to earth, comes in glory to the earth to set up His throne, which is very definitely the throne of the redeemed, repentant, converted, restored people of Israel. The Lord Jesus gathers the nations together, not as God of all the earth, not as a rejected Saviour, but as the King of the Jews. His first act is to judge the nations on the single point of their treatment of the Jews. It is to be noted especially that this is not a judgment of the individuals as individuals but it is a judgment of nations as nations. A judgment may fall upon a nation without falling upon all of the individuals of that nation. In fact, it is even possible for a national judgment to be a personal blessing to some.

We have now seen the principal characters who stand before the throne of the glory of Christ. Those who are His brethren are brought forth as the objects of His tenderest care. There is a sense in which all believers are called His brethren in a spiritual way; indeed, He says that He is not ashamed to call us His brethren (Heb. 2:11). But there is a very special sense in which Israel stands as "the brethren." In one passage Paul cried out that he would, himself, be willing to take eternal punishment if only Israel could be saved, so great was his love for them. He lists some of their privileges, saying, "Who are Israelites; to whom pertaineth the adoption, and the glory, and the covenants, and the giving of the law, and the service of God, and the promises; Whose are the fathers, and of whom as concerning the flesh Christ came, who is over all, God blessed for ever" (Rom. 9:4, 5).

In addition to these, His brethren, there stand the nations, and they are divided into two companies called "the sheep" and "the goats."

They are divided, nationally, with respect to their treatment of Israel. We can draw an analogy from present history. It would be possible in an assembly like that of the United Nations to say: Russia, on the whole you have treated the Jews with terror throughout the centuries. Poland, what pogroms have you not committed upon My people. Germany, how have you made the name of My people to be brought low. Spain, what tortures did you not inflict upon Israel in your iniquitous Inquisition. Thus it would be possible to speak of the nations who have mistreated Israel. But it would be possible to say that, on the whole, France has treated Israel well. Britain has been kind to Israel with brief exceptions in the times of one or two evil monarchs. America has allowed herself to be a haven for Israel in the largest way possible. We can readily understand the basis of such a judgment. It is entirely with respect to the treatment of God's people Israel. And we need not be smug about it because our land has a present history of tolerance toward this people. Germany, so long as the Gospel was in the ascendant, could have been counted among the peoples of kindness to Israel. But Germany forgot God.

In short, this judgment scene does not refer *primarily* to the treatment of Israel during this present age, but to their treatment during the time when the Antichrist is reigning. The 144,000 missionaries of the cross—144,000 St. Pauls, if you will—will all be Jews. How have they been treated as they went to every corner of the world with the Gospel, preaching to every creature on the face of the earth? Evidently they have had harsh treatment in some countries and good treatment in others.

The Lord speaks first to those nations who have done well in this respect. "Then shall the King say unto them on his right hand, Come, ye blessed of my Father, inherit the Kingdom prepared for you from the foundation of the world" (Matt. 25:34). The nations themselves are astonished. They do not realize the basis of the judgment. The scene has been brought to pass with lightning suddenness. Then, when they ask for an explanation, the Lord answers that as they have treated the Jews, so they have treated Him, for they were His ambassadors. The result of the judgment is that these nations are those who are permitted to enter into the earthly Kingdom which is now set up. It is to be noted that there is no question of the salvation of all these nations. It does not say that they are all believers. They are not sent off to destruction, but are permitted to live on into the kingdom, to become the progenitors of those who shall people the earth during the Millennium for the final test. Some of them will, undoubtedly, become saved. Some of them, most certainly, as we shall later see, will be among the lost. But they are indeed blessed of the Father to be the ones chosen for such an opportunity as now lies before them.

The other nations are called the goats. They have mistreated Israel.

They have spurned the message of grace that was brought by these missionaries of the cross of Jesus Christ. They would have none of it. They took the servants of the Lord and put them to death. They gave them neither meat nor drink, and when they were in prison or sick gave them no care nor comfort. So Christ announces, "Inasmuch as ye did it not to one of the least of these [My brethren, Israel], ye did it not unto me" (Matt. 25:45).

The judgment of the nations is ended. This passage in Revelation describes the physical aspect of the judgment of the "goat" nations. "And the rest were killed with the sword of Him that sat upon the horse, the sword which went forth out of His mouth; and all the fowls were gorged with their flesh." Their bodies are thus treated. And what of their souls and spirits? Christ announced it when He was here on earth the first time: "Depart from me, ye cursed, into everlasting fire, prepared for the devil and his angels . . . And these shall go away into everlasting punishment" (Matt. 25:41, 46).

It is to be noted that these are slain by "the sword which went forth out of his mouth." This sword is, of course, the Word of God. Speaking of the wrong use of words in lying propaganda, a columnist said that not only those who took the sword would perish by the sword but that those who took the word would perish by the word. This is an interesting play upon the famous phrase of our Lord. We can be absolutely sure that those who refuse the Word and take but the word shall perish by the Word. This is the final basis of judgment. God has given us the Bible. Those who refuse it and its standards shall perish in accordance with its announced judgments.

PART XI
THE THOUSAND YEARS

CHAPTER 20

Verses 1–3

Satan Bound

¹And I saw a messenger coming down out of Heaven, having the key of the abyss, and a great chain upon his hand. ²And he laid hold on the dragon, the old serpent, which is the Devil and Satan, and bound him for a thousand years, ³And cast him into the abyss, and shut it and sealed it, that he should deceive the nations no more, till the thousand years should be finished; and after that he must be loosed for a little time.
(Rev. 20:1-3, Free Translation)

Dust has been the serpent's meat throughout all the centuries. Always he has grasped at the substance of power and has touched but the shadow. Dust! Always he has desired rule and might. He has staked all on his great rebellion, and has been unable to learn anything from his defeats. He is just as malignant and filled with enmity at the end as he was at the beginning. He had said, "I will ascend . . . I will exalt my throne . . . I will sit . . . I will ascend . . . I will be like the Most High" (Isa. 14:13, 14). But the Word of God was written in the same moment, "Yet thou shalt be brought down to Hell, to the sides of the pit."

Now, at last, it has come to pass. We read, "And I saw a messenger coming down out of Heaven, having the key of the abyss, and a great chain upon his hand. And he laid hold on the dragon, the old serpent, which is the Devil and Satan, and bound him for a thousand years." How are the mighty fallen. This is what Isaiah cries out when he is given the revelation of the plan of God. "How art thou fallen from heaven, O Lucifer, son of the morning! how art thou cut down to the ground, which didst weaken the nations!" (Isa. 14:12).

There is a divine irony in God's dealings with the enemy. He who has been the terror of the nations and the prince of the demons is now led captive by one solitary messenger. There is every evidence that there is a definite order in power and might in the ranks of the angelic beings. We can perceive, even if dimly, the gradation in the orders that God has created when we read of angels, principalities, powers, the archangel, seraphim and cherubim. We know that the angels— if we may say such a thing—the common angels, as we would speak of a common soldier, are the domestic servants of Heaven. "Are they not all ministering spirits, sent forth to minister for them who shall be heirs of salvation?" (Heb. 1:14). It is one of these simple messengers of God who now comes forth with a great chain upon his hand, and whom God uses to take hold of the mighty prince, so long swollen with pride, and bring him to his black doom. Even Michael, the archangel, the mighty power of God who represents the Lord Jehovah in all matters pertaining to the children of Israel (Dan. 12:1), has always dealt with Satan with great respect. When God buried Moses it would appear that Satan attempted to rob the grave, realizing that God must have had a special purpose in thus taking care of the body of the great servant who had dealt the power of Satan such blows. Evidently God sent Michael to take care of the matter and there was some contention between Satan and the archangel. Satan, being of the higher order of the cherubim, was superior in might and power to Michael and we read that "Michael the archangel, when contending with the devil, he disputed about the body of Moses, durst not bring against him a railing accusation, but said, The Lord rebuke thee" (Jude 9).

But now, where once the archangel Michael trod softly, a simple angel comes forth in the power of the God of the universe and lays hold of the rebel to bind him. So God could have done at any moment had it suited His purpose. But this matter of rebellion had to be fully tested. It had to be shown clearly to all the universe that no one had the power to govern apart from God. All of the government of the universe, forever and ever, will be delegated to redeemed sinners, the saints, who will know the pit from which they have been digged. Even though God should permit some saint of the church to create a world and govern it for Him, that saint will never have the thought which Satan had, namely, that he could govern without the power of God. The matter has been given a thorough trial. A simple angel now lays hold upon the one of whom it was said, "Thou sealest up the sum, full of wisdom, and perfect in beauty . . . Thou art the cherub set apart for governing . . . Thou wast perfect in thy ways from the day that thou wast created, till iniquity was found in thee" (Ezek. 28: 12, 14, 15).

A few days before this moment, Satan may have thought that all power was in his grasp and that he was about to have complete victory. All of the hosts of the fallen angels, the hosts of the demons, the Antichrist and the False Prophet, together with all the world of unregenerate men were under his complete domination. All the world wondered after his incarnation, and men worshiped the dragon (Rev.

13:3, 4). Yet a few short months and he has lost all. He is chained by a solitary angel, while his cohorts are scattered, his principal lieutenants are cast into the lake of fire, and the hearts of the redeemed are bursting with the joy and expectancy of the manifestation of Christ and the sons of God.

The time has come.

Forty and two months before this time he was cast forth from Heaven (12:9). The continuing rear guard action has been fought, and now all is lost. He goes to prison, awaiting his final doom.

There are certain characteristics of this judgment scene which need to be examined. First of all, the enemy is named by four different names, all of them indicative of different qualities or offices of the rebel. He is called the dragon. The Greek word is the translation of a Hebrew word that is used many times in the Old Testament for various monsters and a study of the twenty-seven passages in which the Hebrew word is found reveals that uncleanness and foulness was a frequent characteristic of the monster. How fitting, then, that Satan should be called "the monster." But the source of foulness is now arrested by a pure angel and all things that offend are indeed to be taken out of God's kingdom. He is called the old serpent. This refers us to the Garden of Eden and shows us that the day of dust has come for him. He is called the devil, the slanderer, the false accuser of the brethren. God, who announced that no one could lay anything to the charge of His elect, since He had justified the believer (Rom. 8:33), vindicates His Word and silences the accuser for ever. He is called Satan, the adversary, the inveterate foe of God and all that God desired. This was the one who dogged the steps of the Son of God when He was here on earth, tempting Him, working against Him, seeking to destroy Him before His time, and ultimately bringing his mad rage into the frenzied climax of the crucifixion of the Saviour. Now he is to realize that in virtue of that very death he is to go into eternal death.

In the vision of the risen Lord Jesus Christ which God gave to John on the first pages of the Apocalypse, the Lord speaks, saying, "I am he that liveth, and was dead; and, behold, I am alive for evermore, Amen; and have the keys of hell and of death" (Rev. 1:18). One commentator believes that the angel who comes to imprison Satan in the abyss must be Christ because of the possession of one of these keys. But all of us who possess keys have at times entrusted them to others for a certain use, and we need not think otherwise of this instance. But it is to be noticed that Christ's ownership of the keys is stated to be a consequence of His triumphant death. It therefore follows that Satan's imprisonment is a direct result of the crucifixion of the Lord Jesus Christ. Here, then, is the actual execution of the sentence passed upon Satan by God as one of the results of Christ's death. The sentence was pronounced when Christ finished the work which the Father had given Him to do. "Forasmuch then as the children are partakers of flesh and blood, he also himself likewise took part of the same; that through death he might destroy him that had the power of death, that is, the devil" (Heb. 2:14).

The sentence is that the destroyer must be destroyed. Some have attempted to teach from this the annihilation of the Devil. But "destruction" in the Bible never means annihilation. The Revised Version has translated it, "that through death he might bring to naught him that had the power of death." Every step in God's dealings has been toward this purpose. The enemy is being brought to naught. That he is not immediately cast into the lake of fire along with the Antichrist and the false prophet is due to the fact that God has one more use for him.

The temporary prison of Satan is "the abyss." We have already looked into it where we saw the demon hosts come forth. Now it is to put those hosts back in again, with the addition of their prince and chief. Only one commentator that we have found makes mention of the return of the hosts of Satan to their prison house, and he, correctly, we believe, says, "And the demons, who were liberated by Satan are likewise shut up in the bottomless pit, though this is not mentioned because it is self-evident."

One very important detail is to notice that the conquest of Satan and his powers does not come by any human efforts. There are some who have sought to teach that evil shall be put down through the slow spread of the truth. There is nothing of that kind here. In fact, just prior to the coming of the Lord from Heaven, truth has all but vanished from the earth. Here is fulfilled the Word of the Lord, "When the Son of Man cometh, shall he find faith on the earth?" (Luke 18:8). It is in such circumstances that the Lord comes. The enemy is not overthrown by the work of Gospel preaching, but he is put down by the lightning coming of the Lord in glory. From the apex of his might on earth he falls to the pit of the abyss in a moment, even as light always puts out darkness. It is all done suddenly.

Furthermore, the great enemy and his hosts are not only put into the pit of the abyss, but they are sealed there, and since the seal is placed there by the messenger of our Lord, we may be sure that the enemy will not come forth until he is loosed by the same power. Here is the certainty that during the thousand-year period which follows there will be no sign of Satan and his hosts at work in the world of men.

Here is a great illustration of the comparative power of Satan and God. When the Lord Jesus Christ was crucified, Satan had his minions seal the tomb in an attempt to keep the body of the Lord in the grave. But the effort was fruitless, for His soul was not left in hell nor was

His body permitted to see corruption (Acts 2:31). But when God brings Satan to his end, he and his host are put in the abyss and they are sealed within so that they may not deceive the nations any more, till the thousand years should be finished.

Here in this casual phrase there is the evidence that the deception of the nations comes from Satan. Individual sin rises from the heart of man (Matt. 15:18, 19), but national sin comes from the deception of Satan. It is definitely stated that the forces of the devil are the "world-rulers of the darkness of this world, against the spiritual hosts of wickedness in the heavenly places" (Eph. 6:12, ARV). That deception is manifest in the world today. That deception will end only when Satan is bound and sealed in the abyss.

Verses 4–6

The First Resurrection

⁴And I saw thrones and they sat upon them, and judgment was given unto them; and I saw the souls of them who had been hatcheted for the witness of Jesus, and for the Word of God, and which had not worshipped the wild beast, neither his image, neither had received his mark upon their foreheads, or in their hands; and they lived again, and reigned with Christ the thousand years. ⁵But the rest of the dead lived not again until the thousand years should be finished. This is the first resurrection. ⁶Blessed and holy is he that hath part in the first resurrection; over such the second death hath no authority, but they shall be priests of God and of Christ, and shall reign with Him the thousand years.
(Rev. 20:4-6, Free Translation)

We now return to a detailed examination of the phrases which speak of the resurrection of the believers of various ages. In addition to the translation of these verses it might be well to give a paraphrase, beginning with verse four. And I saw thrones and they, the true believers of the Old and New Testament ages, who had already been with Christ for seven years, sat upon them. And, in addition to these, I saw the souls of the tribulation saints, the ones who were beheaded for the witness of Jesus, and for the Word of God, and which had not worshiped the Antichrist, neither his image, neither had received his mark upon their foreheads, or in their hands, and they were resurrected, and participated with Christ in the reign of the thousand years. But the rest of the dead, the unsaved multitudes from Cain on down through the ages, were not raised from the dead at this time. They are not raised until the thousand years are finished. This, of which we have spoken above, concerning the believers of all ages, is the first resurrection. Blessed and holy is he that hath part in the first resurrection:

on such the second death hath no power, but they shall be priests of God and of Christ, and shall partake with Him of the glory of His thousand-year triumph.

There is, first of all, a retrospect covering the resurrection of all who are the elect of God up to this time. The bodies of the Old Testament saints went back to dust, even as the bodies of the New Testament saints, and the bodies of the Tribulation saints. While all bodies are thus accounted for, the abode of the souls and spirits, while waiting for the day of resurrection, has been the subject of much confusion on the part of Bible readers throughout the years. The major cause of this confusion comes from the failure to realize that Hell, the English for the Hebrew Sheol and the Greek Hades, was divided into two compartments, one for the saved and one for the lost, and that between the two there was a great gulf fixed (Luke 16:22-26). Just as there is both desert and plain in Africa, so there was (note the past tense) both Paradise and Torment in Hell. Every person in the world (except Enoch and Elijah), up to the moment that Christ died, went to Hell. The believers went to Paradise in Hell and the unbelievers went to Torment in Hell. When Jesus Christ died on the cross, He told the believing thief that he would be in Paradise with Him on that very day (Luke 23:43).

We do not even take the trouble to explode the ridiculous assertion of some who believe in "soul-sleeping" that Christ said to the thief: I am talking to you today, not yesterday or tomorrow; I say unto thee today, thou shalt be with Me in Paradise (sometime). Such a translation is preposterous. Very clearly the original says, Thou shalt be with Me in Paradise today. So Christ, when He died, descended into Hell as the Apostles' Creed rightly states, but it was to Paradise in Hell. On the day of Pentecost, Peter quoted the Old Testament prophecies to the effect that Christ, though He would surely go to Hell (Paradise), would not remain there: "Thou wilt not leave my soul in hell, neither wilt thou suffer thine Holy One to see corruption" (Acts 2:25-31). Here was a double prophecy which concerned both the spirit and soul of Christ on the one hand and His body on the other.

When He ascended on High (Eph. 4:8) He emptied Hell of Paradise and took it straight to the presence of God. Captivity was taken captive. A first sheaf of the believing dead was given resurrection bodies (Matt. 27:52, 53) and the souls and spirits of all the Old Testament saints were taken to Heaven. From that moment onward there was to be no separation whatsoever for those who believe in Christ. The gates of Hell would nevermore prevail against any believer (Matt. 16:18). Satan might win many a victory on earth over believers, and Satan surely has prevailed in many a place (Galatia, Ephesus, Philippi, Colosse!!), but the individual believer will never know any further separation from Christ. Death can no longer separate us from Him (Rom. 8:38). "To be absent from the body is to be present with the Lord" (II Cor. 5:8); "to depart is to be with Christ which is far better" (Phil. 1:23).

There are two things said about the resurrection which should be carefully compared the one with the other. In the great passage in Thessalonians which speaks of the coming of the Lord for His own we find that it says, "Them also which sleep in Jesus will God *bring with* Him"; and also that "the dead in Christ shall *rise* first" (I Thess. 4:14, 16). It is evident that the first refers to the souls and spirits of the believers which are brought from Heaven with the coming Lord and that the second refers to the bodies of the believers which rise out of the earth.

At the same time there is a great transformation which takes place in the bodies of the believers which are living on the earth at the moment of His appearing for His own. We shall not all sleep, but we shall all be changed . . . the dead shall be raised incorruptible and we shall be changed (I Cor. 15:52, 53). The change consists in the transformation of the body of our humiliation so that it is made like to the glorified body which the Lord Jesus Himself had after His own resurrection (Phil. 3:21).

It must be especially emphasized that our phrase in the Apocalypse covering this resurrection is a retrospect that looks back over all three phases of it. A man on Thanksgiving day may say, with great satisfaction, "All of the harvest is gathered in." That harvest may have included a few handfuls gathered on the first day, then after a long interruption due to a rainstorm, for example, the major part of the harvest may have been gathered, and then after another momentary interruption, the final sheaves are garnered.

The phrase "this is the first resurrection" covers three distinct phases. Our Lord taught us, when He Himself read the Scriptures, that we must be very careful to stop in the right places. Thus when He read what is now the sixty-first chapter of Isaiah He stopped at a point where there is now a comma, and where there is most definitely a continuation. He refused to read the continuation, but rolled up the scroll, gave it to the priest, sat down in the place of teaching and said, "This day is this scripture fulfilled in your ears" (Luke 4:21). We often find thousands of years in a comma in the running narrative of the Scriptures. In no place is it more marked than in the passage covering the resurrection in Paul's first epistle to the Corinthians. "For as in Adam all die [4,000 or 6,000 years in this comma!], so in Christ shall all be made alive. But every man in his own order: Christ, the firstfruits [at least 1,900 years in this comma], afterward they that are Christ's at His coming [and this divided in two parts separated by the period of Antichrist's final rebellion]. Then [and there is a thousand years between the two] cometh the end" (I Cor. 15:22-24). That which is seen in Corinthians in one great prophetic sweep covering all of the order of the resurrection is now seen in retrospect covering the phases of the resurrection of the believers.

Some have declared that all of this is read into the Scriptures, and that it is not really there at all. They must make such a claim in order to bolster up their false theory of a general resurrection and judgment at which everyone from Adam to the last man is supposed to appear in one moment. But the Scriptures will not warrant any such mixing of the saved and the lost. Paul tells us that "the dead *in Christ* shall rise first" (I Thess. 4:16). There is no word about the dead out of Christ, the lost dead, the spiritually dead. And here in the Apocalypse after describing the resurrection of the justified ones, we are specifically told, "The rest of the dead lived not again until the thousand years were finished" (Rev. 20:5). Furthermore, in the great passage which describes the judgment of the believers we are specifically told that there are only two classes of people at the judgment and that both are saved. One group of believers is saved *plus* a reward and the other group is saved, but *minus* the reward. Any believer at this judgment who finds his works burned away is nevertheless told that "he shall suffer loss; but he himself shall be saved, yet so as by fire" (I Cor. 3:15). Christ also promised rewards to be given "at the resurrection of the just" (Luke 14:14). This, all together, proves beyond question that the resurrection cannot be spoken of as a general resurrection of all souls at a given time. "The Lord shall judge the quick and the dead at His appearing and His kingdom" (II Tim. 4:1), the living at His appearing and the dead at the end of His kingdom. There are two definite resurrections.

One other passage remains to be treated. The Lord Jesus said, "Marvel not at this: for the hour is coming, in the which all that are in the graves shall hear his voice, And shall come forth; they that have done good, unto the resurrection of life; and they that have done evil, unto the resurrection of condemnation" (John 5:28, 29). There could never have been any difficulty about verse 29 if some had not wanted to stress to the utmost the fact the Lord said that in the judgment *hour* all that are in the graves shall hear His voice. To attempt to force all resurrection into one moment because of this use of the word *hour* is to ignore that such words are frequently used in a sense covering a whole period of time. (See Luke 22:53; Matt. 24:36, 42; John 4:21, 23, and esp. John 5:25).

The fourth verse of our chapter is especially revealing in its division of the saints into two groups. The first phrase sees thrones and believers to whom is committed judgment sitting upon the thrones. There is a feeling of entering upon something that has already been established. Indeed we recall in the opening of the fourth chapter that there were four and twenty thrones for the four and twenty elders, typical of the twelve tribes of Israel and the twelve Apostles (Rev. 4:4). Here, too, is the fulfillment of the statement given in connection with the command given the believers against going to law with one another. "Do ye not know that the saints shall judge the world?" (I Cor. 6:2).

But there is also a special vindication for the saints of the tribulation period. These are the ones who have been under the lash of the Antichrist, bearing the hatred that began in the enmity which was put between Christ and Satan and the seeds of the two. Now comes their vindication. By faith they had sung it early in their time of trial. "They sung a new song, saying, Thou art worthy to take the book, and to open the seals thereof; for thou wast slain, and hast redeemed us to God by thy blood out of every kindred, and tongue, and people, and nation; And hast made us unto our God kings and priests; and we shall reign on the earth" (Rev. 5:9, 10). In their great worship they had cried out, "And we shall reign on the earth." Here was the scene of Satan's government and early rebellion. Here has been the theater of trial throughout the ages. Here was the scene of our Lord's humiliation, and here has He been humiliated in the person of His saints for centuries. But the cry of faith goes up at the very time it seems Satan is nearest His triumph, "We shall reign on the earth." And now, after Armageddon is over, after Satan is bound for the thousand years, we see the fulfillment. These very ones who were beheaded for the witness of Jesus—the Greek word is that they were *hatcheted*—are the ones who live and reign with Christ.

So all of the believers from righteous Abel down through the very last of the saints of God in the tribulation period will share in the triumph of the Son of God. His is the victory, won at Calvary, but He shares it with all of His redeemed ones. Now comes the proof of that which multitudes have breathed in the midst of earth's trials. "I reckon that the sufferings of this present time are not worthy to be compared with the glory which shall be revealed in us" (Rom. 8:18). Of what matter is the suffering of today? It is for His sake and in His name. Christ's sufferings for sin were completed at Calvary. Christ's suffering for righteousness' sake remains incomplete to this day. It is a suffering which we share with Him. Paul rejoiced in his share of it, filling up, or completing, that which was lacking in the afflictions of Christ (Col. 1:24). The body must not expect better treatment than that which the Head received. But our light affliction is for a moment only, and it worketh for us a far more exceeding and eternal weight of glory (II Cor. 4:17).

> *The saints their watch are keeping,*
> *Their cry goes up, "How long?"*

> *And soon the night of weeping*
> *Shall be the morn of song.*

They lived and reigned with Christ. That is the climax of glory.

The saints are called "blessed" and "holy." The reason for these two titles goes back to the grace of God. We are blessed because we have been saved; we have been the object of God's love and mercy. We, at the first resurrection, enter into the fullness of all the promises made in the many beatitudes throughout the whole of the Word of God. Our delight will then be all in the Word of God. We shall be like planted trees. We shall be blessed. Our distinguishing mark in the midst of this world at the present day is that we are "meek." That is to say, we do not trust in anything of our own for our salvation. We do not glory in man. We have despised and rejected any hope that is in ourselves and have clung to Christ alone, though He is the despised and rejected of men. Thus we have become the meek who shall inherit the earth, and thus are we blessed. It would be possible to carry on through every one of the beatitudes and show that at the first resurrection we shall enter into the fulfillment of that which we now see by faith alone.

Furthermore, we shall be holy. The word "saints" means "the holy ones." But our holiness today is a position that is ours in Christ. Looked upon in ourselves we can lay no claim to holiness as the Word of God defines it. At the very best we are unprofitable servants (Luke 17:10). But the day shall come when "we shall be like Him" (I John 3:2). Then shall we be, at last, truly holy. That for which we have sighed and cried will be ours in completeness, and there shall be no more of the old nature left within us. Its roots will have been taken out for ever and there shall be nothing left within us but the divine nature of which we have already been made partakers (II Pet. 1:4).

Because we are both blessed and holy the second death has no power over us. There are several different words in the Greek which are rendered in our translations by the one English word "power." There is *dunamis* from which we get our words "dynamo," "dynamite," "dynamic." This power is that of great force. There is another word which is very similar to our word "energy." Still another word, *kratos,* gives us the power of ruling, as in our combined words, democrat, aristocrat, autocrat. But there is still another word *exousia* which is translated "power" in such verses as John 1:12, "power to become the sons of God," which might well be translated "authority." This is the word that is used in our text. The second death has no authority whatsoever over those who are the blessed and holy ones through the work of Christ. The judgment of the Great White Throne cannot touch the believers. They have already been told by Christ that they shall not come into condemnation or judgment, but are passed out of

death and into life (John 5:24). Put together, this means that the
believer shall never come into any judgment of condemnation, any
judgment that might endanger his eternal state.

The passage closes with a repetition of the phrase used a few verses
previously. The blessed and holy ones shall reign with Him a thousand
years. Whenever God takes the trouble to repeat something there is
a purpose in it. This repetition is for emphasis of the literal fact that
we shall reign with Christ. On the whole Christians have been last
and not first in earthly affairs throughout the ages. Now there is to be
vindication. The world has hated us because of the great truth of our
election by Christ (John 15:19). When we have claimed that we are
the children of God but that the majority of the world's citizens were
not such children, but were lost souls, the world has laughed at us
and has not known us because it has not known Christ (I John 3:1).
But, even now, we *are* the sons of God and it doth not yet appear
what we shall be. But at the first resurrection it shall appear what
we shall be. We shall be like Christ. We shall be like Him not only
in His attributes of love and holiness, but in His power.

Here we begin to see what God has gained out of the whole trial
of earth history. Man, made a little lower than the angels, is raised
through the redemptive death of the Lord who also was willing to be
made lower than the angels (Heb. 2:7, 9), to a higher position. In
salvation we are not lifted back to the level from which Adam fell,
but higher. We are not lifted to the level of the angels, but higher.
We are not lifted to the eminence from which Lucifer fell, but higher.
We are lifted above all the principalites and powers to the very throne
of Heaven. Now is fulfilled the promise made in the days of the
Church, "To him that overcometh will I grant to sit with me in my
throne even as I also overcame and am set down with my Father
in his throne" (Rev. 3:21).

And still it does not yet appear what we will be, for our reigning
with Christ on earth during the time of His vindication and triumph
is but a prelude to that never-ending eternity when we shall be the instruments of God's government and reign over the universe with our
Lord. As A. B. Simpson once put it, "As I look into the destiny of
the saints I do not put it beyond God that someday He may permit
us to create a world and govern it for Him." Certainly there is more
in the future than we dream.

Verses 7–10

The End of Patience

*⁷And when the thousand years are expired, Satan shall be loosed
out of his prison, ⁸And shall go out to deceive the nations which are*

in the four quarters of the earth, Gog and Magog, to gather them together to battle: the number of whom is as the sand of the sea. ⁹And they went up on the breadth of the earth, and compassed the camp of the saints about, and the beloved city; and fire came down from God out of heaven, and devoured them. ¹⁰And the devil that deceived them was cast into the lake of fire and brimstone, where the beast and the false prophet are, and shall be tormented day and night for ever and ever.

(Rev. 20:7-10, Free Translation)

The final test is over. The thousand years come to an end. The events which now transpire are recorded with a grim factualness which will allow small elaboration. It should be understood, also, that having spent a great deal of thought and consideration on the course and meaning of the thousand years, the final statements of the end must be taken as simple though stupendous happenings that need no further explanation. It may be likened to a great combat in which a noble knight through many phases of battle confronted his opponent at every step, wounding him repeatedly. When the last stroke had been given the only way to describe the end would be that the opponent died. So it is here.

Now Satan is loosed out of his prison. He goes forth to deceive the nations which are spread over all the earth. A thousand years of confinement in the abyss has not changed him. There is not, so far as we know, another line in the Bible to add to our knowledge of this event. That in itself is extraordinary. We do not know what form this deception will take. It is to be doubted that Satan has any new devices, that he can bring forth any deceptive tricks that he has not tried over and over again, so we may be allowed to conclude that there is, once more, a frank offer of freedom from the restraints of God against which the natural heart is at such enmity (Rom. 8:7) and which must have become exceeding irksome during the thousand years. All that he does today is organized on "the principles of force, greed, selfishness, ambition, and sinful pleasure." We need expect nothing new.

The deception of the nations possibly consists in the wild hope that flames through the minds of men that the splendid, resistless sovereign, under whose light they have been living for the thousand years, is capable of being overthrown by their united attack. At all events we see that they take what they may think is only a gambler's chance, but which is no chance at all.

The nations are called "Gog and Magog." Who are these beings? We must eliminate any correspondence between this Gog and the man of that name in the line of Reuben (I Chron. 5:4). But we must look at the character who is mentioned nine times in the thirty-eighth and thirty-ninth chapter of Ezekiel. In like manner, Magog's identity may not be too closely linked with that of the grandson of Noah (Gen. 10:2), though there may be some connection here that has been lost to history. We must turn to the Magog mentioned twice along with Gog in these same chapters of Ezekiel.

We do not think that the portion of Dr. Scofield's note which would make Gog the prince and Magog the land will stand the test of careful scrutiny after reading the chapters. The phrase "the land of Magog" no more means that Magog is land than the phrase "the land of Hitler" would mean that Hitler was the land. We believe that both Gog and Magog must be looked upon as personalities, whether human or of the spirit realm remains to be seen. Adopting the translation of the Revised Versions we find that the lamentation in Ezekiel is against Gog, the land of Magog, Rosh, Meshech and Tubal.

Gog and Magog in Ezekiel clearly refer to personages who are active a thousand years before this scene in the Apocalypse. There can be no doubt whatsoever that the great struggle in which they are involved in the Old Testament prophecy is that which leads up to the battle of Armageddon. This is clearly indicated by the statements that after the destruction of the armies of these leaders, "The house of Israel shall know that I am the Lord their God from that day and forward" (Ezek. 39:22). The thousand years most certainly follow the incidents concerning Gog and Magog in Ezekiel's prophecy.

But we also see, in Ezekiel, that Gog and all his multitude is buried (Ezek. 39:11) at the time he is destroyed. This would give clear indication that there is a human being involved. But we believe that there is more than this. Not from speculation but from legitimate inference we can discern one or two other details. In Ezekiel we have two beings, Gog and Magog, who are leaders in the revolt against God and His people. They come under the wrath of God and their forces are destroyed. But a thousand years later, in the end of the final test of man, we find Satan loosed from his prison and somehow involved with characters with these same names. We believe, therefore, that just as Satan entered into Judas (John 13:27), whether personally or through one of his mighty principalities and powers we do not know, and as Satan clothed the human being called the wild beast, with his power, his throne, and great authority (Rev. 13:2), thus making him the Antichrist, so Satan possesses some princeling, perhaps named Gog, through one of his mighty angels who own his sway. A more striking example may be found elsewhere in Ezekiel where we see a being who is clearly a man, the prince of Tyre, leading us on to a description of another being, the king of Tyre, who is clearly Satan.

That, then, which has satisfied our minds in this matter, is that some of Satan's mighty angels, principalities, or powers which rule the darkness of this world (Eph. 6:12), take hold of earth dictators, use them for their ends, and are defeated by God at the great conflict of the destruction at Armageddon. The human instrumentalities are destroyed, but the demon forces live on, held back by the power of God until Satan is released after the thousand years. Whereupon they seize again some willing earthling and seek to lead the peoples against God in their final rebellion.

It is a frightful commentary upon the nature of mankind that this showy rebellion is able to muster millions and millions of followers who gladly join in a last desperate effort to strike at God. Truly the carnal mind is *enmity* against God. The number is as the sands of the sea.

The goal of their enmity is the nearest thing to them that represents God. They cannot, of course, reach the throne of Heaven to fight against the Creator, the Most High God, possessor of Heaven and earth. They cannot reach the lower heavens where the cherubim and the hosts of holy angels are now united forever in faithfulness to God. They cannot reach the Lord Jesus Christ who is ruling earth from above. So they do the one thing that is in their power. They surround the camp of the saints and the beloved city. The camp of the saints is a phrase that covers the headquarters of the believers who are aiding the Lord in His government of the earth. The hosts of men make war on these saints. He had promised that Israel should be restored to human government, and throughout the thousand years He had been governing the earth by means of a righteous human government composed of the children of Israel and centered at Jerusalem, fulfilling all of the scores of promises to that effect throughout the Old Testament. The hosts of natural men invest that city, symbol of the government of God, to make war upon these representatives of God.

The day of God's patience is over. Earth is to see its last iniquity. God will not temporize with them any longer. The biblical account is terse and terrible in its simplicity. Fire came down out of Heaven and devoured them. That is the end of rebellion in this universe. Now, in one climactic judgment the God of patience and grace shows Himself to be the God of power. He destroys all of sin's outbreak forever. No other rebellion shall ever crop out in the universe.

Someone may ask why God did not thus act when Satan first rebelled. A careful, and continued reading of the whole Bible gives us the definite answer. God has all power and has always had all power. He was neither astonished or nonplussed when Satan rebelled. He had known it would happen. He could have destroyed him with a word. But if He had done so, every other angelic spirit which He created anywhere near His own throne in magnificence and wisdom would have, ultimately, formed the idea of ruling independently of the unseen, invisible God, who is Spirit. So God took the other alternative. He allowed Satan's rebellion to run the full gamut of its experiment.

Out of the fall of man and the redemption in Christ God has raised a race of saints whom He has lifted—not to the level of unfallen Adam —not to the level of the angels—not to the level of the cherubs—not to the level of Lucifer, the anointed cherub—but to the very throne of Heaven. A great company has been redeemed. They have received God's own righteousness and will be associated with Him in fellowship forever, for truly our fellowship is with the Father and with His Son Jesus Christ (I John 1:3). This is the company of the overcomers, who have overcome by the blood of the Lamb and by the Word of their testimony (Rev. 12:11). To them were all the promises made, and recorded in the letters to the seven churches. Never, never in all eternity will the thought possess any heart that it can act independently of God. Though seated on the very throne of the reigning Christ (3: 21) they will have no desire for a glory apart from His. A race of re- deemed ones, a bride in truth, will govern the universe for God, with all power derived from Him and all glory going to Him. The little moment called "time" which lies between the eternity past before there were two wills, and the eternity future which runs on forever from this moment when the one will is firmly reestablished forever, will, as seen from eternity, take on its proportions of brevity in the whole plan of God. Also it will appear as that point of light which saw the incarnation of God in Christ and the redemption of the in- numerable company of brethren whom He has brought to glory through His sufferings (Heb. 2:10).

Satan's doom is now come. He is cast into the lake of fire and brimstone, where the wild beast and the false prophet are, and he shall be tormented day and night forever and ever. This passage must be read in its naked simplicity. No comment can enhance its literalness. It is stark fact. The thousand years in the abyss have wrought no change in the devil. He is not in the slightest melted toward the righteousness of God. He is quick and eager to show his enmity against God, and his doom is sure.

At all events the doctrine of conscious, eternal torment for impeni- tent men is clearly revealed in the Word of God. Whether we can defend it on philosophic grounds or not, it is our business to believe it; and leave it to the clearer light of eternity to explain what we cannot now understand, realizing that God has infinitely wise reasons for doing things for which we in our ignorance can see no sufficient reason at all. It is the most ludicrous conceit for beings so limited and foolish as the wisest of men are, to attempt to dogmatize how a God of infinite wisdom must act. All we know as to how God will act is what God has seen fit to tell us.

Verses 11–15

The Final Judgment

¹¹And I saw a great white throne, and Him that sat on it, from whose face the earth and the heaven fled away; and there was found no place for them. ¹²And I saw the dead, small and great, stand before God; and the books were opened: and another book was opened, which is the book of life: and the dead were judged out of those things which were written in the books, according to their works. ¹³And the sea gave up the dead which were in it; and death and hell delivered up the dead which were in them: and they were judged every man according to their works. ¹⁴And death and hell were cast into the lake of fire. This is the second death. ¹⁵And whosoever was not found written in the book of life was cast into the lake of fire.
(Rev. 20:11-15, Free Translation)

The great moment has come. Time is to end and eternity, the new eternity is to begin. There remains but the settling of accounts against all evil on earth. God has dealt with the leading rebel, the prince of this world. Now he deals with the world and its inhabitants.

The scene takes place in Heaven—that is, in the Heaven of God's throne. John sees a great white throne and the Lord God who sits upon it. This is undoubtedly the Lord God, Jesus Christ, since He has told us that the Father has "given him authority to execute judgment also, because he is the Son of man" (John 5:27). But very probably it is all three of the Godhead. This is the scene of the "resurrection of condemnation" (John 5:29), which He warned His enemies would surely come. The judgment of the believers, of course, has long since taken place, for when this judgment of the great white throne takes place we shall already have been with the Lord Jesus for more than a thousand years. A believer was once asked if he would not be afraid to stand before the great white throne. He answered with real knowledge of the Word, that he did not know for sure whether he would be present at the judgment of the great white throne, but that he was absolutely certain that if he were there he would be on the throne as the bride of the Judge and not before it for condemnation. Only one group will be seen at this judgment, the dead—the spiritually dead.

Before we proceed to the judgment itself, however, we must note that this earth and its immediate heavens disappear. Many of the commentators of the Reformation time and after have imagined that the earth on which we now are is merely "purified" by fire. But the Bible will not leave place for any such theory. A "new heaven and a new earth" are to be created, "and the former shall not be remembered, nor come into mind" (Isa. 65:17). The Lord Jesus declared with final simplicity, "Heaven and earth shall pass away" (Matt. 24:35). During the day of the Lord, Peter tells us, "the heavens shall pass away with a great noise, and the elements shall melt with fervent heat, the earth also and the works that are therein shall be burned up . . . all these things shall be dissolved . . . the day of God, wherein the heavens being on fire shall be dissolved, and the elements shall melt with fervent heat . . ." (II Pet. 3:10-12). The writer of the epistle to the Hebrews says, "Thou, Lord, in the beginning hast laid the foundation of the earth; and the heavens are the works of thine hands: They shall perish; but thou remainest; and they shall all wax old as doth a garment; And as a vesture shalt thou fold them up, and they shall be changed . . ." (Heb. 1:10-12). Further in this same epistle we read, "Yet once more I shake not the earth only, but also heaven. And this word, Yet once more, signifieth the removing of those things that are made, that those things which cannot be shaken may remain" (Heb. 12:26, 27). Back in the Old Testament there is one more passage that belongs with this same teaching. "And all the host of heaven shall be dissolved, and the heavens shall be rolled together as a scroll: and all their host shall fall down, as the leaf falleth off from the vine, and as a falling fig from the fig tree" (Isa. 34:4). All of these passages show us that there is to be an end of the material heavens and earth which we know. It is not that they are to be purified and rehabilitated, but that the reverse of creation is to take place. They are to be un-created. As they came from nothing at the word of God, they are to be sucked back into nothingness by this same word of God. Science may say that matter cannot be made and that matter cannot be destroyed, but such an attitude does not believe in the God of creation. Once we truly believe in *creation* we shall have no difficulty in believing that God is able to put the process into reverse. Matter is dissolved, folded up, perishes. "The things which are seen are temporal" (II Cor. 4:18).

The unsaved man may tremble at the thought of having no earth to stand on, but that is but a symbol that there will be no support for him whatsoever. He appears before the throne of God, not for a trial, for the trial is over. He comes to be sentenced and plunged to his doom. The throne is called the great white throne. This is to be distinguished from all other aspects of the throne of God, no matter in what part of the Bible they may be described. This is something new, different. It has been well summarized as follows: "Weigh each word. *Great*—it is the Infinite before whom the finite must stand; *White*—it is the unveiled, undimmed blaze of the divine holiness and purity and justice; *Throne*—it is majesty unlimited, in which inheres utter right to dispose of the destiny of creatures. Before such a throne, creatures cannot stand; but they *shall stand*—even the lost!"

And now there comes the word that rings through the rest of this scene like the muffled tolling of a bell. Again and again the word appears, "the dead," "the dead," "the dead," "the dead," coupled with the similar word "death," "death." There are two reasons, one positive and the other negative, why we may be sure that only lost souls are before this throne of judgment. The positive reason is that our Lord Jesus Christ said in definite terms that those who believed on Him should not come into judgment—condemnation (John 5:24). "He that believeth is not condemned" (John 3:18). The second death has no power, no authority, no jurisdiction over the believer who is raised from the dead at the resurrection of the believers (Rev. 20:6). The negative reason includes the deduction from all of these passages, that the unbeliever shall come into condemnation, is condemned already, and that the second death does have jurisdiction over him.

Back in the garden of Eden, God had said to Adam, "In the day that thou eatest thereof, thou shalt surely die" (Gen. 2:17). Satan gave the lie to God and said to the woman, "Ye shall not surely die" (Gen. 3:4). But death did pass upon all the race (Rom. 5:12), and now the moment of the condemnation comes upon those who died in Adam and who were never made alive in Christ. This is the moment of their resurrection, for verse five tells us that they were to be raised at the close of the thousand years, and now that time has passed and the hour of the condemnation has come.

All are there, small and great. God is no respecter of persons, and the fact that some men have been kings or emperors, the fact that they have commanded armies and ruled peoples will not hold any comfort for them in this hour. The fact that some have been preachers and prophets will not avail anything. Some undoubtedly were in amazement when they were plunged from religious work to Hell upon their death, and the echo of their cry has been sent back to us through Christ, "Lord, Lord, have we not prophesied in thy name? and in thy name have cast out demons? and in thy name done many wonderful works?" (Matt. 7:22). And the answer of the Lord is definite, "I never knew you; depart from me, ye that work iniquity" (Matt. 7:23). Thus the great unbelievers meet their doom. The fact that others of the dead were insignificant in their places in this world will not avail anymore than the greatness of the mighty availed for them. No one can get by God on the ground that his life was not important. God placed every man in the circumstances in which his life was lived. A farmer like Job, unknown to human history, is shown by the Word of God to have gained much honor and glory for His Lord by his faithfulness to his creator. So those who have not been known to history, but who lived for self or Satan will come to their doom at last.

The announcement of the basis of judgment is enough to strike terror into the soul of any unbeliever. If God had announced that the basis of judgment was their acceptance or rejection of His Christ, there might be many recriminations, and some might even hold an argument against the justice of God. For some did not have the chance to hear, and some had their minds warped by false education. A thousand and one arguments might be brought up if God had announced that the judgment of the lost would be on the standard of salvation in Christ. But he does not do this. He opens books and men are judged according to their own standards. It is demonstrated that on the low level of their own knowledge and their own standards, no man has ever lived up to the light that he has had. The only objection seems to be that of religious leaders who make an appeal to their good works, especially their religious works, but they are told to depart, that the Lord had never known them (Matt. 7:22, 23). All the secrets of men will be made known (Rom. 2:16).

It is to be noted that "books" is a plural form. There is more than one set of books kept in Heaven. There are at least two records in Heaven concerning the believers in the Lord Jesus Christ. There is one which is the roll of the elect, chosen in Christ before the foundation of the world, and this is called "the Lamb's book of life" (Rev. 21:27) or simply, "the book of life" (Phil. 4:3; Rev. 13:8, etc.). The Lord spoke of this book to His disciples when He told them that they were to rejoice that their names were written in Heaven (Luke 10:20). There is another book concerning the believers which is the record of all of their thoughts and meditations concerning their Lord. We read of this in the beautiful passage in Malachi, "Then they that feared the Lord spake often one to another; and the Lord hearkened, and heard it, and a book of remembrance was written before him for them that feared the Lord, and that thought upon his name" (Mal. 3:16). It is very possible that this book contains the difference between those who are saved plus the reward of a crown and those who are saved so as by fire with all of their works burned away (I Cor. 3:14, 15).

In our passage it is also evident that there are books which concern the unsaved, though one writer, at least, sees the "Book" to be the Book of the Bible. The easiest to describe is the Book of the records of the life and works of the unsaved. Here we read in no uncertain terms that the deeds of the unbelievers are recorded in Heaven. How this is done we do not claim to know or venture to guess. It is hidden in God, but there should be no difficulty in believing this when man himself is able to record great symphonies and speeches on tape and reduce whole libraries to microfilm. The fact is there, God states it. The unbeliever may scoff at it, but he will be judged by it. Then there is another book which definitely concerns the unbeliever and which is called, also "the book of life," though it is evidently very different from "the Lamb's book of life." The names of the unbelievers are in this book, but are blotted out of the book. This is evident from a study of certain passages of the Scriptures. It would seem that there is a book, something like a census record, in which the names of every individual to whom physical life is given are recorded, and that these names are blotted out of the book, leaving, at the end, a check-list which would be identical with the list in the book of the elect, chosen in Christ before the foundation of the world. We have already seen (3:5) that one of the promises made to the born-again ones, for who is the overcomer but he that believeth that Jesus is the Son of God (I John 5:4, 5), is that their names shall never be blotted out of the book of life. This would indicate that some names are blotted out, and since the names of the elect cannot be blotted out, it must be that the names of the lost are in that particular book, along with the saved, and that the names of the lost are blotted out. This would be further indicated by the statement in the last paragraph of the Bible (Rev. 22:19) that the names of those who subtract anything from the whole of God's revelation in the Scriptures shall be subtracted from the book of life. There are two books, one the census record of all, from which the names of the lost are blotted, and the Lamb's book of life in which the names of the righteous, the elect, are written.

On the phrase "and the sea gave up the dead that were in it," most commentators have confined themselves to some simple statement such as the fact that those drowned at sea are no different from those dying in any other manner. Milligan thinks that the sea means "the sea of the troubled and sinful world." Very many commentators pass the phrase by without reference as though the meaning were on the surface and not in the depths of the sea! There are two possibilities that must be considered. The sea, in Scripture, often signifies the Gentile nations (e.g., Dan. 7:3, etc.). We know that all Israel is saved before the thousand years (Rom. 11:26), so that all the unsaved in the millennial kingdom shall be among the nations. May this have reference to the fact and mean that the remaining lost from the earth which has just been dissolved pour their number along with the dead of all other ages? The other possibility is mentioned by Pember who points out that the Lord rebuked demon forces that had agitated the sea (Matt. 8:26), and that the demons who took refuge for a moment in the swine rushed into the sea (Matt. 8:30), and he wonders if there may not be some reference here to the judgment of the vast numbers of demons, whom he links in his argument with the disembodied spirits of the earth's first inhabitants who followed Lucifer in his fall, as being markedly different from the angels who fell with Satan. At all events we are sure that there is more than the mere yielding of the bodies of those who have died at sea. For there are multitudes of born-again ones who have been buried at sea, and they shall have risen long ere this passage finds fulfillment.

The fact that death and Hades are bracketed together, yielding up their dead is also significant. We know from our Lord's teaching in the story (not parable) of the rich man and Lazarus, that the spirits of the lost are conscious in the torment of Hades, while we know from many passages of Scriptures that their bodies have gone back to the dust of the earth, even as God announced after the entrance of sin (Gen. 3:19). To say that death and Hades are to yield their dead is to announce that the bodies and the spirits of the lost will be united in a resurrection body. The resurrection of Christ guaranteed that *all* should be made alive (I Cor. 15:22). In successive scenes we have seen the promised "order" fulfilled. They that are Christ's came forth at the first resurrection, and now, they that are not Christ's come forth at this moment, announced by Paul in the passage describing the order of the resurrection as, "then cometh the end." Earlier in Revelation we saw that the judgments are poured upon the earth in consequence of the death of Christ (Rev. 8:5); it is not astonishing that resurrection comes to the lost for their eternal doom in consequence of the resurrection of Christ.

In their eternal bodies of shame the doomed stand before the judgment bar of God to receive their sentence. Every mouth is now stopped, and all the world is brought guilty before God (Rom. 3:19). And in their eternal bodies (death) their eternal spirits (Hades) are cast into the lake of fire. This is the second death. The Antichrist and the false prophet were there first. Satan and his host of high ones were next, and the lost of earth are last. It is all over. He has finished casting out of His kingdom all things that offend and them that do iniquity (Matt. 13:41). This is the second death. This is the death of death.

PART XII
ALL THINGS NEW

CHAPTER 21

Verses 1–8

The Utopia of God

¹And I saw a new heaven and a new earth, for the former heaven, and the former earth had passed away, and the sea was no more. ²And the holy city, the new Jerusalem, I saw descending out of heaven from God, prepared as a bride who has been made beautiful for her husband. ³And I heard a great voice from the throne saying: "Behold, the tabernacle of God with men, and he will tabernacle with them, and they will be his people; and God, himself will be with them. ⁴And he will wipe away every tear out of their eyes, and death will be no more; neither mourning, nor crying, nor distress will be any more. For the former things are passed away."

⁵And the one who sat upon the throne said: "Behold, I make new all things." And he said to me: "Write that these words are faithful and true." ⁶And he said to me: "It has come to pass. I am the Alpha and the Omega, the beginning and the end, and I will give to the thirsty ones freely out of the spring of the water of life. ⁷The one who overcomes will inherit these things, and I will be to him, God, and he will be to me a son. ⁸But to the cowardly and unbelieving, and to the abominable and to the murderers, and to the homosexuals and to the poisoners, and to the idolaters and liars, there will be a portion in the lake which burns with fire and brimstone."

(Rev. 21:1-8, Free Translation)

The Word of God does not leave us in darkness as to the fulfillment of God's plan for the world. When God planned for the ideal society in eternity, He knew it would involve a number of things. Men would become sinners and reject Him. No matter what He did for them, they would despise Him. They would merit His judgment and destruction. To form a perfect society out of sinful men would take redemption. Before a single man was created in time, in eternity, God planned redemption in His Son Jesus Christ in order that His perfect society—His Utopia—might be realized. Though in each stage of man's history there is great failure, yet there was a remnant who loved God and who determined to do His will.

In this chapter we see that the history of time is finished; the history of eternity is about to begin. The earth as we now know it is no longer. This chapter deals with the history of the new earth and the new heaven; no longer are we dealing with Adam's sinful race, now we are dealing with all the redeemed of the ages who, at last, find themselves in God's Utopia—the holy city, the new Jerusalem. The wicked are no more. They have been judged at the great white throne and have been cast into the lake which burns with fire and brimstone (Rev. 20:11-15). God's Day has come; the earth has been physically and morally cleansed of all evil (II Pet. 3:10-13). Now the heirs of eternal life begin to live in all fullness.

One of the first details that John brings to our attention is that "the sea is no more" (Rev. 21:1). Throughout God's Word, the sea has been the symbol of the Gentile nations who were not in a covenant relationship with God. Isaiah speaks of their conversion (Isa. 60: 3, 5). The wicked are likened to the troubled sea when it cannot rest, "whose waters cast up mire and dirt, for there is no peace . . . for the wicked" (Isa. 57:20, 21). Daniel's dream of the parade of empires causes him to see the mighty kings of the earth come out of the sea (Dan. 7:1-3, 17). John's vision of the coming Antichrist shows him coming out of the sea (Rev. 13:1, 6-9). Now, the sea is quiet. It is like glass (Rev. 4:6). The activities of the Gentiles and the Gentile nations are over.

In his vision, John sees the holy city slowly descending out of heaven. It is the "holy city," the city of the saints. God had desired such a city for His ancient people Israel. He had hoped to establish His temple there, and from it the blessings of righteousness and justice were to flow to all the earth. It was to be the city of peace, that is why it was called "Jerusalem"—the city of peace in Hebrew—but instead, it became an unfaithful city, disobedient, rebellious. It was the city over which the Lord wept: "O Jerusalem, Jerusalem, thou that killest the prophets, and stonest them which are sent unto thee, how often would I have gathered thy children together, even as a hen gathereth her chickens under her wings, and ye would not! Behold, your house is left unto you desolate. For I say unto you, Ye shall not see me henceforth, till ye shall say, Blessed is he that cometh in the name of the Lord" (Matt. 23:37-39).

John, in speaking of the holy city, is not speaking of a mere political unity of society, but of a spiritual people, "the bride made beautiful for her husband." Throughout the Old and New Testaments, the relationship between God and His people has been spoken of in terms of marriage; Israel is the bride of Jehovah, and the church as the bride of Christ. When the spiritual relationship is broken, the bride is but a harlot. Thus God speaks through Isaiah: "How is the faithful city become a harlot! It was full of judgment; righteousness lodged in it; but now murderers. Thy silver is become dross, thy wine mixed with water: Thy princes are rebellious, and companions of thieves: everyone loveth gifts, and followeth after rewards: they judge not the fatherless, neither doth the cause of the widow come unto them" (Isa. 1:21-23). In speaking to the New Testament believers, Paul makes it definitely clear that any one who is engaged in conduct not befitting the gospel of Christ is engaged in spiritual harlotry (I Cor. 6:15-18).

But now, all that is passed, the bride has been made beautiful for her husband. The work of salvation is complete. God, Himself, is to dwell with His people.

In days gone by, God had made His presence known to His people in various ways. He appeared to the Patriarchs in theophanies; He spoke to Moses personally; and when Israel was ready to make their exodus from Egypt, God assured them of His guiding presence. "And the LORD went before them by day in a pillar of a cloud, to lead them on the way; and by night in a pillar of fire, to give them light; to go by day and night: He took not away the pillar of the cloud by day, nor the pillar of fire by night from before the people" (Exod. 13:21, 22). When our Lord Jesus Christ came to earth, we read: "And the Word was made flesh, and dwelt among us, (and we beheld His glory, the glory as of the only begotten of the Father), full of grace and truth. . . . No man hath seen God at any time; the only begotten Son, who is in the bosom of the Father, He hath declared Him" (John 1: 14, 18). In this present time, along with His Word, God's Holy Spirit dwells within each believer to reveal the presence of God (I Cor. 6: 19, 20). In the Millennial Kingdom, God makes His presence known through His reigning Son, the Lord Jesus Christ (Rev. 20:6).

Now, God, Himself, joins His Son to dwell with His people. "And I heard a great voice from the throne saying: "Behold, the tabernacle of God with men; and he will tabernacle with them; and they will be his people, *and God, Himself, will be with them*'" (Rev. 21:3). The work of Christ is truly finished. The work of the Mediator has been accomplished; sin is no more. The hope of every believer is now realized: "Beloved, now are we the sons of God, and it doth not yet appear what we shall be: but we know that when he shall appear, we shall be like him; for we shall see him as he is" (I John 3:2).

John does not tell us the nature of this eternal relationship with God the Father and God the Son, but he does tell us of the glorious joy which will be ours. Death has been turned to life; sorrow into joy; distress into peace. For the former things are passed away and all things have been made new (Rev. 21:4, 5). And in this new eternal city, there will be no thirst, for the saints will drink freely out of the springs of the water of life. And in the seventh verse, John emphasizes that this new relationship with God will be personal as well as corporate: "The one who overcomes will inherit these things (the joys of the preceding verses), *and I will be to him God, and he will be to me a son."*

After describing the joys of the New Jerusalem, God makes it very clear concerning those who will be excluded from it. "But to the cowardly, and the unbelieving, and to the abominable and to the murderers, and to the homosexuals and purveyor of 'pot' (dispenser of drugs—sorcerer), and to the idolaters and liars, there will be a portion in the lake which burns with fire and brimstone" (Rev. 21:8). When eternity begins, their doom will have been sealed, but God realizes that in the writings of this prophecy, John is still in time, and for this reason He indicates to John that the door of grace is still open. This is indicated in verse seven. "The one who overcomes [present tense] will inherit [future tense] these things."

CHAPTER 21, 22

Verses 21:9–22:5

The City Foursquare

⁹*And one of the seven angels who had the seven bowls which were full of the seven last plagues, came and spoke with me, saying: "Come here! And I will show you the bride, the wife of the Lamb."* ¹⁰*And he carried me away in the Spirit to a great and high mountain, and he showed me the holy city, Jerusalem, descending out of heaven from God.* ¹¹*Having the glory of God; the light of the city was like a most precious stone, like a jasper stone, sparkling like crystal.* ¹²*And the city had a great and high wall which had twelve gateways; and there were at the gateways twelve angels, and there had been engraven on the gateways names, which were names of the twelve tribes of the sons of Israel.* ¹³*On the east, there were three gates; on the north, three gates; on the west, three gates; and on the south, three gates.* ¹⁴*And the wall of the city had twelve foundations, and upon them the names of the twelve apostles of the Lamb.*

¹⁵*And the one who spoke with me had a golden measuring rod in order to measure the city and its gateways and its walls.* ¹⁶*And the city lay foursquare; and its length was equal to its width. And he measured the city with his measuring rod fifteen hundred miles;—the length, the width, and the height of the city were equal.* ¹⁷*He measured the wall of the city to be seventy-two yards—reckoning by a human cubit, the measure the angel used.*

¹⁸*And the material of the wall was jasper, and the city was like pure gold, even like pure glass.* ¹⁹*The foundations of the city's wall were made beautiful with all kinds of precious stones; the first foundation was jasper; the second, sapphire; the third, chalcedony; the fourth, an emerald;* ²⁰*The fifth, a sardonyx; the sixth, a sardius stone; the seventh, a gold colored stone; the eighth, a beryl; the ninth, a topaz; the tenth, a clear stone sprinkled with gold; the eleventh, a blue sapphire; and the twelfth, an amethyst.* ²¹*And the twelve gateways were twelve pearls; each one of the gateways was one pearl throughout, and the boulevard of the city was of pure gold, like transparent glass.*

²²*And I did not see a temple in it, for the Lord God Almighty and the Lamb are the temple in it.* ²³*And the city had no need for the sun, nor for the moon that they should shine in it, for the glory of God illumined it, and the Lamb was its lamp.* ²⁴*And the nations will walk by its light, and the kings of the earth will bring their glory to it.* ²⁵*Its*

gates will not be closed by day since there is no night there. ²⁶*And they will bring the glory and honor of the nations into it.* ²⁷*And there will not enter into the city any vulgar thing; neither one who does abominable things, nor liars, but only those who have been written in the Lamb's book of life.*

Chapter 22

¹*And he showed me the river of water of life, clear as crystal, flowing out from the throne of God and the Lamb,* ²*Through the middle of the boulevard of the city: And on both sides of the river was the tree of life bearing fruit twelve times a season; each month it gave off its fruit, and the leaves of the tree were for the healing of the nations.* ³*And there will be a curse no more. And the throne of God and of the Lamb will be in it, and his servants will serve him.* ⁴*And they will see his face and his name will be upon their foreheads.* ⁵*And there will be no more night; and there will be no need of lamplight, nor of the light of the sun, because the Lord God will be the light upon them, and they will reign for ever and ever.*
(Rev. 21:9–22:5, Free Translation)

In these verses, John gives us a fuller description of the new Jerusalem. First of all he describes its nature (21:9-21), then he focuses our attention upon the temple of the city (21:22-27), and he closes his account of the city by refreshing us with the water of life which flows through the center of the heavenly metropolis (Rev. 22:1-5).

John is impressed with the brilliance of the city (21:9-14), the size of the city (21:15-17), and the beauty of the precious stones of which the city is built (Rev. 21:18-21). There is a contrast between the light of the city of men and the light in the city of God; the former is from God's judgment, the latter is from God's glory.

The light from the fires of judgment does not light the holy city; rather it is the glory of God and of the Lamb. God had given to the world glimpses of His light; to His ancient people Israel His glorious light shone in the temple; through the incarnation, Christ became the Light of the world; and in the Millennial Kingdom, through God's anointed Messiah, the light shone in royal brilliance. But now, at last, in the heavenly city, the prophecy of Isaiah comes to its complete fulfillment. "Arise, shine: for thy light is come. And the glory of the LORD is risen upon thee. For behold, the darkness shall cover the earth, and gross darkness the people, but the LORD shall arise upon thee, and his glory shall be seen upon thee. And the Gentiles shall come to thy light, and kings to the brightness of thy rising" (Isa. 60:1-3).

In studying the city, there is a problem of interpretation. Two lines of thought are presented to us. We are given the description of a city in terms of material: walls, streets, foundations, gateways, precious stones, trees and a river. And yet we are twice told that the city is made up of people, the bride made ready for her husband. How are these two lines of thought to be reconciled? If we keep in mind that the book of the Revelation is a "code" book, and that much of the "code" grows out of the Old Testament, and if we seek to decode the cypher from the Old Testament, we shall be on safe ground in our intrepretation. Also, we shall avoid ludicrous conclusions when we steer a middle course between the literal and figurative meanings of our text. Of several things we can be sure, we have before us the description of a real, heavenly community of the saints from all the ages; in the midst of the city dwells God the Father with the Lord Jesus Christ; and finally, this fellowship will not be broken for the author of wickedness and evil is barred from this holy city.

As we approach the city we discover that it is surrounded by a very high wall. This was a customary feature of the cities of the East for walls served as a means of protection for the people. This wall doubtless was a memorial to God's protection of His people throughout their long history. The New Testament saints would well remember how their lives were "hid with Christ in God" (Col. 3:3). Now, the wall does not need to serve as a means of protection for God Himself dwells in the city. This is further proven by the fact that each of the four walls of the city has three gateways which never will be shut. This is true for two reasons; there is no night in the city to conceal the wickedness of men (Rev. 21:25), and there are no evil men to molest the saints (Rev. 20:11-15). Furthermore, at each of the gateways there is stationed a guarding angel keeping watch at the gate. But, perhaps, it would be more apt to think of these angelic guardians as true gatekeepers—porters—with a welcoming message for the blessed who will enter the city by these gates. For John learns that this is the purpose of the gateways: "Blessed are they that do his commandments, that they may have the right to the tree of life, and may enter in through the gates into the city" (Rev. 22:14). Thus the duty of the gatekeepers is to welcome people into the city, not to keep them out. Men are excluded by their rejection of Jesus Christ and because their names are not written in the Lamb's book of life.

Along with the twelve gates in the wall of the city, there are twelve foundations supporting the wall. The gateways and the foundations were inscribed with twelve names each: the gateways were inscribed with the names of the twelve tribes of the sons of Israel; the foundations were inscribed with the names of the twelve apostles of the Lamb (Rev. 21:12, 14). These two sets of inscriptions are further memorials of God's elective grace. God's ancient covenant people consisted of the twelve tribes of Israel. They were His people; not by merit, but by sovereign election (Deut. 7:6-8). It was only through the covenant that God had promised to bless the world. Circumcision was the sign of that covenant (Gen. 17:11). No one could be blessed by God apart from the covenant. The Jews were to make a great point of this in

New Testament times (Eph. 2:11, 12). However, a careful reading of the covenant will show that God made provision whereby non-Jews —"strangers"—could enter the covenant and avail themselves of the blessings and promises which God had given to Israel. Thus the covenant was the "gateway" to God, and the "sons of the covenant"— God's *B'nai B'rith,* were its trustees. Thus it is fitting that their names should be inscribed over the gateways of the heavenly city as a memorial of ancient Israel's privileged position.

The inscription on the foundation stones of the wall is also a reminder of a great New Testament truth. The apostles were given the doctrine of justification by faith alone in all of its fullness. It was hinted at in the Old Testament but was fully set forth in the New. Christ Jesus is the Chief Cornerstone of these foundation stones. Paul speaks of this relationship: "Now therefore, you are no more strangers and foreigners, but fellowcitizens with the saints, and of the household of God; And are built upon the foundation of the apostles and prophets, Jesus Christ himself being the chief corner stone; In whom all the building fitly framed together grows to a holy temple in the Lord: In whom you also are builded together for an habitation of God through the Spirit" (Eph. 2:19-22).

What God did through Christ in making one new man of Jew and Gentile, He now does in all its fullness by making the saints of all the ages one in Himself. There is no "middle wall" in the heavenly city. What the Church of Christ began, the heavenly city finishes. "For he is our peace, who hath made both one, and hath broken down the middle wall of partition between us; Having abolished in his flesh the enmity, even the law of commandments contained in ordinances; for to make in himself of twain one new man, so making peace; And that he might reconcile both unto God in one body by the cross, having slain the enmity thereby: And came and preached peace to you which were afar off, and to them that were nigh. For through him we both have access by one Spirit unto the Father" (Eph. 2:14-18). Thus we can see in these two inscriptions a memorial to the fact that Christ began the work of destroying the hostility between Jew and Gentile, making of them one new man in Himself. In the heavenly city the work is complete; the saved of Israel and the members of the body of Christ are one in the New Jerusalem, in fellowship with God the Father and God the Son.

In his vision, John now observes the angel about to measure the city with his golden measuring rod (Rev. 21:15-17). The city is tetragonal—foursquare—in shape. In fact it is a perfect cube since its width, length, and height are equal. Since there were several kinds of "cubits" used as units of measurement, John sees that the angel is using the human cubit to measure the city which was the length of one's forearm from the elbow to the center finger. (This is indicated by the phrase "the cubit of a man." The term comes from the Latin *cubitus* which is the Latin word for "elbow.")

Following the measurement of the city, John is impressed by the materials which have gone into the building of the city. The walls are of jasper and each foundation is studded with a different precious stone. A close study of the colors of these precious stones will bring to mind the colors of the rainbow, and how God used the rainbow as a promise to Noah that he would never again destroy the earth by water (Gen. 9:12-17).

After the messages to the seven churches, John had his attention turned to the throne in heaven where God the Father and the Son of God, the Lion of Judah, the slain Lamb were seated. Surrounding the throne was a rainbow which assured the saints that judgment was over. Thus they could rest secure in Him who was slain for them.

The precious stones themselves have a very interesting biblical history. On the breastplate of judgment which the high priest wore when he went into the holy of holies, there were four rows of three precious stones each. These precious stones were like signets for inscribed on each was a name of one of the tribes of Israel. These stones were similar to those which we discovered in the foundations of the heavenly city. The shape of the breastplate was similar to that of the heavenly city, tetragonal — foursquare — indicating God's perfect work. These stones became the sign of Israel's peace, security and joy. "And Aaron shall bear the names of the children of Israel in the breastplate of judgment upon his heart, when he goeth in unto the holy place, for a memorial before the LORD continually" (Exod. 28:29). They were taken into the presence of the LORD to receive His mercy; not His judgment. The precious stones again appear in Israel's history when she was punished by the LORD for her sins, as recorded by Isaiah.

Having seen the nature and the size of the heavenly city, and having been impressed with its colorful beauty, John turns his attention to the temple in the new Jerusalem (Rev. 21:22-27). To his amazement he finds none. There is no need for any. The Father and the Son are the temple in the new city. In our previous study, we saw how God had made His presence known to Israel by means of the *Shekinah* glory, and how the disciples beheld the glory of God in the person of Jesus Christ at the incarnation (John 1:14). No longer is God to be worshiped in a place made with hands; He is to be worshiped face to face from the heart. Our Lord Jesus anticipated this when speaking to the woman at the well. He pointed out to her that the hour would come when God would not be worshiped in a temple or upon a mountain, but those who would worship God would worship Him in Spirit and in truth (John 4:21-24).

On the throne are seated the Father and the Son. Each time the Son is referred to He is spoken of as "the Lamb." Well is this for it was He who was slain before the foundation of the world (I Pet. 1: 18-20). The raptured saints sing of this before His throne in heaven (Rev. 5:6). Four times the Father and the Son are closely linked together in our passage (Rev. 21:22, 23; 22:1, 3). Here one of the greatest petitions in our Lord's high priestly prayer is answered. He had prayed: "Father, I will that they also, whom thou hast given me, be with me where I am; that they may behold my glory, which thou hast given me: for thou lovedst me before the foundation of the world" (John 17:24). Although the Lord was praying from the Garden physically, spiritually He was praying from the throne in heaven as though the cross, to which He had yet to go, were already passed (John 17: 1-5). Now the saints see Him victoriously enthroned with His Father in the heavenly city.

Every great city has its main street or avenue. John sees the holy city from heaven has its great boulevard too. Though generally the Greek term *plateia* is translated "street," it has in view a broad central avenue or boulevard. In the passage before us (Rev. 22:1-3), the street turns out to be a boulevard with a river of water—the river of the water of eternal life—running through its center from the throne of God and the Lamb. The banks of the river are adorned by the tree of life, the fruit of which nourishes the saints and the leaves of which furnish healing for the nations.

The tree of life is a miraculous tree in that it bears twelve times a year, each month it gives fruit. All the saints may partake of this tree. Eternal life is the portion of those who have been written in the Lamb's book of life. Sin will not keep them from this tree as it kept Adam and Eve from Eden's tree (Gen. 3:22-24).

There will be no more curse; there will be no more night (Rev. 22: 3, 5). Nothing will ever defile the city. Judgment no more will be necessary. Righteousness has come *to dwell* in the city; it has not merely come *to reign* as in the millennial city. The darkness of time has passed into eternity's day. The saints see the face of their God; His name is upon their foreheads; they serve and worship Him (Rev. 22:3, 4). At last, the saints can see by sight what they have held by faith through God's Word: "And the light shineth in darkness; and the darkness comprehended it not" (John 1:5). Now there is no darkness; nor is there need for the light of the sun. For the Light that is God the Father, and the "sun of righteousness" who is God the Son, light the city with Divine brilliance as the heavenly glory shines all around. At last, the saint can *really* sing:

> *Sun of my soul, Thou Saviour dear,*
> *It is not night if Thou be near;*
> *O may no earth-born cloud arise*
> *To hide Thee from Thy servant's eyes.*

Verses 6–21

Christ's Last Word

⁶And he said to me: "These words are faithful and true: And the Lord, the God of the spirits of the prophets sent his angel to show his servants what must come to pass speedily. ⁷And behold, I come speedily. Happy is the one who keeps the words of the prophecy of this book."

⁸And I, John, also heard and saw these things. And when I heard and saw these things, I fell down and worshiped before the feet of the angel who continued to show me these things. ⁹And he said to me: "See that you do not do it; I am your fellowservant, and brother of the prophets, and of those who keep the words of this book; let your worship be to God."

¹⁰And he said to me: "Do not seal the words of the prophecy of this book for the time has come. ¹¹He that is unrighteous, let him be unrighteous still; and the one who is filthy, let him be filthy still; and the one who is righteous, let him be righteous still; and the one who is holy, let him be holy still. ¹²Behold, I come speedily, and my reward is with me, to give to every one according as his work will be. ¹³I am the Alpha and the Omega, the First and the Last, the Beginning and the End."

¹⁴"Happy are they who have washed their robes in order that they may have their right to the tree of life, and that they might enter into the city through its gateways. ¹⁵Outside are the dogs, and the poisoners, and the fornicators, and the murderers, and the idolaters, and every one who loves and tells lies. ¹⁶And I, Jesus, send my angel to bear witness to you, of these things to the churches. I am the root and the offspring of David, the bright and morning star. ¹⁷And the Spirit and the bride say, 'Come!' And he who hears says, 'Come!' And the one who is thirsty, let him come, even the one who wishes to take of the water of life freely. ¹⁸I bear witness to every man who hears the words of the prophecy of this book. If any one adds to them, God will add to him the plagues which have been written in this book. ¹⁹And if any one takes away from the prophecy of this book, God will take away his part from the tree of life, and from the holy city, which has been written in this book."

²⁰The One who bears witness to these things, says: "Sure, I come speedily!" Amen! Come, Lord Jesus. ²¹The grace of our Lord Jesus Christ be with you all.

(Rev. 22:6-21, Free Translation)

The prophetic visions of John are completed. John is brought back to the present and through him our Lord gives His last invitation to all men in order that they might be prepared to enter the heavenly, holy city and to partake of the water of life.

In this final message, the Lord Jesus Christ, the living Word of God, pays great honor to the written Word of God. This fact we should mark very carefully, for we are living in a day when men are attempting to downgrade the written Word in favor of the living Word. Our Lord Jesus Christ in every phase of His ministry was careful to honor the written Word and to submit Himself to it. There can be no doubt of the fact that our Lord joined Himself with God the Father by magnifying the written Word. Thus the psalmist bears witness: "I will worship toward thy holy temple, and praise thy name for thy lovingkindness and for thy truth: *for thou hast magnified thy word above all thy name"* (Ps. 138:2). We also remember how the Lord Jesus made it abundantly clear that by His coming He did not intend to destroy, nor even loosen up, the Word of God, but to fulfill it in every jot and tittle.

John is assured that the prophetic visions which he has just seen and heard are trustworthy (22:6). These visions and the messages which accompanied them are from the Lord God Himself as given to His prophets through His Spirit. Furthermore, these prophetic truths are to show to God's servants what must come to pass speedily. God would have us understand that John is the agent of objective truth and not the victim of some religious experience which is nothing more than psychological subjectivism. John was "born along by the Holy Spirit" as the prophets of old (II Pet. 1:21). And this book of the Revelation, having God's own certification, is a book to be open to all and its readers are instructed to give heed to it (22:7, 10). We must give careful consideration to this exhortation, for *God's Last Word* is not only a book of prophetic vision, but it is His revelation that gives true meanings to history. There is an entire branch of philosophy which seeks to discover the meaning of history; in fact, philosophy is not sure as to whether history has meaning. God's revelation not only declares that history has meaning, but that He has revealed it in the Holy Scriptures, and in this last book of the Bible, He describes its culmination. For from God's point of view, history is nothing more nor less than the record of man's complete ruin in sin and God's perfect remedy in Christ—which is the sum and substance of the Gospel on a world scale.

The outstanding feature of our Lord's last words to John is "Behold, I come speedily!" (22:7, 12, 20). In verse six, our Lord had told John that the things written in this book must "come to pass speedily." When John uses the word *speedily,* he is not using it in the sense of time in terms of hours, days, months, years, but in the sense of a series of events happening in rapid succession once they start. We do not know when our Lord will return, nor when the prophetic visions of John will be fulfilled (Mark 13:32), but we can know that when the time arrives the events will follow one another in rapid succession.

We must note the time expression in the tenth verse of our chapter. "Do not seal the words of the prophecy of this book for the *time* has come." Our Lord, here, is not using the word "time" in the sense of hours, days, weeks, months, and years. If He were, the word for "time" which He would have used would be *chronos* from which we get our English word "chronometer." Instead, He uses the word *kairos,* which has to do with the proper time, the opportune moment, the correct season. Thus what He is saying to us is that now the prophetic truth is to be unsealed; God's people are to be made aware of it; now is the time to know what the future holds, and by knowing the future we can be prepared to meet it. This invitation to open the book of prophecy is in sharp contrast to God's admonition to Daniel when He ordered Daniel to seal the prophecy for the time was not yet (Dan. 8:26; 12: 4, 9).

It is important that John is told that the Lord Jesus Christ will return, for everything that will occur hinges upon His coming. Many, today, do not believe in the second coming of our Lord Jesus Christ. One of the reasons for this unbelief is that there are some theologians who, in their thought, have never allowed the Lord Jesus Christ to rise from the dead. And, consequently, there can be no returning Christ without a risen Christ. Then there are those who have been overwhelmed by the monotonous law of history's continuity that they cannot conceive that Eternity will again break into Time by the return of our Lord. Peter describes this group as follows: "This second epistle, beloved, I now write unto you; in both which I stir up your pure minds by way of remembrance: That ye may be mindful of the words which were spoken before by the holy prophets, and of the commandment of us the apostles of the Lord and Saviour: Knowing this first, that there will come in the last days scoffers, walking after their own lusts, And saying, Where is the promise of his coming? For since the fathers fell asleep, all things continue as they were from the beginning of the creation" (II Pet. 3:1-4). All of the prophetic events which are described in the book of the Revelation, and the facts concerning our Lord's return, we, as true believers, take by faith. Thus, when the Lord Jesus Christ returns, He will vindicate us by demonstrating to the world's sight that which we have accepted by faith. And in so doing, He will vindicate Himself by proving that His Word was trustworthy. And furthermore, His return vindicates the Father who through the Lord's return has proven faithful to His Word.

Our Lord is very realistic in His invitation of salvation. He knows that men will reject this final invitation to escape judgment and to know the mercy of God. Though He is still willing to invite them, He will not beg them to come to Him. Thus He declares to John: "He that is unrighteous, let him be unrighteous still; and he that is filthy, let him be filthy still; . . . Behold, I come quickly, and my reward is with me, to give every one according as his work will be. . . . For without are the dogs, and the sorcerers, and the fornicators, and the murderers, and the idolaters, and every one who loveth and maketh a lie" (22:11, 12, 15). Men resent the holiness of God, they will not respond to the righteousness of God, and they are not only indifferent to the love of God, they despise it, misreading it as a sign of God's weakness instead of His grace. But this last invitation is an invitation of mercy before judgment falls. This prophetic book is opened that men may read and give heed, that they may come to know that the days of grace are about to end and that the days of God's damnation are about to begin. For the dam of God's mercy will break and the floods of His judgment will rush forth to sweep the lost before it into the lake which burns forever and ever. Thus they will be eternally separated from the God whom they have rebelliously rejected.

It is also interesting to note that our Lord reviews for John those who will be excluded from the heavenly city (22:11). We must not forget that in describing the citizens of the heavenly city, John was specifically told who would be included and who would be excluded (21:7, 8). Upon reflection, the reason for this accounting is very simple. The Bible presents a faith that is false and a faith that is true; the former is formal, a mere mental assent; the latter is genuine which has an effect on the conduct of the believer. The devil is a good illustration of a formal faith; he believed everything that is true concerning God and His Son. He believed that Jesus Christ was God and that He could do miracles. He even knew that Jesus Christ would not worship Him. Yet these truths which the devil believed had no affect upon his life (Matt. 4:1-11). His belief was false. True biblical belief demands an absolute change in conduct. This is why James writes: "Thou believest that there is one God; thou doest well: The demons also believe and tremble. But wilt thou know, O vain man, that faith without works is dead?" (James 2:19, 20). Thus, by pointing out the workers of iniquity who will be excluded from the heavenly city, our Lord is not teaching salvation by works, but He is showing that real faith demands a change in one's life, for in the words of the Apostle Paul "with the heart man believeth unto righteousness" (Rom. 10:10).

Someone may raise the question as to how seriously is the declaration of our Lord to be taken. In the earthly order of things, men try to find loopholes within the law in order to escape the penalty for their misdeeds. But in God's court, there will be absolute justice. God is holy and no one will be able to point a finger at Him which will cause Him to violate His law. God is not like men who lie; what He says He will do (Num. 23:19). And every man who will stand before the bar of God's just judgment, will do so with the knowledge that he has rejected God's mercy of forgiveness by throwing it in the face of the Saviour, the Lord Jesus Christ.

The seriousness with which the judgment of God is to be taken is further shown by the warning that God gives to those who would tamper with His Word. "For I testify unto every man that heareth the words of the prophecy of this book, If any man shall add unto these things, God shall add unto him the plagues that are written in this book: And if any man shall take away from the words of the book of this prophecy, God shall take away his part out of the book of life, and out of the holy city, and from the things which are written in this book" (22:18, 19). Let us not forget that the Apocalypse was written not only to inform the believer of the events which close the history of time and open the history of eternity, but it was also written to warn the lost of their eternal doom and to bid them seek the Saviour who alone can deliver them from a godless eternity.

In the closing verses of our study, the Lord Jesus Christ identifies Himself and then reaffirms His coming again. He says to John: "And I, Jesus, send my angel to bear witness to you, of these things to the churches. I am the root and the offspring of David, the bright and morning star." By the personal pronoun "I," He emphasizes the fact that He Himself is speaking. By identifying Himself as "Jesus," He not only brings to our attention that He is the Saviour of the world, but also that His witness is the spirit of prophecy (Rev. 19:10). As the "root and offspring of David," we see Him as Israel's greater David—Israel's Messiah, as promised to King David in the covenant which God had made with him (II Sam. 7:12-16). Lastly, Christ refers to Himself as "the bright and morning star." To the people of the East, the stars had great meaning for they were the heavenly time pieces by which the shepherds told the different seasons of the year, and the various watches of the night. It was the "morning star" which heralded the sunrise and the breaking of a new day. Thus how fitting it is that our Lord Jesus in relation to His return should be spoken of as "the bright and morning star," for He will usher in God's eternal day. And while we await the coming of our Morning Star, we heed the word of Peter regarding God's Word: "We have also a more sure word of prophecy, whereunto ye do well that you take heed as unto a light that shines in a dark place, until the day dawn, and the day-star arise in your hearts" (II Pet. 1:19).

And as we heed God's Word, and while we await His coming, we pray with John: "Even so come, Lord Jesus."

APPENDIX

APPENDIX

The Millennium, Literal or Symbolic

[2]*. . . a thousand years . . .* [3]*. . . the thousand years . . .* [4]*. . . a thousand years . . .* [5]*. . . the thousand years . . .* [6]*. . . a thousand years . . .* [7]*. . . the thousand years . . .*
(Rev. 20:2-7)

The Latin phrase for thousand years has given us the English word "millennium," and the theological world has been divided between post-millennial, pre-millennial, and a-millennial interpretations of the Bible.

Before we go to the Scriptures, let us clear the ground of one or two matters that will lessen confusion when we come to the subject. There have been protagonists on the one side and on the other who have attempted to bolster up their theory by an appeal to theology or church history. One claims that the other is a modern addition to the field of theology and the other claims the reverse. To us, all such arguments are worthless. Had the Romanists of the sixteenth century claimed that the doctrine of justification by faith, apart from the works of the law was a new doctrine, not supported by weight of theologians, Luther and Calvin would have well answered: What have we to do with theologians? To the Word of God! What is the answer of the Scriptures?

We are quite certain that forty different answers could be found among the theologians, but we are equally sure that the Scriptures, when *fully* understood, and when *all* of the teaching of the Word is taken into consideration, can not contradict themselves, and that there is but one answer to the question. We are equally sure that devout minds in all ages have come to this same conclusion. We can also trace the reasons, psychological and otherwise, which led Catholic theologians to one position, and we can trace the reasons, psychological and otherwise, which led certain theologians of the Reformation to adopt the Catholic point of view in this point while rejecting that same point of view in so many other matters.

417

Since it would take a lengthy volume to discuss the matter from this angle, and since such a study would belong rather to the field of the history of dogma, or to the history of theological controversy, it is entirely outside our field in a volume which is dedicated to the devotional study of the Apocalypse. For these reasons, we lay aside all the books which have been written on these phases of the matter and set ourselves directly to the definition of the subject, and then to the answer to the question in our title, which answer will, in itself, constitute the devotional application of the matter to our private lives, since these verses are a part of the "all scripture" which is God-breathed and "profitable for doctrine, for reproof, for correction, for instruction in righteousness" so that every born-again child of God may, indeed, be perfect, and thoroughly furnished to every good work (II Tim. 3:16).

There is little doubt, historically, that theologians have taken the thousand years as descriptive of a period of time, literal or symbolized by this measure, that would some day be upon earth. During this time, it was generally agreed, righteousness would rule upon the earth. The main division between theologians concerned the matter of how the millennial reign of Christ would be brought about. The post-millenarians believed that the Church, little by little, would bring righteousness on the earth, until the whole world would be converted, all would be under the sway of the church, and that Christ would rule the earth spiritually through the church on earth during this period of time. Then after (post) the millennium, He would come forth from Heaven to judge the world, and would bring in the new Heavens and the new earth for the eternal state. The pre-millenarians believed that conditions would continue much as they are today, with good and bad continuing side by side until the end of the present age, when Christ would come forth from Heaven personally, before (pre) the millennium, and would reign upon the earth personally, through the glorified church, after which the wicked would be judged and the new Heavens and the new earth would be established in their eternal state.

The nineteenth century and the first third of the present century witnessed the practical death of the post-millennial idea. Many of the older theologians, true believers in the Lord Jesus Christ, who yet held this view, have died, and their places have not been filled except, perhaps, in one denomination. The exponents of this idea today are mostly aged men whose concept has not changed in their lifetime from that which they adopted in youth, or else the men who hold this idea have adopted so many ideas of unbelief in the person and the work of Christ, and have preached "the social gospel" to the exclusion of the gospel of grace to such an extent that their place is no longer found in conservative, evangelical circles. The post-millenarian theory

was the first name on the casualty list that followed the great recru-
descence of prophetic study which broke out about a century ago.

If this theory were held for the slightest moment it would be necessary to throw great sections of the Bible away. All the promises made
to literal Israel would have to be nullified, and explained in terms of
some supposed spiritual application to the Church, contradicting, thereby, many other promises to the Church.

Taking the place of post-millenarianism there arose a new school.
It may have had proponents in earlier centuries, but people did not
bother too much about prophecy before a hundred years ago, and
certainly this new school had few followers before the rapid break-up
of the post-millenarian school. The new theory is called a-millenarian-
ism. The followers of this school believe, like the pre-millenarians, that
conditions will continue much as they are today, with good and bad
continuing side by side until the end of the present age, when Christ
will come forth from Heaven, personally; but at this point they depart
and say that there will be no (a-) millennium at all, and that the
phrase is merely a figure of something spiritual, and that we are not
to expect Christ to have any earthly reign. It is obvious that this theory
is much closer to the Bible than the one it has so largely replaced,
but we believe that its errors can be definitely established also.

We wish to emphasize the unity there is between the pre-millenarian
position and that of the a-millenarians as to the course of this present
age and the necessity of the return of Christ to right the wrongs of
earth. From a textbook written by a professor in an important theological seminary, we take the following a-millenarian statement which
would be acceptable to almost any pre-millenarian. The only difficulty
might be in the first sentence, but after that is passed it is almost entirely Scriptural. "The Kingdom of God comes as a developing process;
but the process culminates in a catastrophic coming. In the course of
human history the Church in each generation is a witnessing Church,
a missionary agency. In proportion as the Church is true to her mis-
sion the principles of Christ become more and more operative in human
society and civilization. The number of Christian individuals and
groups will increase (exception may be taken here). The Church will
ever be the medium through which the light of the world shines out
upon and enlightens the darkness of the world. As the Church witnesses and works she also waits and watches for the coming of the
Lord. The world, however, will not be completely Christianized by
the work of the Church and by the preaching of the Gospel. The conflict between the good and the evil will continue until the end of the
age. The disciples of Christ are commissioned to preach the Gospel in
all the world for a witness unto all nations; but they are not promised
that all the world will be converted by their preaching. They themselves will be hated and despised and persecuted even until the end.

Wars shall continue, all the results of evil will be manifest, there will be no lasting peace preceding the *parousia* (appearance of Christ). There will be tribulations and trials and distress down to the end; and there shall be the falling away of many. The golden age of the world, the ideal society, will never be the result of purely evolutionary forces, nor the product of human plans and policies. The holy city, the new Jerusalem, comes down from God. And so at the end of the age Christ will come in power and great glory for the completion of the conquest of the good over the evil."

It can be seen that this a-millenarian professor concedes most of the main points of the pre-millenarian position. Even the phrase to which we have taken exception, which states flatly that the number of Christian individuals and groups will increase, is counter-balanced by a clear picture which shows that the control of society is in the hands of those able to use it for war, tribulations, trials and distress, while these Christian groups, however numerous, will be hated, despised, and persecuted even until the end. So the points of agreement are tremendous. They are so numerous, in fact, that many may be moved to ask: What is the importance of the disagreement? The importance lies in the fact that the whole of the Bible moves consistently on toward a given culmination and this is a definite part of the culmination. Without it there are hundreds of verses in the Scripture that are robbed of their meaning. If some theologian would say that God would not have made so much devolve on so few verses, we would reply that, at the other end of the Bible, there is a brief paragraph describing the fall of man, without which the Bible would be incomprehensible.

The same professor whom we have quoted above says of the passage we are considering: "In our Bibles there are 66 books; 1189 chapters; 31,173 verses. Nowhere else in all these books and chapters and verses does the idea of a millennium occur. Only in the twentieth chapter of Revelation, verses two, three, four, five, six, and seven, do we find this mystic word. If verses four, five, and six had been omitted from this chapter, no one would have dreamed of a literal thousand years of Christ's reign on earth; of His setting up a temporal throne in Jerusalem and inaugurating a millennial reign as an earthly monarch. To build an entire system of eschatology and a philosophy of history on these three highly figurative verses is a precarious thing to do." We must state, frankly, that we are amazed that anyone with such knowledge of the Bible could make such a statement. In the first place, we can see how an unbeliever would delight to turn this statement against the scene in the Garden of Eden describing the fall of man. Faithful theologians of all generations have fought against any attempt to interpret the fall in any other than a literal fashion. The doctrine of sin and the consequent necessity of the atonement are based on those few short verses.

But most astonishing of all is the idea that there is no other mention of a literal kingdom of Christ on earth. What were the Jews expecting when Christ came the first time? How are we to read the hundreds of verses in the Old Testament which speak of a literal kingdom and a literal throne? It can readily be seen that this thrust against the passage under discussion is ill-considered, not fully thought out, and, to say the least, is a baseless assumption without the evidence of Scripture to back it up.

Much of the disagreement between the non-millenarian and the believer in the literal reign of Christ is that extremists have muddied the waters. There have been some, who are called dispensationalists, who have taken positions which are not tenable in the light of Scripture. There is one great passage of Scripture which, we believe, clears up many of these difficulties that arise out of various uses of the word "kingdom" in the Bible. That the Old Testament contains hundreds of references to a kingdom over which Messiah is to rule is as obvious as though we should state that there was water in the ocean. A-millenarians have attempted to take all of these passages and to apply them to the church. It was Dr. James H. Brookes who stated that the "spiritualizing" of Scripture to give it another meaning than the plain and the evident, should really be called by another name, for the Holy Spirit would never treat Scripture that way. This "spiritualizing" is one extreme position. The other extreme position is that of the dispensationalist who attempts to take much of the Scripture away from the believer by saying that there is no such thing as the kingdom of Christ on earth today because he believes that there will be a literal kingdom, yet to come. He would take away the Gospels, especially Matthew, and say that this is not for the Church but that it is future.

Between these two extremes there is the centrality of truth. If certain passages in Matthew had been properly understood, neither side could have gone to these extremes. When our Lord first began to teach in parables He was immediately questioned by His followers who began to wonder why He used such a teaching method. "Why speakest thou unto them in parables?" they asked, and He answered, "Because it is given unto you to know the mysteries of the kingdom of heaven, but to them it is not given . . ." (Matt. 13:11). Later on, in the same chapter, it is announced, "All these things spake Jesus unto the multitude in parables; and without a parable spake he not unto them: That it might be fulfilled which was spoken by the prophet, saying, I will open my mouth in parables; I will utter things which have been kept secret from the foundation of the world" (Matt. 13:34, 35).

This passage states definitely that the parables of the Lord Jesus Christ, or at least these parables of the thirteenth chapter of Matthew, are entirely new matter, that the teaching is on a subject of which the Old Testament has nothing whatsoever to say.

The mysteries of the kingdom of Heaven, according to this, refer to matters unknown in the Old Testament, and, therefore, there are two absolutely distinct phases of the kingdom. When this is understood, it does away with the theories of the non-millenarians on the one side and the extreme dispensationalists on the other side. The non-millenarians are wrong when they apply Old Testament kingdom passages to the church and the dispensationalists are wrong when they say that the church is in no wise a kingdom. The truth is that there is a literal kingdom, announced in hundreds of passages in the Old Testament, and ardently expected by the Jews in the day of Christ, but announced as postponed until after the Church age, and there is the kingdom in its mystery aspect, moving today from heart to heart among those who are born again. The saved of our day can truly pray, as children, "Our Father, which art in heaven, Hallowed be thy name." As members of this mystery-aspect of the kingdom, they can truly pray, "Thy kingdom come." As servants of God we can pray, "Thy will be done on earth [in me] as it is in heaven." As dependents we can pray, "Give us this day our daily bread." As redeemed sinners who still possess an old nature capable of breaking out, we can pray, "Forgive us our debts, as we forgive our debtors." And while there is a sense in which this is reversed in Ephesians 4:32, in which our forgiveness of others is manifested as an outgrowth of divine grace provided for us, there is a sense in which our maintenance in fellowship is dependent upon a surrender of our being to the Lord, which will involve a spirit of forgiveness of others, which makes it possible for us to come confessing our sins that they may be forgiven. So when the believer prays in these various capacities he throws himself on the mercy of God, pleading to be kept from the place of testing and to be delivered from the evil one. The supreme acknowledgment is that we have refused Satan's claim to possess the rights of the kingdom, the power and the glory (Luke 4:5, 6), and that we acknowledge that these belong to our Lord forever.

So we come back to the fact that there are hundreds of promises in the Old Testament which concern a literal kingdom. We must not be led away from them by the errors of the non-millenarian or by the errors of the extreme dispensationalist.

In the first place, there are to be considered all the promises which refer to a literal gift of the land of Palestine to Israel. The Lord God told Abraham that He had brought him out of Ur of the Chaldees in order that He might give him that land for a possession (Gen. 15:7). When Abraham asked God, "Whereby shall I know that I shall inherit it?" the Lord gave to Abraham a pageant of sacrifice which is a pure picture of the death of the Lord Jesus Christ on the cross as a proof that the land should belong to his seed, even as it had been promised.

In the thirty-third chapter of Jeremiah, God gives to the prophet promises so literal concerning the earthly kingdom of Israel that it is impossible to get around them. It must be understood that we do not for a moment follow those dispensationalists who have said that there are no spiritual promises to Israel, or that Israel was not the elect people of God. There is the larger Israel, including both saved and unsaved, including all of the physical posterity of Abraham through Isaac. Then there is the spiritual Israel, objects of the loving grace of God, saved through faith in God's great redemptive work by looking forward to Christ even as we are saved by looking backward to Christ. We would even be willing to concede that the word "church" might be used in a large sense covering all the elect of God out of this earth from the dawn of time, providing that a narrower sense of the word would also be allowed covering the body of those whose bodies became the temples of the Holy Spirit in the age since the day of the resurrection of our Lord.

When all of these balancing truths are seen in their proper sphere the whole of God's great plan begins to take on more of its splendid and unutterable majesty. But we must not overlook the definite, literal, earthly, kingdom promises of the Word. To Jeremiah God promised that "this city" (Jer. 33:4), the very one that had been polluted by dead bodies of victims of the anger of God and had caused Him to hide His face from "this city," should be cured and cleansed. "There shall be heard in this place . . . the voice of joy, and the voice of gladness . . . Thus saith the Lord of Hosts, Again in this place . . . shall be an habitation . . . and the flocks shall pass again . . . Behold the days come, saith the Lord, that I will perform that good thing which I have promised . . . In those days and at that time, will I cause the Branch of righteousness to grow up unto David; and he shall execute judgment and righteousness in the land. In those days shall Judah be saved, and Jerusalem shall dwell safely: and this is the name wherewith she shall be called, The Lord our righteousness. For thus saith the Lord: David shall never want a man to sit upon the throne of the house of Israel . . ." (Jer. 33:10-17). And just as the original promise to Abraham was confirmed by a symbol of the cross of Jesus Christ, so these promises are confirmed by one of the mightiest of God's comparisons of truth. "Thus saith the Lord; If ye can break my covenant of the day, and my covenant of the night, and that there should not be day and night in their season; Then may also my covenant be broken with David my servant, that he should not have a son to reign upon his throne . . ." (Jer. 33:20, 21). In other words, the promises of a literal, earthly kingdom cannot be broken until someone has found a way to stop the earth turning on its axis, so that day and night can be brought to an end.

We have quoted enough to show that the belief of Christians in a literal, earthly kingdom is not built on six verses in the book of Revelation, but that it is a theme that runs through the entire Word of God. Having established the fact of such a kingdom, we shall go on to show the urgent necessity for it, and the nature of this kingdom when the Lord will fulfill His Word.

Why the Millennium Must Be Literal

If there is to be no earthly kingdom, then man has an excuse that he can offer to God, and every mouth will not be stopped, as the Word of God tells us that it will be (Rom. 3:19). The successive dealings of God with men have been wrought for the purpose of bringing man down to the realization of his own nothingness and his absolute dependence upon the grace of God.

When God put a mark on Cain so that no one finding him would kill him (Gen. 4:15), the way was open for an argument against God's plan. Man could say to God: You protected the murderer. If we had had the right of taking judgment into our hands, we would have made such an example of Cain that murder would not have broken out again. It is Your fault that Lamech murdered the young man who had wounded him. We could have taken care of such things.

Man did not realize that what was taking place was a further testing of man, and a further consequent judgment upon him. Man had received the knowledge of good and evil at the fall. This must now be given a thorough test. If man can follow the good and avoid the evil, all will be well. But it is demonstrated that with the mere knowledge of the good and the evil, man is unable to establish himself in right living before God. Something else has to be done.

It is noteworthy, in the light of the above, that God's first dealings with Noah after the flood are on the basis of establishing man in a collective society to which will be committed the responsibility of government. There shall now be a thorough test of man, collectively responsible, to see if it be possible to have true righteousness upon earth as a result of man's operations. "Whoso sheddeth man's blood, by man shall his blood be shed" (Gen. 9:6). This is, most certainly, the commission to man of the highest functions of government. What will man be able to do with it?

The history of subsequent society demonstrates that man is not able to control his fellows, and there are many who would admit the need of a super-government from above, although man, in his unchanged condition, does not wish Christ to reign over him any more today than he did when he cried out for His crucifixion. But though man's insufficiency for self-government had been demonstrated, there were still points where man could attack God in argument. Man could say: The trouble is that we do not know what You want us to do. Tell us exactly what You want done and we will take care of it properly. The real difficulty is that we are left alone here without sufficient light to work out our problems.

Again God answers the cry of man. The law is given by Moses. In reality it is a divine code for living that includes everything. It tells a man how he must live in relation to God, in relation with his fellows, in his relationship with wife and children, servants and foreigners. It tells him how he is to plough his fields and sew his garments, how he is to cook his food and dispose of his refuse. As the law was a divine code, it was absolutely impossible for man to keep it, and once more he was shut off from the grace of God. No one could have been saved had not God continued His purposes in grace. Even Peter testified that the law was a "yoke . . . which neither our fathers nor we were able to bear" (Acts 15:10).

Today man is living in a situation that may be simply described as a free offer of salvation through grace without any limitations or conditions whatsoever. "Him that cometh unto me I will in no wise cast out" (John 6:37). But man does not accept this offer of free grace. Instead there are a thousand excuses and there are innumerable plans for the proper government of all mankind by man himself.

Most important of the excuses, from a spiritual point of view, is the statement that God cannot hold man responsible since man was seduced by Satan, and that Satan, therefore, must be responsible. It is true that the Bible definitely denies this and places the full responsibility on man himself. The situation may be put in the form of an analogy. A huntsman shoots a deer which, wounded bounds away over the hill and is lost to the track of the follower. The deer, weakened by loss of blood, and fevered with its wound, plunges into a stream to quench its thirst and cool its fever. Too weak to rise, it dies in the stream and its body turns to corruption, polluting the stream below. We will assume that the deer was infected with the germ of typhoid and that this germ, multiplying greatly on the carcass, pollutes all the water of a town which draws its supply from the stream. An epidemic of typhoid breaks out in the town. What is the cause of the malady? There might well be two parties who would put up strong arguments the one against the other. The one party blames the hunter, the other party blames the deer.

In resolving the analogy we will let the huntsman represent Satan and the deer mankind. It is true that the Bible tells us that man originally fell through the seductions of Satan. But the Bible definitely teaches us that man became corrupted by sin and that all of the evils that are now in the world come definitely and directly from man and that Satan can not be blamed for them. It is the corrupt heart of man that is the cause of all of the ills of the world. "That which cometh out of the man, that defileth the man. For from within, out of the heart of men, proceed evil thoughts, adulteries, fornications, murders, thefts, covetousness, wickedness, deceit, lasciviousness, an evil eye, blasphemy, pride, foolishness; all these evil things come from within, and defile the man" (Mark 7:20-23). "From whence come wars and fightings among you? come they not hence, even of your lusts that war in your members?" (James 4:1).

Mankind, however, is not willing to admit this fact. Men are constantly evolving utopian schemes for bringing economic and social righteousness upon the earth. Preachers, even, state that there is good in human nature. Those who have departed from the finality of the Word of God are at work even today planning a future society that will not have the ills of our present society. It is absolutely necessary, according to the Bible, that there be a period in which fallen man is left on this earth without any temptation from without. There will be no power of Satan or of his principalities and powers which now rule this world darkness (Eph. 6:12).

The millennium, then, will be the final test of man, of fallen man without any interference from without. We shall see man's failure under such conditions.

Besides this social necessity for a millennial period, there are also necessities that are based on the nature of the struggle between God and the usurper, Satan. When Satan fell there were two ways in which God might have treated the rebellion. He had the power to put it down with a word and to crush Satan fully and completely. Had He done this, He could never have created another mighty angelic power that would not have been subject to the same spontaneous (Ezek. 28:15) outbreak of sin, unless He wanted to remain forever in a universe of automatons. The other alternative was to give to the rebel a complete and free field to do as he pleased, and to demonstrate before a universe, palpitatingly interested, that the enemy would be an utter failure, and that dust should always be his meat.

The field of the conflict has always been this world which was the original province of the unfallen Lucifer. He was "set" as the governing cherub (Ezek. 28:14) by God Himsef, and was able to claim this to the very face of Christ (Luke 4:6). It is on this ground that he has been called "the prince of this world" even by Christ (John 14:30). Because of Satan's rebellion this world has seen three successive catastrophes. The world was smashed to chaos and became without form and void, waste and desolate, at the time of the first introduction of sin (Gen. 1:2 cf. Isa. 45:18, same Hebrew words). The refashioned world was cursed at the time of Satan's seduction of newly created man (Gen. 3:17), and has brought forth its thorns and thistles from that time to this. Finally, when Satan sought to corrupt the race with mass demon possession God sent the flood which probably swung the oceans from their beds and piled former seafloors on top of what are now mountain ranges and created all of the illusions of strata which confuse the modern geologists.

The Bible everywhere teaches that the results of these various judgments will be reversed and that the earth itself will see the victory of God after so much of the triumph of Satan. It is necessary that there be a period such as the millennium in order that these victories will be displayed before the universe, even as God is now manifesting His manifold wisdom before the principalities and powers by means of the Church (Eph. 3:10). That this period of triumph is to be on this earth before the final judgment, and that the prophecies may not be applied to the new Heavens and the new earth, will be brought out fully when we come to the final paragraphs of the Apocalypse.

Not only is the earthly reign of Christ a necessity from the point of view of the conflict with the rebel Satan, and from the point of view of the redemption of the earth from its groaning curse, but it is necessary from the point of view of God's definite covenant with David. It is beyond our present purpose to argue this point extensively, as many chapters could be written on the subject. It will be sufficient to point the reader to the definite covenant promises of an earthly kingdom and an earthly throne that are to be found throughout the Scriptures. The student may consult II Samuel 7:11-17; Psalm 89:20-37; Jeremiah 33:20, 21 among the Old Testament passages, and Luke 1: 32; Acts 2:25-31; 15:15-17; and Revelation 3:21 in the New Testament.

There is one further item in the argument for the necessity of the literal kingdom of Christ on earth that grows out of all of the utopian literature that has been created by unbelieving man. From Thomas More's "Utopia," there has been a stream of literary dreamings—Butler's "Erewhon," Bellamy's "Looking Backward," Hilton's "Lost Horizon." There has been a whole gamut of socialistic and communistic writings—Marx, Engels, Lenin and the lesser satellites. There have been serious efforts to establish utopian colonies, such as those of Hopedale, Mass., Economy, Penna., Utopia, Ohio, the more pretentious effort of Robert Owen from England to New Harmony, Ind., and Dana's effort at Brook Farm, as well as the gigantic effort of Tolstoy in Russia. Many theological modernists have adopted these various dreams and speak of a classless society without violence and ultimately without a state. William Morris has written:

> *Nor shall any lack a share*
> *In the days when the world grows fair . . .*

We have never seen a line in any biblical commentator which deals with the definite fact that the Word of God prophesies conditions that are similar to those hoped for by these literary, political or social idealists.

This leads naturally from the above considerations of the necessity for a literal reign of Christ on earth to the nature of that reign. We believe that it can be demonstrated that everything ever imagined by man as a possible solution of the world's problems will be brought into the conditions set up at that time, and that the millennium will be the perfect trial period for every device which the natural heart has imagined as a possible cure for the ills of mankind.

We turn to the Bible for an outline of the nature of the future kingdom period. First of all, as we have seen, it is to be a period without the presence of any supernatural power of enmity. Satan and all his hosts will be out of the way, bound for the thousand-year period. The kingdom rule of Christ, therefore, shall be the fullest test of the natural heart of unbelief with all its enmity against God.

Second, the framework of the final test of mankind will be a world from which all the curse upon the material world shall have been removed. One of the key passages to this line of teaching is found in the eighth of Romans. "For the earnest expectation of the creation waiteth for the manifestation of the sons of God. For the creation was made subject to vanity, not willingly, but by reason of him who hath subjected the same in hope. Because the creation itself also shall be delivered from the bondage of corruption into the glorious liberty of the children of God. For we know that the whole creation groaneth and travaileth in pain together until now. And not only the creation, but . . . even we ourselves groan within ourselves, waiting for the adoption, the redemption of our body" (Rom. 8:19-23). This passage teaches very definitely that the material world is to be released from the bondage which came upon it at the time of the curse, and that this is to happen at the time when the sons of God are manifested and their bodies redeemed. This, of course, dates the prophecy as being fulfilled at the time of the first resurrection, and at the moment of the completion of that first resurrection in its various stages.

There are many passages in the Bible which speak of the nature of that change and the removal of the curse. It is to affect the earth itself. There are many passages corresponding to Isaiah's great revelation: "For ye shall go out with joy, and be led forth with peace: the mountains and the hills shall break forth before you into singing, and all the trees of the field shall clap their hands. Instead of the thorn shall come up the fir tree, and instead of the brier shall come up the myrtle tree: and it shall be to the Lord for a name, for an everlasting sign that shall not be cut off" (Isa. 55:12, 13). And again, "I will open rivers in high places, and fountains in the midst of the valleys: I will make the wilderness a pool of water, and the dry land springs of water. I will plant in the wilderness the cedar, the shittah tree, and the myrtle, and the oil tree; I will set in the desert the fir tree, and the pine, and the box tree together. That they may see, and know, and consider, and understand together, that the hand of the Lord hath done this, and the Holy One of Israel hath created it" (Isa. 41:18-20).

To argue that, botanically speaking, some of these growths cannot live in tropical climates, as one commentator, at least, has done, is to argue against the divine element in all this fulfillment. He who is able to subdue all things unto Himself (Phil. 3:21) will take care of the details. There are to be profound astronomical changes, since the powers of the sun and the moon are to be definitely changed (Isa. 30:26).

There will be definite geographical changes that will play their part. While we cannot know all that shall come to pass at that time, we are given to see dimly certain of the changes. The Mount of Olives is to be divided, and there shall be a "very great valley," probably bringing the Mediterranean to the doors of Jerusalem, and part of the land that is now below the sea shall be lifted up to a higher level (Zech. 14:4, 10). A river shall flow out of the sanctuary at Jerusalem, dividing into two branches, one flowing to the Mediterranean (Zech. 14:8), and the other flowing down into what is now the Dead Sea, bringing those waters to a height where they shall flow into the Red Sea, healing the waters of the Dead Sea so that they shall be alive with fish (Ezek. 47:8-10). The fertility of the ground and the productivity of crops will be enormously increased, possibly to the extent of a new crop each month (Ezek. 47:12). This will make possible a vastly increased population, so that there may be billions and billions of people living on the earth.

Not only will the material earth be changed, but the nature of the animals on the earth will be changed. Those that are now carnivorous shall become herbivorous, the lion eating straw like the ox. "The wolf also shall dwell with the lamb, and the leopard shall lie down with the kid; and the calf and the young lion and the fatling together; and a little child shall lead them. And the cow and the bear shall feed; their young ones shall lie down together: and the lion shall eat straw like the ox" (Isa. 11:6, 7). There shall be no more poison in those insects or reptiles that now have the power to kill, for "the sucking child shall play on the hole of the asp, and the weaned child shall put his hand on the cockatrice's den. They shall not hurt nor destroy in all my holy mountain" (Isa. 11:8, 9). The only mark of the curse that will remain in the natural world is that the serpent will still go rampant (Isa. 65:25). This will be one of two awful symbols that will be present to the eyes of the world's peoples. We shall see the reason for this when we come to the second of the remaining symbols.

The peoples who inhabit the earth at the beginning of this kingdom on the transformed earth are of two kinds. We have already seen that the judgment of the nations excludes from participation in the kingdom all of the nations which have rejected the Lord in His messengers during the tribulation period. The "sheep" nations are taken into the kingdom, and thus are blessed of the Father (Matt. 25:34). It should be definitely realized that there is no hint that these nations are composed of individuals who are all redeemed. There can be no doubt that there are many who are still "natural" men, receiving not the things of the Spirit (I Cor. 2:14), with the carnal mind, which is enmity against God (Rom. 8:7).

There are several proofs of this existence of sin in the millennial kingdom. We have seen that one of its outstanding purposes is the complete test of human nature under perfect conditions to reveal its corrupt inwardness. It is to be noted, also, that the Bible definitely teaches that there shall be sin and physical death during this period of Christ's reign. That this in no wise contradicts the statements of an all-pervading righteousness will come out in a moment. We know that man, before the flood, lived for centuries. So shall it be in the millennial kingdom. Anyone dying at a hundred shall be as a child, and the sinner, at a hundred years of age shall be accursed (Isa. 65:20).

Not only will there be these tremendous physical advantages for man in the millennium, but there will be great economic and social advantages. These grow out of the governmental aspects of the millennium. The Lord shall break and rule with a rod of iron, and shall dash His enemies to pieces as a potter's vessel (Psalm 2:9). He shall do this by means of the saints of the Old Testament and New Testament periods, who shall be given exactly the same power that He received of the Father (Rev. 2:27), and who shall rule from the newly erected throne of Christ (Rev. 3:21; Matt. 25:31). Then shall be fulfilled the definite prophecy that was used by Paul as an exhortation for the saints of his and our day, "Do ye not know that the saints shall judge the world?" (I Cor. 6:2). In accordance with the capacities developed during this life, to the one shall be given rule over one city, to another over five, to another over ten, even as Christ said (Luke 19:16-24). Some have complained that this would be a step down from the present glory of the saints in their disembodied state in Heaven. The answer, of course, is that it is to the honor and glory of the Lord Jesus Christ, and is a faint picture of the use to which God will put His saints in His government for ever and ever.

It is possible that the New Jerusalem, a literal city 1,500 miles in length, in breadth and in height, will already hang suspended above the earthly Jerusalem, as the earthly residence of the resurrected and transformed saints. At all events, the government of Christ will be exercised, primarily, through the saints ruling as His agents.

The secondary delegation of power shall be from the saints, already in their eternal bodies, to the Jews on earth, now born again and receiving all the promises that were sworn to them in Abraham and David. "For the gifts and calling of God are without repentance . . . And so all Israel [living at the time of the Lord's return in glory] shall be saved: as it is written, There shall come out of Zion the Deliverer, and shall turn away ungodliness from Jacob: for this is my covenant unto them, when I shall take away their sins" (Rom. 11: 29, 26, 27).

It can readily be understood, from this governmental set-up, that righteousness shall cover the earth as the waters cover the seas. There will be sinful, rebellious hearts, hating the government of God, but there shall be a prohibition of all evil, and any outward manifestation of evil shall be dealt with by the immediate presence and flashing power of God's righteous instruments of government. It would appear that physical death would be the immediate portion of those who persist in open sin. There shall be a full prohibition of outward evil, and it shall be a prohibition that will really prohibit.

The economic and social results of such a system of government are immediately apparent. There shall be no more wars. "He shall judge among the nations, and shall rebuke many people: and they shall beat their swords into plowshares, and their spears into pruninghooks: nation shall not lift up sword against nation, neither shall they learn war any more" (Isa. 2:4). But that does not mean that the selfishness, the true cause of war (James 4:1), shall have disappeared from the human heart.

There will be no more economic exploitation. Every man will be a land owner. They shall all sit, every man under his own vine and fig tree (Micah 4:4). Here is the ideal state according to socialistic principles.

There remains one further aspect of the kingdom time to be discussed. Just as there will be no national power, whatsoever, that shall be in opposition to the kingdom power of the Messiah, so there shall be no spiritual or religious power in opposition to Him. It will be impossible for there to be a mental unbeliever upon the earth. Among the increasing billions that shall fill the transformed earth, there shall not be one atheist, one agnostic, one skeptic. There shall be neither leader nor follower of any false cult. The earth shall be filled with the knowledge of the Lord . . .

Every human being upon the earth shall know that the Bible is the Word of God. Every human being shall see the flashing saints as they go about their government for God. Every human being shall look upon the Lord Jesus Christ. But many, many will be hating Him, even as they look.

The Gospel shall be preached, even as it is preached today. There will be talk about sin and redemption. The story of the fall and the curse will be told, and the serpent, though robbed of its poison (Isa. 11:8), shall still have its crawling body that brings a chill to hearts as they behold it. The serpent will be visible as a reminder of the fall and the curse which hearts, though knowing it to be true, will not wish to admit. Thus the depravity of the human heart is brought out in sharpest relief. Men shall be told that Christ died. These words would have little effect in a world where there is no longer any death by violence. There will, therefore, be the visible symbol of that death, seen on the altar at Jerusalem, and visible, no doubt by television, to every soul on earth. A young bullock, a kid, a ram and a goat will be killed at various times, and the nations of the world shall see the blood flow. The literal interpretation of the prophecy of the killing of these sacrifices (Ezek. 43:19-27) has been bitterly fought by many because they did not understand the nature of the millennium, but when seen against the background which we have painted, their offering is a logical part of the whole picture of the final test of man.